ORWELL

George Orwell lived in the first half of the twentieth century, and *Orwell* contains offensive and racist language which reflects some of the attitudes and prejudices of the period.

First published in English in 2021
by SelfMadeHero
139–141 Pancras Road
London NW1 1UN
www.selfmadehero.com

Written by Pierre Christin
Illustrated by Sébastien Verdier
Translated from the French edition by Edward Gauvin

Publishing Director: Emma Hayley
Editorial & Production Director: Guillaume Rater
Designer: Txabi Jones
Publishing Assistant: Stefano Mancin
UK Publicist: Paul Smith
US Publicist: Maya Bradford
Textual Consultant: Nick de Somogyi

ROYAUME-UNI

This book is supported by the Institut français (Royaume-Uni)
as part of the Burgess programme

Orwell © DARGAUD 2019, by Christin, Verdier
www.dargaud.com
All rights reserved

Extracts of Orwell's writing reproduced by kind permission
of AM Heath Literary Agents and Houghton Mifflin Harcourt.
With thanks to Bill Hamilton and Ron Hussey.

A CIP record for this book is available from the British Library

ISBN: 978-1-910593-87-5

10 9 8 7 6 5 4 3 2 1

Printed and bound in Slovenia

Pierre Christin   Sébastien Verdier

ORWELL

Old Etonian, copper, prole, dandy, militiaman, journalist, rebel,
novelist, eccentric, socialist, patriot, gardener, hermit, visionary

With special contributions from
André Juillard, Olivier Balez, Manu Larcenet,
Blutch, Juanjo Guarnido, and Enki Bilal

SELF
MADE
HERO

CHAPTER I

ORWELL BEFORE ORWELL

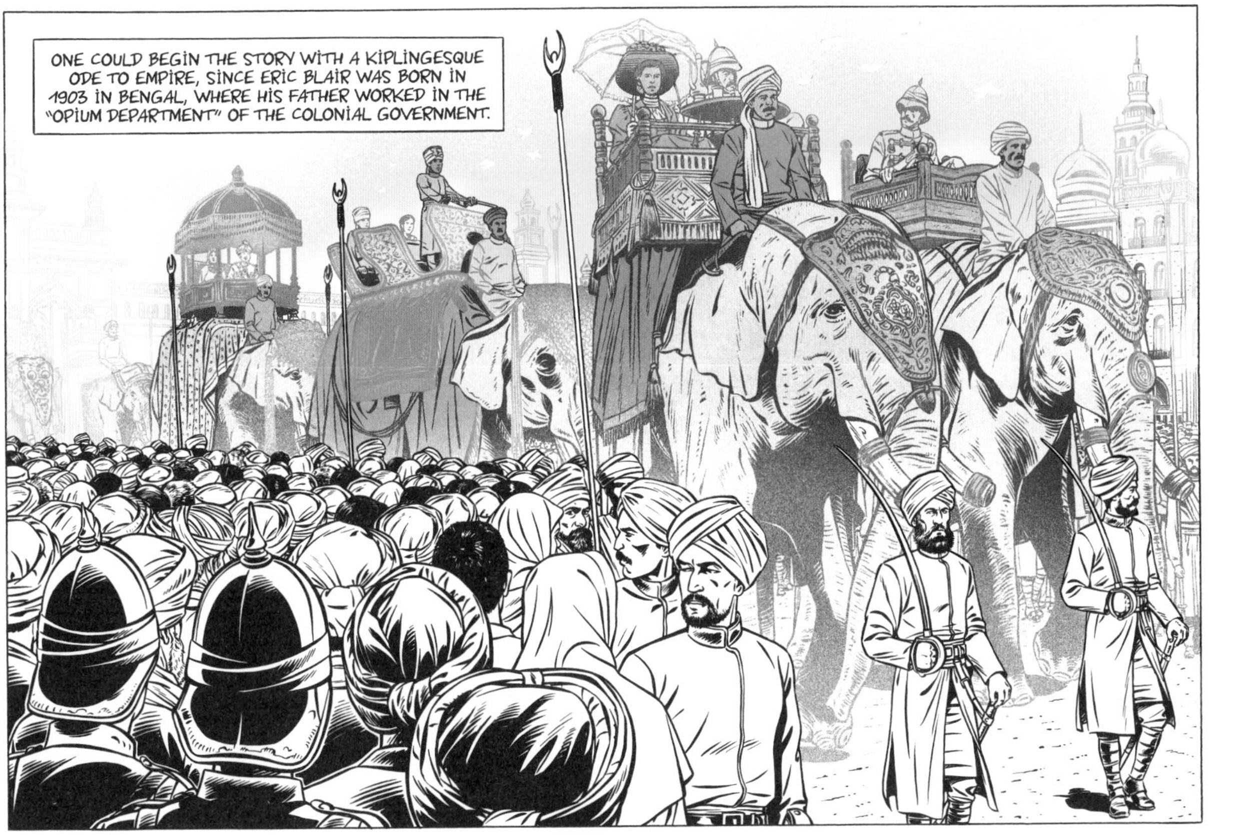
ONE COULD BEGIN THE STORY WITH A KIPLINGESQUE ODE TO EMPIRE, SINCE ERIC BLAIR WAS BORN IN 1903 IN BENGAL, WHERE HIS FATHER WORKED IN THE "OPIUM DEPARTMENT" OF THE COLONIAL GOVERNMENT.

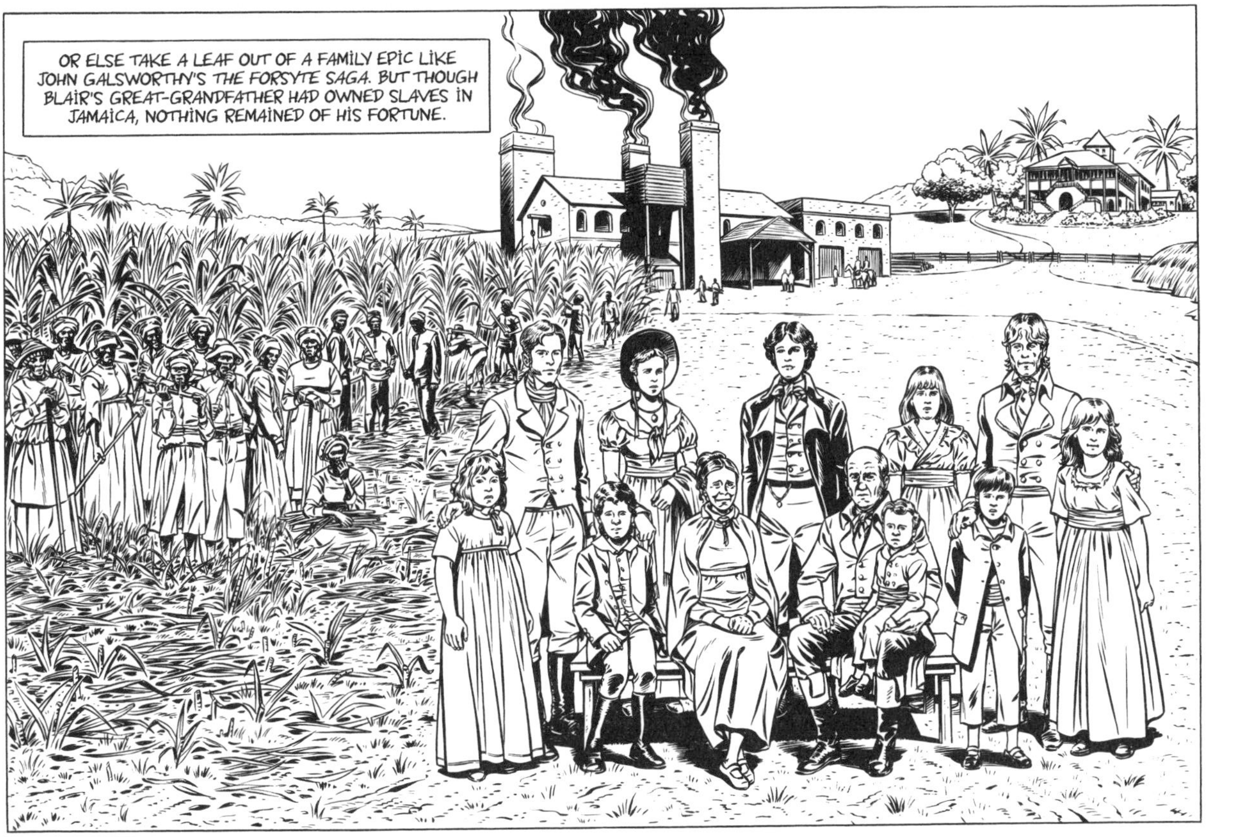
OR ELSE TAKE A LEAF OUT OF A FAMILY EPIC LIKE JOHN GALSWORTHY'S *THE FORSYTE SAGA*. BUT THOUGH BLAIR'S GREAT-GRANDFATHER HAD OWNED SLAVES IN JAMAICA, NOTHING REMAINED OF HIS FORTUNE.

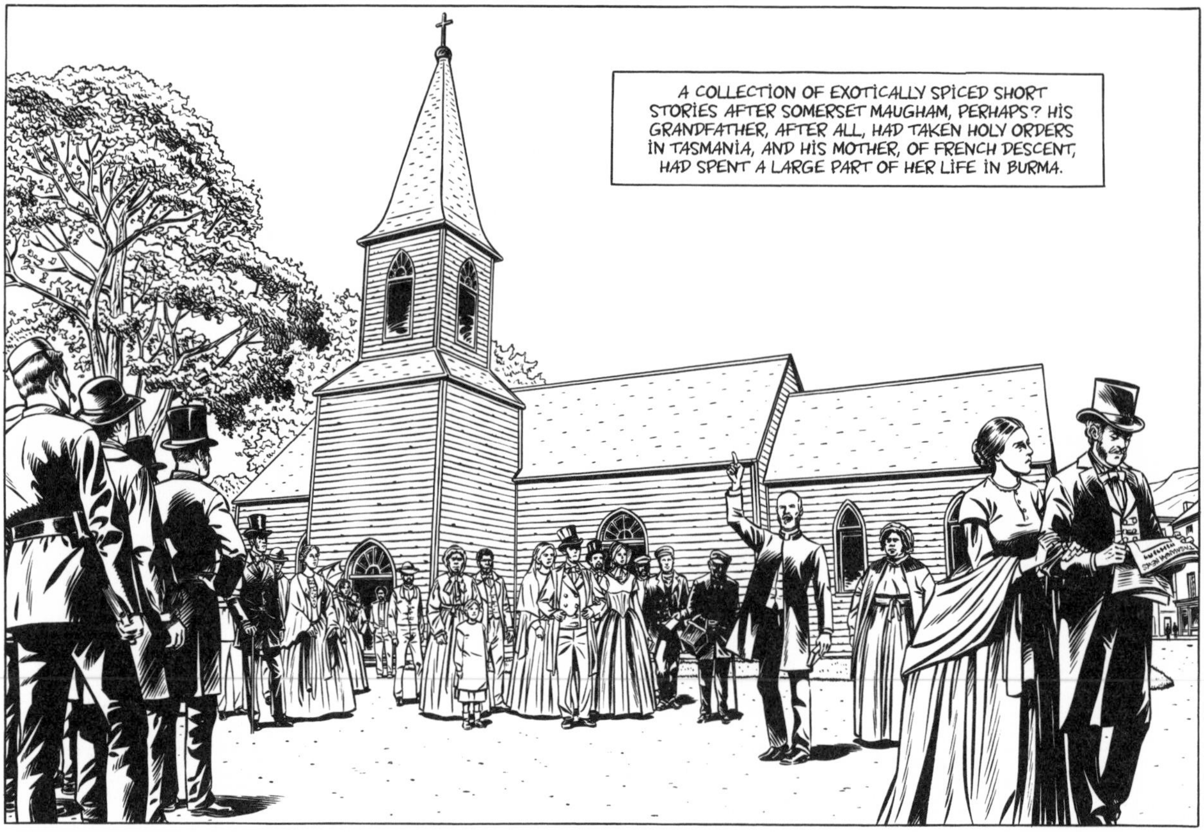
A COLLECTION OF EXOTICALLY SPICED SHORT STORIES AFTER SOMERSET MAUGHAM, PERHAPS? HIS GRANDFATHER, AFTER ALL, HAD TAKEN HOLY ORDERS IN TASMANIA, AND HIS MOTHER, OF FRENCH DESCENT, HAD SPENT A LARGE PART OF HER LIFE IN BURMA.

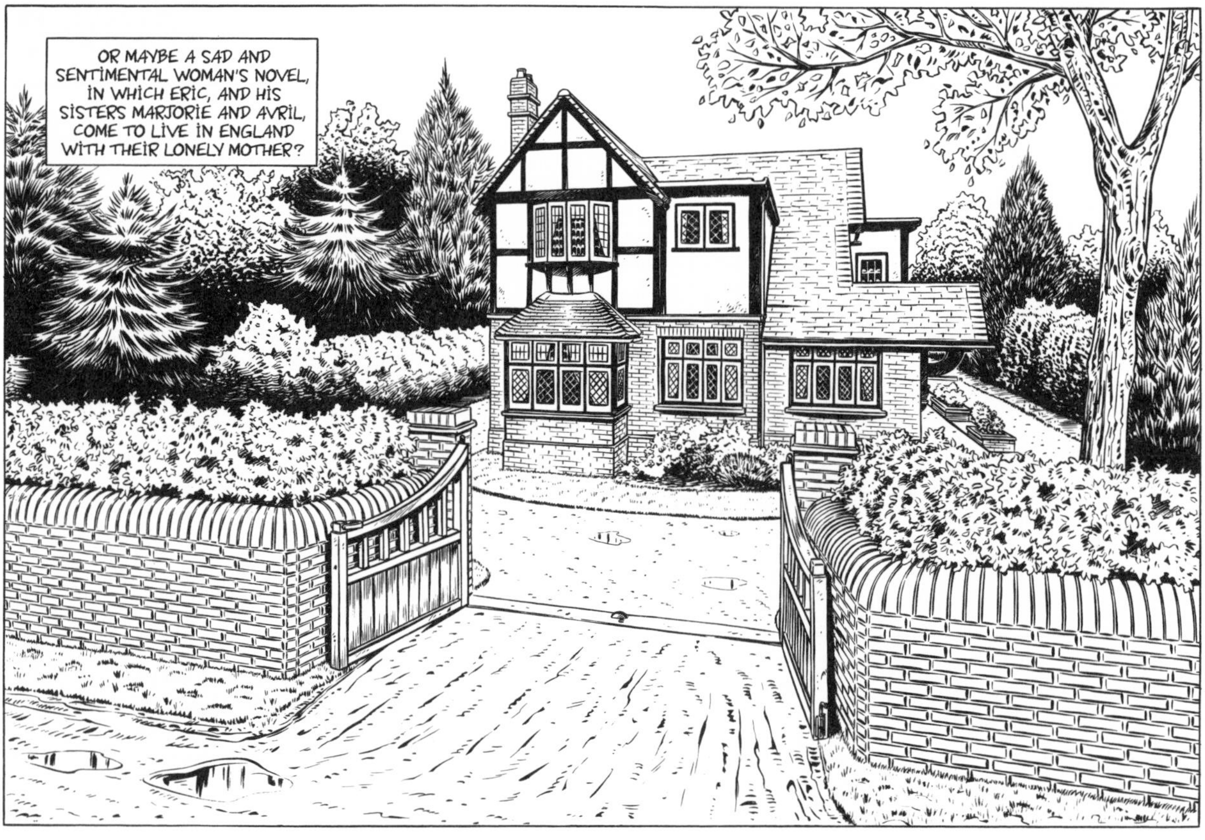
OR MAYBE A SAD AND SENTIMENTAL WOMAN'S NOVEL, IN WHICH ERIC, AND HIS SISTERS MARJORIE AND AVRIL, COME TO LIVE IN ENGLAND WITH THEIR LONELY MOTHER?

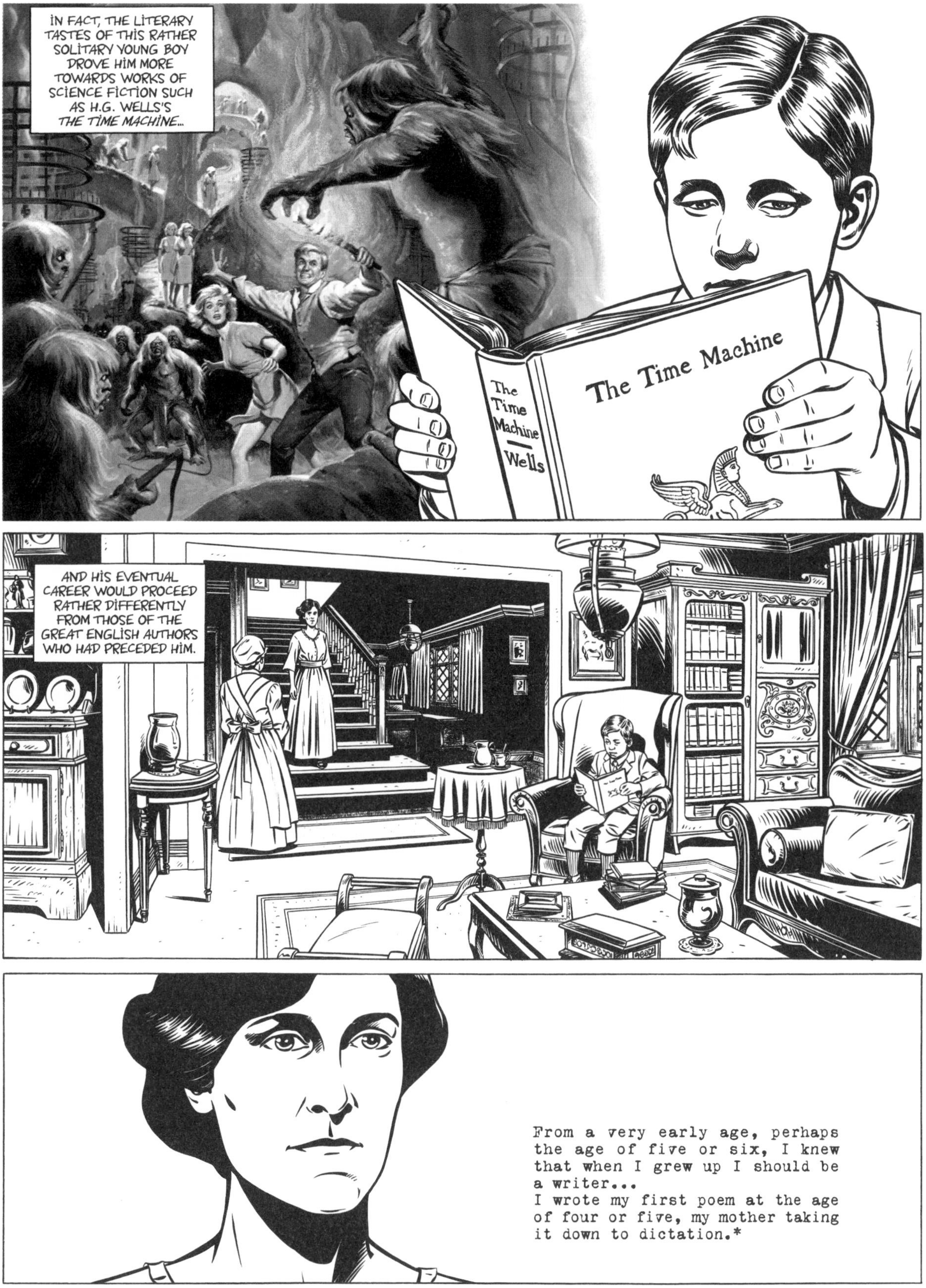
IN FACT, THE LITERARY TASTES OF THIS RATHER SOLITARY YOUNG BOY DROVE HIM MORE TOWARDS WORKS OF SCIENCE FICTION SUCH AS H.G. WELLS'S *THE TIME MACHINE*...
The Time Machine Wells
The Time Machine
AND HIS EVENTUAL CAREER WOULD PROCEED RATHER DIFFERENTLY FROM THOSE OF THE GREAT ENGLISH AUTHORS WHO HAD PRECEDED HIM.
From a very early age, perhaps the age of five or six, I knew that when I grew up I should be a writer...
I wrote my first poem at the age of four or five, my mother taking it down to dictation.*

* All typewritten text is quoted directly from Orwell himself.

AS ORWELL HIMSELF WOULD LATER EXPLAIN, THE BLAIRS BELONGED TO THE "LOWER-UPPER-MIDDLE CLASS", AND SETTLED IN SHIPLAKE, OXFORDSHIRE.

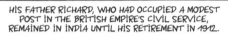

HIS FATHER RICHARD, WHO HAD OCCUPIED A MODEST POST IN THE BRITISH EMPIRE'S CIVIL SERVICE, REMAINED IN INDIA UNTIL HIS RETIREMENT IN 1912.

HIS MUCH YOUNGER WIFE IDA, ORWELL'S MOTHER, HAD AN ACTIVE SOCIAL LIFE, AND SO WAS OFTEN AWAY FROM HOME.

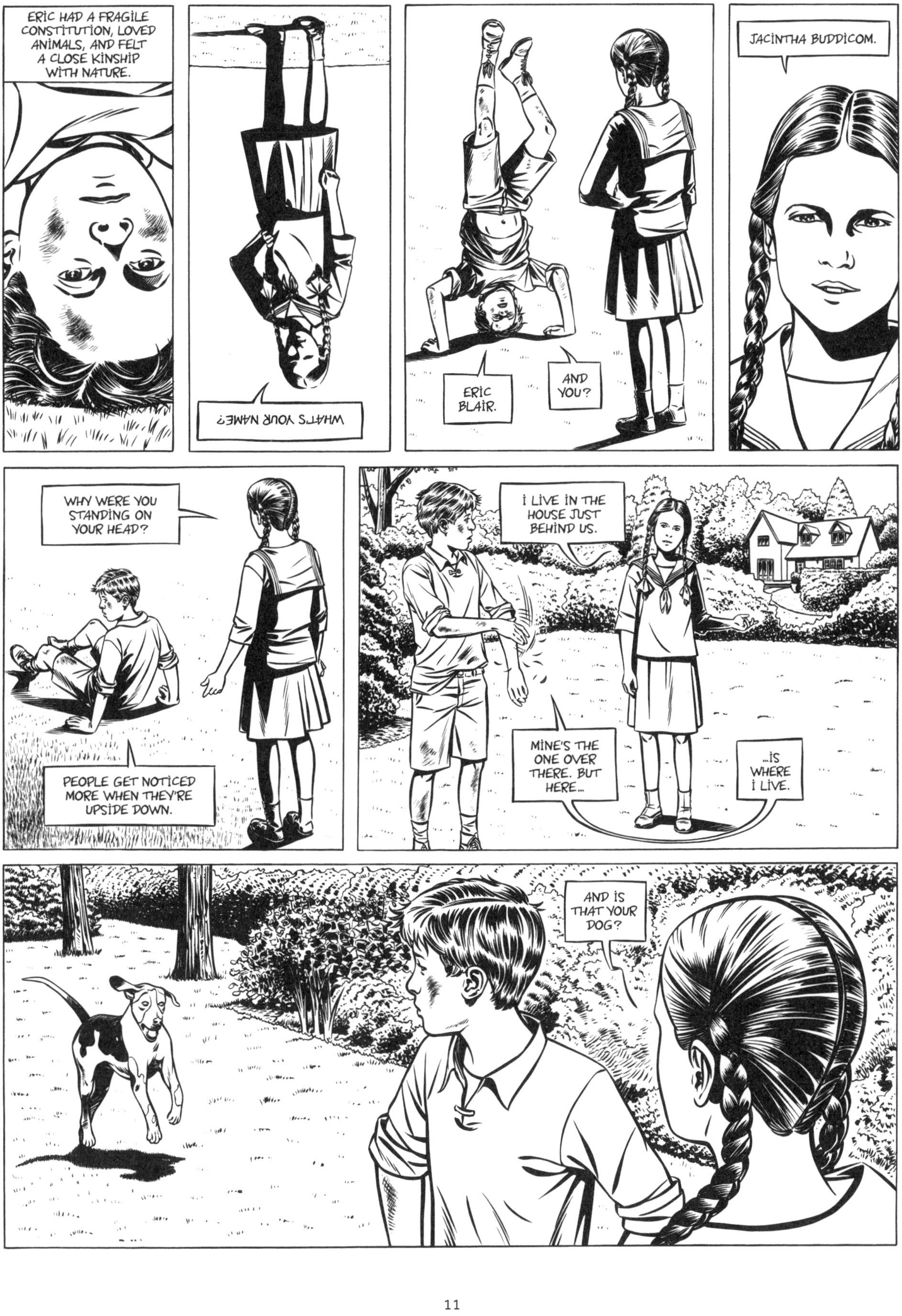
ERIC HAD A FRAGILE CONSTITUTION, LOVED ANIMALS, AND FELT A CLOSE KINSHIP WITH NATURE.
WHAT'S YOUR NAME?
ERIC BLAIR.
AND YOU?
JACINTHA BUDDICOM.
WHY WERE YOU STANDING ON YOUR HEAD?
PEOPLE GET NOTICED MORE WHEN THEY'RE UPSIDE DOWN.
I LIVE IN THE HOUSE JUST BEHIND US.
MINE'S THE ONE OVER THERE. BUT HERE...
...IS WHERE I LIVE.
AND IS THAT YOUR DOG?

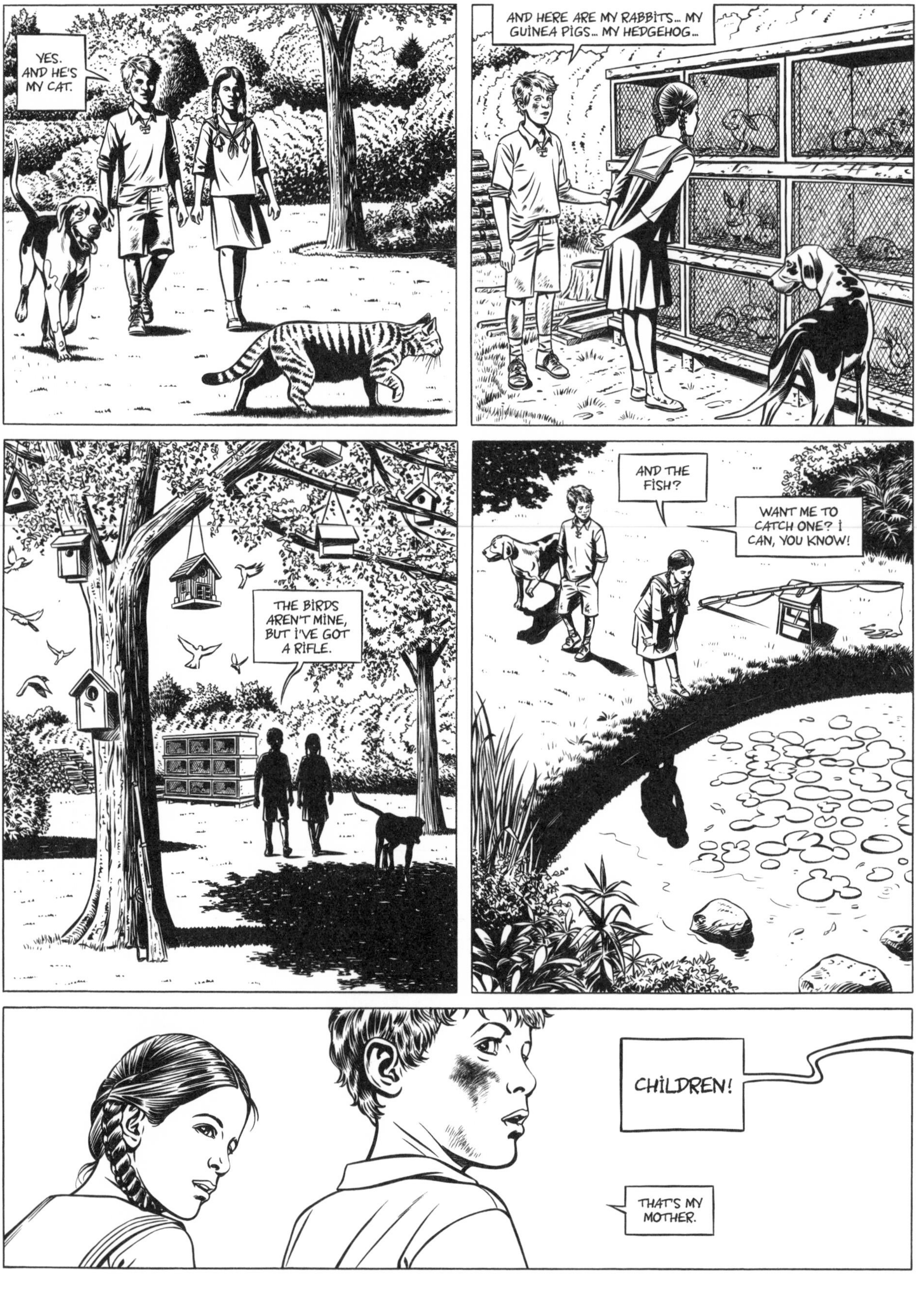
YES. AND HE'S MY CAT.
AND HERE ARE MY RABBITS... MY GUINEA PIGS... MY HEDGEHOG...
THE BIRDS AREN'T MINE, BUT I'VE GOT A RIFLE.
AND THE FISH?
WANT ME TO CATCH ONE? I CAN, YOU KNOW!
CHILDREN!
THAT'S MY MOTHER.

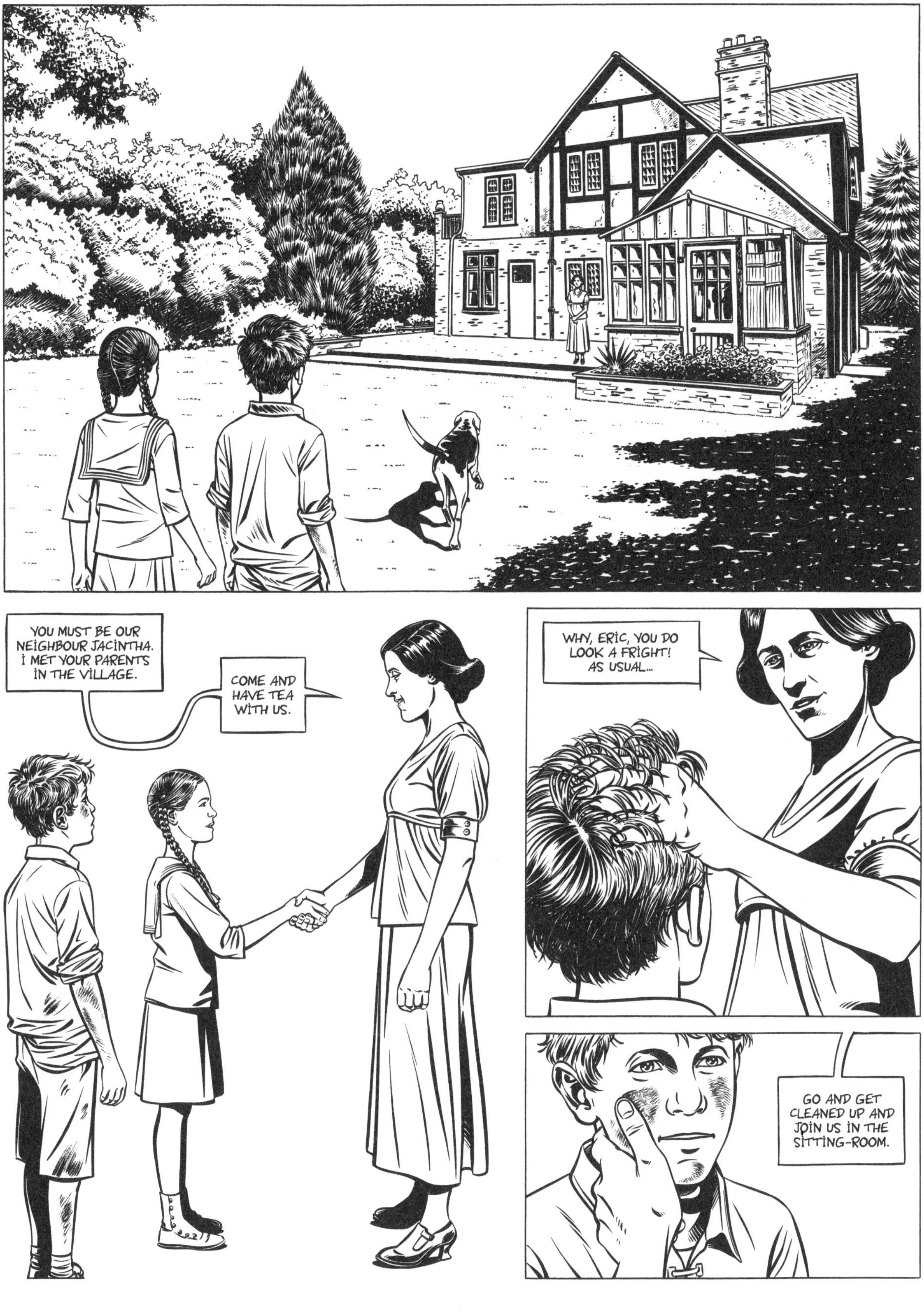
YOU MUST BE OUR NEIGHBOUR JACINTHA. I MET YOUR PARENTS IN THE VILLAGE.
COME AND HAVE TEA WITH US.
WHY, ERIC, YOU DO LOOK A FRIGHT! AS USUAL...
GO AND GET CLEANED UP AND JOIN US IN THE SITTING-ROOM.

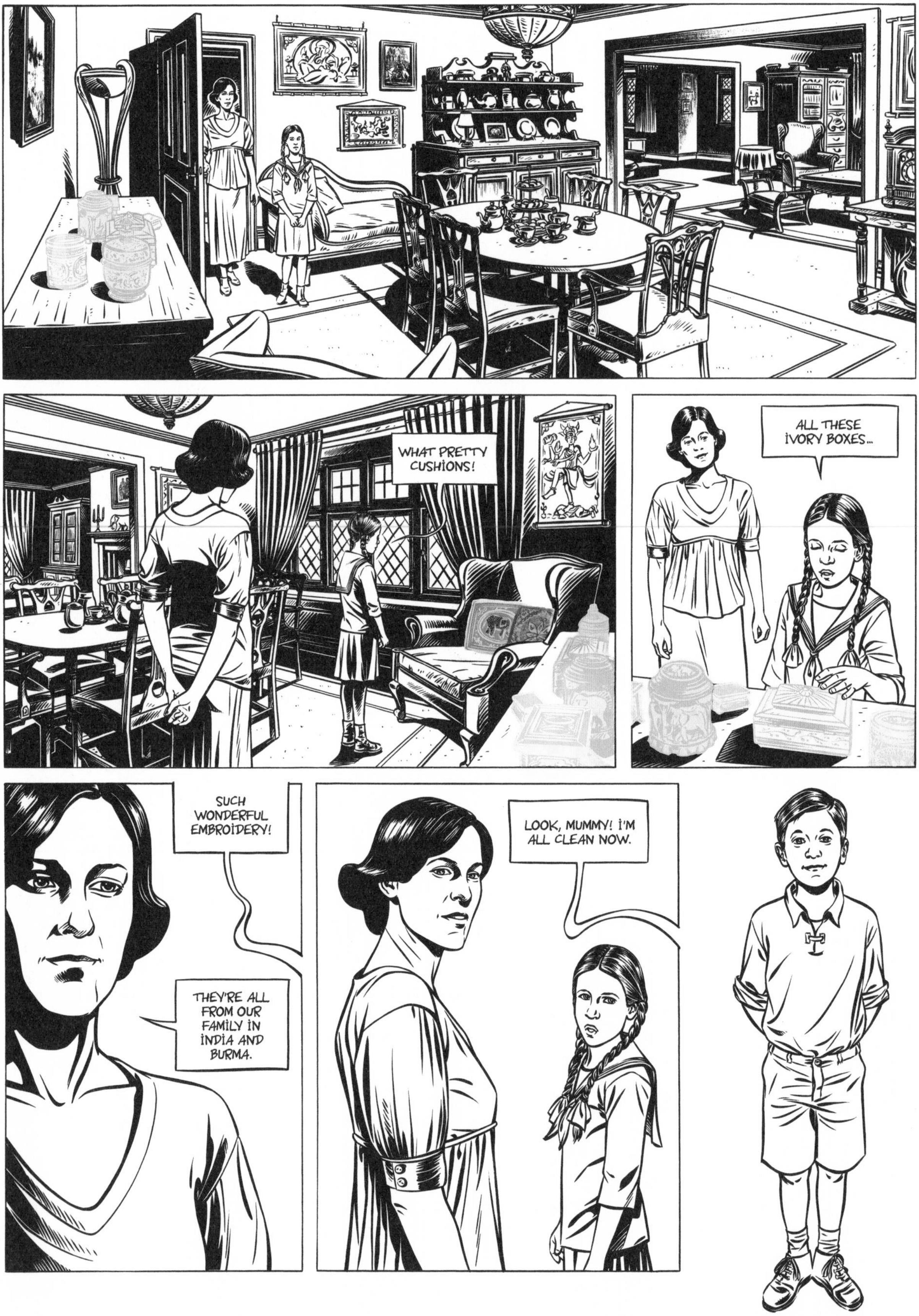
WHAT PRETTY CUSHIONS!
ALL THESE IVORY BOXES...
SUCH WONDERFUL EMBROIDERY!
THEY'RE ALL FROM OUR FAMILY IN INDIA AND BURMA.
LOOK, MUMMY! I'M ALL CLEAN NOW.

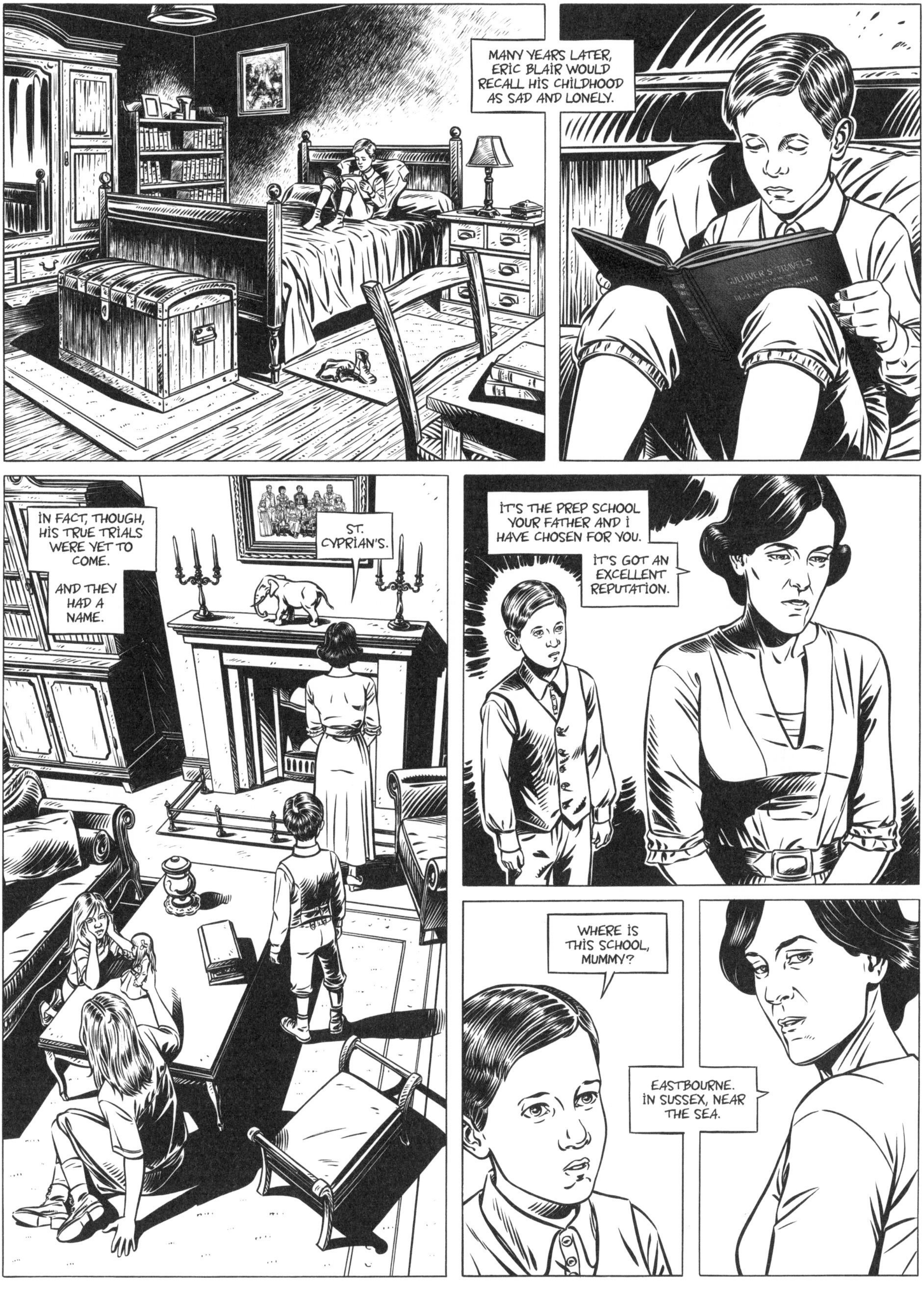
MANY YEARS LATER, ERIC BLAIR WOULD RECALL HIS CHILDHOOD AS SAD AND LONELY.
GULLIVER'S TRAVELS
IN FACT, THOUGH, HIS TRUE TRIALS WERE YET TO COME.
AND THEY HAD A NAME.
ST. CYPRIAN'S.
IT'S THE PREP SCHOOL YOUR FATHER AND I HAVE CHOSEN FOR YOU.
IT'S GOT AN EXCELLENT REPUTATION.
WHERE IS THIS SCHOOL, MUMMY?
EASTBOURNE. IN SUSSEX, NEAR THE SEA.

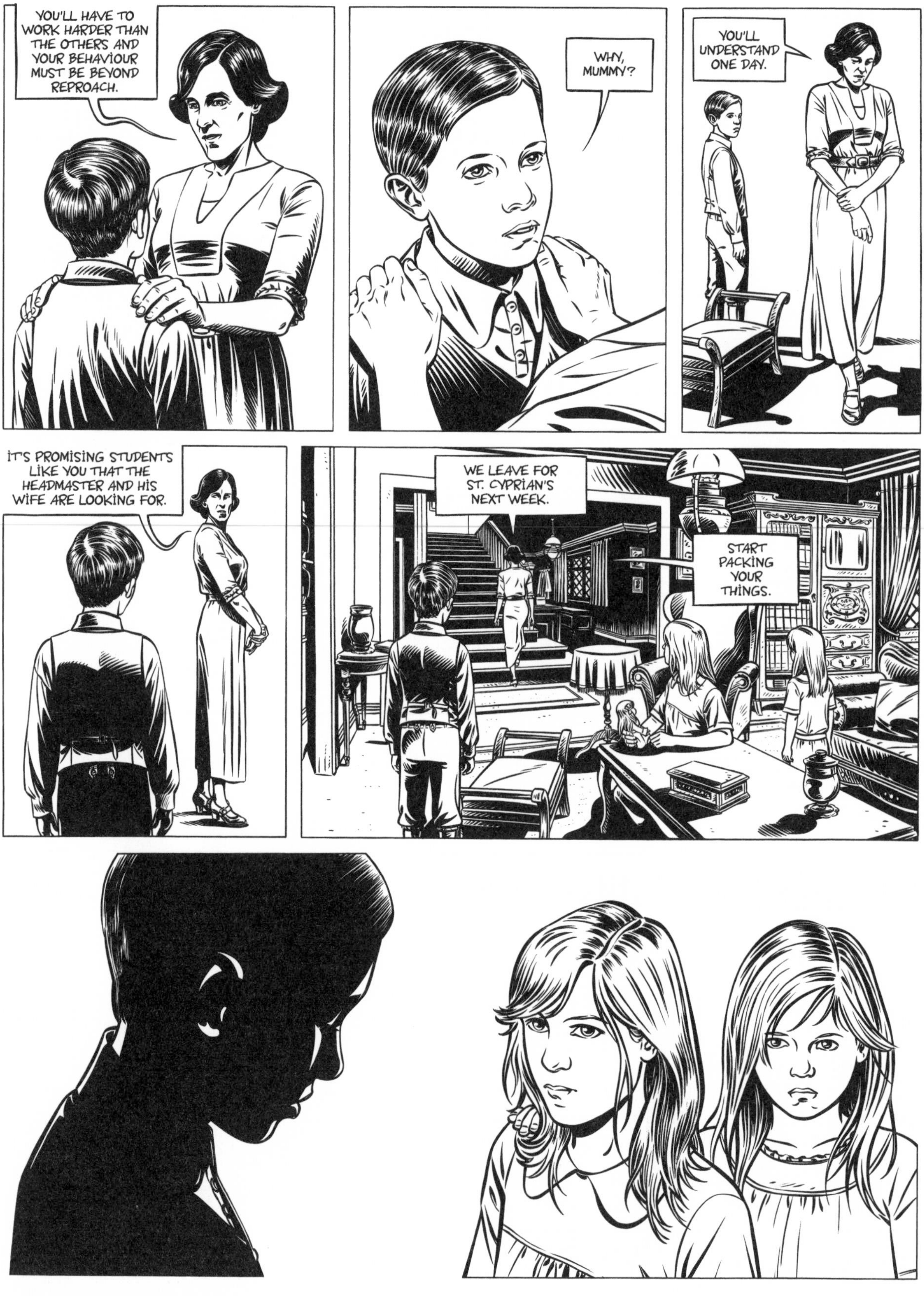
YOU'LL HAVE TO WORK HARDER THAN THE OTHERS AND YOUR BEHAVIOUR MUST BE BEYOND REPROACH.
WHY, MUMMY?
YOU'LL UNDERSTAND ONE DAY.
IT'S PROMISING STUDENTS LIKE YOU THAT THE HEADMASTER AND HIS WIFE ARE LOOKING FOR.
WE LEAVE FOR ST. CYPRIAN'S NEXT WEEK.
START PACKING YOUR THINGS.

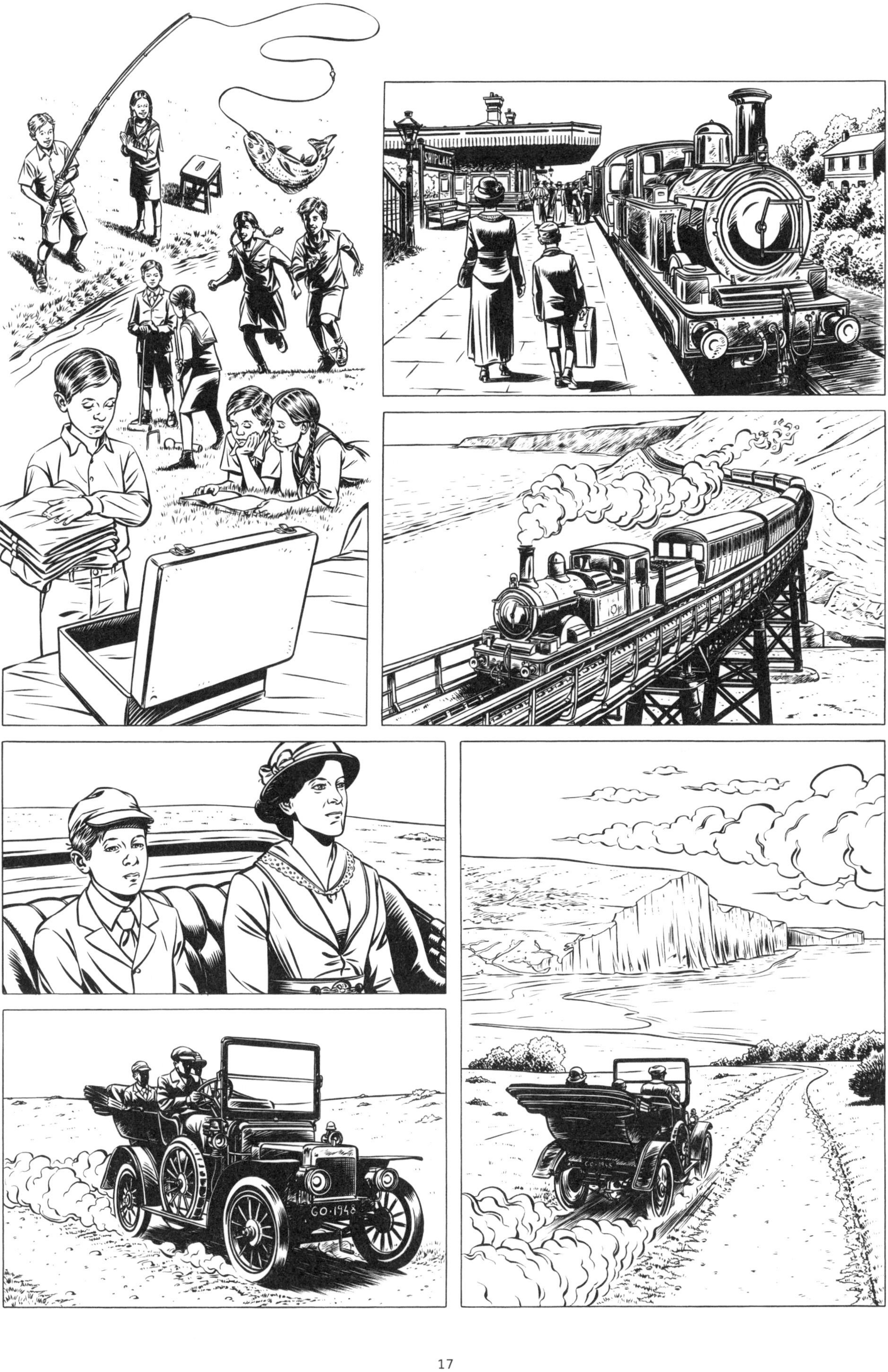
SHIPLAKE
GO·1948

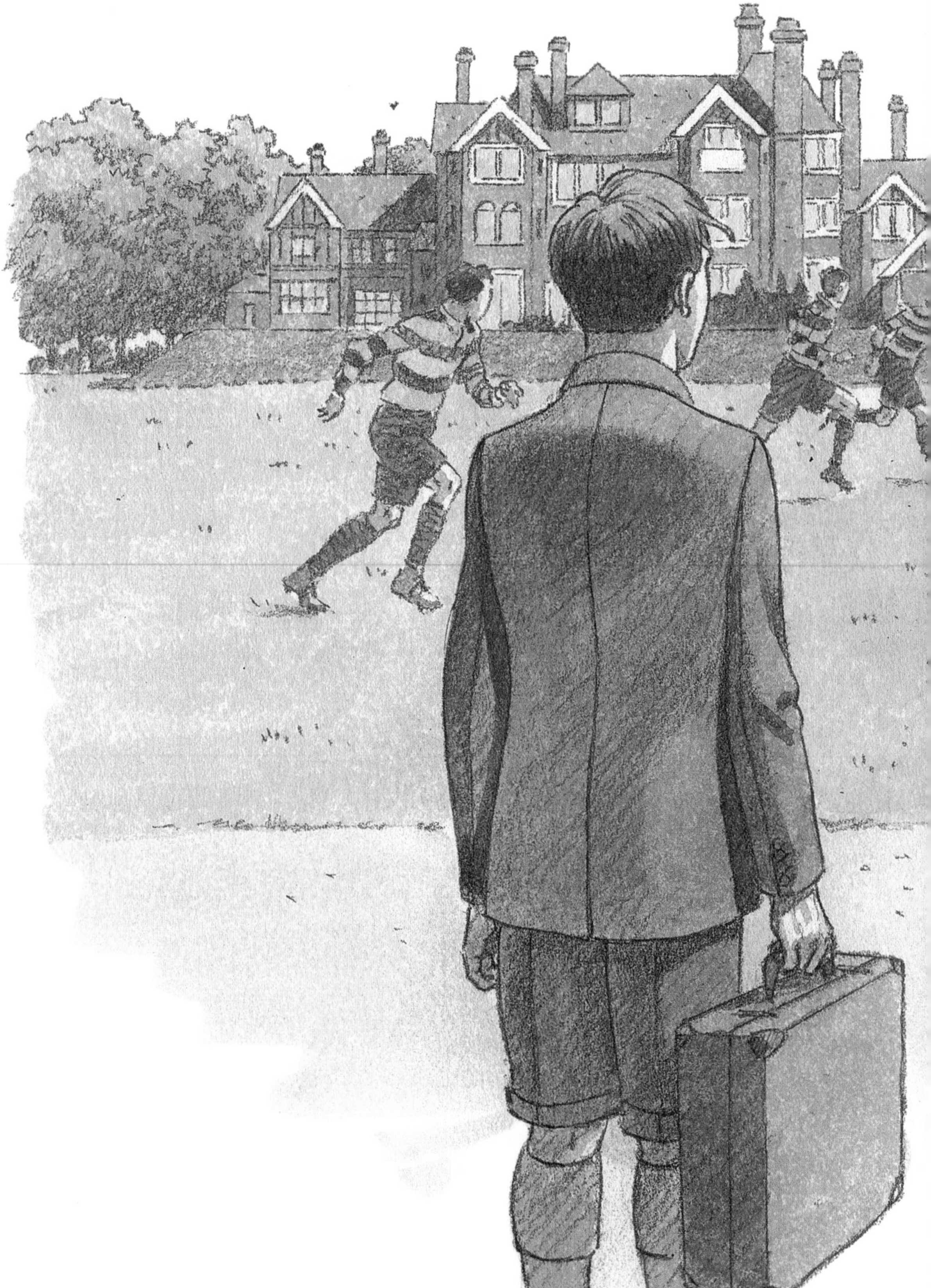

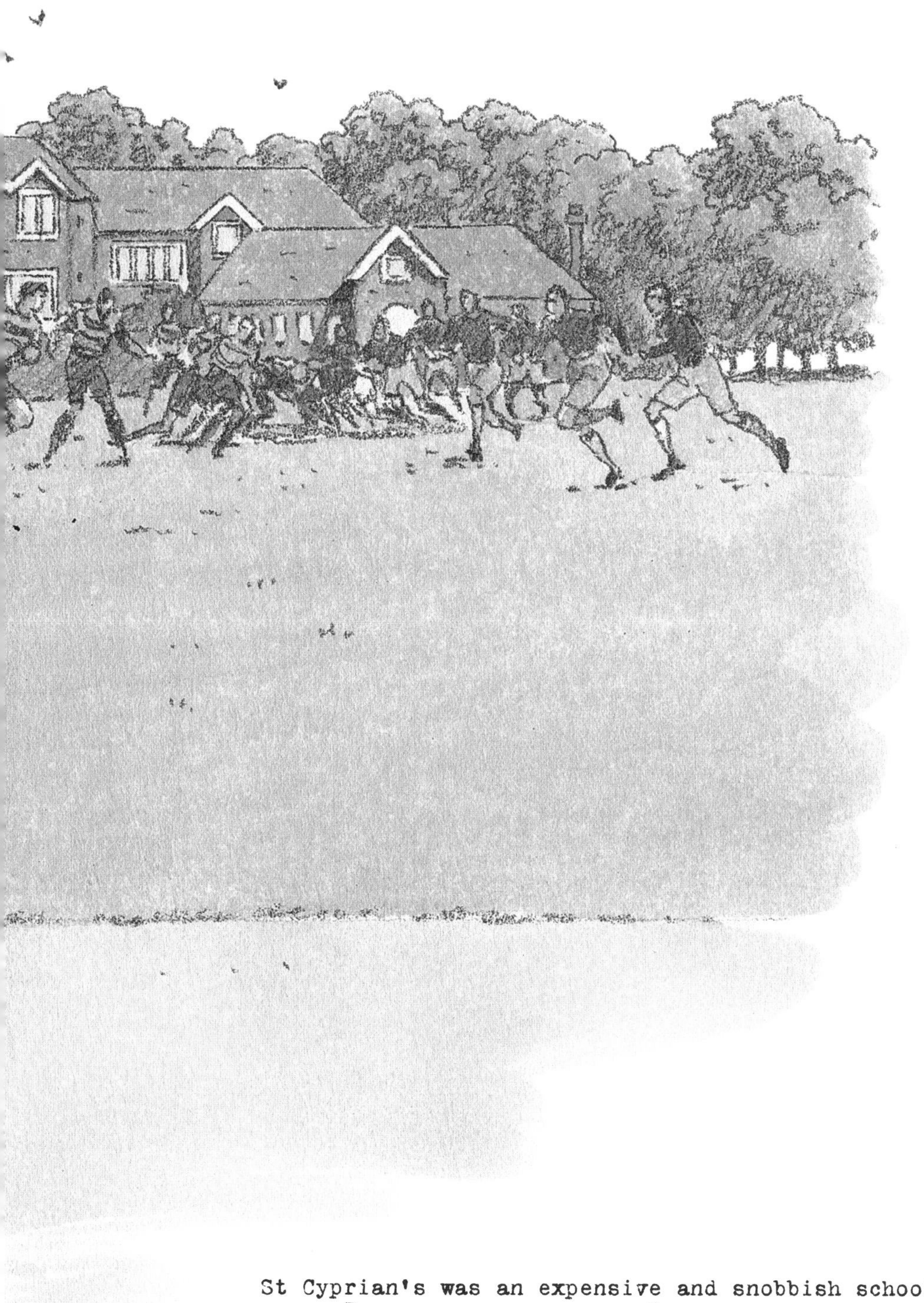

St Cyprian's was an expensive and snobbish school...
Sambo [Mr. W, the headmaster] had two great ambitions. One was to attract titled boys to the school, and the other was to train up pupils to win scholarships at public schools, above all at Eton.

I did not at first understand that I was being taken at reduced fees; it was only when I was about eleven that Flip and Sambo began throwing the fact in my teeth.

Mrs. W[ilkes] was nicknamed Flip... Although a great
deal of the time she was full of false heartiness...
her eyes never lost their anxious, accusing look.
"Here is a little boy," said Flip, indicating me to
the strange lady, "who wets his bed every night. Do
you know what I am going to do if you wet your bed
again?" she added, turning to me, "I am going to
get the Sixth Form to beat you." The strange lady
put on an air of being inexpressibly shocked, and
exclaimed "I-should-think-so!"

Sambo seized me by the scruff of the neck, twisted
me over and began beating me with the riding-
crop... He continued for a length of time... ending
up by breaking the riding-crop. The bone handle
went flying across the room... If a boy were the
son of rich parents... Sambo would goad him along
in a comparatively fatherly way, with jokes and
digs in the ribs and perhaps an occasional tap
with the pencil. It was the poor but "clever" boys
who suffered... But there is one more thing to be
remarked. This is that I did not wet my bed again.

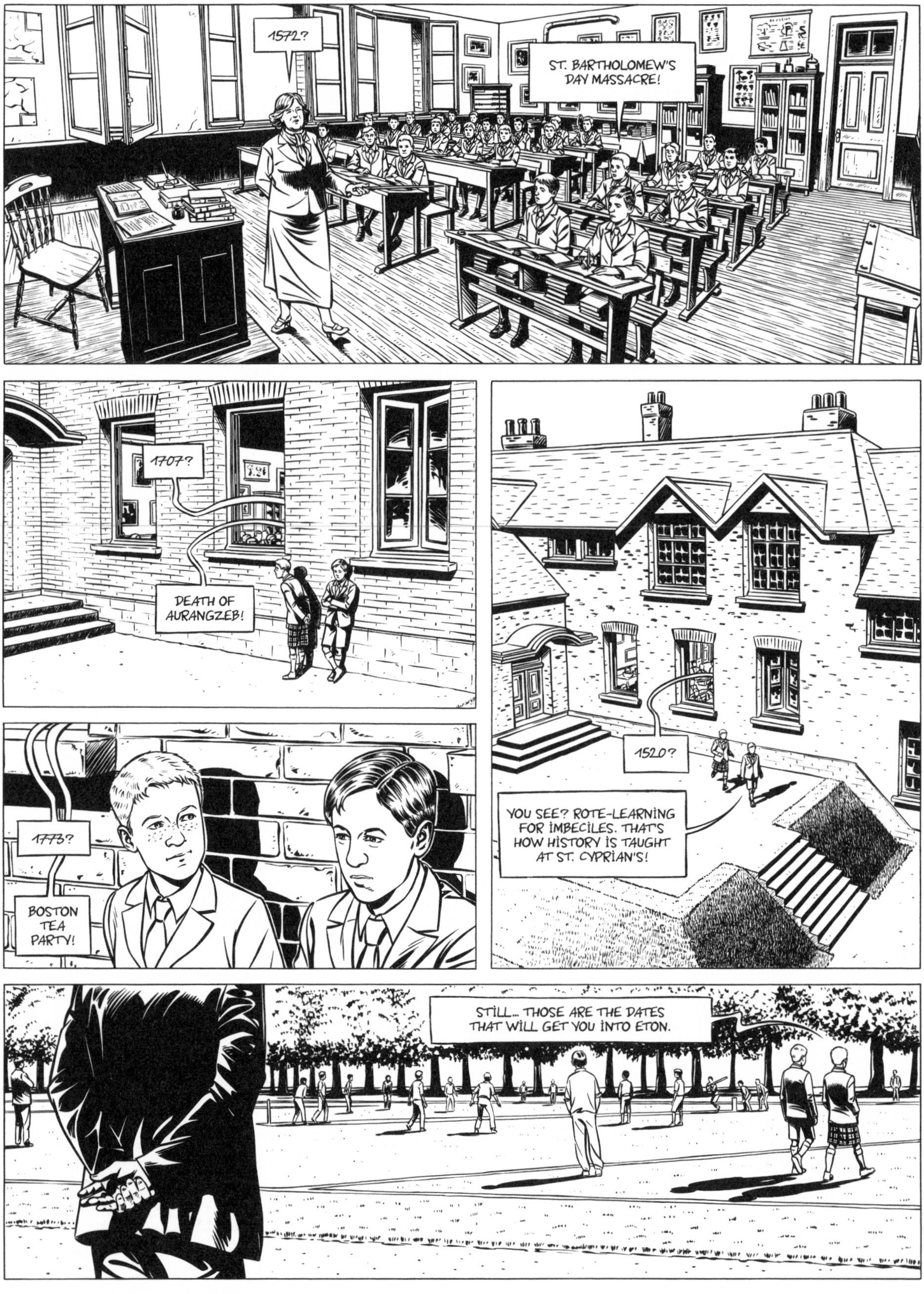
1572?
ST. BARTHOLOMEW'S DAY MASSACRE!
1707?
DEATH OF AURANGZEB!
1773?
BOSTON TEA PARTY!
1520?
YOU SEE? ROTE-LEARNING FOR IMBECILES. THAT'S HOW HISTORY IS TAUGHT AT ST. CYPRIAN'S!
STILL... THOSE ARE THE DATES THAT WILL GET YOU INTO ETON.

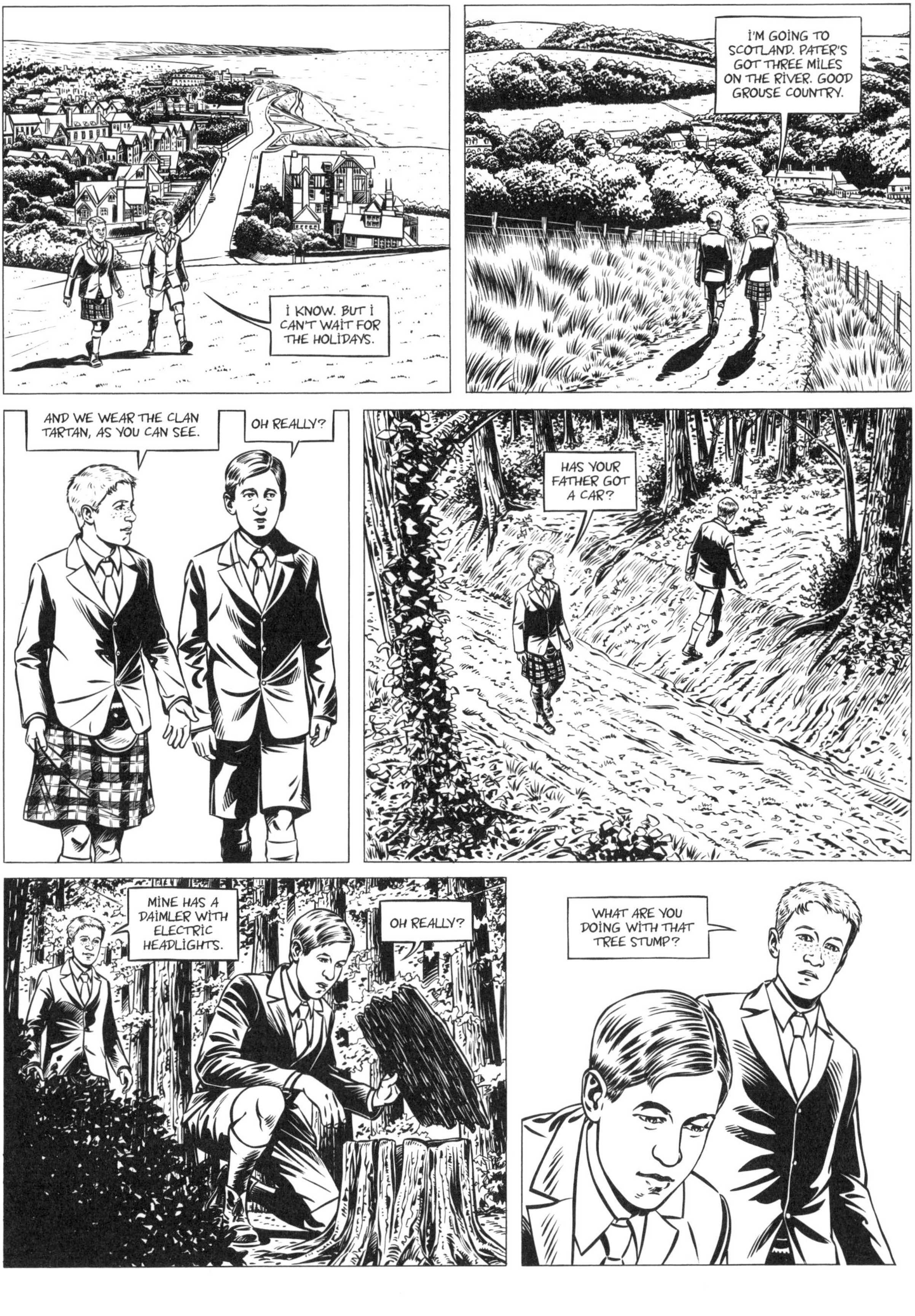
I KNOW. BUT I CAN'T WAIT FOR THE HOLIDAYS.
I'M GOING TO SCOTLAND. PATER'S GOT THREE MILES ON THE RIVER. GOOD GROUSE COUNTRY.
AND WE WEAR THE CLAN TARTAN, AS YOU CAN SEE.
OH REALLY?
HAS YOUR FATHER GOT A CAR?
MINE HAS A DAIMLER WITH ELECTRIC HEADLIGHTS.
OH REALLY?
WHAT ARE YOU DOING WITH THAT TREE STUMP?

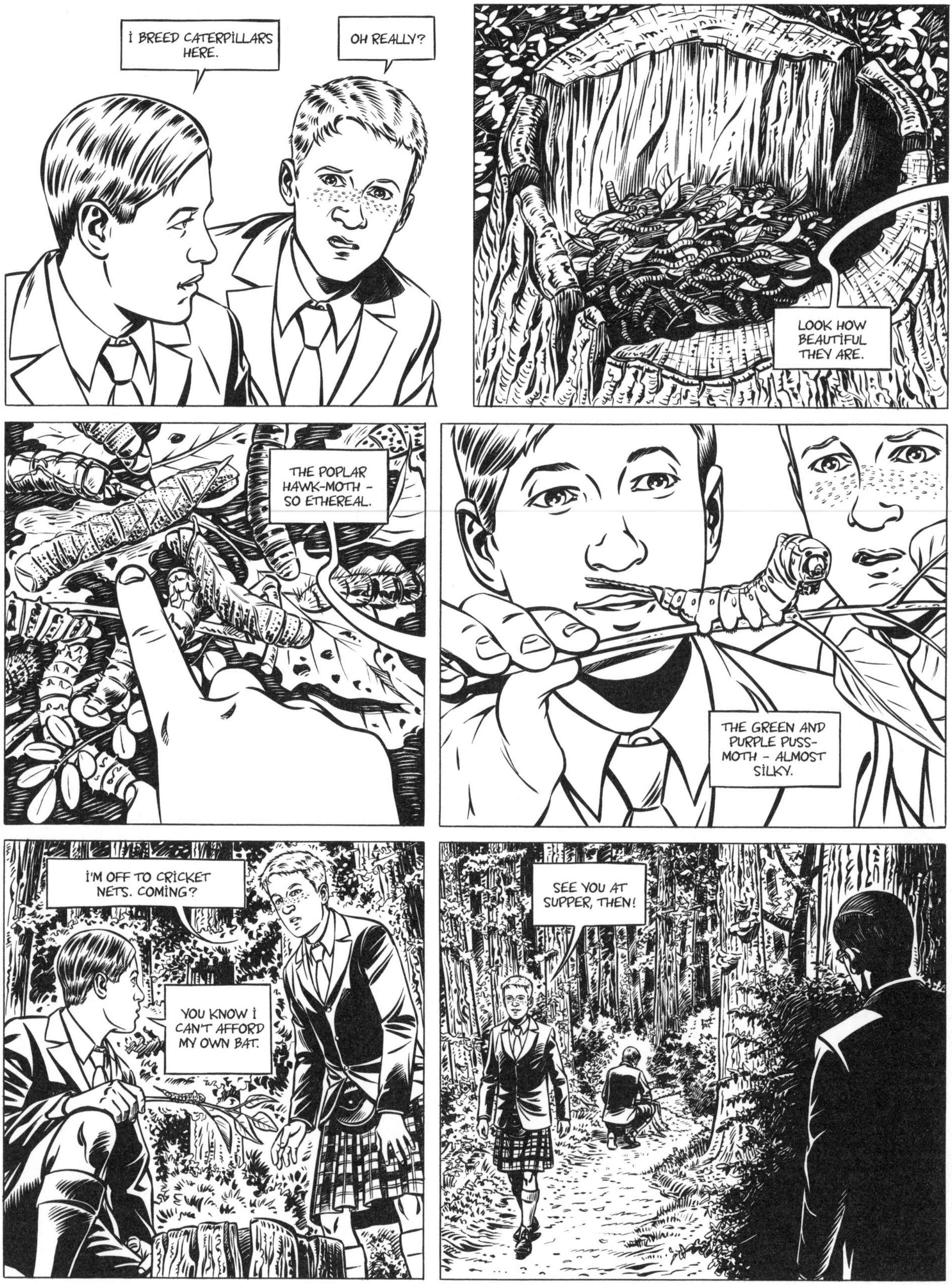
I BREED CATERPILLARS HERE.
OH REALLY?
LOOK HOW BEAUTIFUL THEY ARE.
THE POPLAR HAWK-MOTH - SO ETHEREAL.
THE GREEN AND PURPLE PUSS-MOTH - ALMOST SILKY.
I'M OFF TO CRICKET NETS. COMING?
YOU KNOW I CAN'T AFFORD MY OWN BAT.
SEE YOU AT SUPPER, THEN!

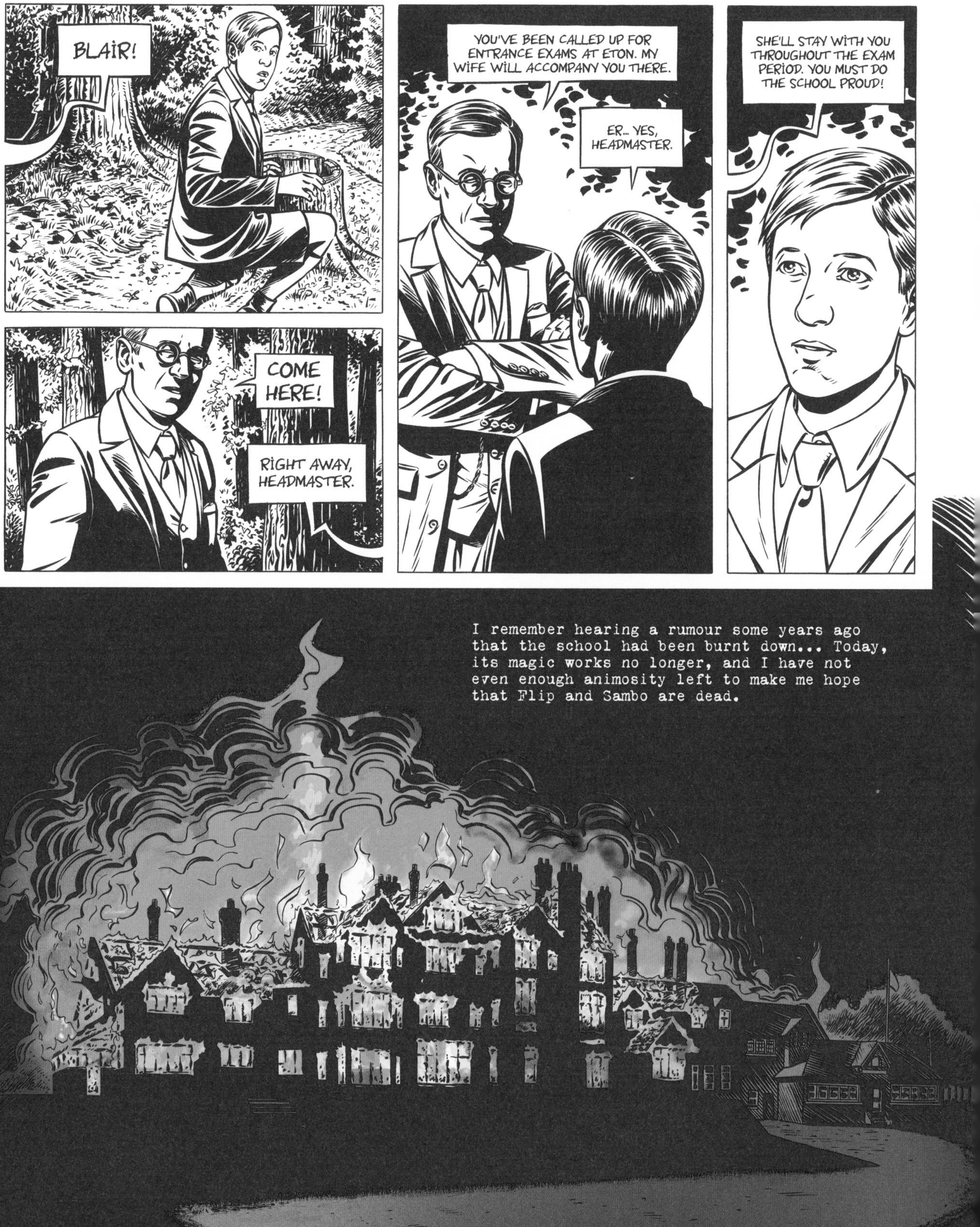
BLAIR!
COME HERE!
RIGHT AWAY, HEADMASTER.
YOU'VE BEEN CALLED UP FOR ENTRANCE EXAMS AT ETON. MY WIFE WILL ACCOMPANY YOU THERE.
ER... YES, HEADMASTER.
SHE'LL STAY WITH YOU THROUGHOUT THE EXAM PERIOD. YOU MUST DO THE SCHOOL PROUD!
I remember hearing a rumour some years ago that the school had been burnt down... Today, its magic works no longer, and I have not even enough animosity left to make me hope that Flip and Sambo are dead.

AT ETON, ERIC BLAIR'S EDUCATION PROCEEDED IN A MORE HARMONIOUS FASHION.

BUT HE HAD DECIDED TO DO AS LITTLE WORK AS POSSIBLE, AND THE WAR RAGING ON THE CONTINENT SEEMED FAR AWAY...

NEGLECTING THE FORMAL CURRICULUM AND HIS TUTORS' WARNINGS, BUT ENGAGING IN SEVERAL SPORTS...

...HE DEVOURED THE WRITERS HE ADMIRED: H.G. WELLS – ALWAYS H.G. WELLS – BUT ALSO ALDOUS HUXLEY, CHARLES DICKENS, LEO TOLSTOY, JACK LONDON...

AND THERE HE ALSO PICKED UP THE INIMITABLE ACCENT THAT HE WOULD NEVER QUITE SHED, DESPITE HIS MANY FUTURE DISGUISES...

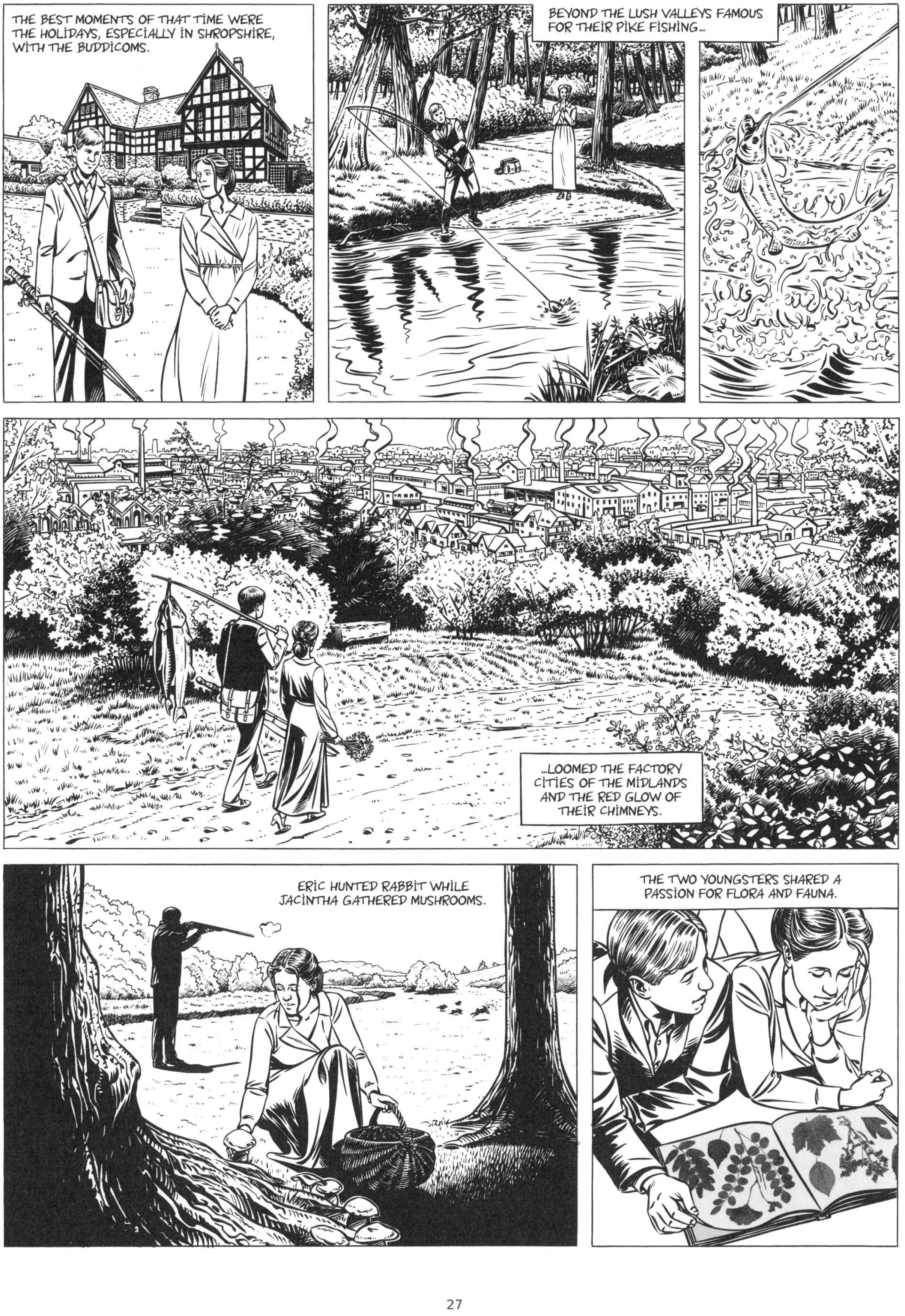
THE BEST MOMENTS OF THAT TIME WERE THE HOLIDAYS, ESPECIALLY IN SHROPSHIRE, WITH THE BUDDICOMS.
BEYOND THE LUSH VALLEYS FAMOUS FOR THEIR PIKE FISHING...
...LOOMED THE FACTORY CITIES OF THE MIDLANDS AND THE RED GLOW OF THEIR CHIMNEYS.
ERIC HUNTED RABBIT WHILE JACINTHA GATHERED MUSHROOMS.
THE TWO YOUNGSTERS SHARED A PASSION FOR FLORA AND FAUNA.

UNLIKE MANY OF HIS CLASSMATES, ERIC WOULD NOT GO TO OXFORD.

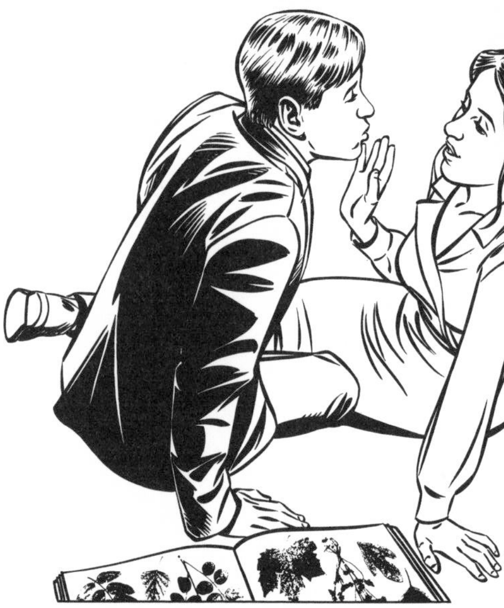

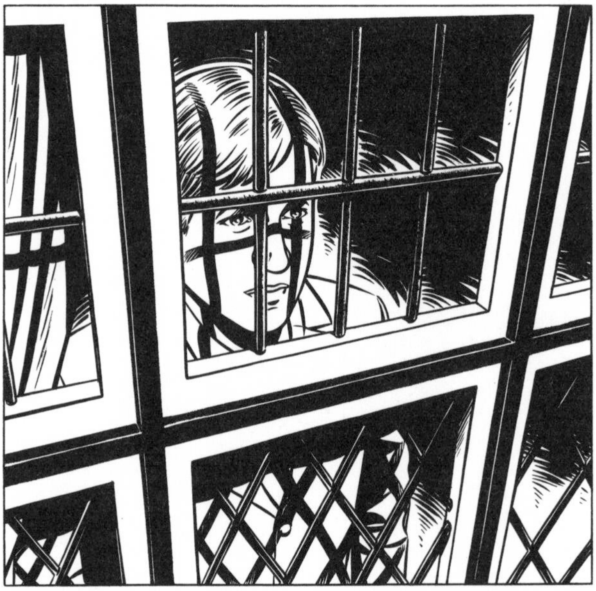

PERHAPS INFLUENCED BY THE FAMILY STORIES THAT HAD PASSED DOWN, HE MADE A RATHER ODD CHOICE: TO JOIN THE IMPERIAL POLICE IN BURMA.

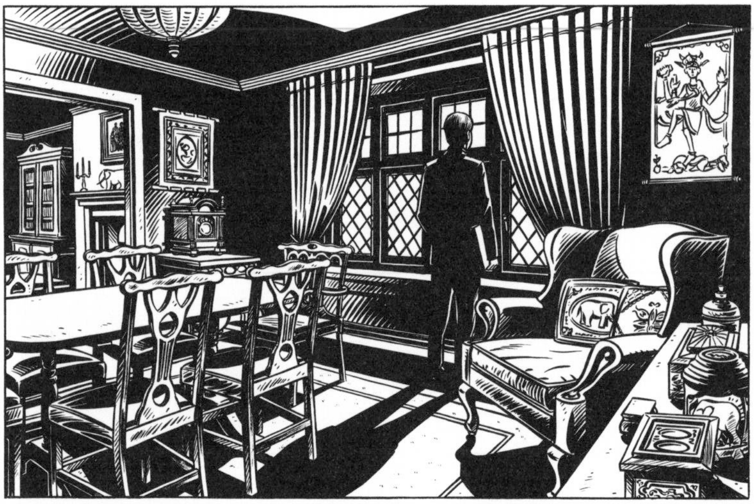

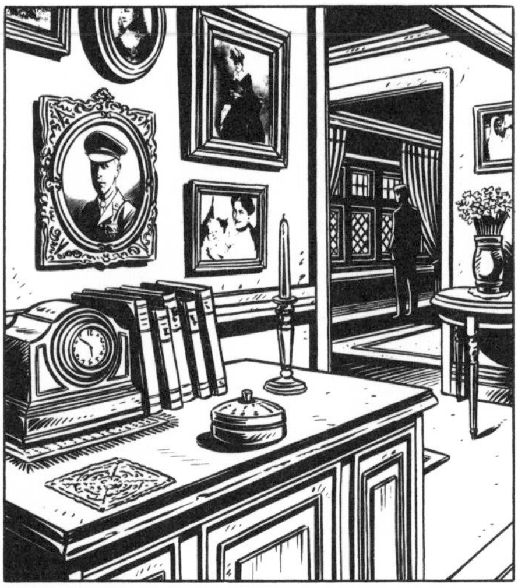

HE WENT TO AN ACADEMY WHERE HE ALWAYS STOOD OUT AS THE TALLEST BOY, AS IN THE PHOTOGRAPH BELOW.

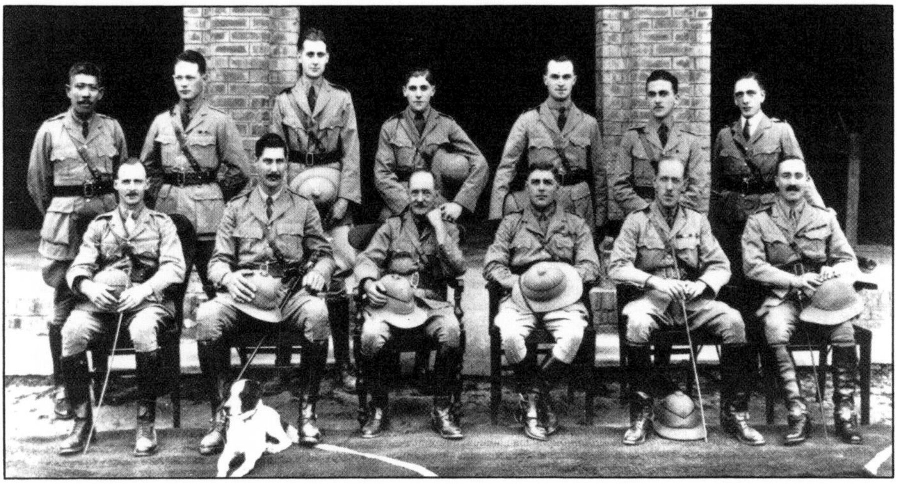

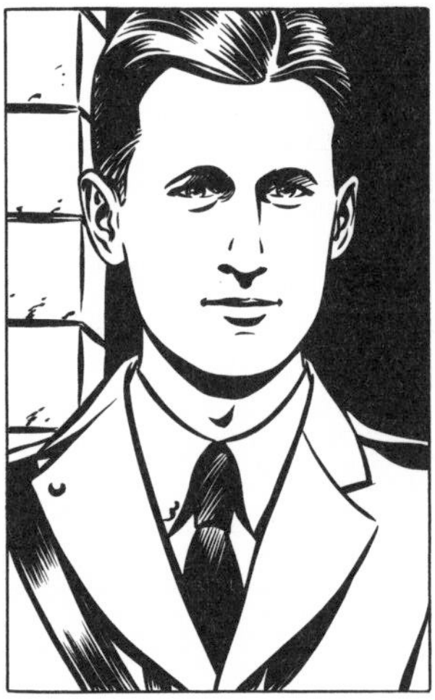

IT WAS ON A LONG VOYAGE BY SEA TO ASIA IN 1922 THAT HE FIRST BECAME AWARE OF CLASS DIFFERENCE.

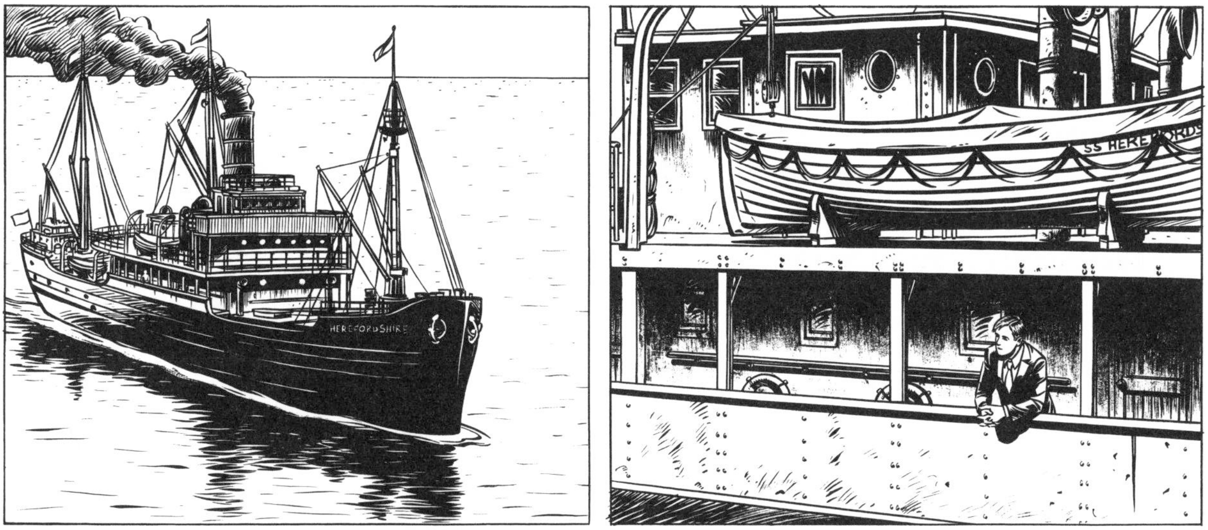
HEREFORDSHIRE

WHILE HE HAD LOOKED UP TO PETTY OFFICERS AT THE WHEEL AS "GODLIKE BEINGS", ONE DAY HE SURPRISED ONE...

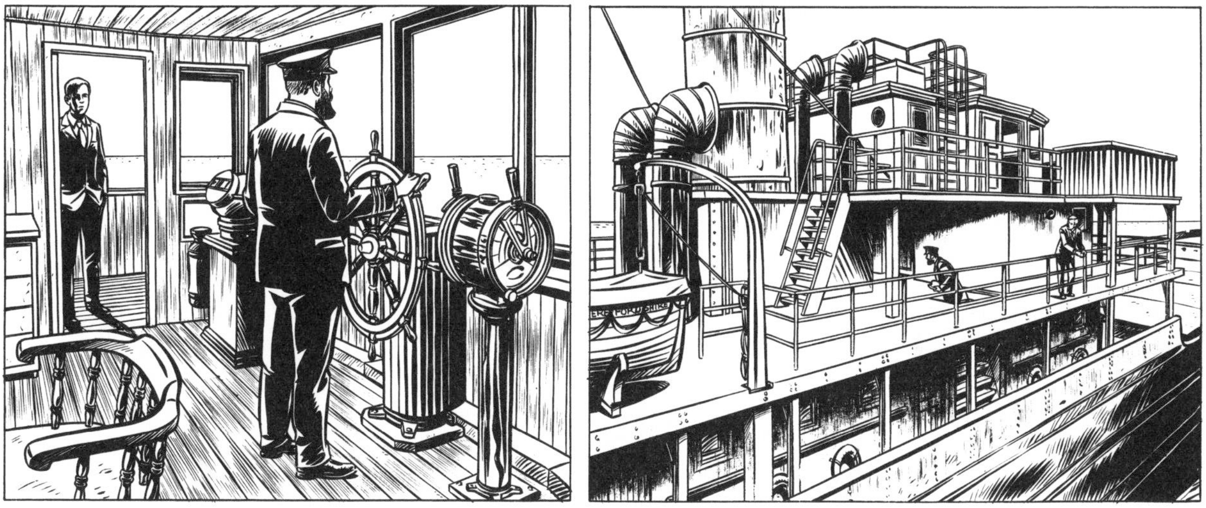

...scurrying like a rat along the side of the deck-houses with... a half-eaten baked custard pudding... from the passengers' tables.

The astonishment that struck me then taught me more than I could have learned from half a dozen Socialist pamphlets.

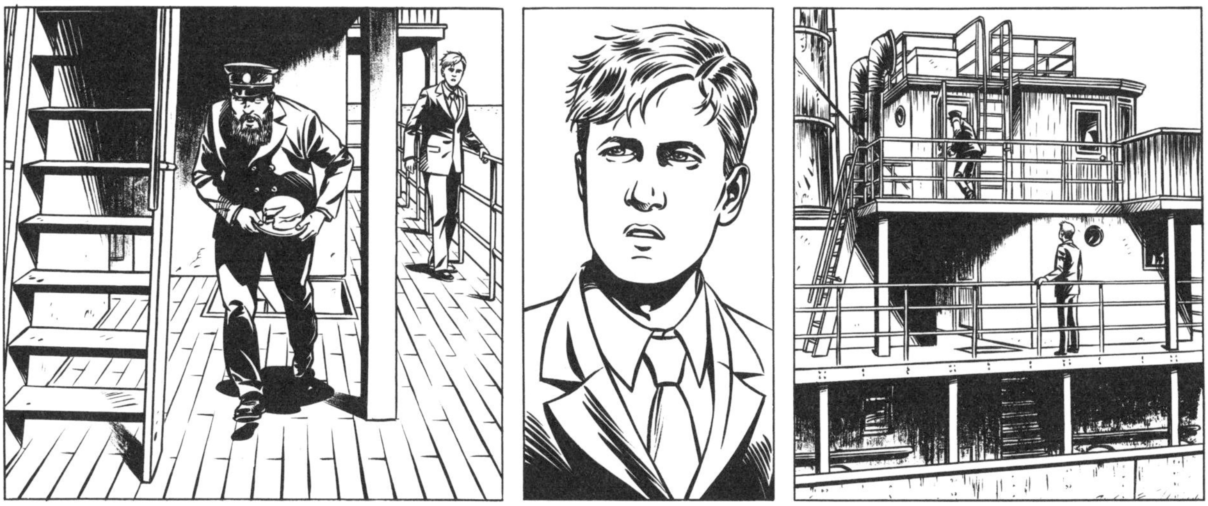

SAHIB, COME QUICK!

RIGHT AWAY, SAHIB! BRING THE CARBINE!

A TAMED ELEPHANT WENT "MUSTH" AND RAVAGED THE BAZAAR!

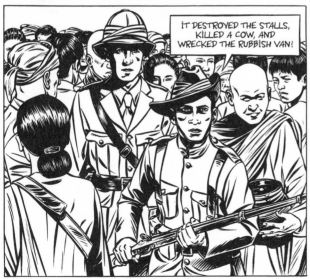

IT DESTROYED THE STALLS, KILLED A COW, AND WRECKED THE RUBBISH VAN!

IT TRAMPLED A COOLIE UNDERFOOT!

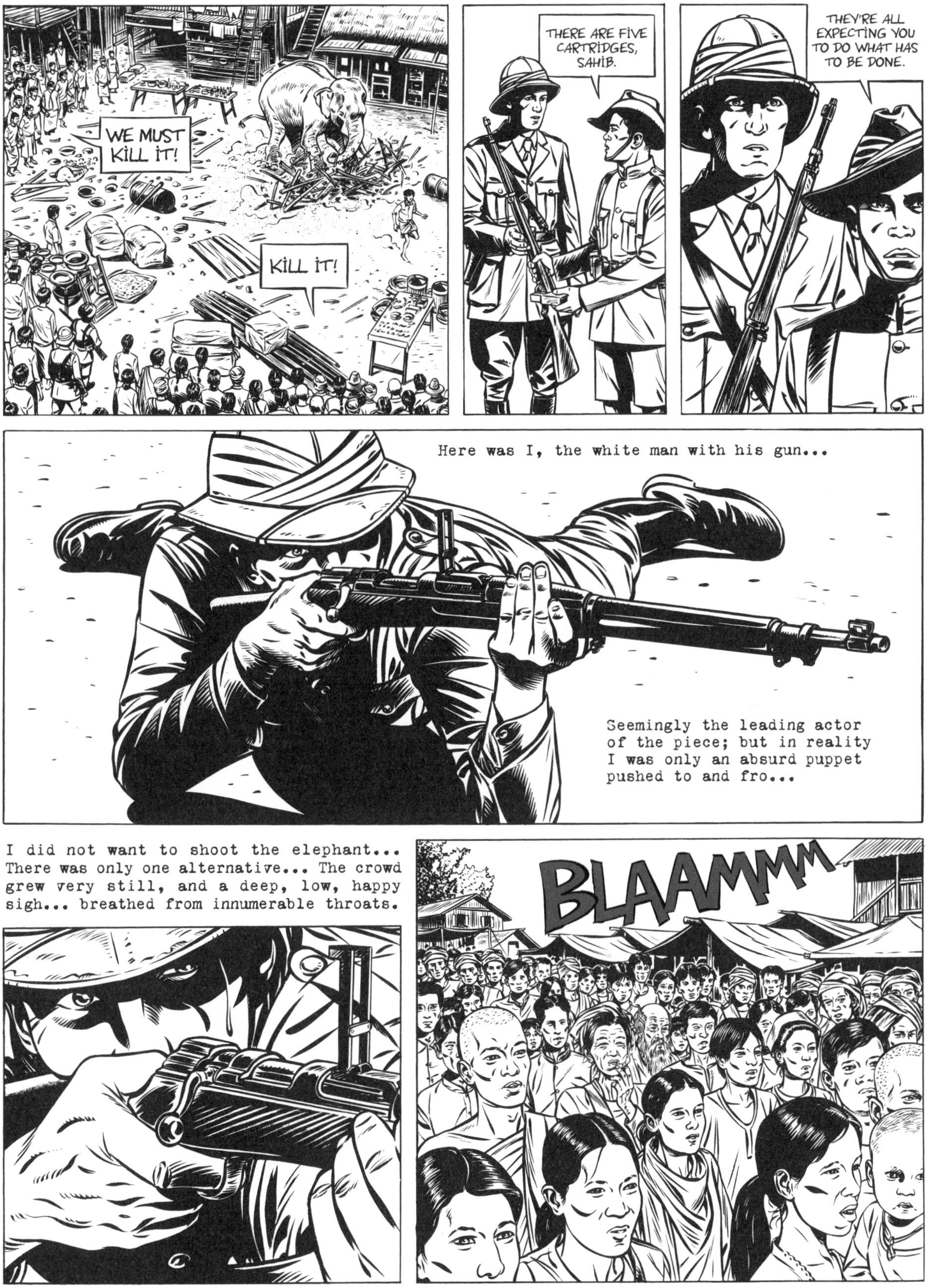
WE MUST KILL IT!
KILL IT!
THERE ARE FIVE CARTRIDGES, SAHIB.
THEY'RE ALL EXPECTING YOU TO DO WHAT HAS TO BE DONE.
Here was I, the white man with his gun...
Seemingly the leading actor of the piece; but in reality I was only an absurd puppet pushed to and fro...
I did not want to shoot the elephant... There was only one alternative... The crowd grew very still, and a deep, low, happy sigh... breathed from innumerable throats.
BLAAMMM

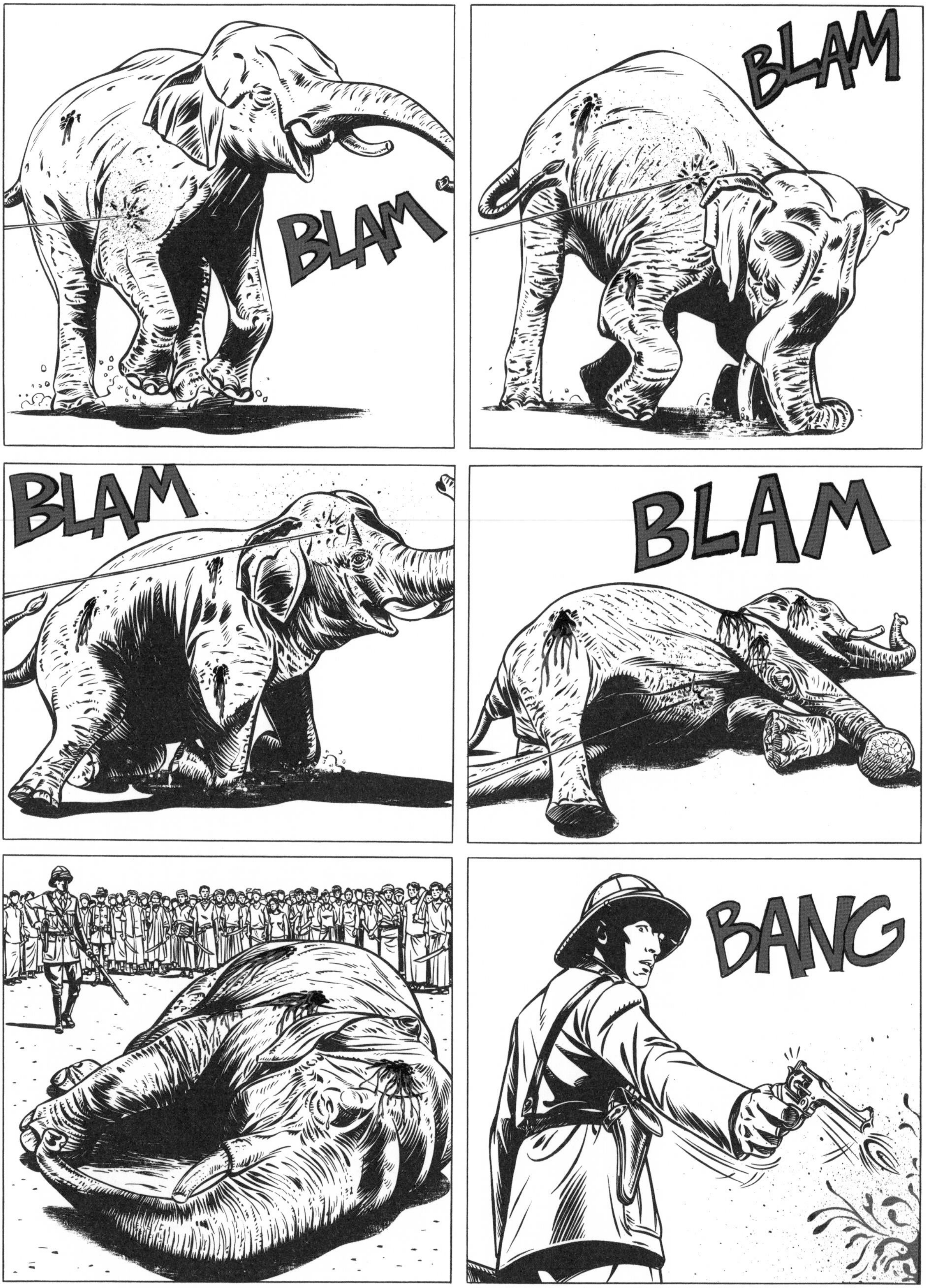
BLAM
BLAM
BLAM
BLAM
BANG

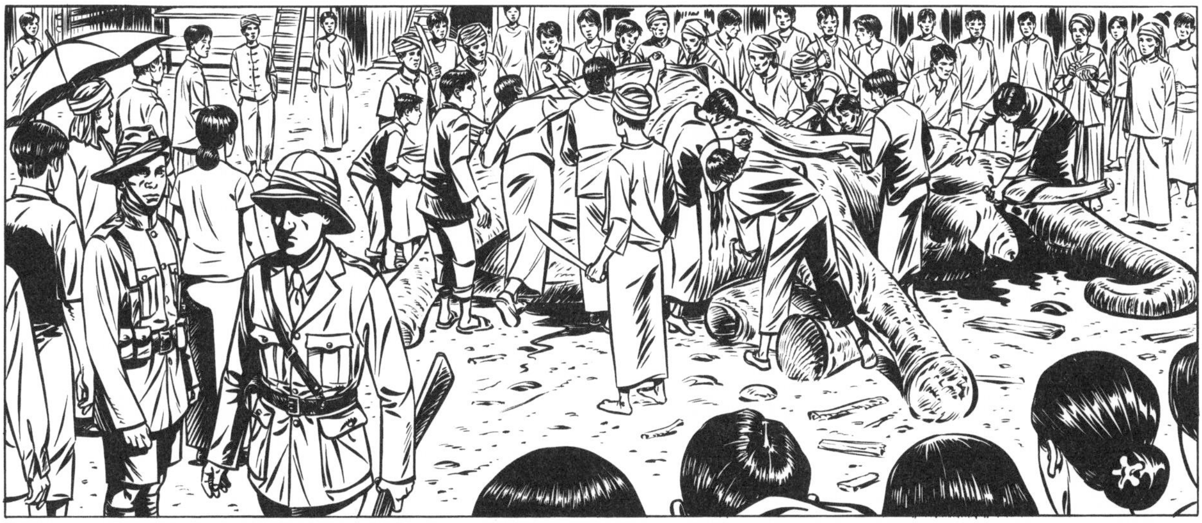

I often wondered whether any of the others grasped that I had done it solely to avoid looking a fool.

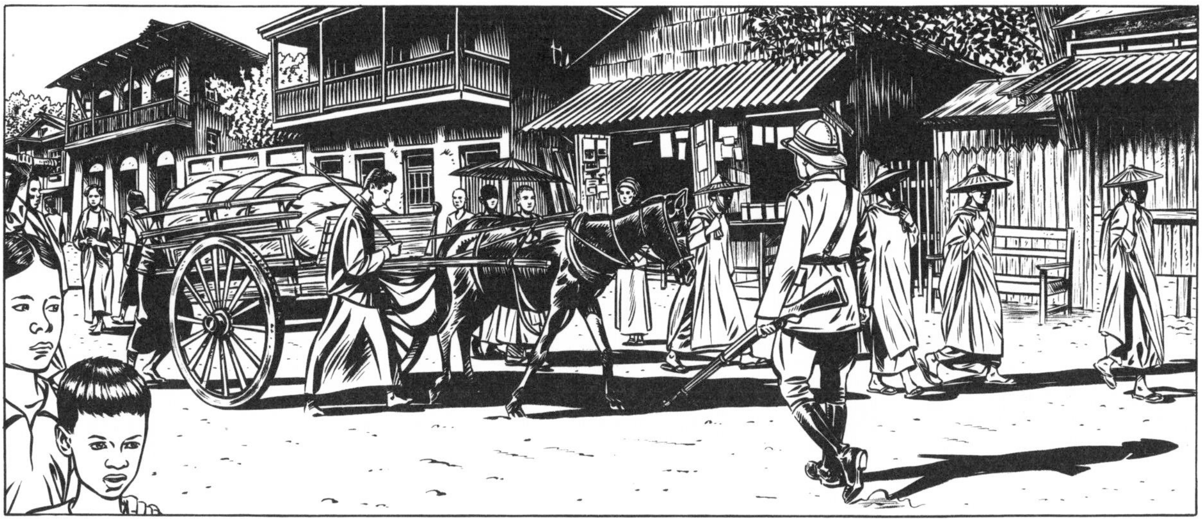

For at that time I had already made up my mind that imperialism was an evil thing and the sooner I chucked up my job and got out of it the better.

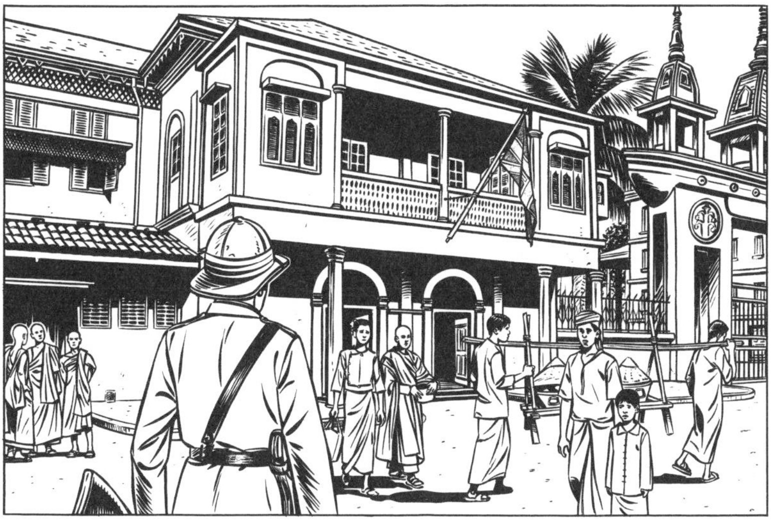

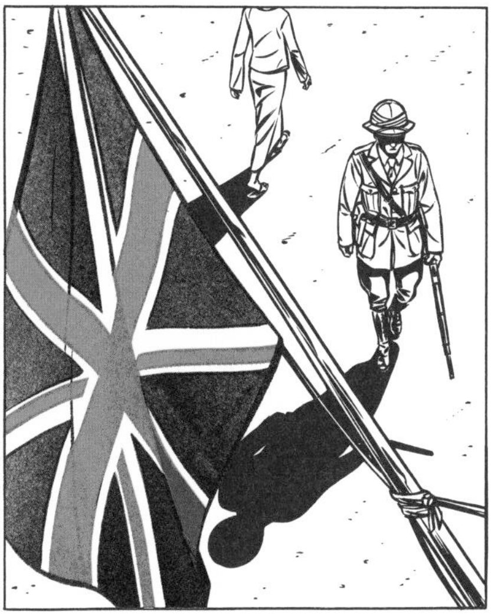

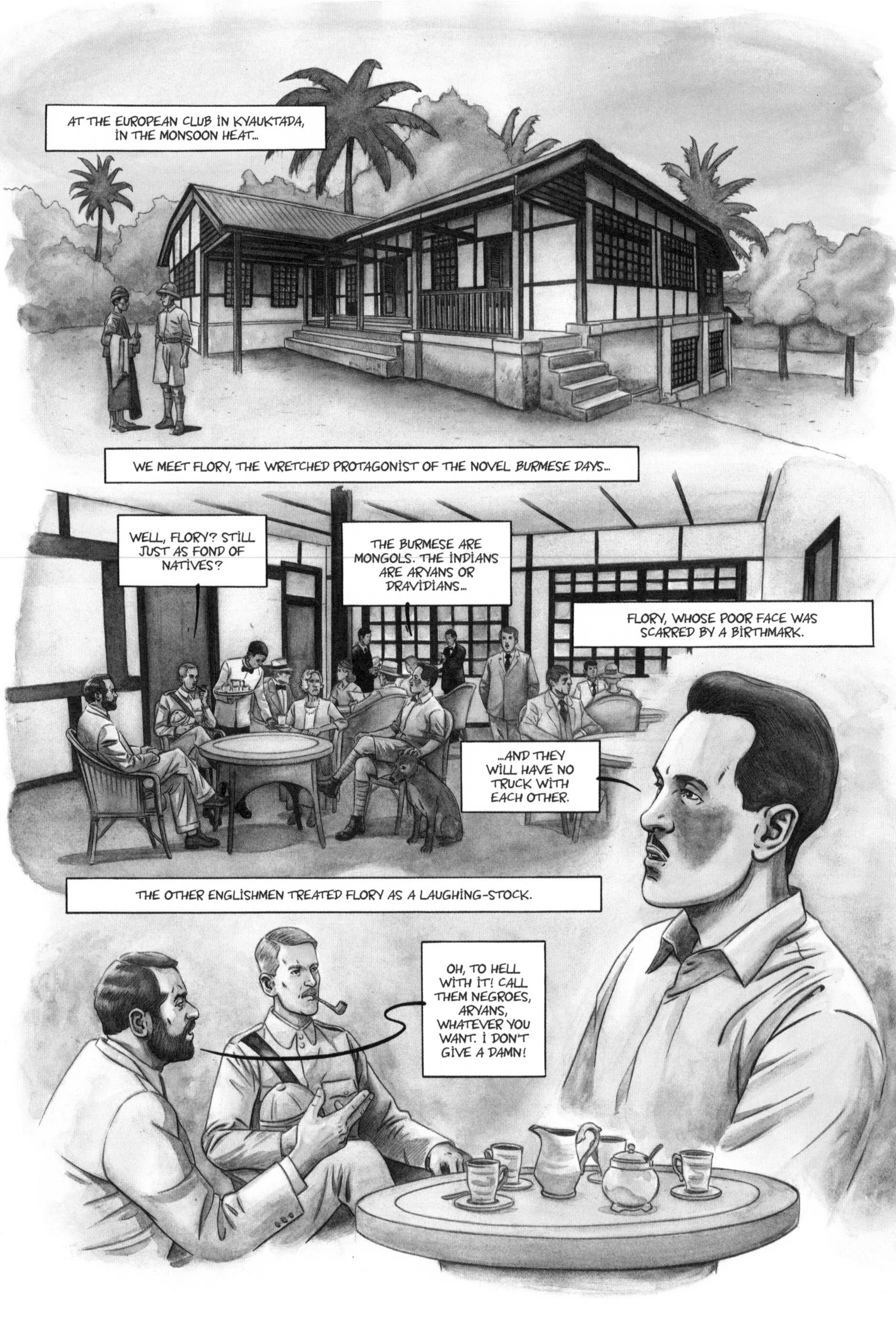
AT THE EUROPEAN CLUB IN KYAUKTADA, IN THE MONSOON HEAT...
WE MEET FLORY, THE WRETCHED PROTAGONIST OF THE NOVEL BURMESE DAYS...
WELL, FLORY? STILL JUST AS FOND OF NATIVES?
THE BURMESE ARE MONGOLS. THE INDIANS ARE ARYANS OR DRAVIDIANS...
FLORY, WHOSE POOR FACE WAS SCARRED BY A BIRTHMARK.
...AND THEY WILL HAVE NO TRUCK WITH EACH OTHER.
THE OTHER ENGLISHMEN TREATED FLORY AS A LAUGHING-STOCK.
OH, TO HELL WITH IT! CALL THEM NEGROES, ARYANS, WHATEVER YOU WANT. I DON'T GIVE A DAMN!

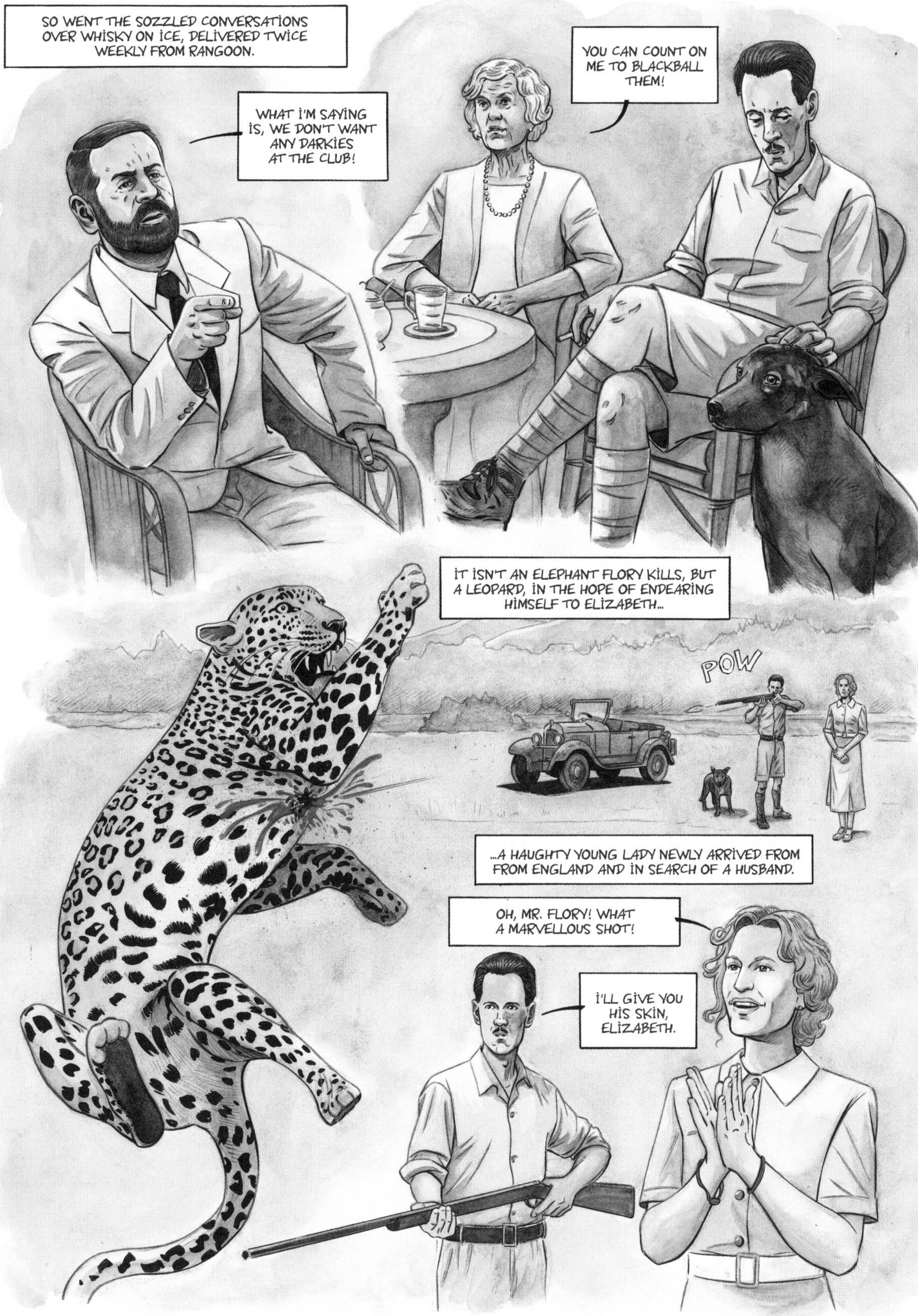
SO WENT THE SOZZLED CONVERSATIONS OVER WHISKY ON ICE, DELIVERED TWICE WEEKLY FROM RANGOON.
WHAT I'M SAYING IS, WE DON'T WANT ANY DARKIES AT THE CLUB!
YOU CAN COUNT ON ME TO BLACKBALL THEM!
IT ISN'T AN ELEPHANT FLORY KILLS, BUT A LEOPARD, IN THE HOPE OF ENDEARING HIMSELF TO ELIZABETH...
POW
...A HAUGHTY YOUNG LADY NEWLY ARRIVED FROM FROM ENGLAND AND IN SEARCH OF A HUSBAND.
OH, MR. FLORY! WHAT A MARVELLOUS SHOT!
I'LL GIVE YOU HIS SKIN, ELIZABETH.

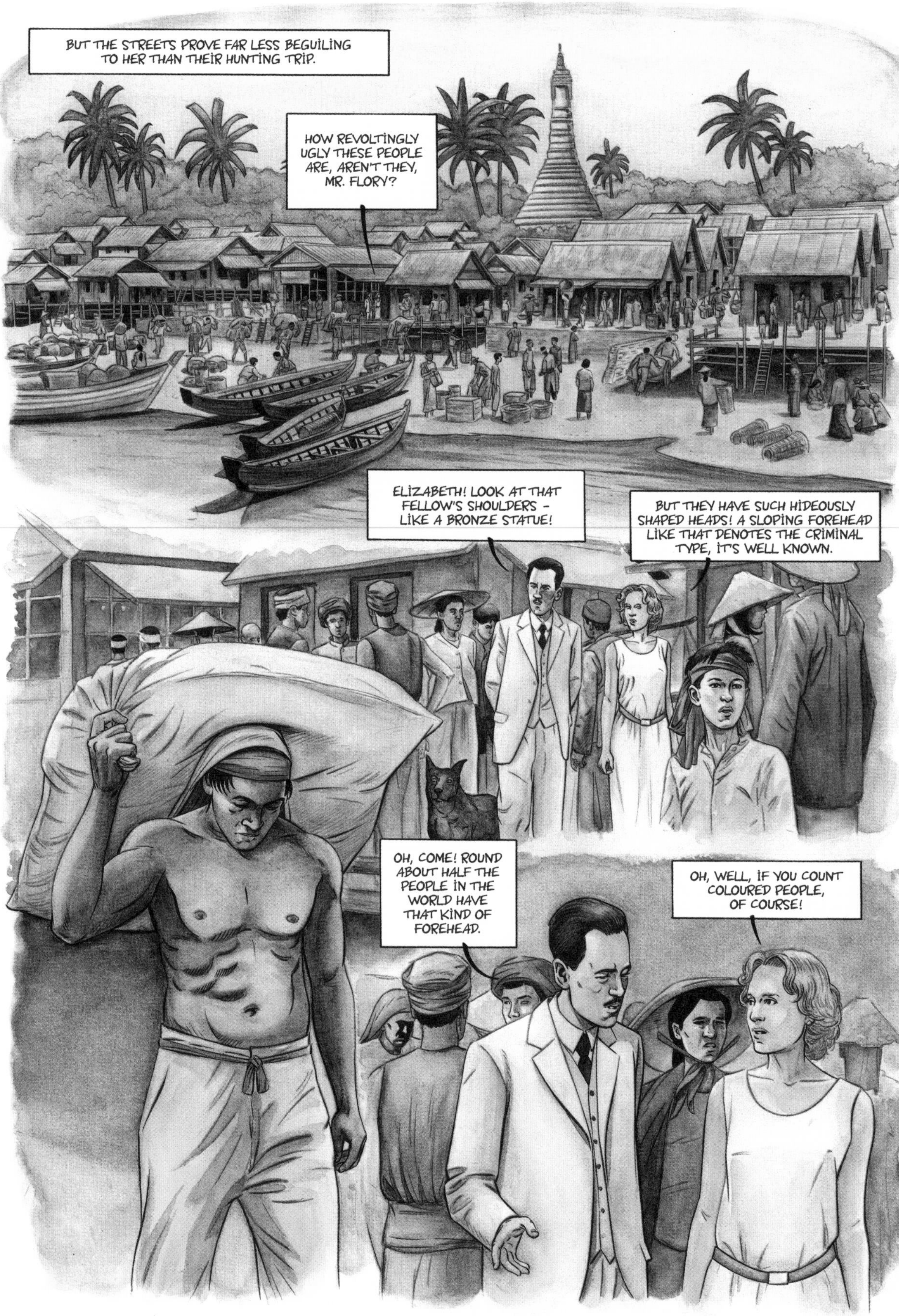
BUT THE STREETS PROVE FAR LESS BEGUILING TO HER THAN THEIR HUNTING TRIP.
HOW REVOLTINGLY UGLY THESE PEOPLE ARE, AREN'T THEY, MR. FLORY?
ELIZABETH! LOOK AT THAT FELLOW'S SHOULDERS - LIKE A BRONZE STATUE!
BUT THEY HAVE SUCH HIDEOUSLY SHAPED HEADS! A SLOPING FOREHEAD LIKE THAT DENOTES THE CRIMINAL TYPE, IT'S WELL KNOWN.
OH, COME! ROUND ABOUT HALF THE PEOPLE IN THE WORLD HAVE THAT KIND OF FOREHEAD.
OH, WELL, IF YOU COUNT COLOURED PEOPLE, OF COURSE!

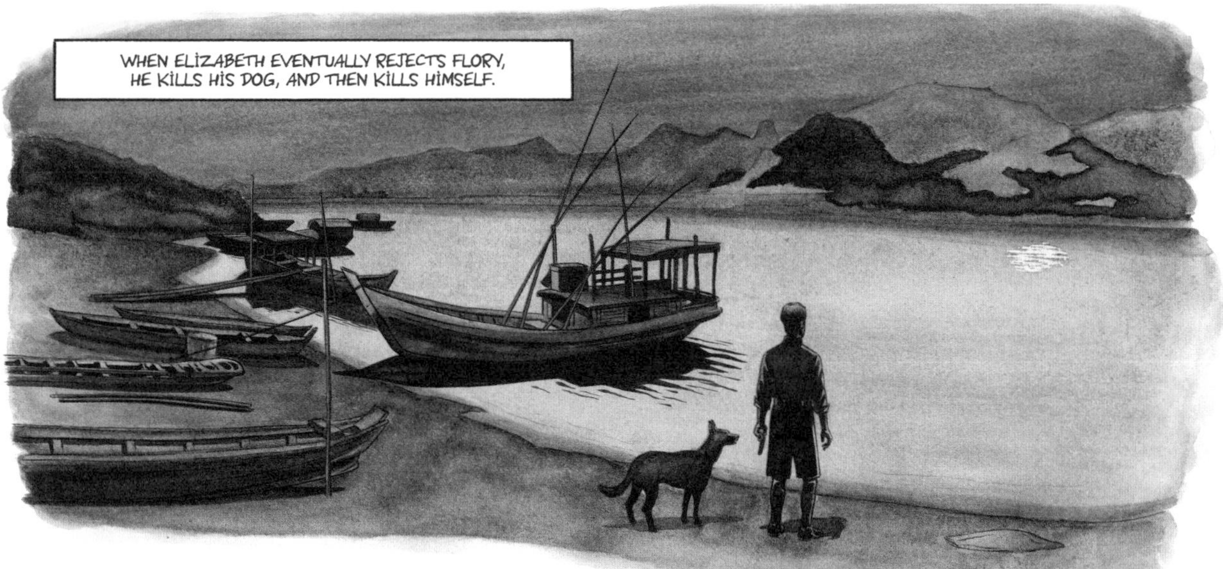
WHEN ELIZABETH EVENTUALLY REJECTS FLORY, HE KILLS HIS DOG, AND THEN KILLS HIMSELF.

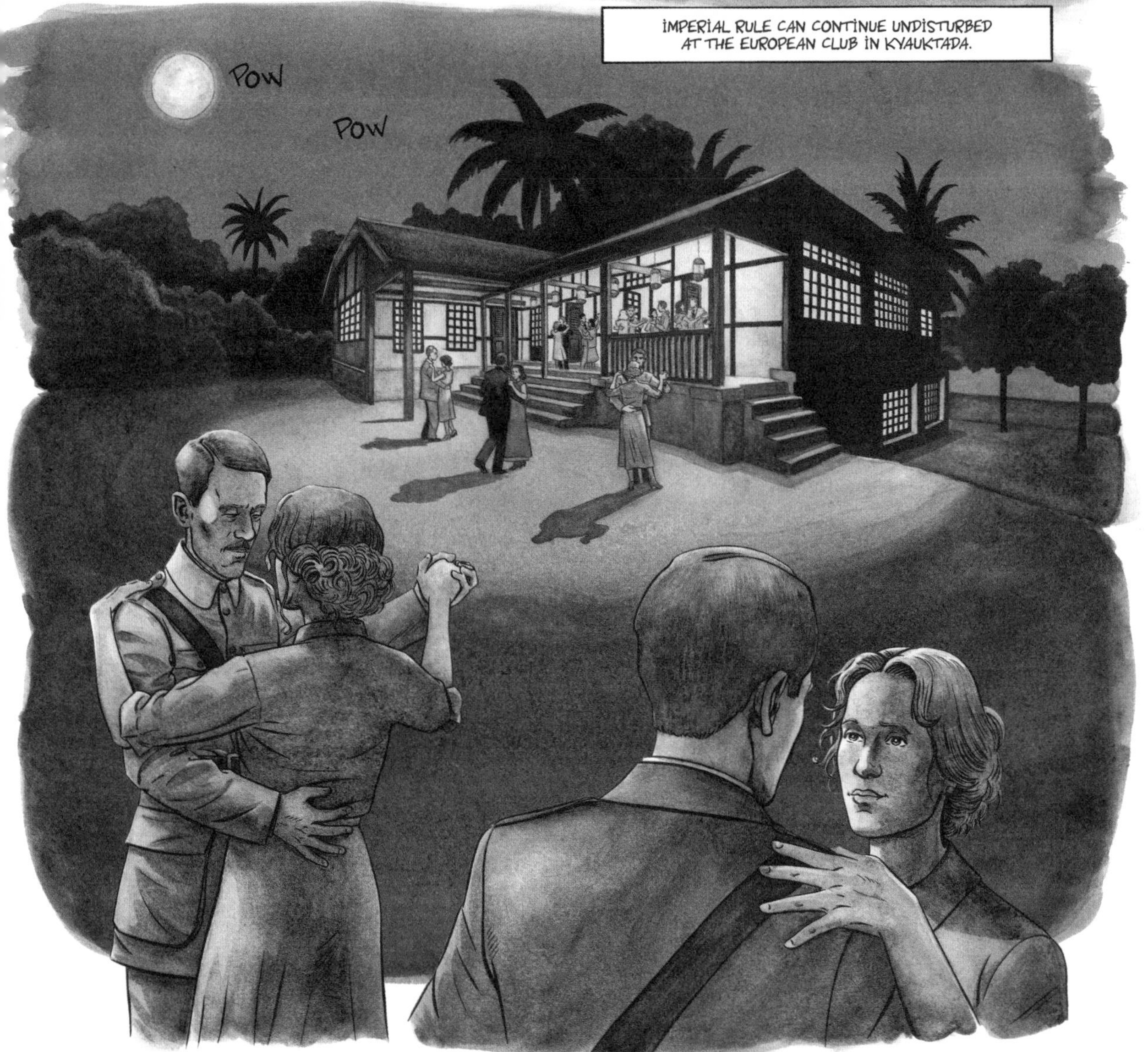
IMPERIAL RULE CAN CONTINUE UNDISTURBED AT THE EUROPEAN CLUB IN KYAUKTADA.
POW
POW

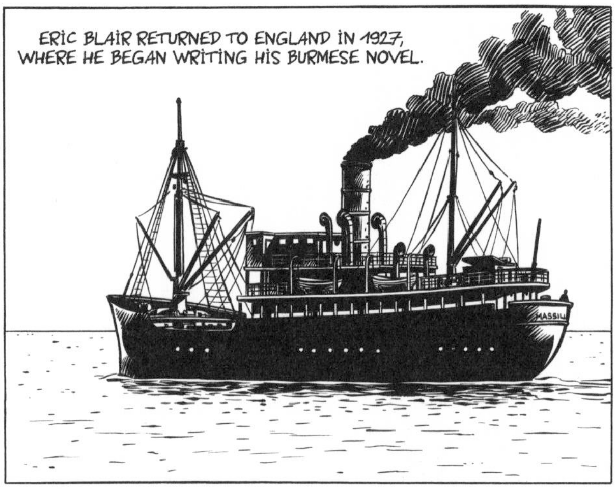
ERIC BLAIR RETURNED TO ENGLAND IN 1927, WHERE HE BEGAN WRITING HIS BURMESE NOVEL.
MASSILI

OF HIS TIME IN THE FAR EAST, HE RETAINED ONLY THE MOUSTACHE FAVOURED BY OFFICERS OF THE BRITISH RAJ, AND A HATRED OF IMPERIALISM.

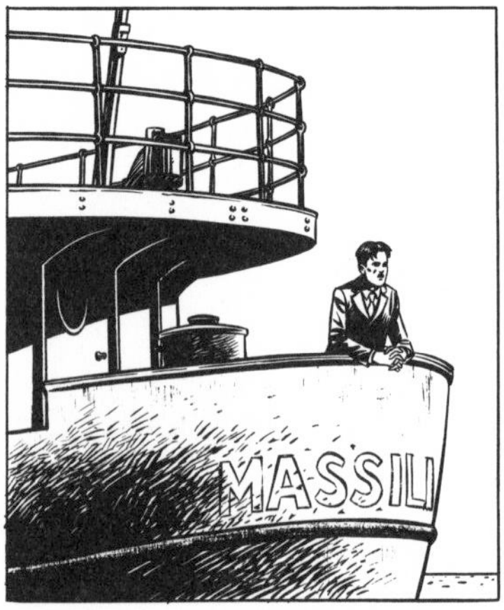
MASSILI

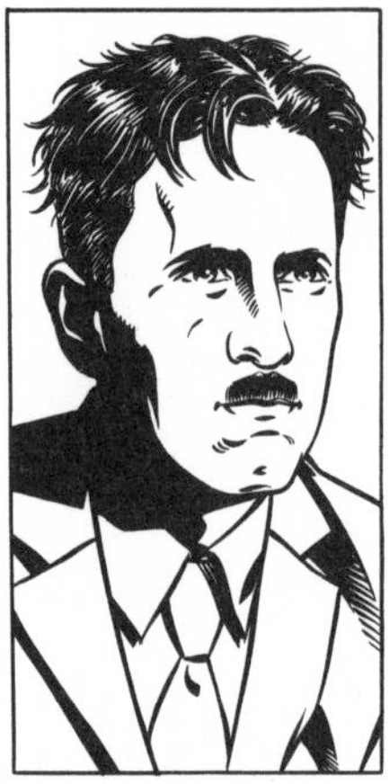

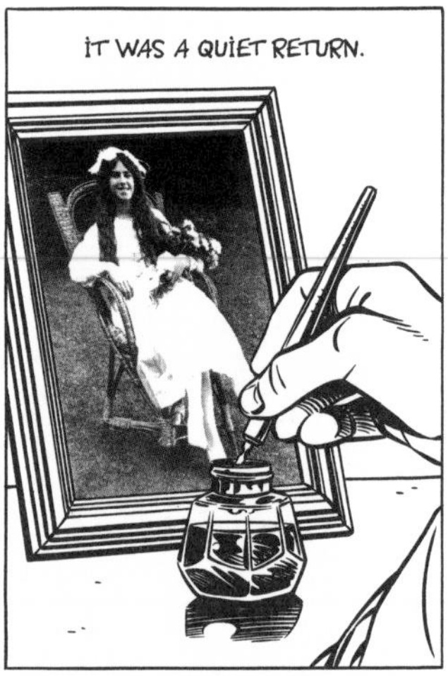
IT WAS A QUIET RETURN.

JACINTHA BUDDICOM DRIFTED AWAY FROM HIM. HE LIVED WITH HIS PARENTS IN SOUTHWOLD AND BEGAN TO WRITE.

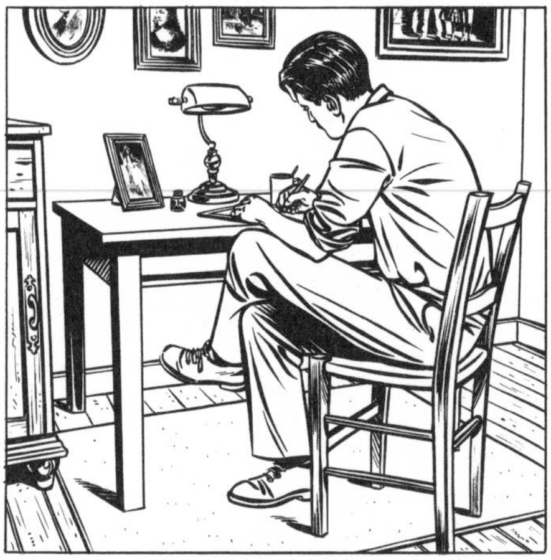

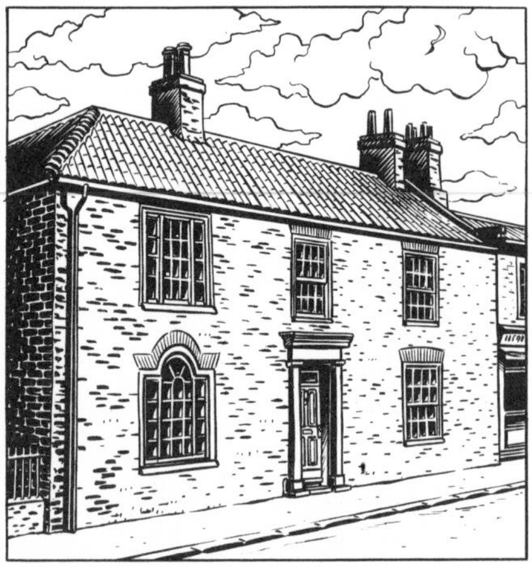

PENNILESS, OUT OF WORK, BUT HIGHLY OPINIONATED, SOME OF HIS FRIENDS CONSIDERED HIM A TORY ANARCHIST.

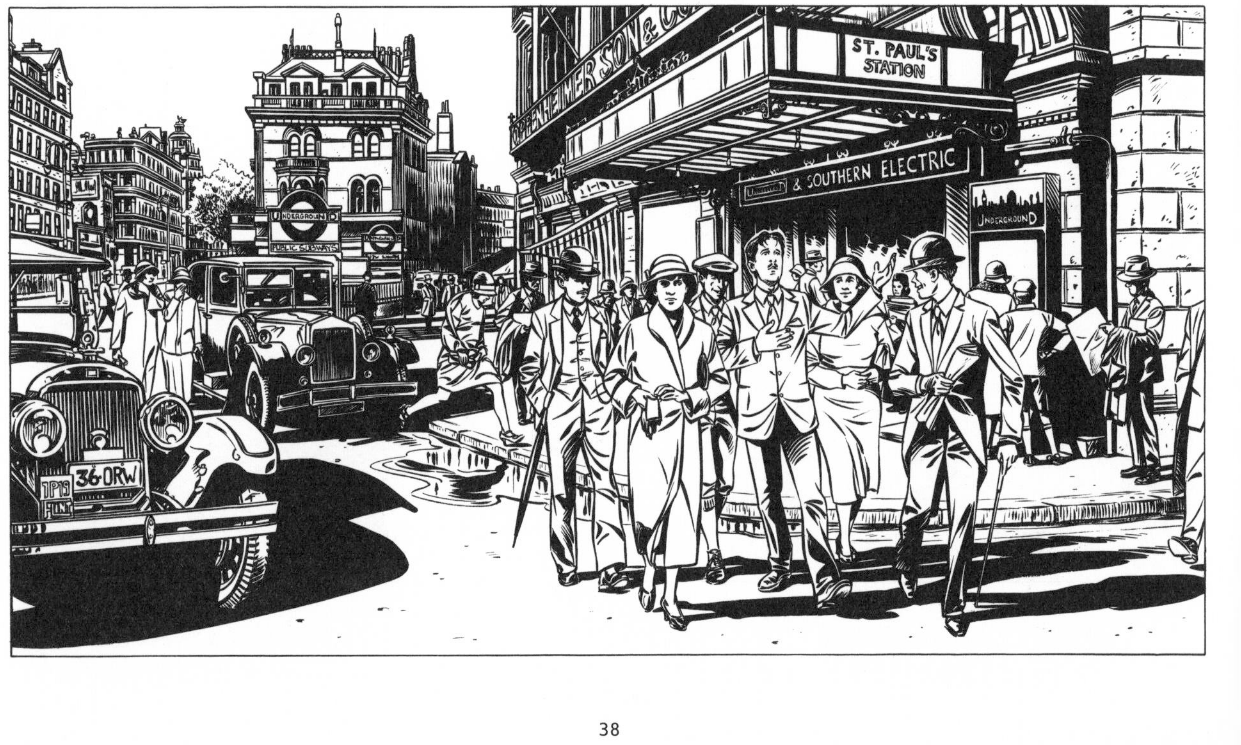
ST. PAUL'S STATION
& SOUTHERN ELECTRIC
UNDERGROUND
36·ORW

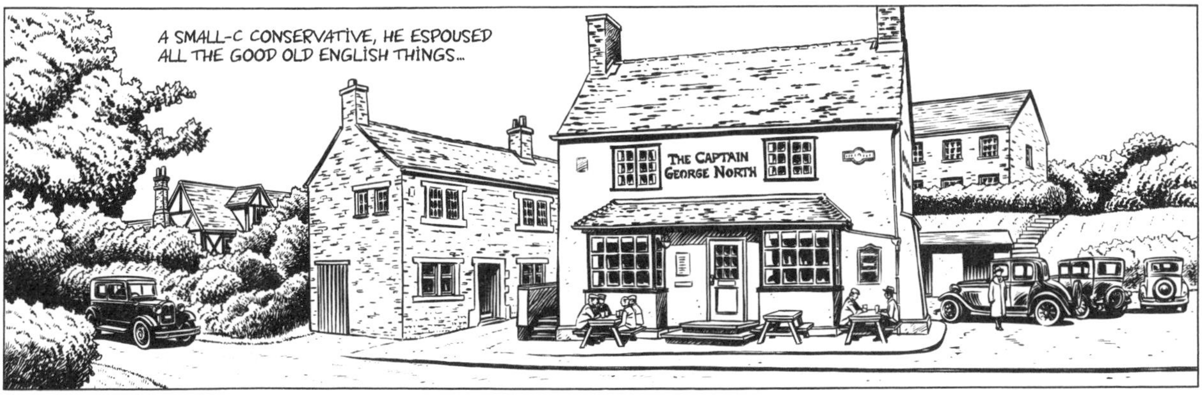
A SMALL-C CONSERVATIVE, HE ESPOUSED ALL THE GOOD OLD ENGLISH THINGS...
THE CAPTAIN GEORGE NORTH

FROM PINTS OF BEER IN CROWDED PUBS (WHICH HE LIKED A GREAT DEAL)...

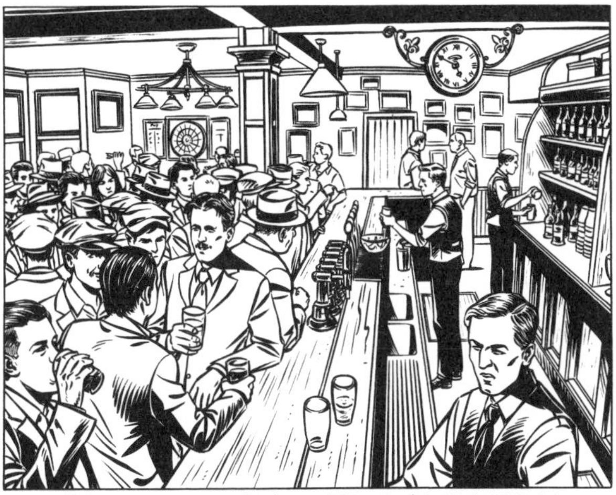

TO THE MUSTY RITUALS OF THE ANGLICAN CHURCH (WHICH HE DIDN'T, REALLY).

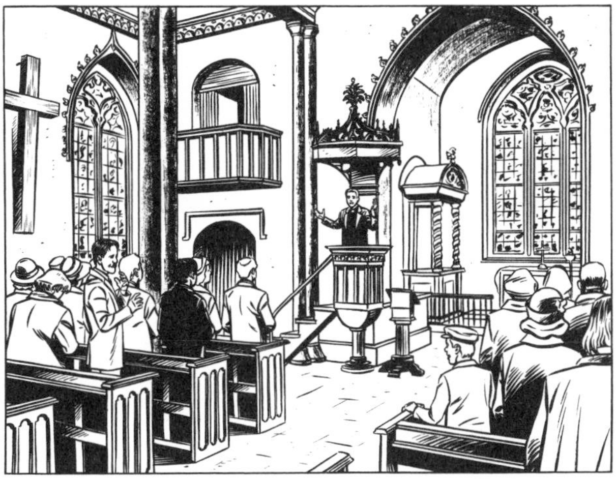

BUT THERE WAS ALSO AN ANARCHIST STREAK TO HIM, OR AT LEAST A NONCONFORMIST ONE, FREQUENTING THE ROUGHER PARTS OF LONDON WHILST LIVING ON THE PORTOBELLO ROAD.

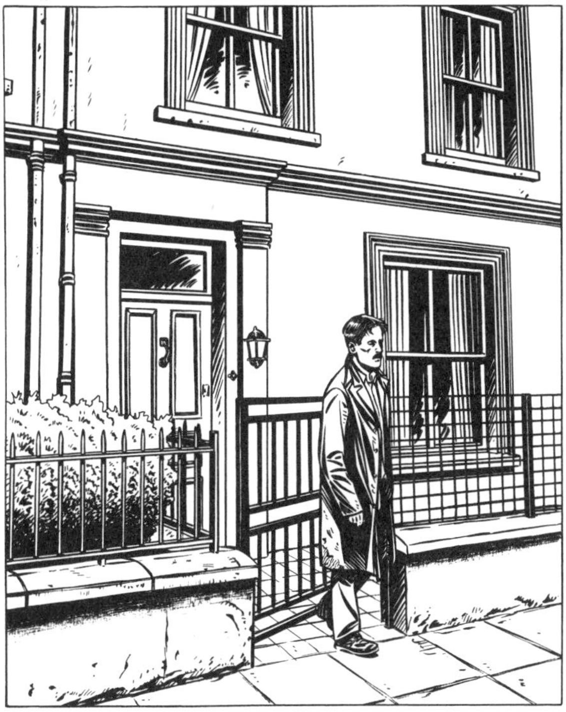

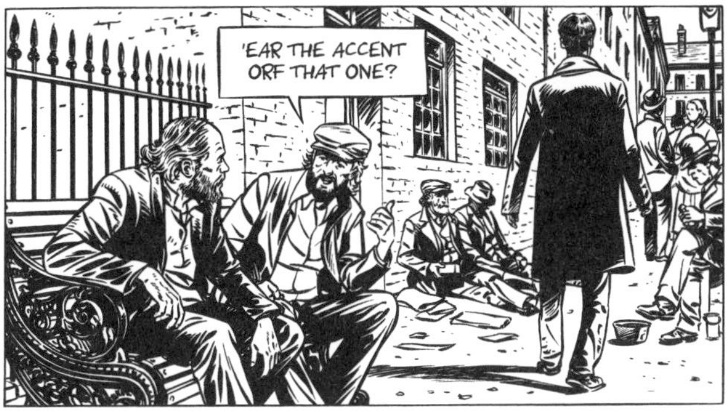
'EAR THE ACCENT ORF THAT ONE?

COMBINING BOHEMIAN ECCENTRICITY AND SOCIAL COMPASSION, HE "WENT NATIVE" IN HIS OWN COUNTRY.

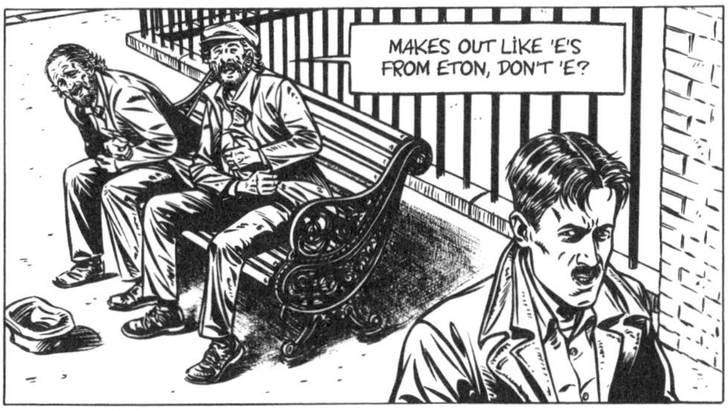
MAKES OUT LIKE 'E'S FROM ETON, DON'T 'E?

IN 1929, HE LEFT FOR FRANCE AND SETTLED ON RUE DE POT-DE-FER, LIVING "DOWN AND OUT" IN PARIS, AS HE WOULD LATER RECOUNT IN HIS 1933 BOOK.

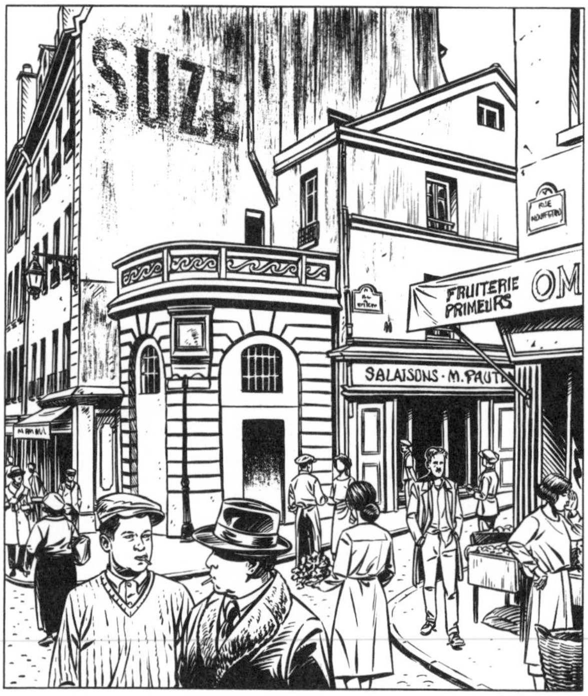
SUZE
FRUITERIE PRIMEURS
SALAISONS M.PAUT

HIS ACCOUNT OF LITERALLY STARVING AMONG THE IMPOVERISHED WORKING CLASS RECALLED BOTH EMILE ZOLA AND JACK LONDON.

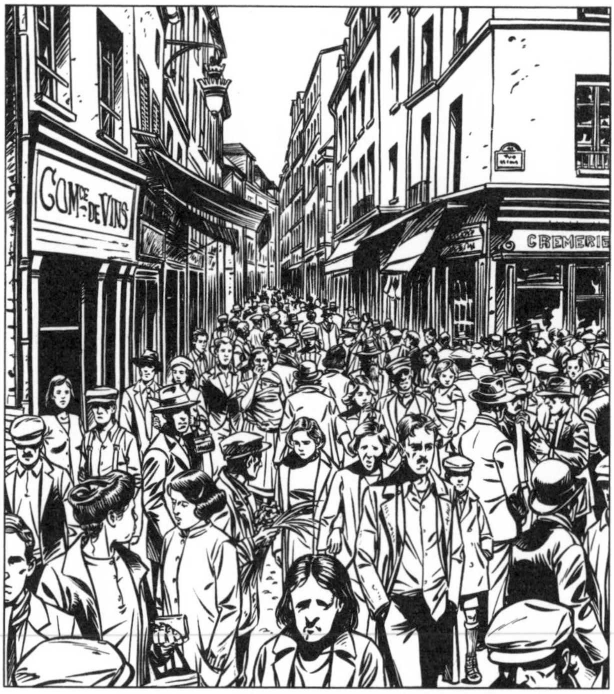
CREMERIE

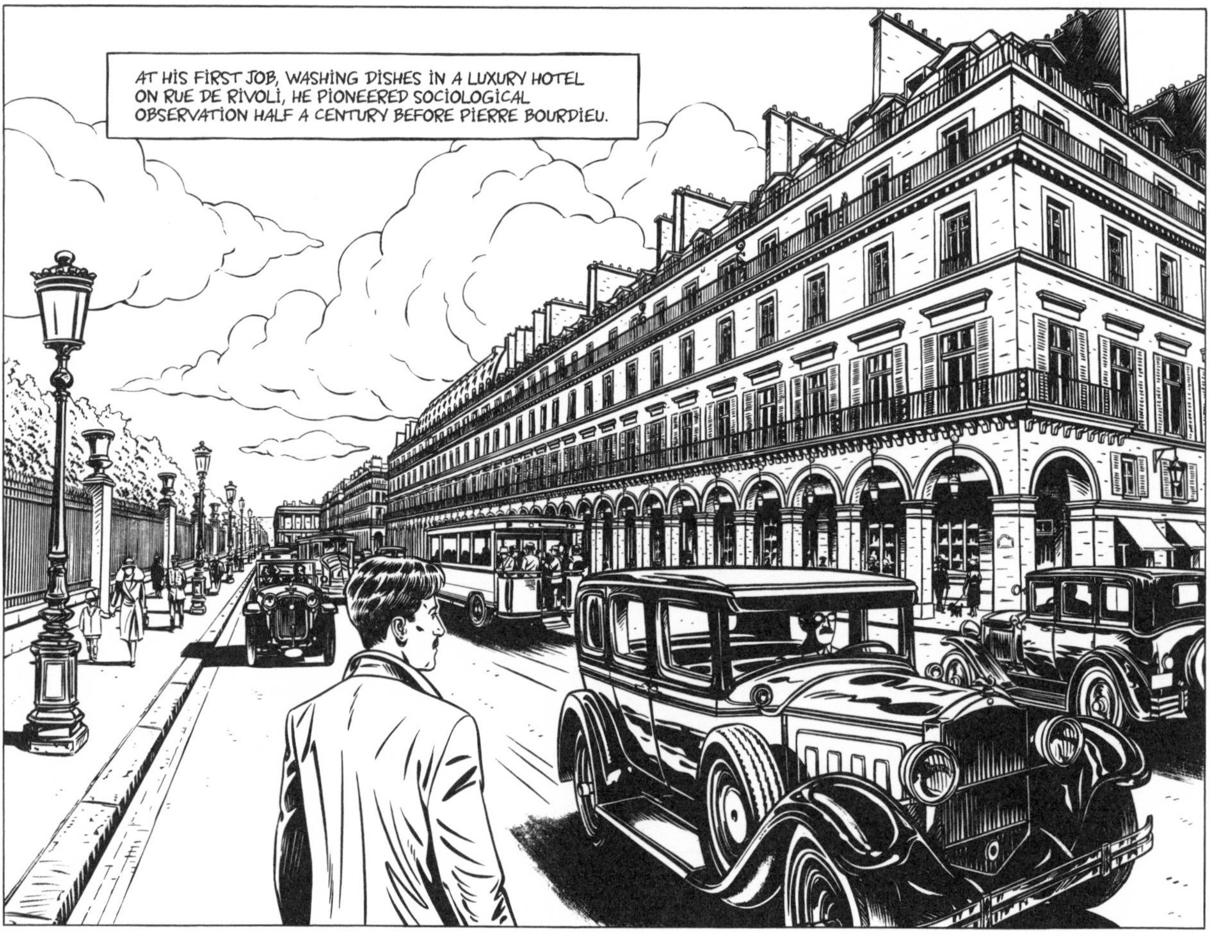
AT HIS FIRST JOB, WASHING DISHES IN A LUXURY HOTEL ON RUE DE RIVOLI, HE PIONEERED SOCIOLOGICAL OBSERVATION HALF A CENTURY BEFORE PIERRE BOURDIEU.

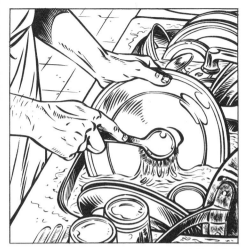

HEY, ENGLISHMAN! DISHWASHER!

ME?

THAT MOUSTACHE HAS TO COME OFF.

BUT... WHY?

DIDN'T YOU KNOW THAT ONLY CHEFS ARE ALLOWED TO HAVE MOUSTACHES AROUND HERE?

This gives some idea of the elaborate caste system existing in a hotel... Our staff... had their prestige graded as accurately as that of soldiers.

Highest of all came the... MAITRE D'HOTEL. He did not serve at table... but directed the other waiters and helped with the catering. He was in a position quite apart from the rest of the staff, and took his meals in a private room.

The head cook drew about five thousand francs a month; he dined in the kitchen, but at a separate table, and one of the apprentice cooks waited on him.

Then came the CHEF DU PERSONNEL; he drew only fifteen hundred francs a month, but he wore a black coat and did no manual work.

It is an instructive sight to see a waiter going into a hotel dining-room... All the dirt and hurry and irritation have dropped off in an instant. He glides over the carpet, with a solemn priest-like air.

The waiter's outlook is quite different... his skill is chiefly in being servile. His work gives him the mentality... of a snob. He lives perpetually in sight of rich people... The result is that... the waiter comes to identify himself to some extent with his employers.

There were also maids, laundrywomen, café managers, cellarmen, bellhops, warehouse clerks, porters, ice-cream vendors, bakers, night-watchmen, doorkeeper.

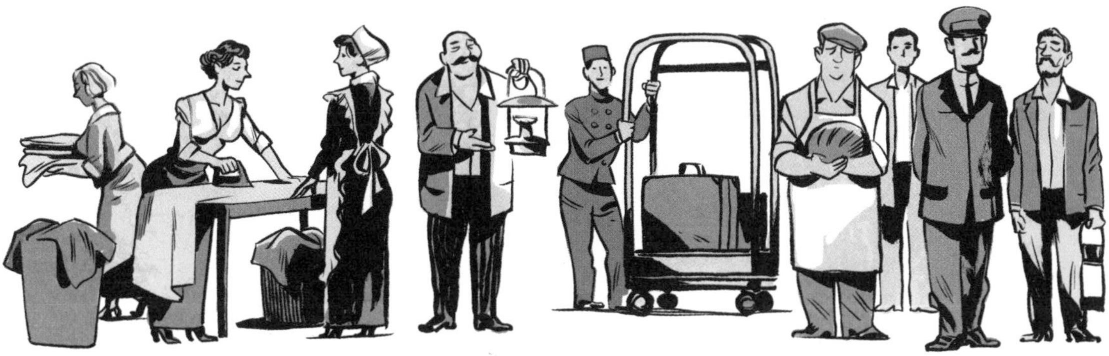

The PLONGEURS were of every race in Europe... We of the cafeterie were the very dregs of the hotel... We were stuck down in the kitchens where there reigned a nauseating stench of swill and sweat.

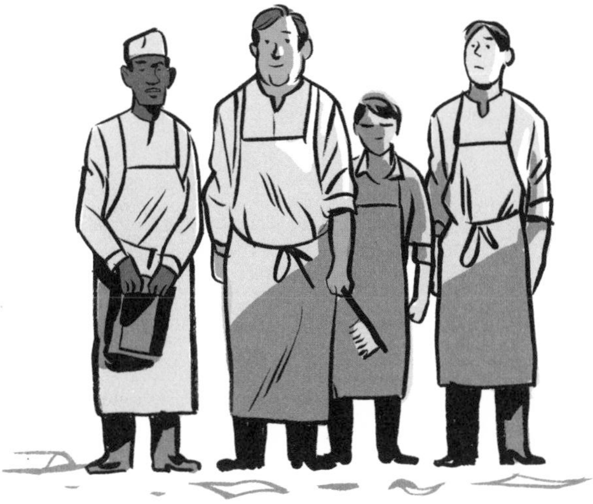

Everywhere in the cupboards... were squalid stores of food that the waiters had stolen... It was nothing unusual for a waiter to wash his face in the water in which clean crockery was rinsing.

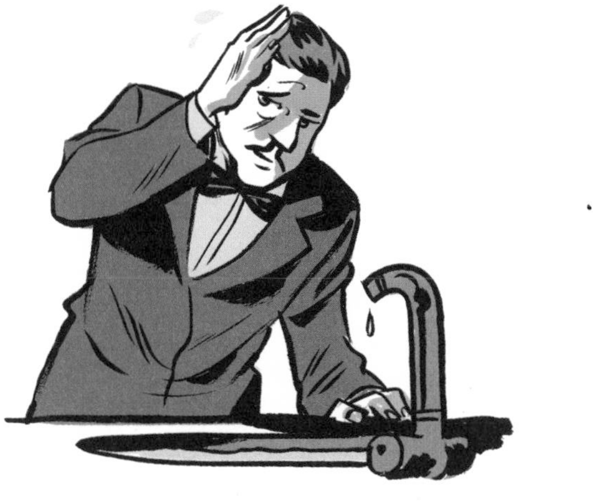

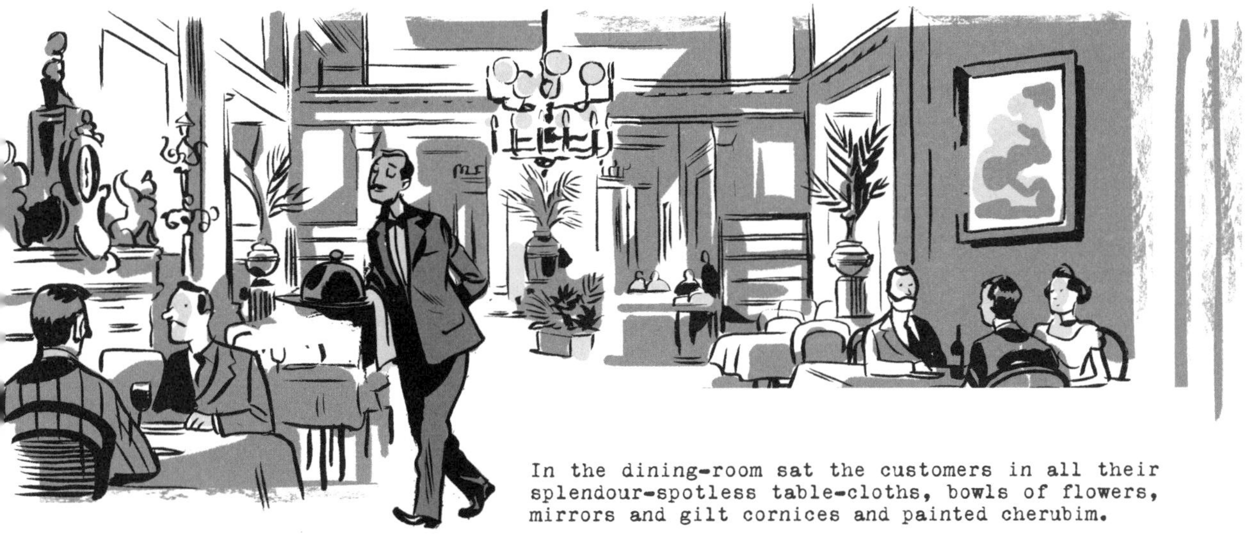

In the dining-room sat the customers in all their splendour-spotless table-cloths, bowls of flowers, mirrors and gilt cornices and painted cherubim.

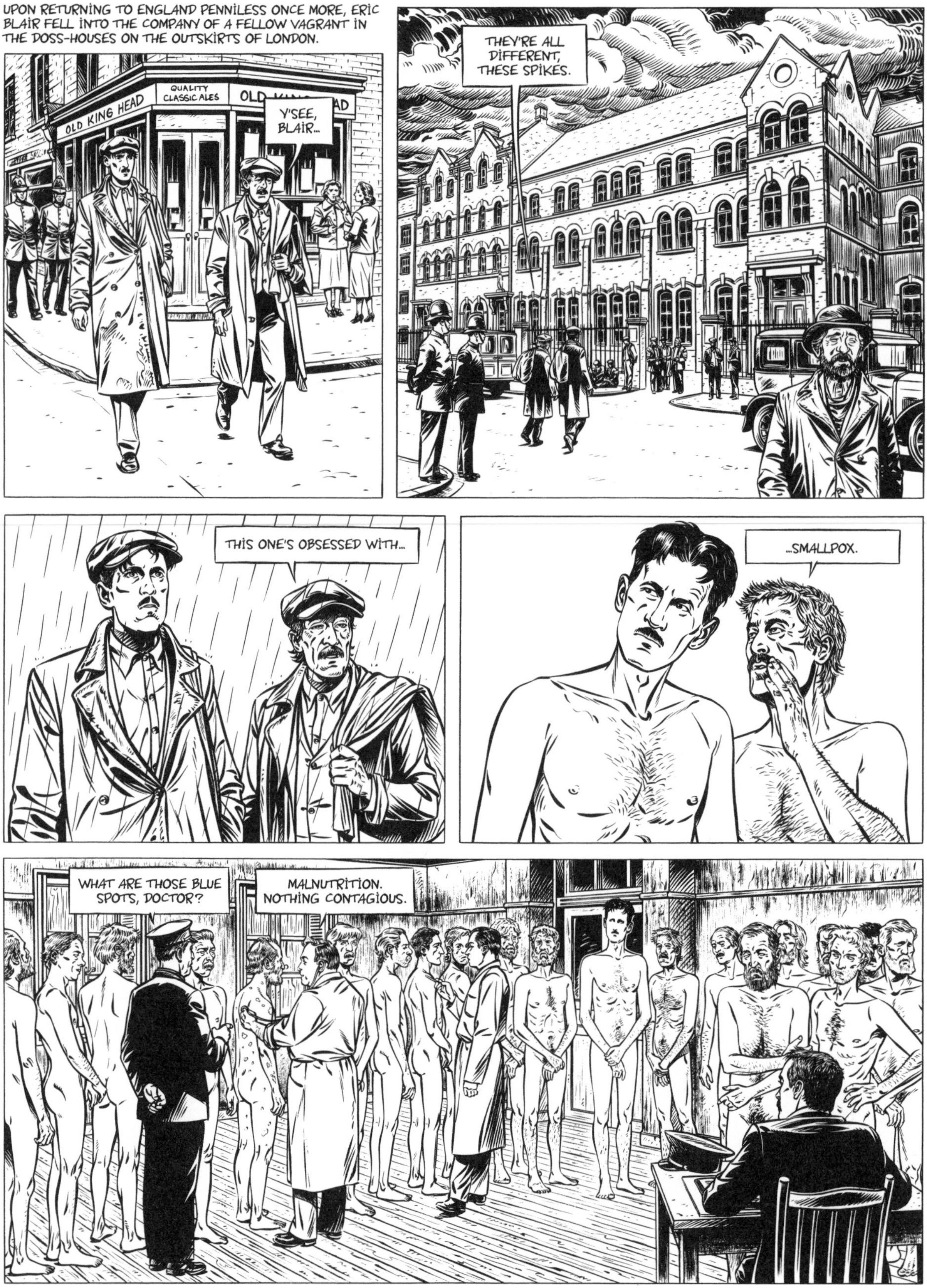
UPON RETURNING TO ENGLAND PENNILESS ONCE MORE, ERIC BLAIR FELL INTO THE COMPANY OF A FELLOW VAGRANT IN THE DOSS-HOUSES ON THE OUTSKIRTS OF LONDON.
OLD KING HEAD
QUALITY CLASSIC ALES
Y'SEE, BLAIR...
THEY'RE ALL DIFFERENT, THESE SPIKES.
THIS ONE'S OBSESSED WITH...
...SMALLPOX.
WHAT ARE THOSE BLUE SPOTS, DOCTOR?
MALNUTRITION. NOTHING CONTAGIOUS.

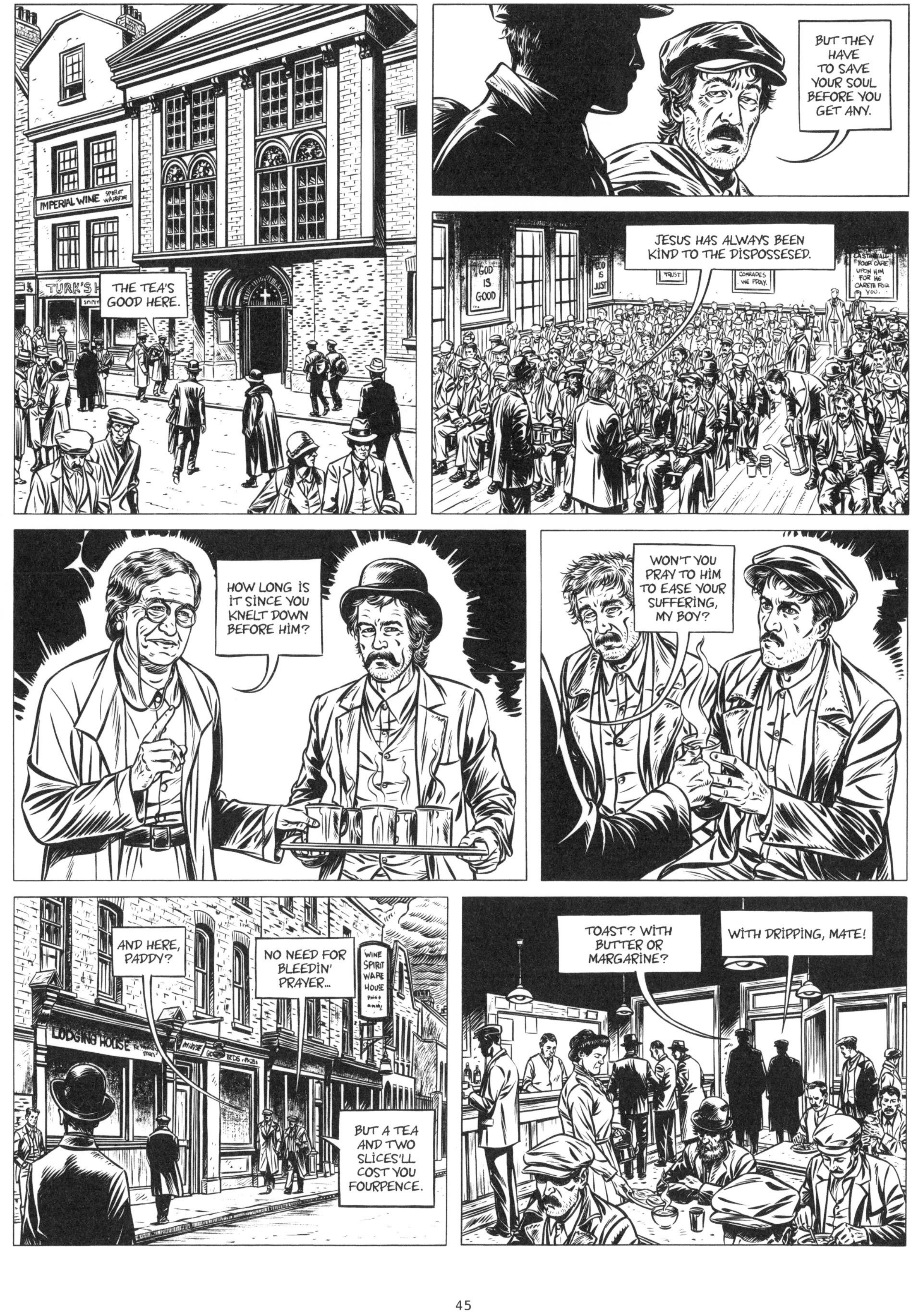
IMPERIAL WINE
THE TEA'S GOOD HERE.
BUT THEY HAVE TO SAVE YOUR SOUL BEFORE YOU GET ANY.
JESUS HAS ALWAYS BEEN KIND TO THE DISPOSSESED.
GOD IS GOOD
GOD IS JUST
TRUST
COMRADES WE PRAY.
HOW LONG IS IT SINCE YOU KNELT DOWN BEFORE HIM?
WON'T YOU PRAY TO HIM TO EASE YOUR SUFFERING, MY BOY?
AND HERE, PADDY?
NO NEED FOR BLEEDIN' PRAYER...
LODGING HOUSE
BUT A TEA AND TWO SLICES'LL COST YOU FOURPENCE.
TOAST? WITH BUTTER OR MARGARINE?
WITH DRIPPING, MATE!

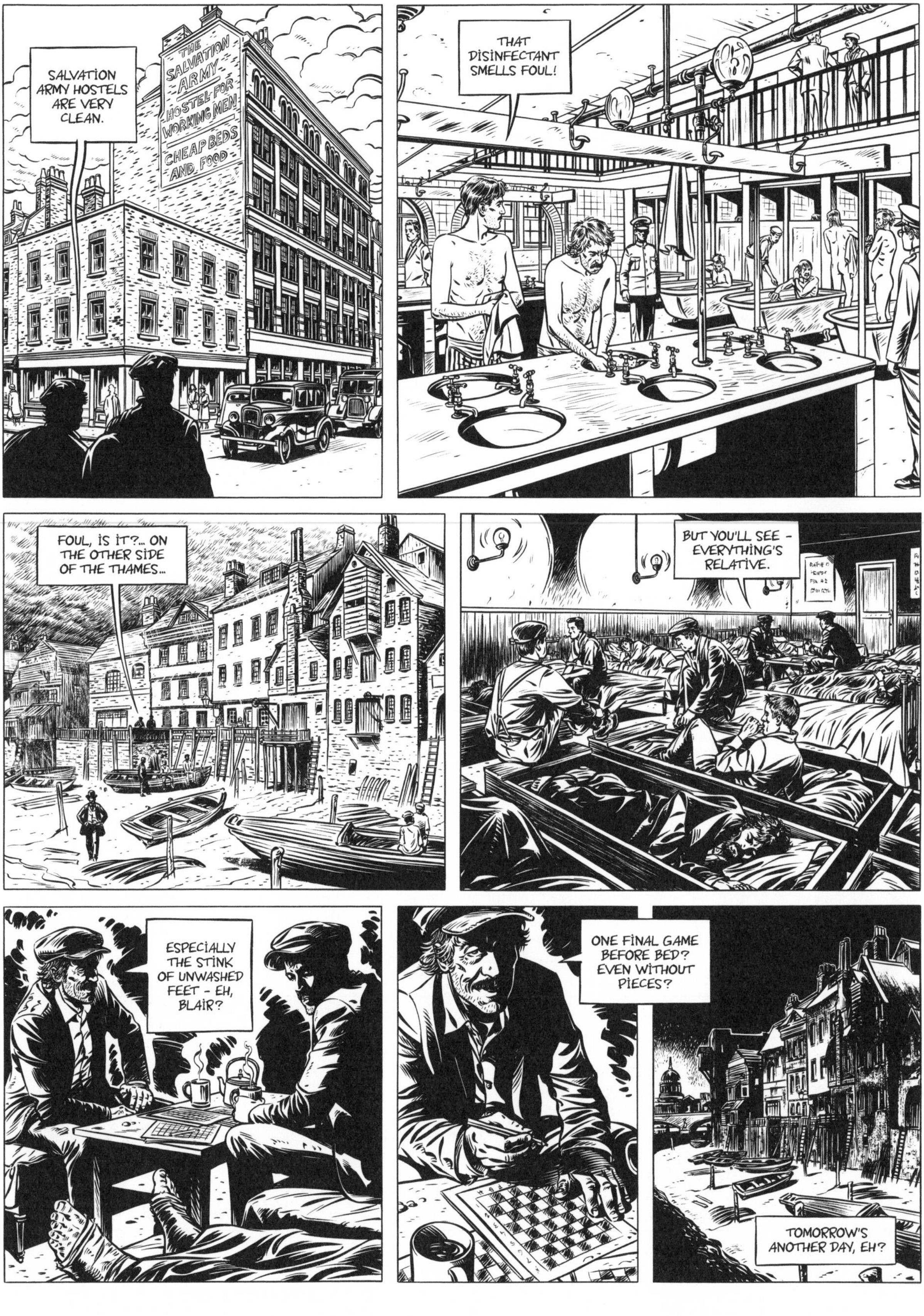
SALVATION ARMY HOSTELS ARE VERY CLEAN.
THE SALVATION ARMY HOSTEL FOR WORKING MEN CHEAP BEDS AND FOOD
THAT DISINFECTANT SMELLS FOUL!
FOUL, IS IT?... ON THE OTHER SIDE OF THE THAMES...
BUT YOU'LL SEE - EVERYTHING'S RELATIVE.
ESPECIALLY THE STINK OF UNWASHED FEET - EH, BLAIR?
ONE FINAL GAME BEFORE BED? EVEN WITHOUT PIECES?
TOMORROW'S ANOTHER DAY, EH?

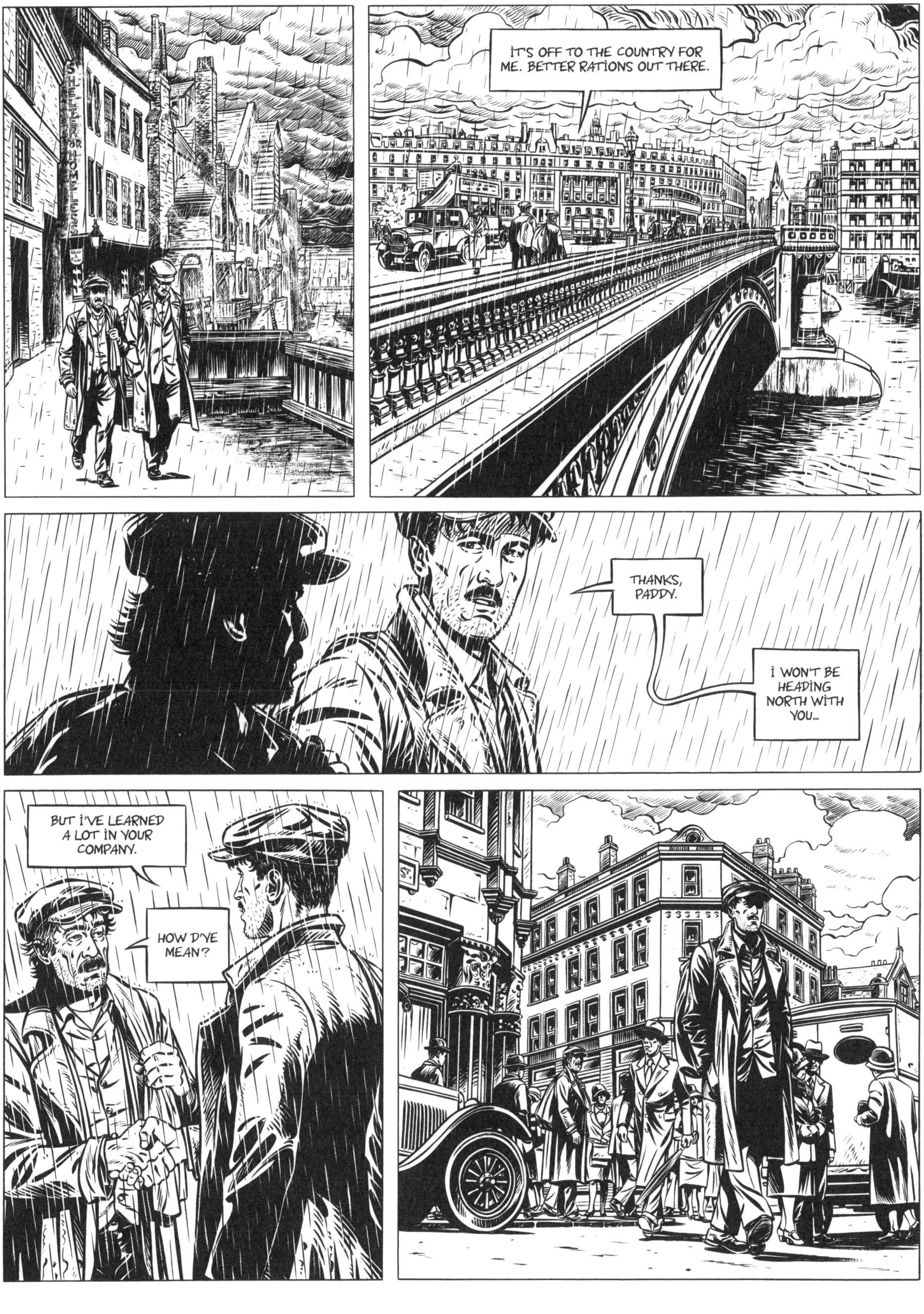
SHELTER FOR HOMELESS
IT'S OFF TO THE COUNTRY FOR ME. BETTER RATIONS OUT THERE.
THANKS, PADDY.
I WON'T BE HEADING NORTH WITH YOU...
BUT I'VE LEARNED A LOT IN YOUR COMPANY.
HOW D'YE MEAN?

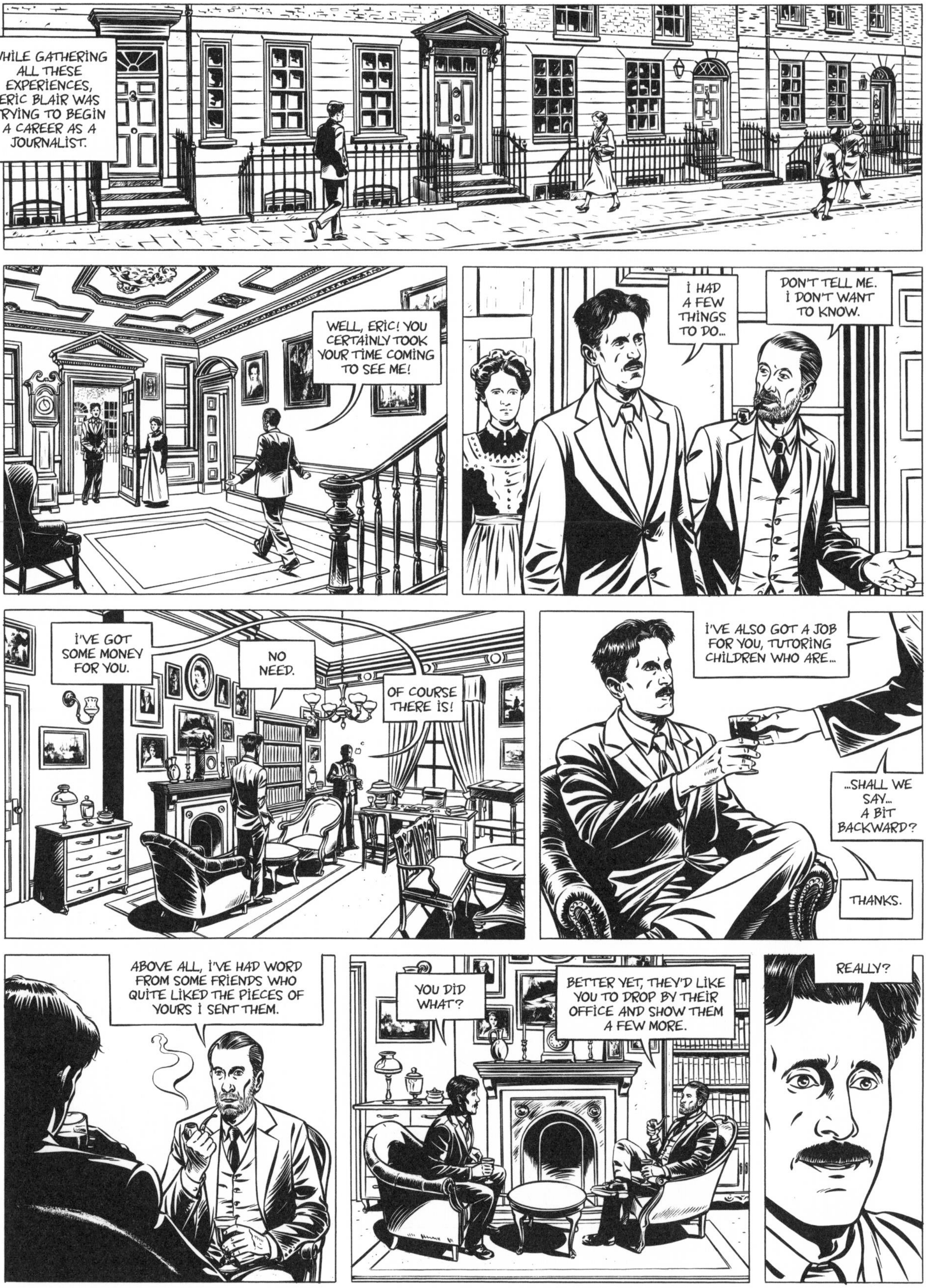
WHILE GATHERING ALL THESE EXPERIENCES, ERIC BLAIR WAS TRYING TO BEGIN A CAREER AS A JOURNALIST.
WELL, ERIC! YOU CERTAINLY TOOK YOUR TIME COMING TO SEE ME!
I HAD A FEW THINGS TO DO...
DON'T TELL ME. I DON'T WANT TO KNOW.
I'VE GOT SOME MONEY FOR YOU.
NO NEED.
OF COURSE THERE IS!
I'VE ALSO GOT A JOB FOR YOU, TUTORING CHILDREN WHO ARE...
...SHALL WE SAY... A BIT BACKWARD?
THANKS.
ABOVE ALL, I'VE HAD WORD FROM SOME FRIENDS WHO QUITE LIKED THE PIECES OF YOURS I SENT THEM.
YOU DID WHAT?
BETTER YET, THEY'D LIKE YOU TO DROP BY THEIR OFFICE AND SHOW THEM A FEW MORE.
REALLY?

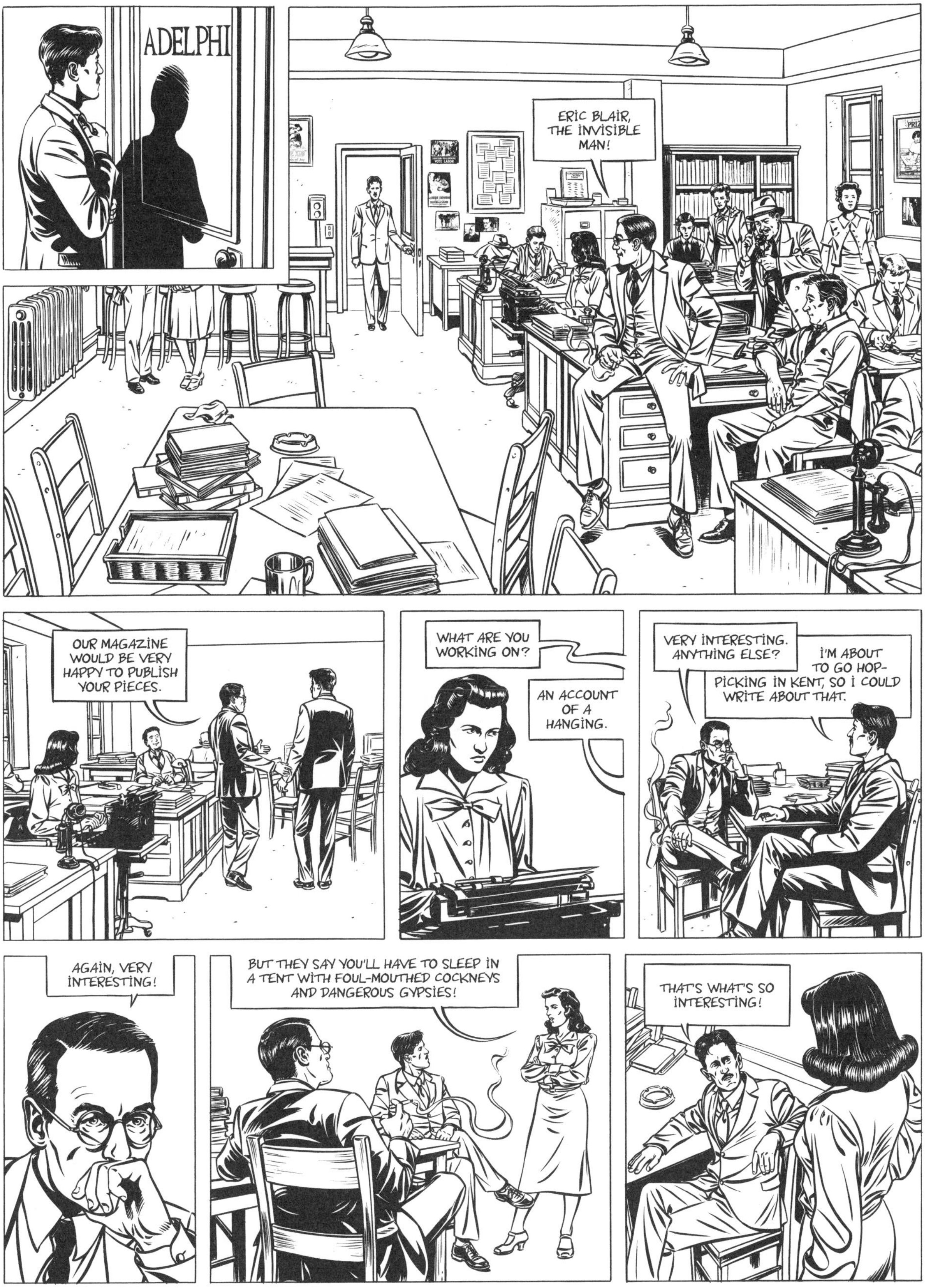
ADELPHI
ERIC BLAIR, THE INVISIBLE MAN!
OUR MAGAZINE WOULD BE VERY HAPPY TO PUBLISH YOUR PIECES.
WHAT ARE YOU WORKING ON?
AN ACCOUNT OF A HANGING.
VERY INTERESTING. ANYTHING ELSE?
I'M ABOUT TO GO HOP-PICKING IN KENT, SO I COULD WRITE ABOUT THAT.
AGAIN, VERY INTERESTING!
BUT THEY SAY YOU'LL HAVE TO SLEEP IN A TENT WITH FOUL-MOUTHED COCKNEYS AND DANGEROUS GYPSIES!
THAT'S WHAT'S SO INTERESTING!

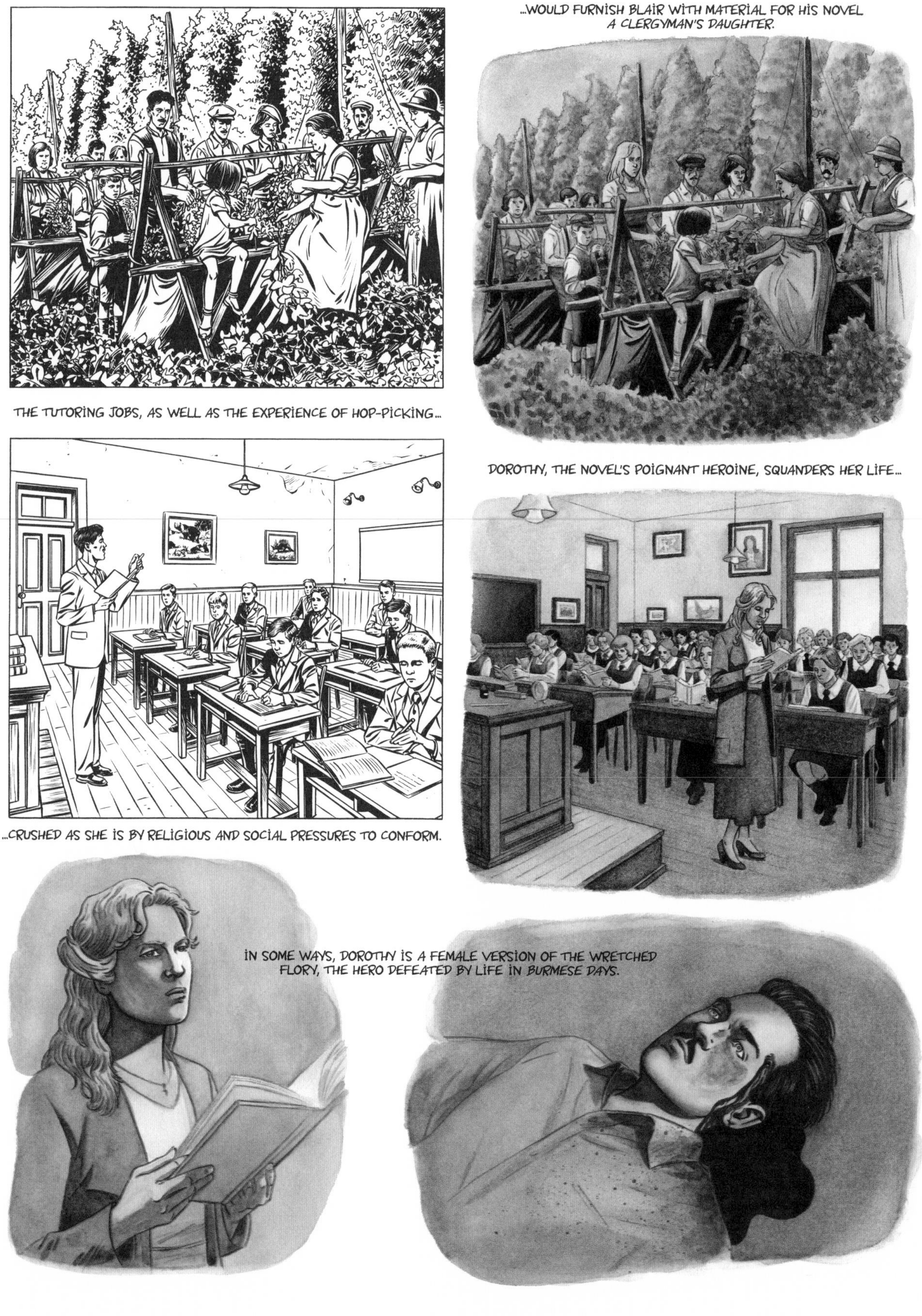
THE TUTORING JOBS, AS WELL AS THE EXPERIENCE OF HOP-PICKING...
...WOULD FURNISH BLAIR WITH MATERIAL FOR HIS NOVEL *A CLERGYMAN'S DAUGHTER.*
DOROTHY, THE NOVEL'S POIGNANT HEROINE, SQUANDERS HER LIFE...
...CRUSHED AS SHE IS BY RELIGIOUS AND SOCIAL PRESSURES TO CONFORM.
IN SOME WAYS, DOROTHY IS A FEMALE VERSION OF THE WRETCHED FLORY, THE HERO DEFEATED BY LIFE IN *BURMESE DAYS.*

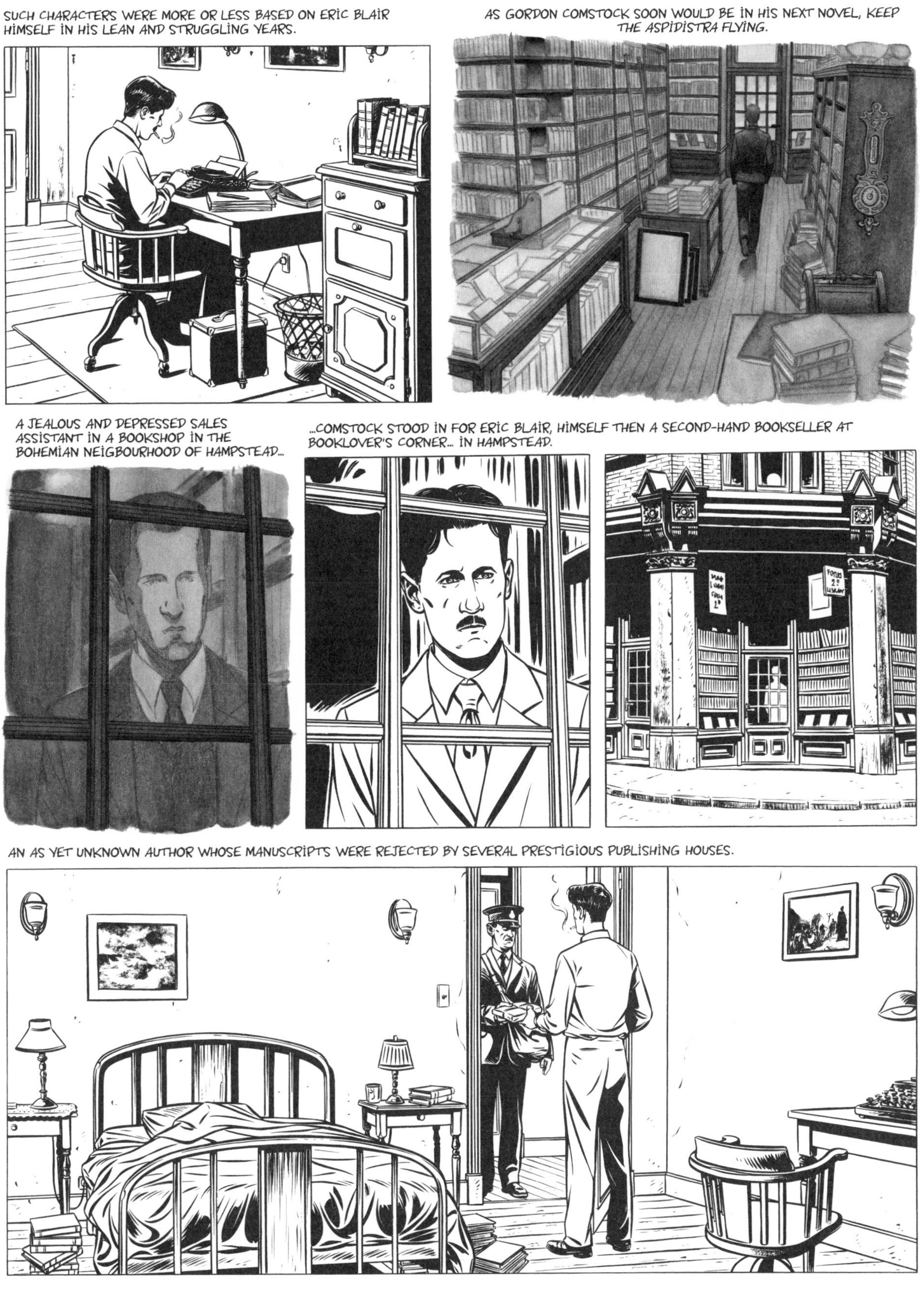
SUCH CHARACTERS WERE MORE OR LESS BASED ON ERIC BLAIR HIMSELF IN HIS LEAN AND STRUGGLING YEARS.
AS GORDON COMSTOCK SOON WOULD BE IN HIS NEXT NOVEL, KEEP THE ASPIDISTRA FLYING.
A JEALOUS AND DEPRESSED SALES ASSISTANT IN A BOOKSHOP IN THE BOHEMIAN NEIGBOURHOOD OF HAMPSTEAD...
...COMSTOCK STOOD IN FOR ERIC BLAIR, HIMSELF THEN A SECOND-HAND BOOKSELLER AT BOOKLOVER'S CORNER... IN HAMPSTEAD.
AN AS YET UNKNOWN AUTHOR WHOSE MANUSCRIPTS WERE REJECTED BY SEVERAL PRESTIGIOUS PUBLISHING HOUSES.

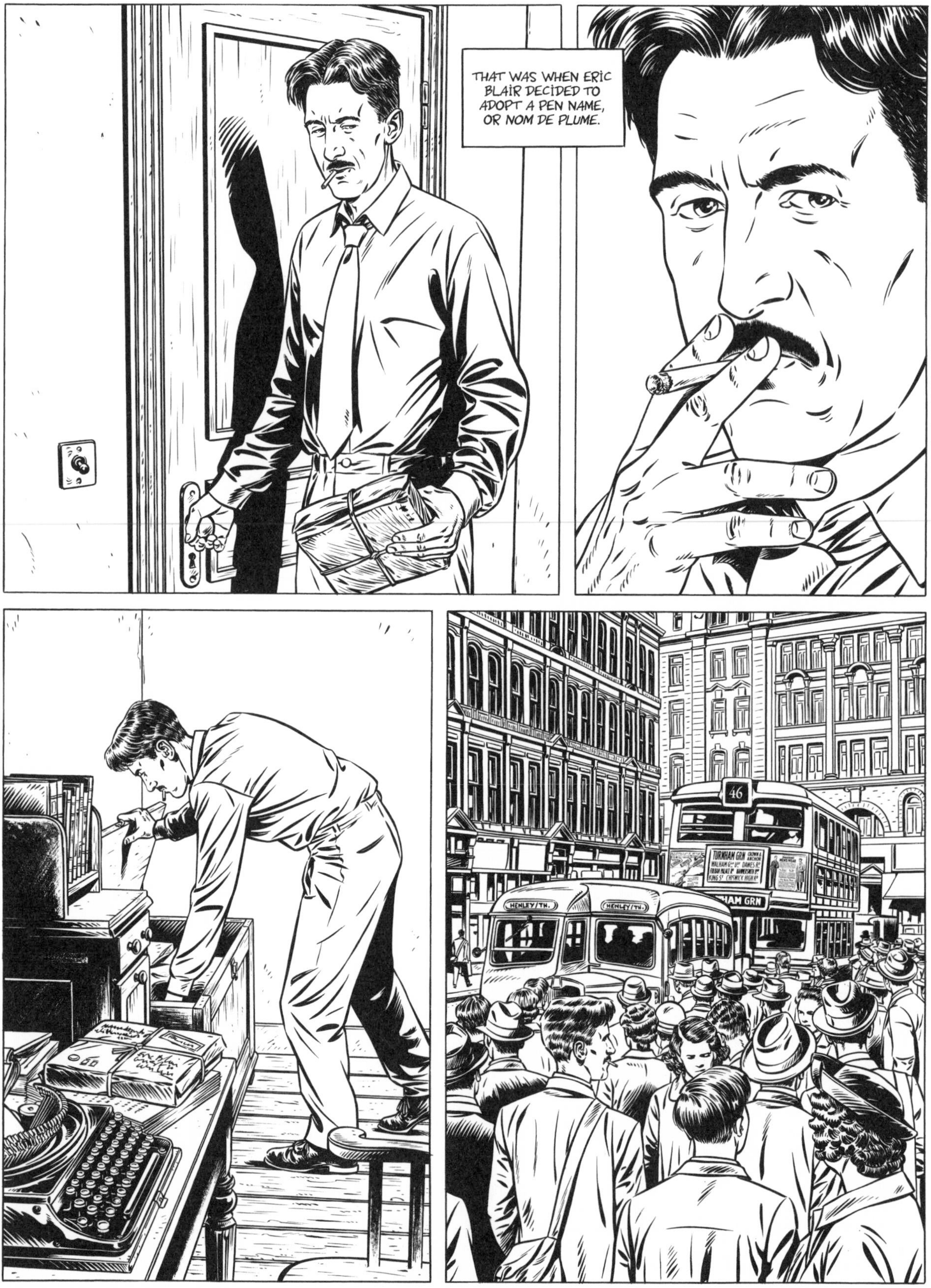
THAT WAS WHEN ERIC BLAIR DECIDED TO ADOPT A PEN NAME, OR NOM DE PLUME.
46
TURNHAM GRN
HENLEY/TH.
HENLEY/TH.

WELL MIGHT WE WONDER WHAT SORT OF BOOKS HE WOULD HAVE WRITTEN IF HE HAD CALLED HIMSELF P.S. BURTON, AN ALIAS HE SOMETIMES USED IN THE SLUMS.

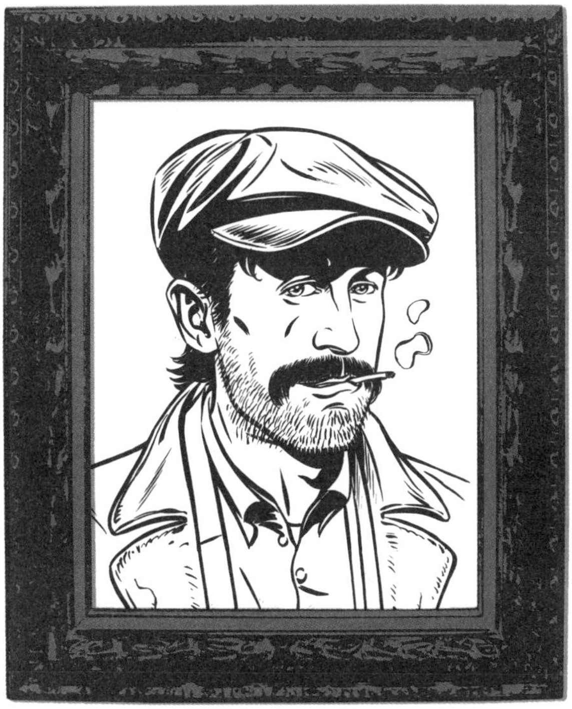

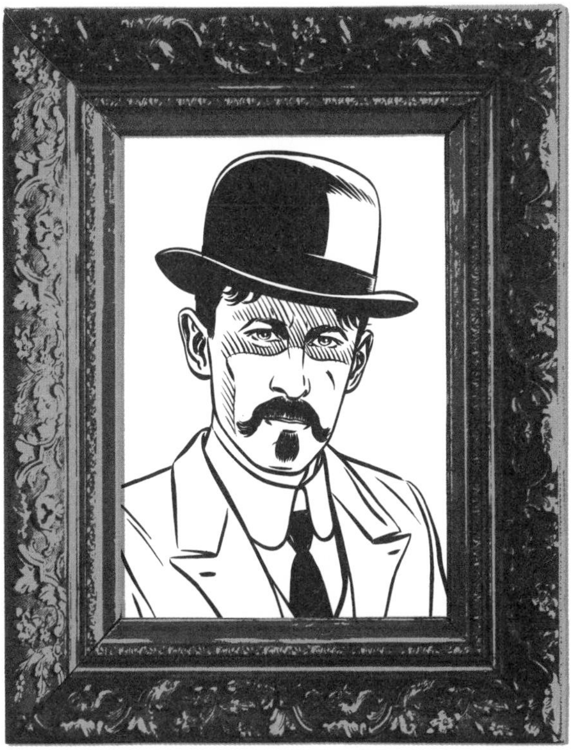

WHAT WOULD SOMEONE NAMED H. LEWIS ALLWAYS HAVE LIVED THROUGH OR WRITTEN ABOUT?

AND THE SAME GOES FOR KENNETH MILES: AN AUTHOR, OR SOMETHING ELSE ENTIRELY?

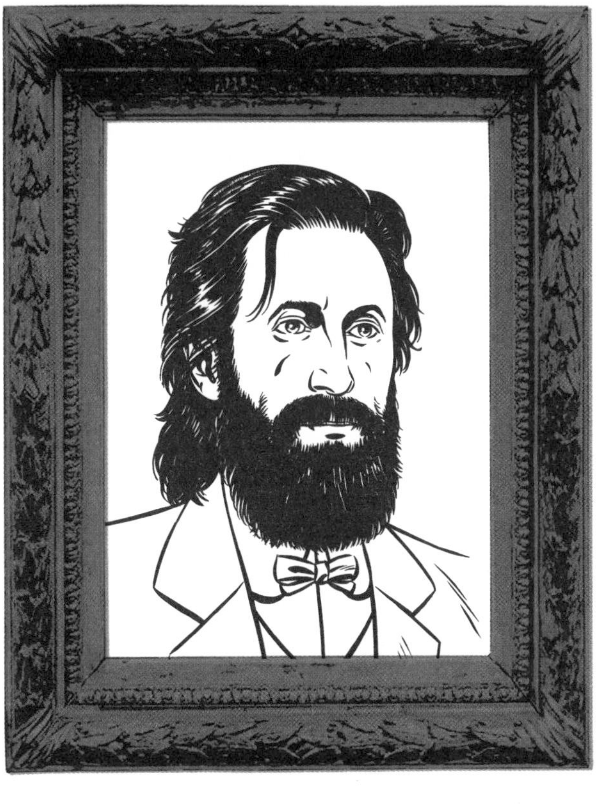

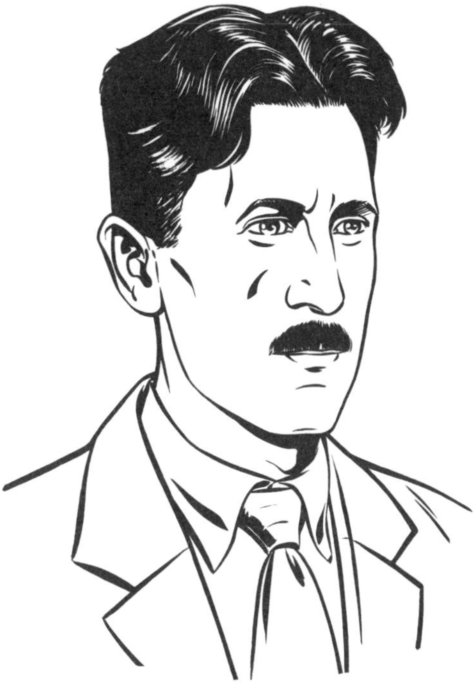

IN THE END, HE OPTED FOR GEORGE ORWELL, THE NAME BY WHICH HE WAS TO FIND FAME.

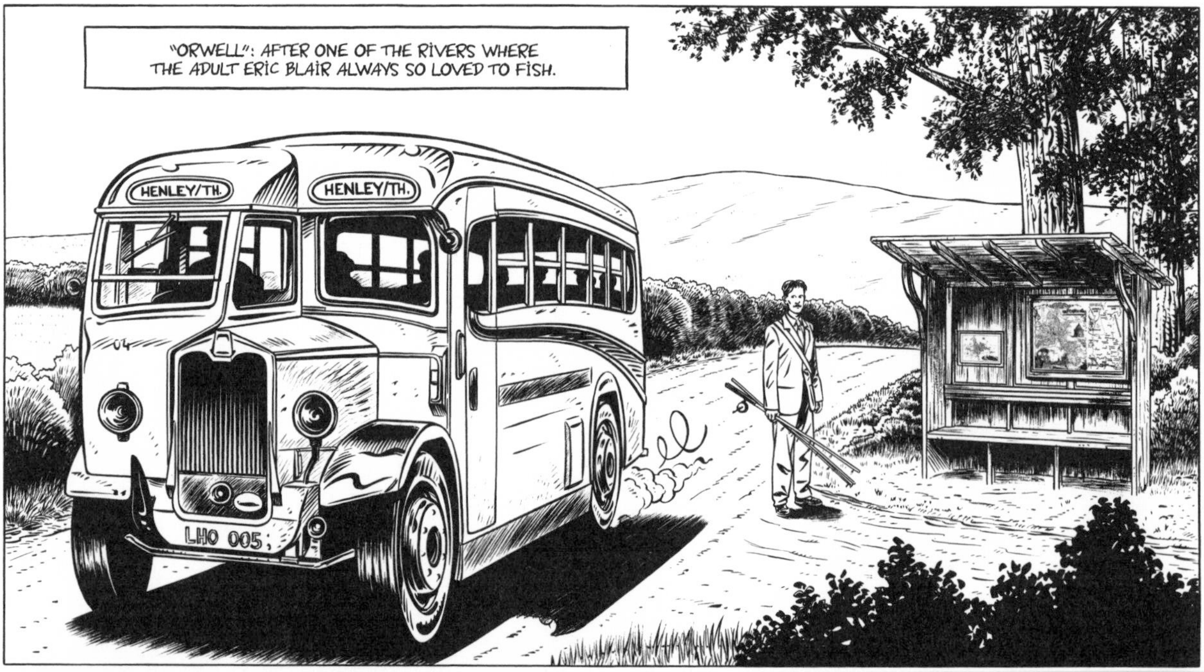
"ORWELL": AFTER ONE OF THE RIVERS WHERE THE ADULT ERIC BLAIR ALWAYS SO LOVED TO FISH.
HENLEY/TH.
HENLEY/TH.
LHO 005

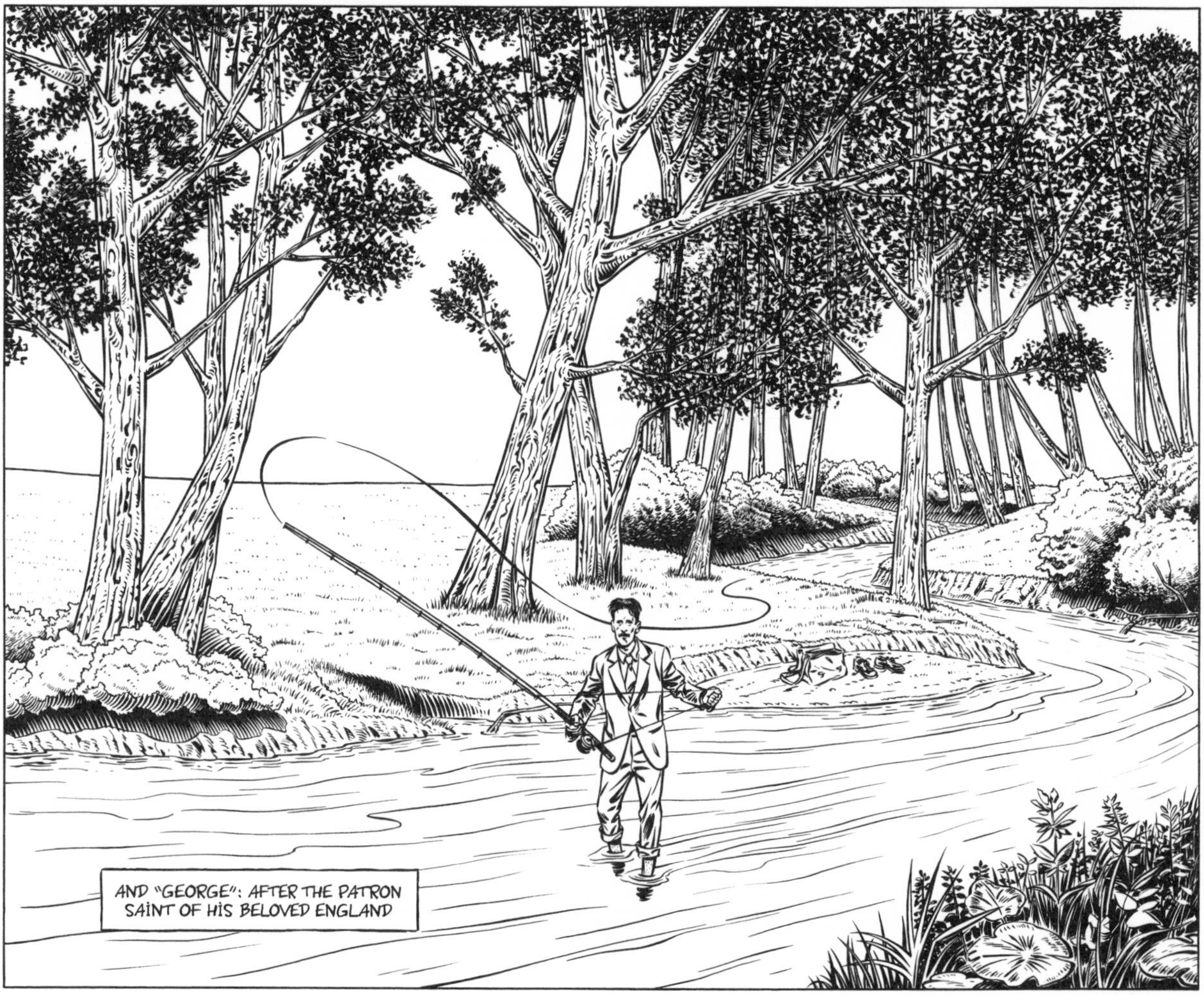
AND "GEORGE": AFTER THE PATRON SAINT OF HIS BELOVED ENGLAND

CHAPTER II

BLAIR INVENTS ORWELL

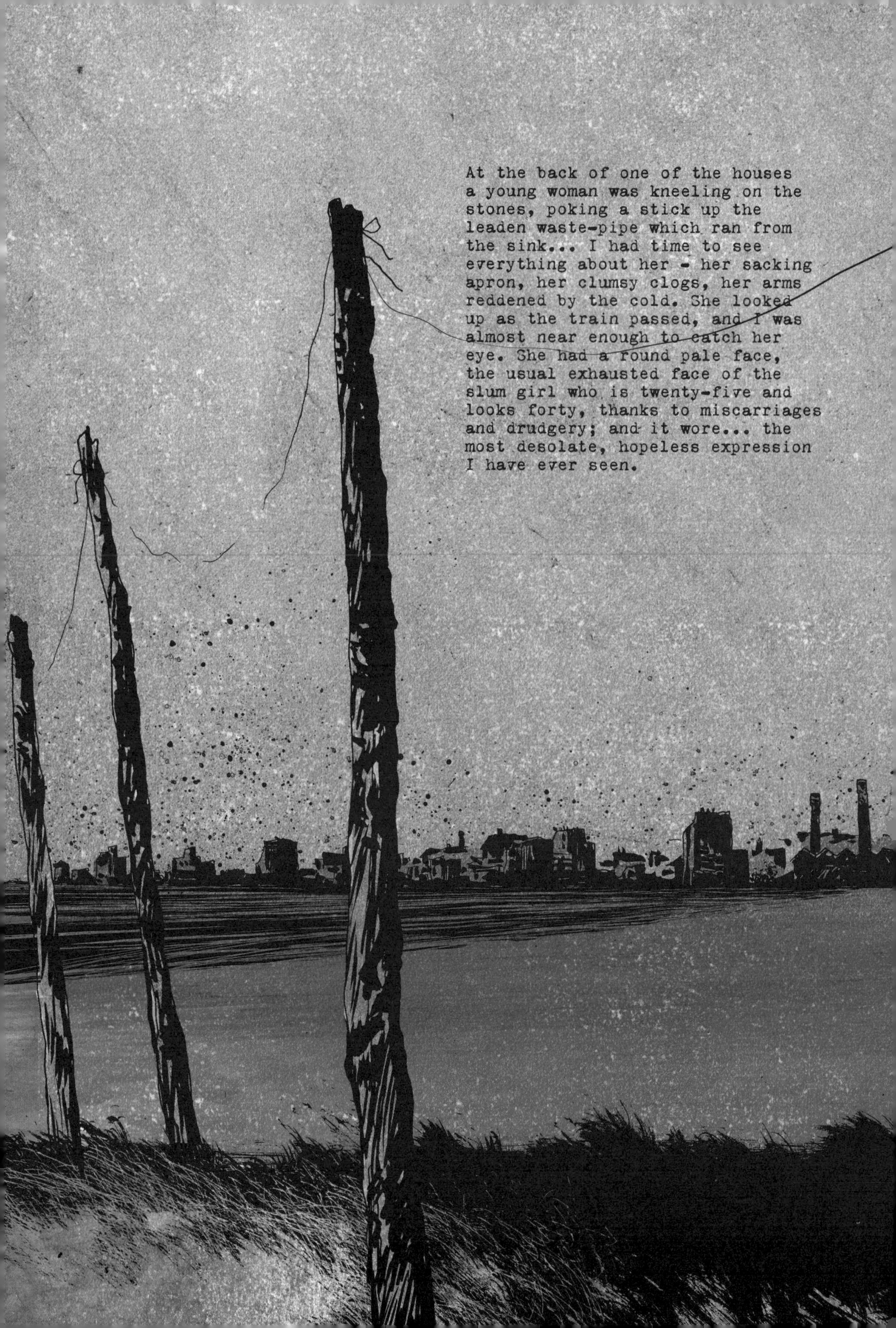
At the back of one of the houses a young woman was kneeling on the stones, poking a stick up the leaden waste-pipe which ran from the sink... I had time to see everything about her - her sacking apron, her clumsy clogs, her arms reddened by the cold. She looked up as the train passed, and I was almost near enough to catch her eye. She had a round pale face, the usual exhausted face of the slum girl who is twenty-five and looks forty, thanks to miscarriages and drudgery; and it wore... the most desolate, hopeless expression I have ever seen.

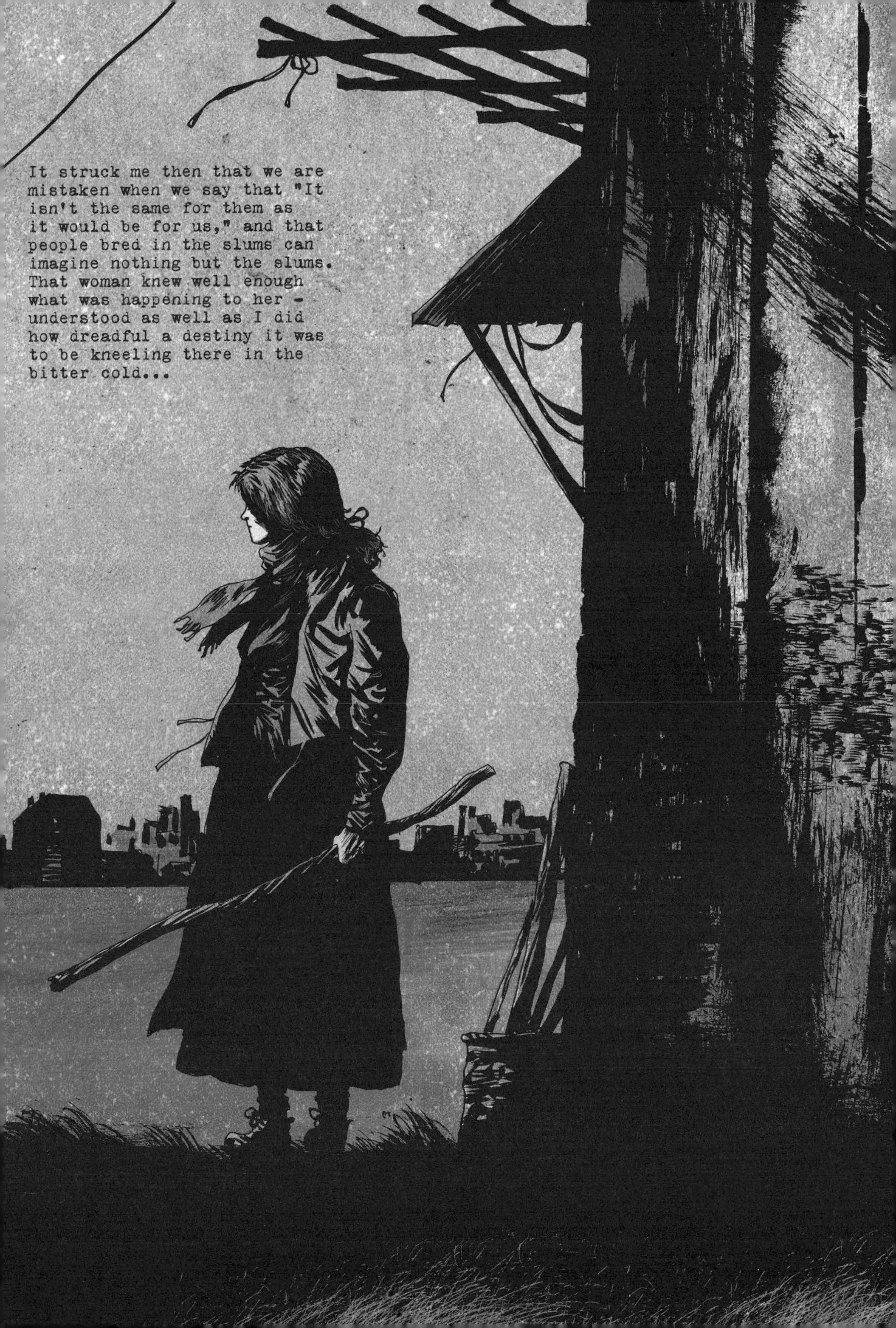
It struck me then that we are mistaken when we say that "It isn't the same for them as it would be for us," and that people bred in the slums can imagine nothing but the slums. That woman knew well enough what was happening to her - understood as well as I did how dreadful a destiny it was to be kneeling there in the bitter cold...

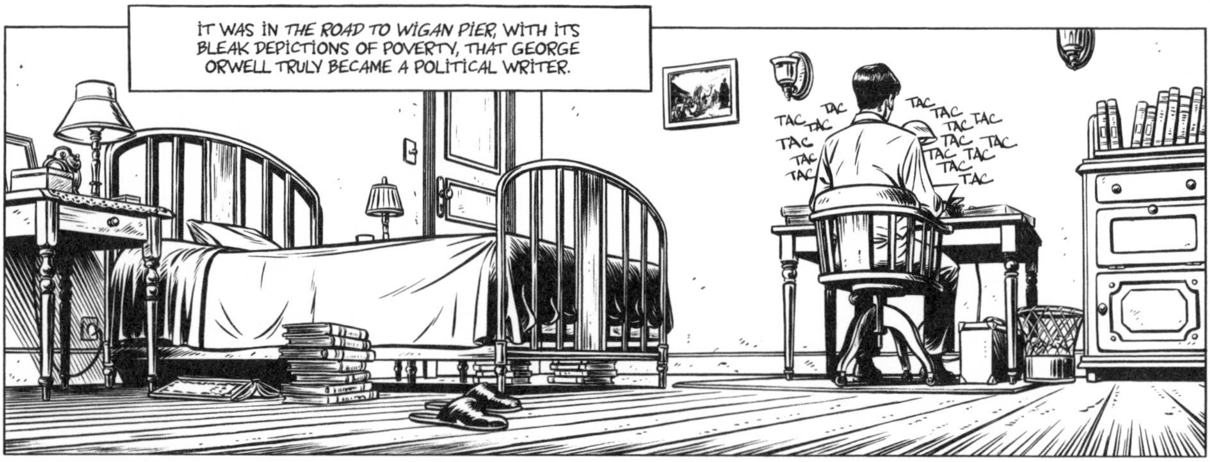
IT WAS IN *THE ROAD TO WIGAN PIER*, WITH ITS BLEAK DEPICTIONS OF POVERTY, THAT GEORGE ORWELL TRULY BECAME A POLITICAL WRITER.
TAC TAC TAC TAC TAC TAC TAC TAC TAC TAC TAC TAC TAC TAC TAC TAC

But I knew nothing about working-class conditions... Therefore my mind turned immediately towards the extreme cases... "the lowest of the low", and these were the people with whom I wanted to get in contact.

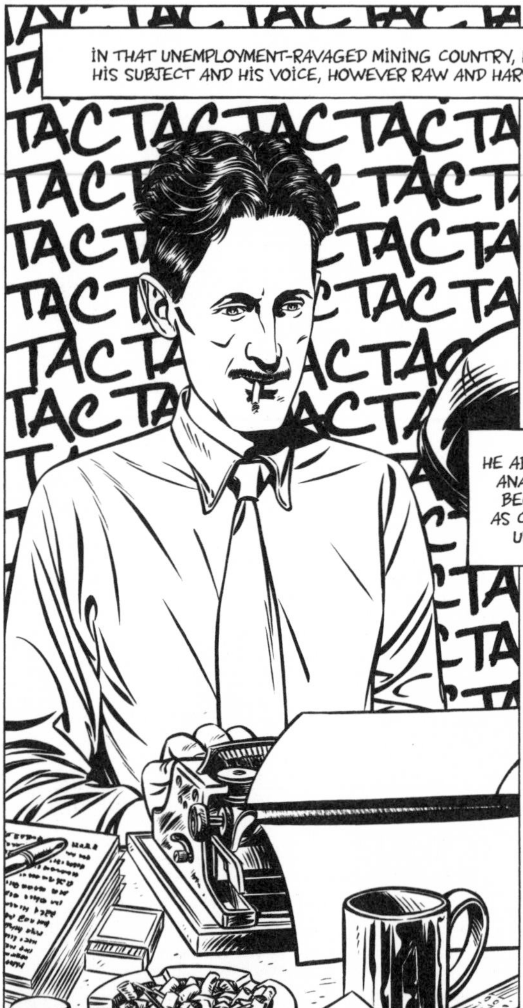
IN THAT UNEMPLOYMENT-RAVAGED MINING COUNTRY, HE FOUND BOTH HIS SUBJECT AND HIS VOICE, HOWEVER RAW AND HARSH IT SOUNDED.
TACTACTACTACTA

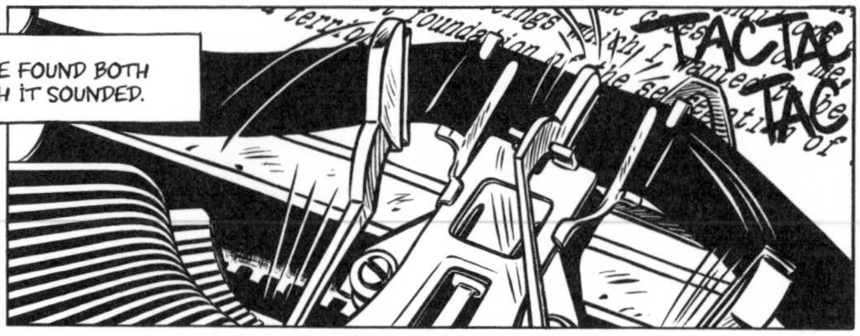
TACTAC TAC

Here you come to the real secret of class distinctions... It is summed up in four frightful words: The lower classes smell. It was rubbing shoulders with the tramps that cured me of it.

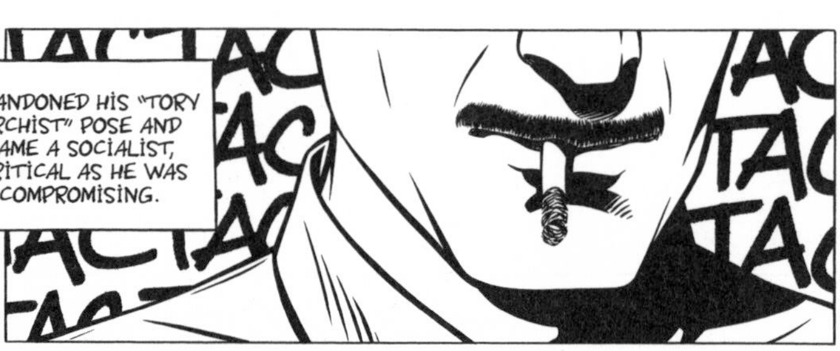
HE ABANDONED HIS "TORY ANARCHIST" POSE AND BECAME A SOCIALIST, AS CRITICAL AS HE WAS UNCOMPROMISING.
TAC TAC

Look at Comrade X, member of the C.P.G.B. and author of *Marxism for Infants*... I have known numbers of bourgeois Socialists, I have listened by the hour to their tirades against their own class, and yet never, not even once, have I met one who had picked up proletarian table-manners.

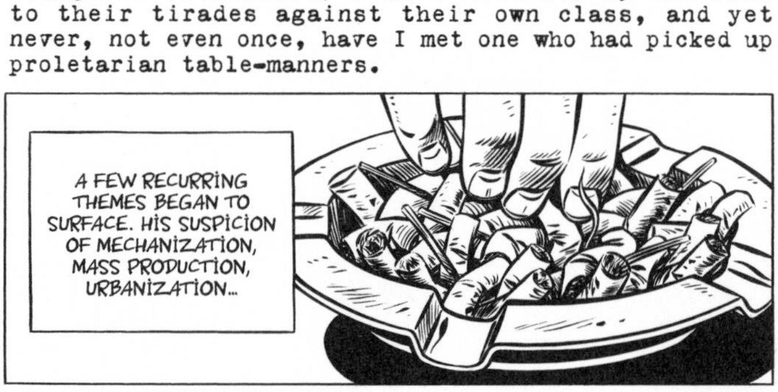
A FEW RECURRING THEMES BEGAN TO SURFACE. HIS SUSPICION OF MECHANIZATION, MASS PRODUCTION, URBANIZATION...

It is quite likely that fish-and-chips, art-silk stockings, tinned salmon... the movies, the radio... the Football Pools have between them averted revolution... We are sometimes told that the whole thing is an astute manoeuvre by the governing class... What I have seen of our governing class does not convince me that they have that much intelligence.

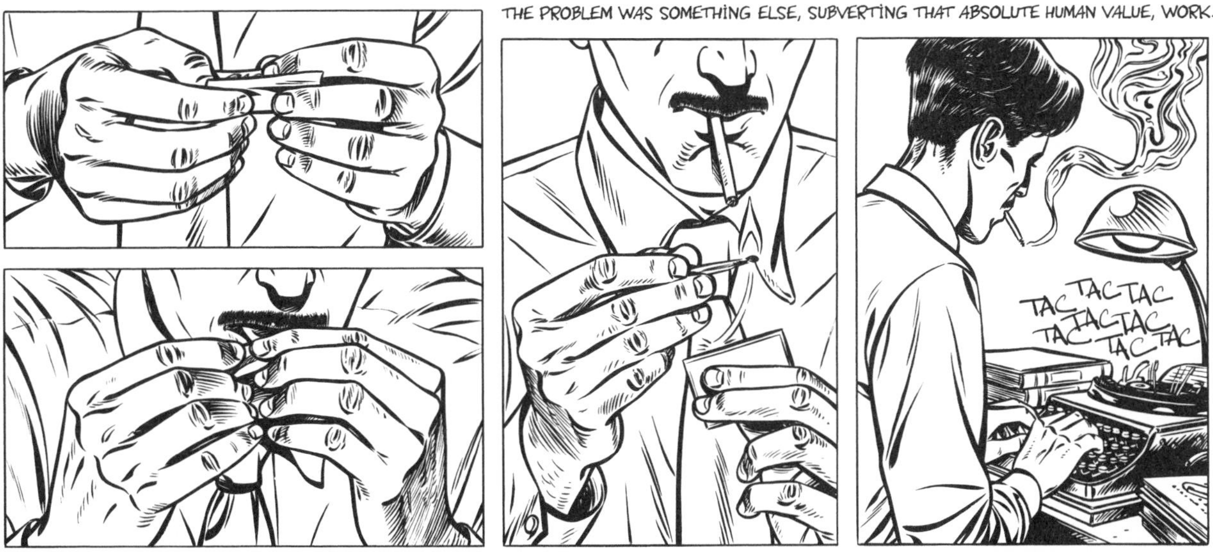
THE PROBLEM WAS SOMETHING ELSE, SUBVERTING THAT ABSOLUTE HUMAN VALUE, WORK.
TAC TAC TAC TAC TAC TAC TAC TAC TAC TAC

But there is no doubt about the deadening, debilitating effect of unemployment upon everybody, married or single, and upon men more than upon women.

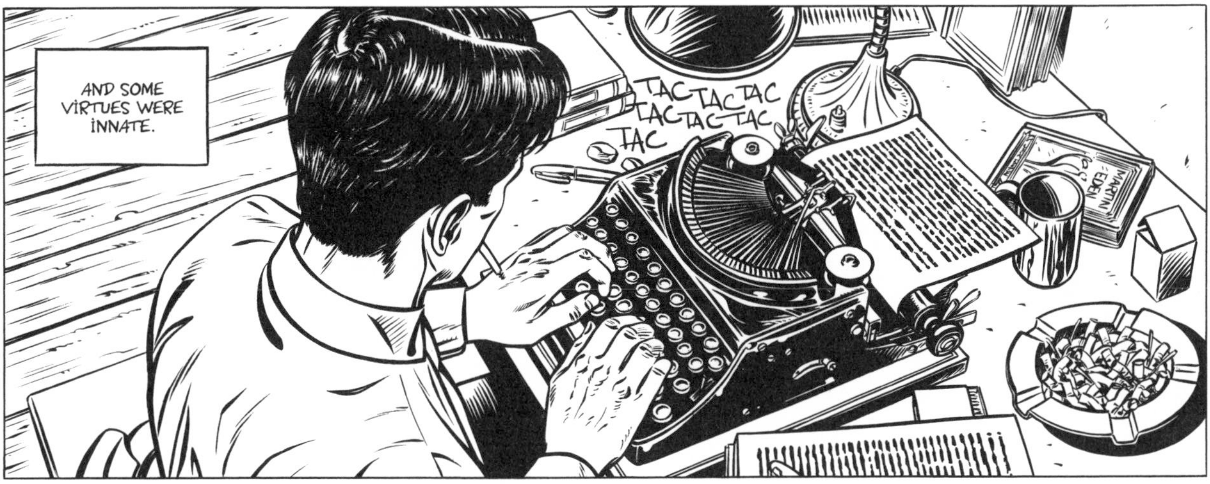
AND SOME VIRTUES WERE INNATE.
TAC TAC TAC TAC TAC TAC TAC
MARTIN EDEN

In a working-class home - I am not thinking at the moment of the unemployed... you breathe a warm, decent, deeply human atmosphere which it is not so easy to find elsewhere. I should say that a manual worker... has a better chance of being happy than an "educated" man.

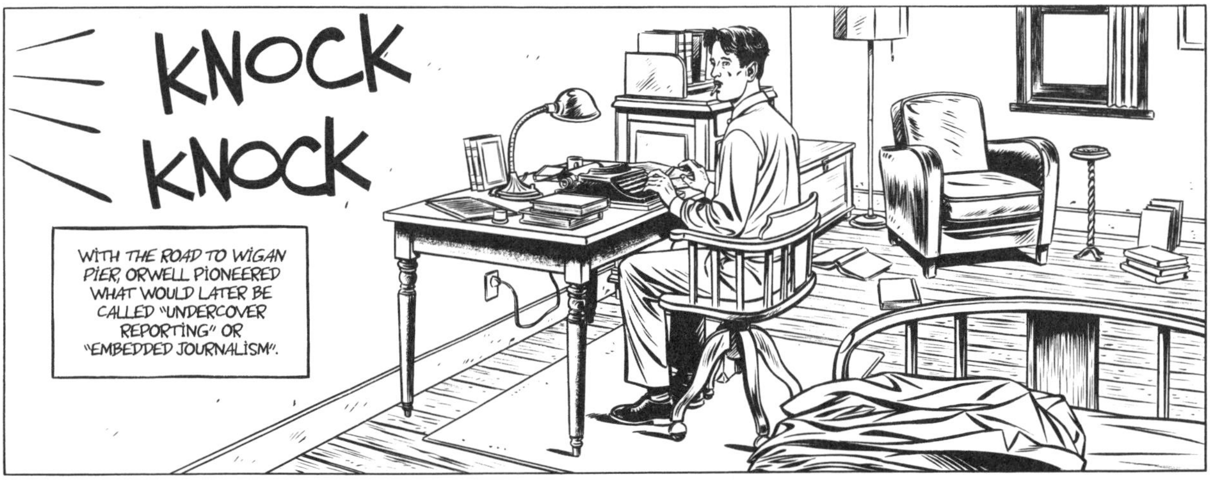
KNOCK
KNOCK
WITH *THE ROAD TO WIGAN PIER*, ORWELL PIONEERED WHAT WOULD LATER BE CALLED "UNDERCOVER REPORTING" OR "EMBEDDED JOURNALISM".

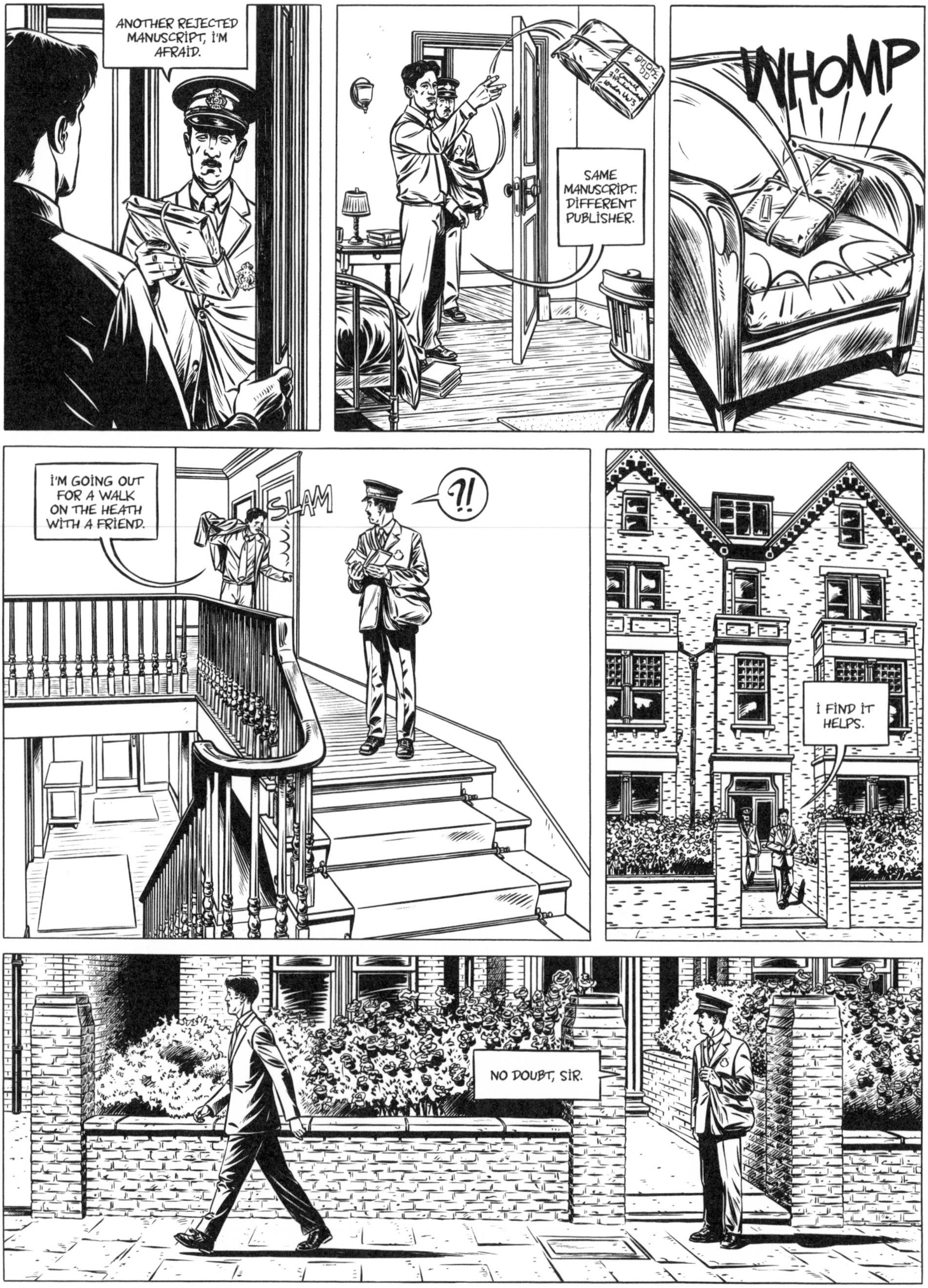
ANOTHER REJECTED MANUSCRIPT, I'M AFRAID.
SAME MANUSCRIPT. DIFFERENT PUBLISHER.
WHOMP
I'M GOING OUT FOR A WALK ON THE HEATH WITH A FRIEND.
SLAM
?!
I FIND IT HELPS.
NO DOUBT, SIR.

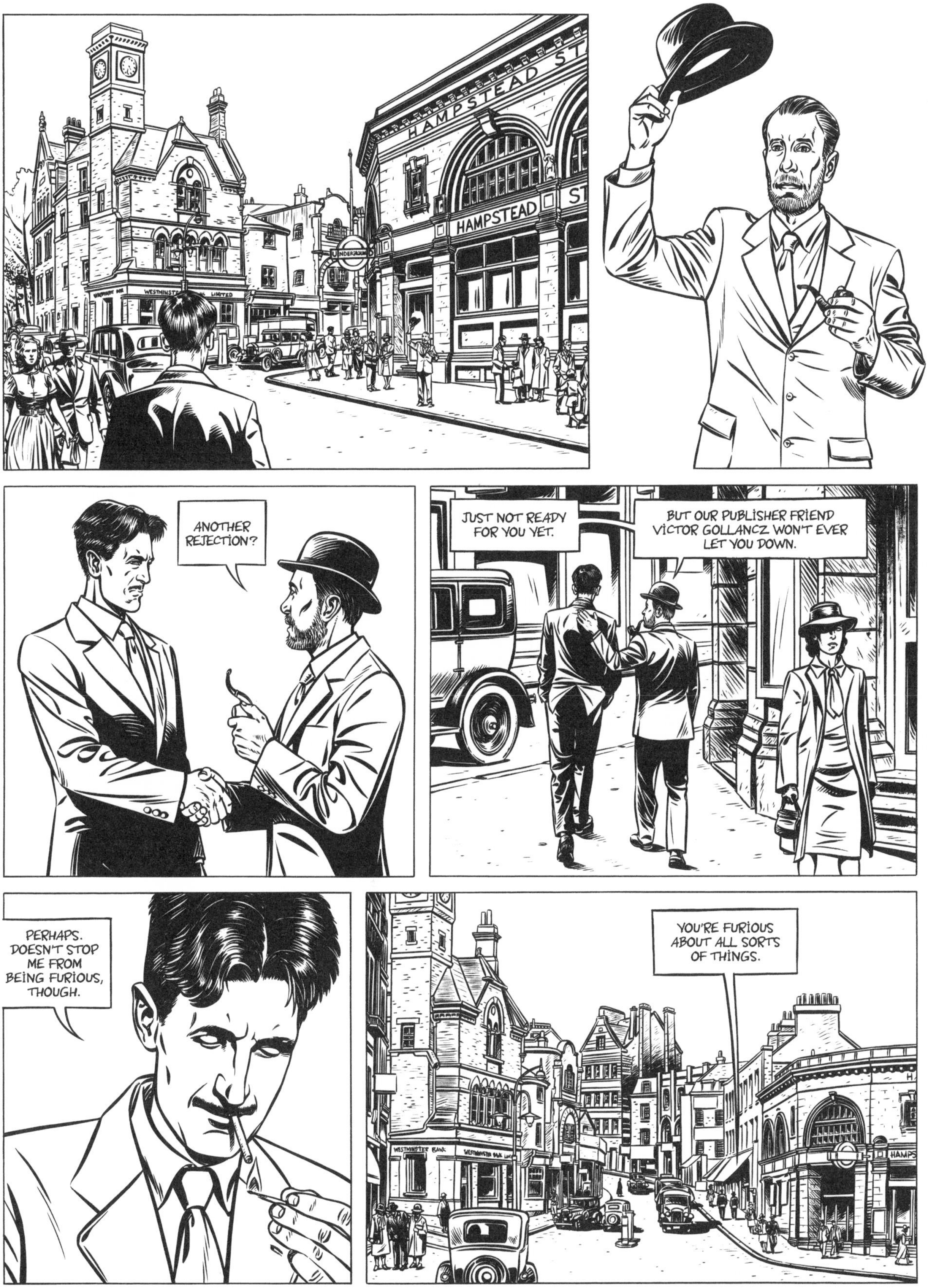
HAMPSTEAD ST
HAMPSTEAD
ANOTHER REJECTION?
JUST NOT READY FOR YOU YET.
BUT OUR PUBLISHER FRIEND VICTOR GOLLANCZ WON'T EVER LET YOU DOWN.
PERHAPS. DOESN'T STOP ME FROM BEING FURIOUS, THOUGH.
YOU'RE FURIOUS ABOUT ALL SORTS OF THINGS.

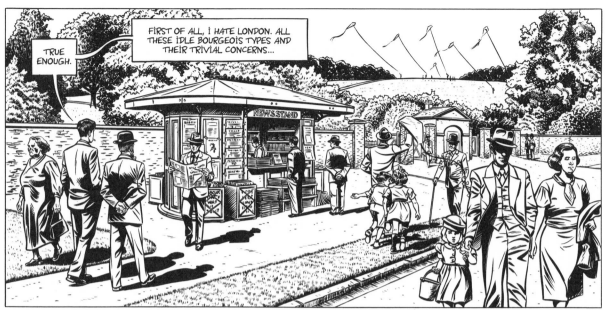

FIRST OF ALL, I HATE LONDON. ALL THESE IDLE BOURGEOIS TYPES AND THEIR TRIVIAL CONCERNS...
TRUE ENOUGH.
NEWSSTAND
I ALSO HATE LABOUR POLITICIANS - THEY'VE BECOME CAPITALIST LACKEYS WITHOUT EVEN REALIZING IT.
THE DAILY WORKER
LABOUR PARTY WINS
I HATE THEM ALMOST AS MUCH AS THOSE BLACK-SHIRT FASCISTS OFF TO OSWALD MOSLEY'S DEMONSTRATION.
BUT THE PEOPLE I HATE THE MOST ARE ALL THOSE DRUNKEN SCOTS RULING OVER THE COLONIAL EMPIRE.
LET ME STOP YOU THERE. YOUR ANTI-SCOTS OBSESSION VERGES ON MADNESS.
YOU'RE RIGHT.
WE ALL HAVE OUR CONTRA-DICTIONS.

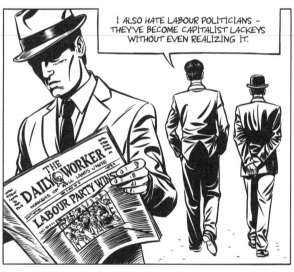

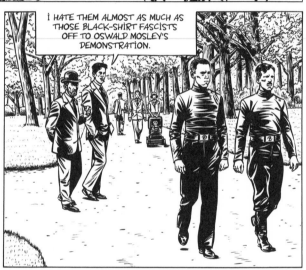

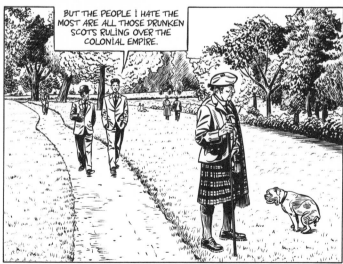

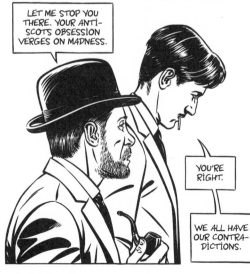

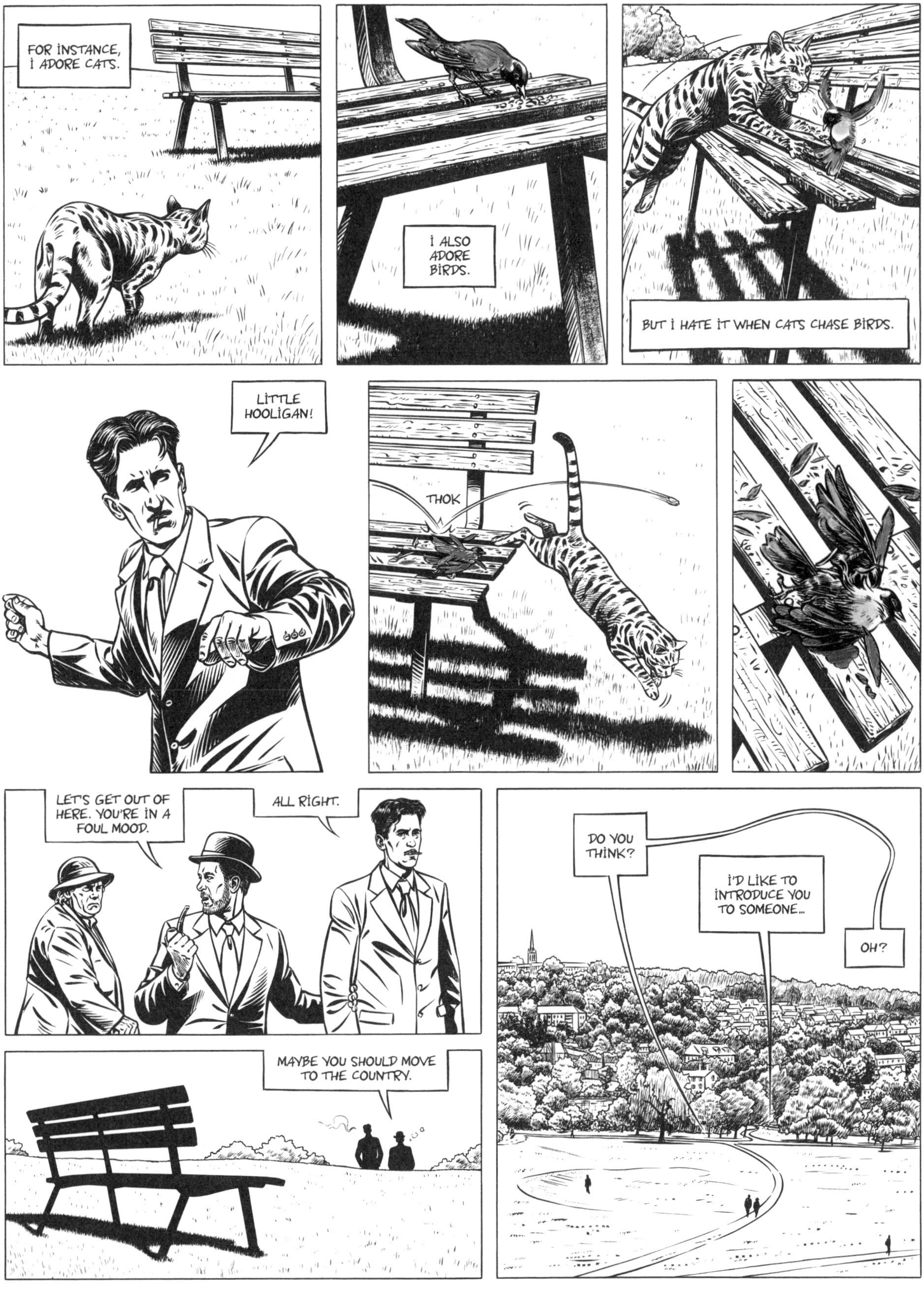

FOR INSTANCE, I ADORE CATS.
I ALSO ADORE BIRDS.
BUT I HATE IT WHEN CATS CHASE BIRDS.
LITTLE HOOLIGAN!
THOK
LET'S GET OUT OF HERE. YOU'RE IN A FOUL MOOD.
ALL RIGHT.
MAYBE YOU SHOULD MOVE TO THE COUNTRY.
DO YOU THINK?
I'D LIKE TO INTRODUCE YOU TO SOMEONE...
OH?

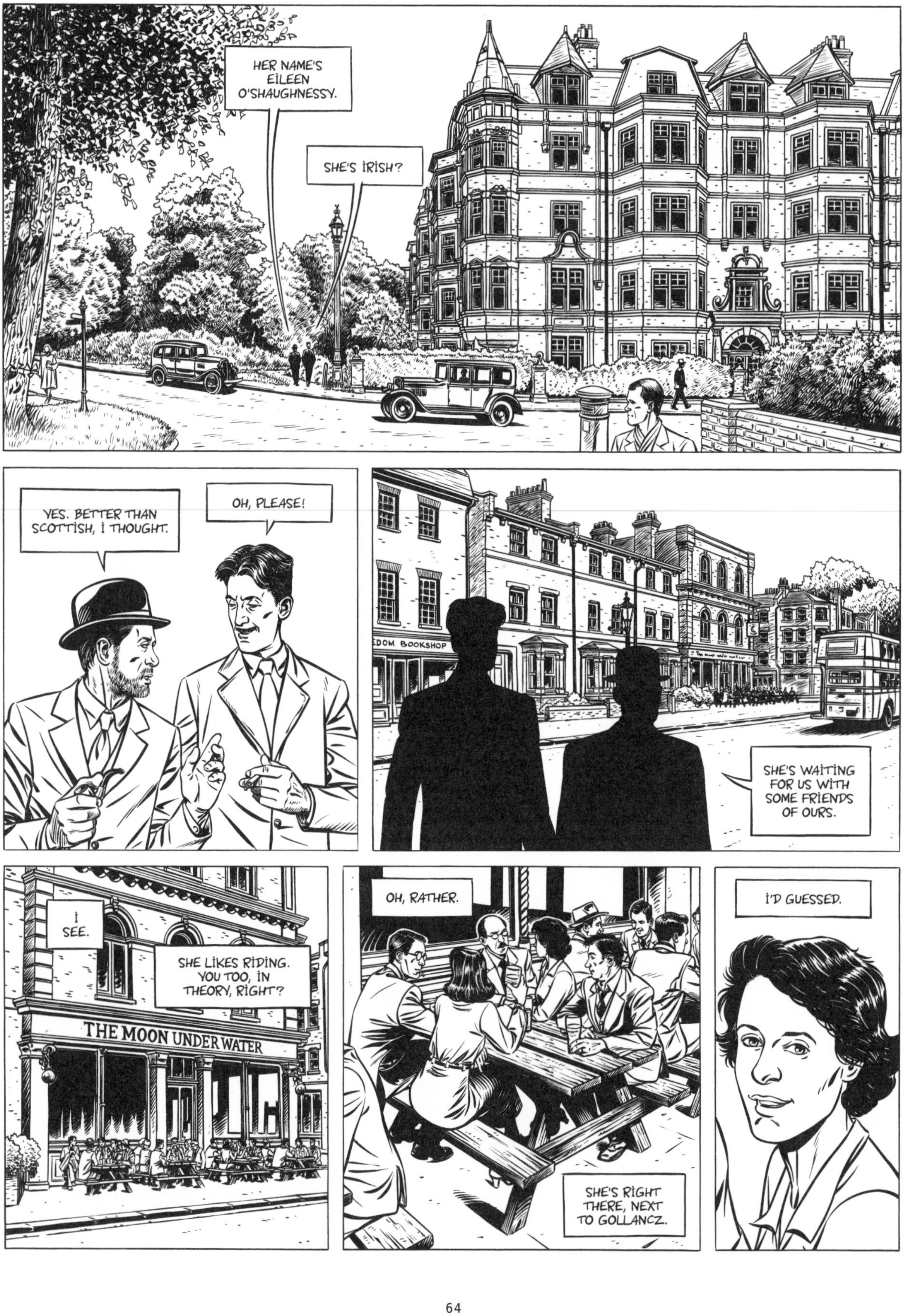
HER NAME'S EILEEN O'SHAUGHNESSY.
SHE'S IRISH?
YES. BETTER THAN SCOTTISH, I THOUGHT.
OH, PLEASE!
EDOM BOOKSHOP
SHE'S WAITING FOR US WITH SOME FRIENDS OF OURS.
I SEE.
SHE LIKES RIDING. YOU TOO, IN THEORY, RIGHT?
THE MOON UNDER WATER
OH, RATHER.
SHE'S RIGHT THERE, NEXT TO GOLLANCZ.
I'D GUESSED.

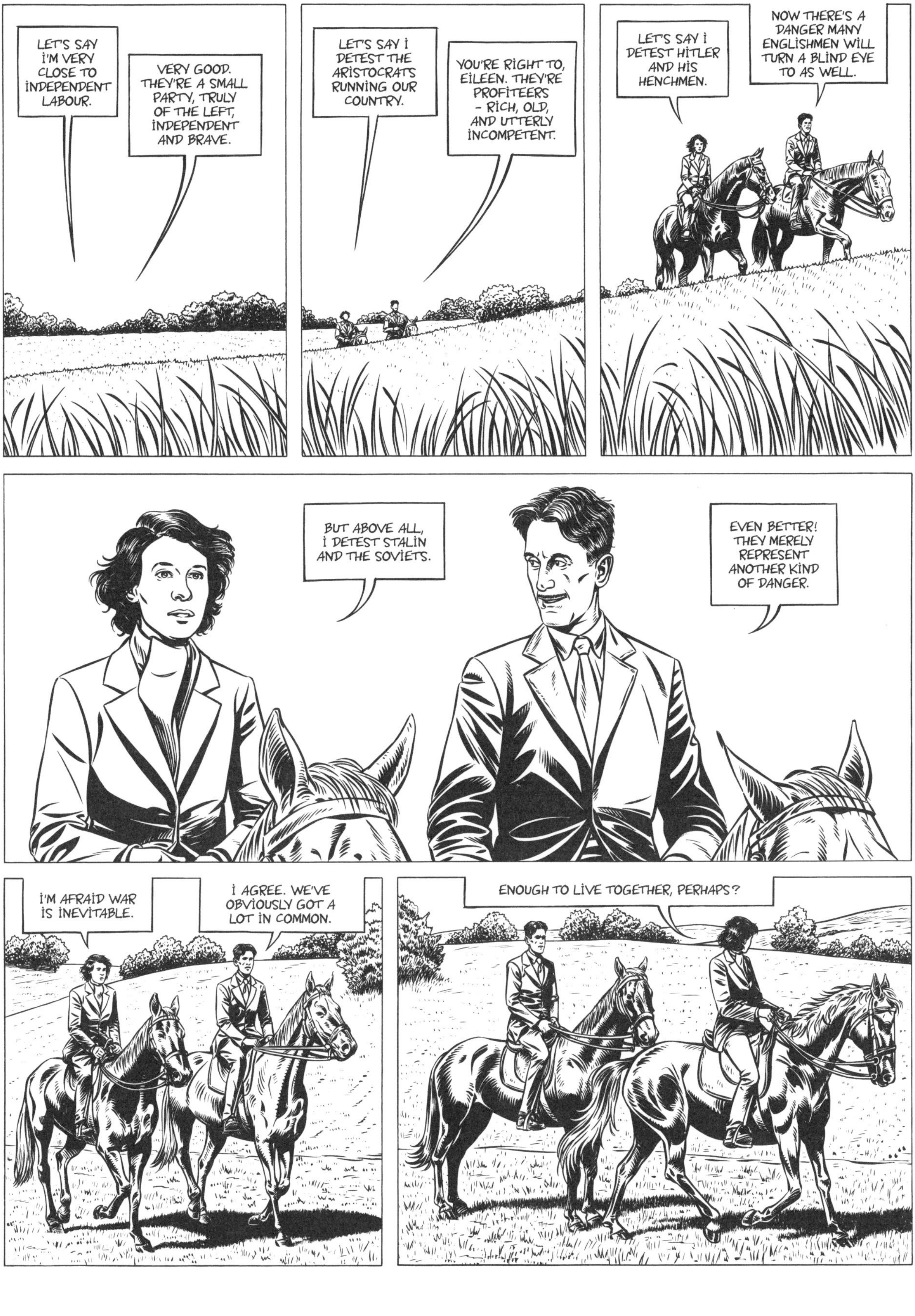
LET'S SAY I'M VERY CLOSE TO INDEPENDENT LABOUR.
VERY GOOD. THEY'RE A SMALL PARTY, TRULY OF THE LEFT, INDEPENDENT AND BRAVE.
LET'S SAY I DETEST THE ARISTOCRATS RUNNING OUR COUNTRY.
YOU'RE RIGHT TO, EILEEN. THEY'RE PROFITEERS - RICH, OLD, AND UTTERLY INCOMPETENT.
LET'S SAY I DETEST HITLER AND HIS HENCHMEN.
NOW THERE'S A DANGER MANY ENGLISHMEN WILL TURN A BLIND EYE TO AS WELL.
BUT ABOVE ALL, I DETEST STALIN AND THE SOVIETS.
EVEN BETTER! THEY MERELY REPRESENT ANOTHER KIND OF DANGER.
I'M AFRAID WAR IS INEVITABLE.
I AGREE. WE'VE OBVIOUSLY GOT A LOT IN COMMON.
ENOUGH TO LIVE TOGETHER, PERHAPS?

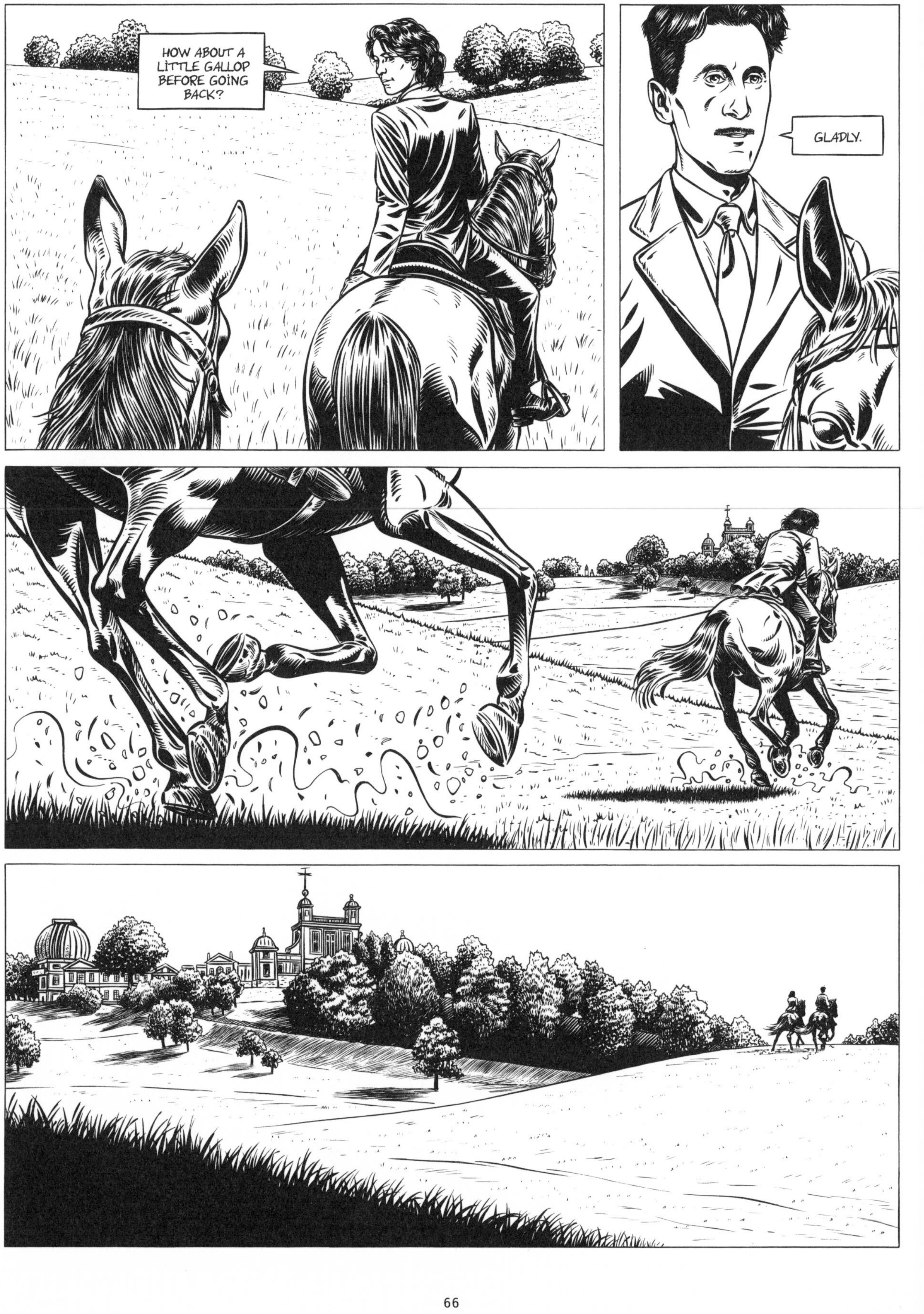
HOW ABOUT A LITTLE GALLOP BEFORE GOING BACK?
GLADLY.

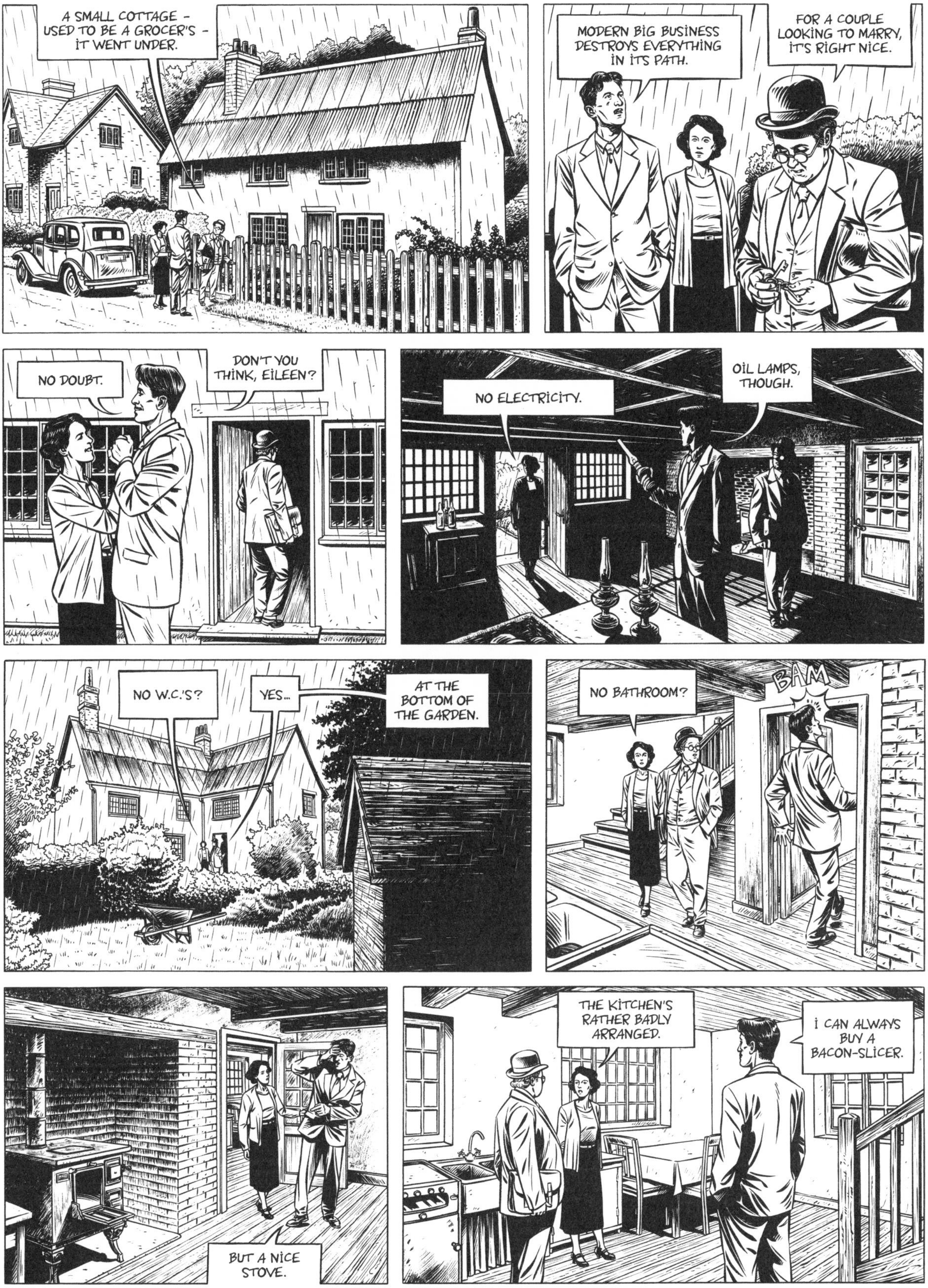
A SMALL COTTAGE - USED TO BE A GROCER'S - IT WENT UNDER.
MODERN BIG BUSINESS DESTROYS EVERYTHING IN ITS PATH.
FOR A COUPLE LOOKING TO MARRY, IT'S RIGHT NICE.
NO DOUBT.
DON'T YOU THINK, EILEEN?
NO ELECTRICITY.
OIL LAMPS, THOUGH.
NO W.C.'S?
YES...
AT THE BOTTOM OF THE GARDEN.
NO BATHROOM?
BAM
BUT A NICE STOVE.
THE KITCHEN'S RATHER BADLY ARRANGED.
I CAN ALWAYS BUY A BACON-SLICER.

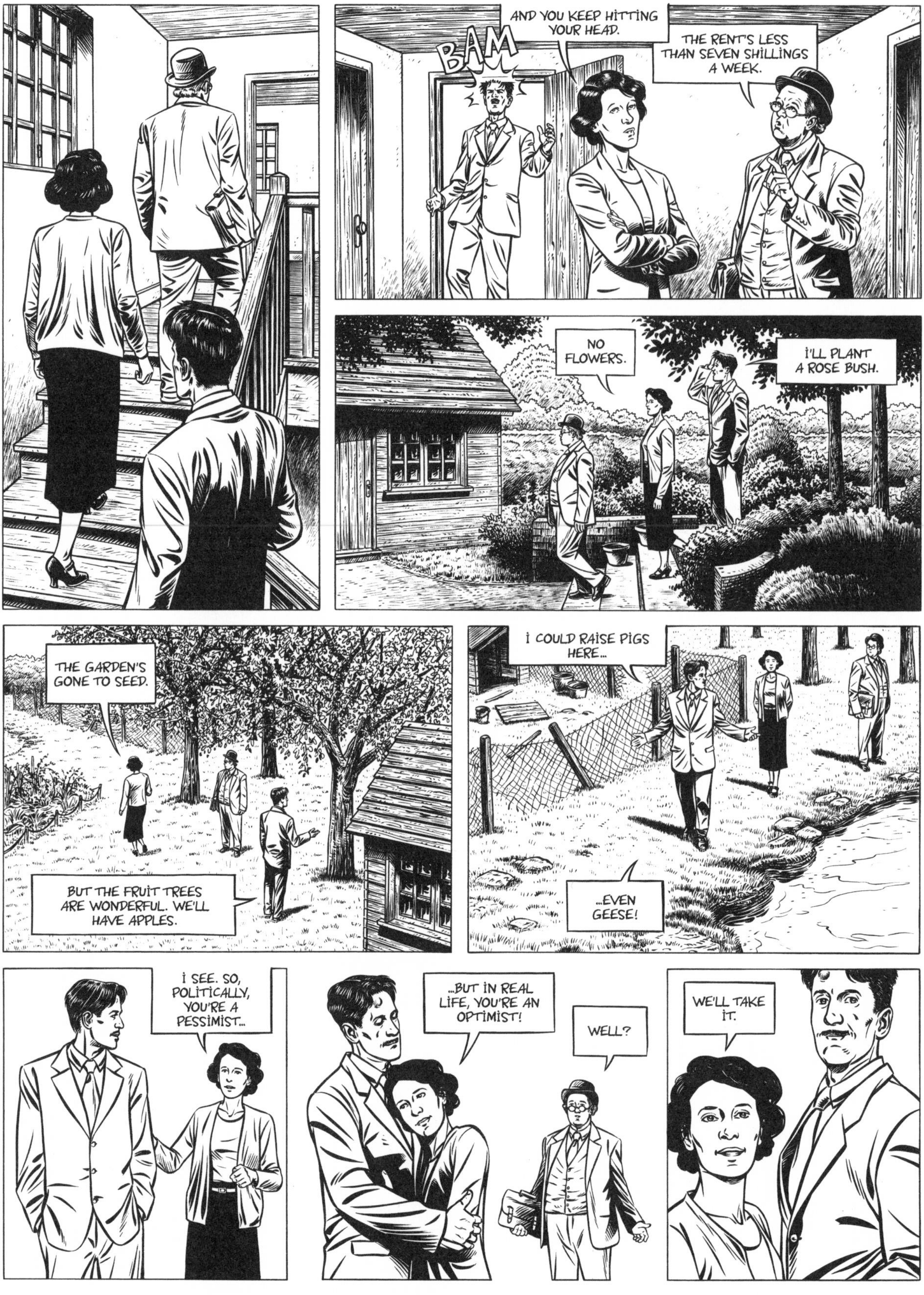

BAM
AND YOU KEEP HITTING YOUR HEAD.
THE RENT'S LESS THAN SEVEN SHILLINGS A WEEK.
NO FLOWERS.
I'LL PLANT A ROSE BUSH.
THE GARDEN'S GONE TO SEED.
BUT THE FRUIT TREES ARE WONDERFUL. WE'LL HAVE APPLES.
I COULD RAISE PIGS HERE...
...EVEN GEESE!
I SEE. SO, POLITICALLY, YOU'RE A PESSIMIST...
...BUT IN REAL LIFE, YOU'RE AN OPTIMIST!
WELL?
WE'LL TAKE IT.

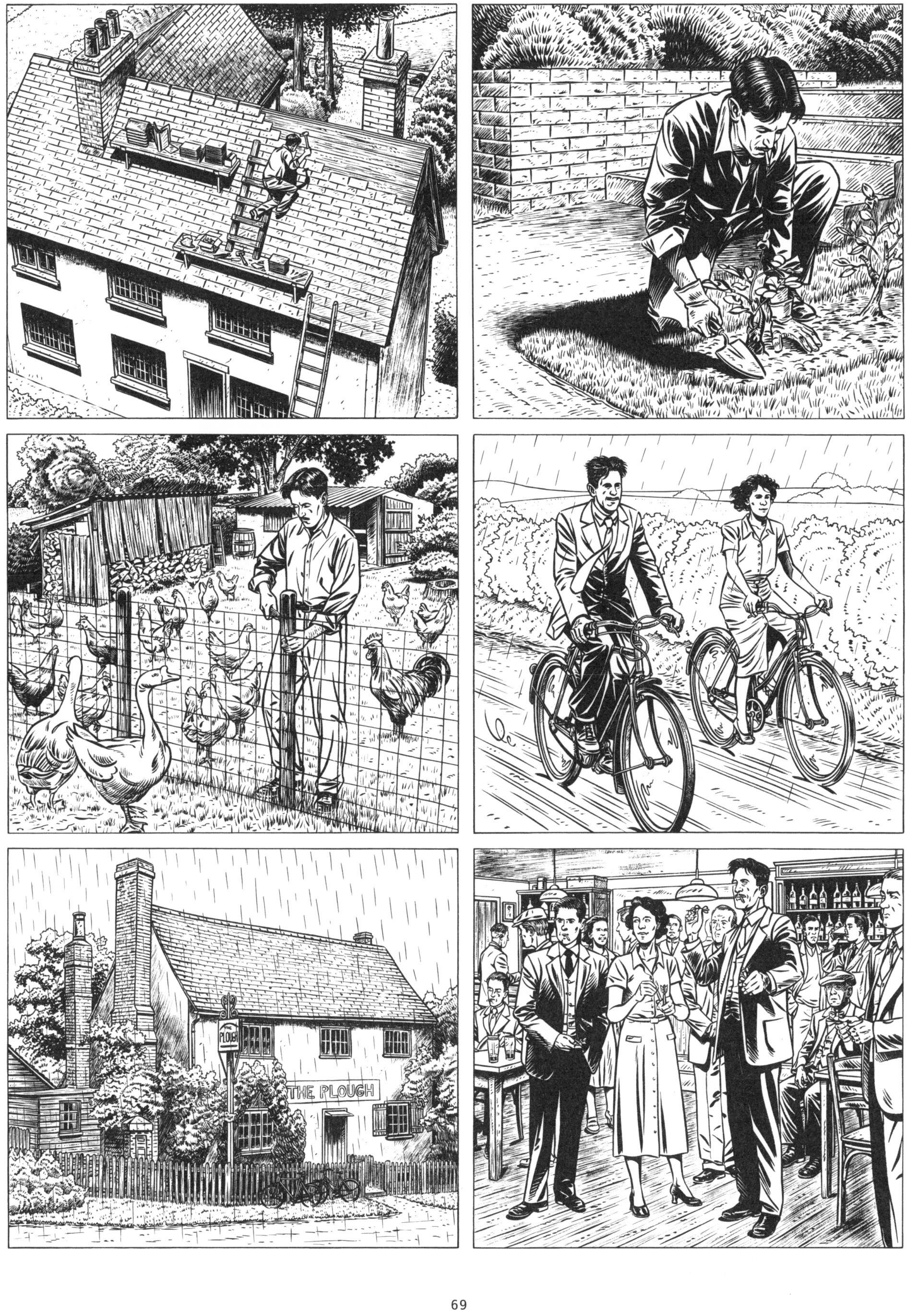
THE PLOUGH
THE PLOUGH

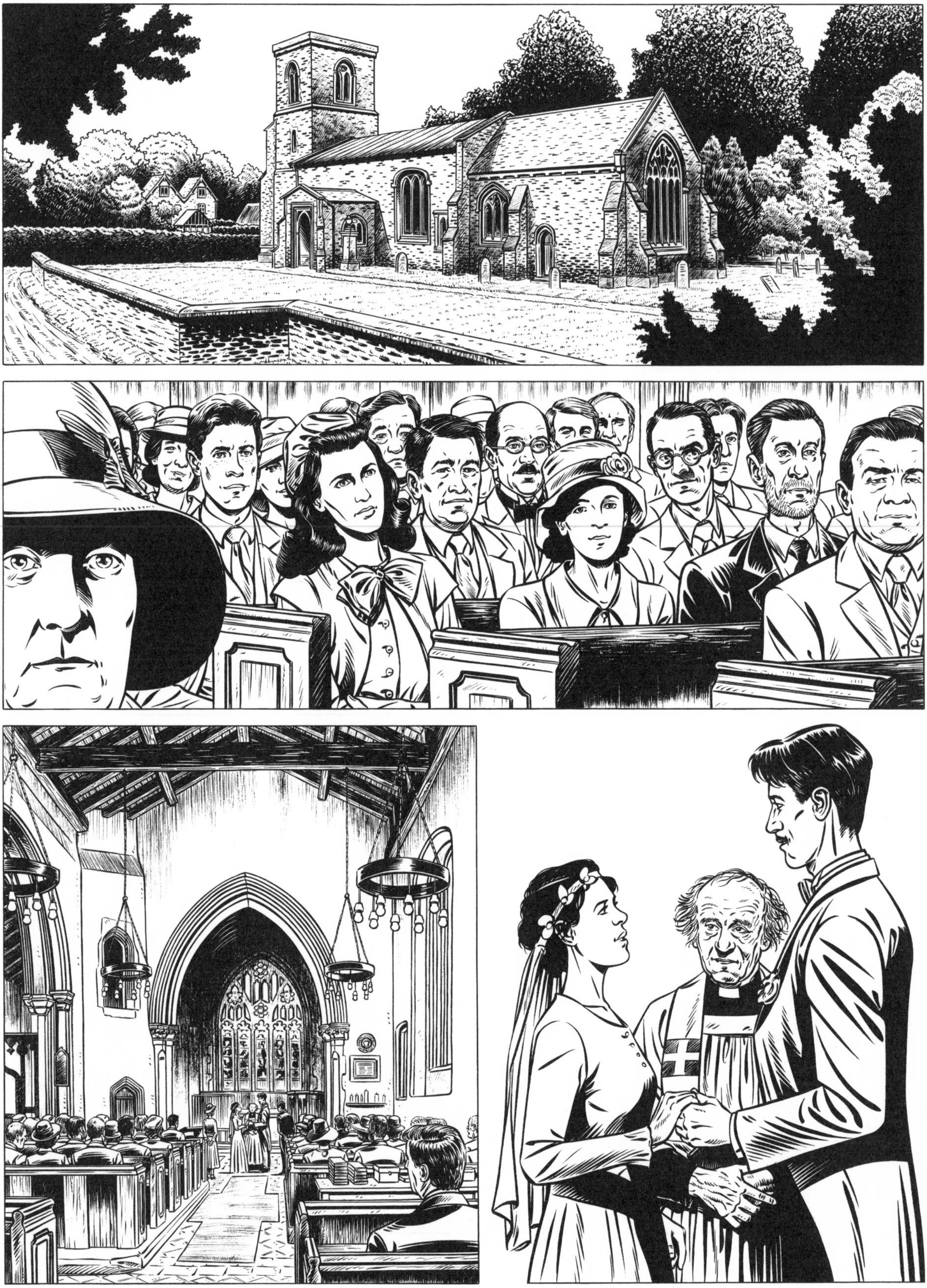

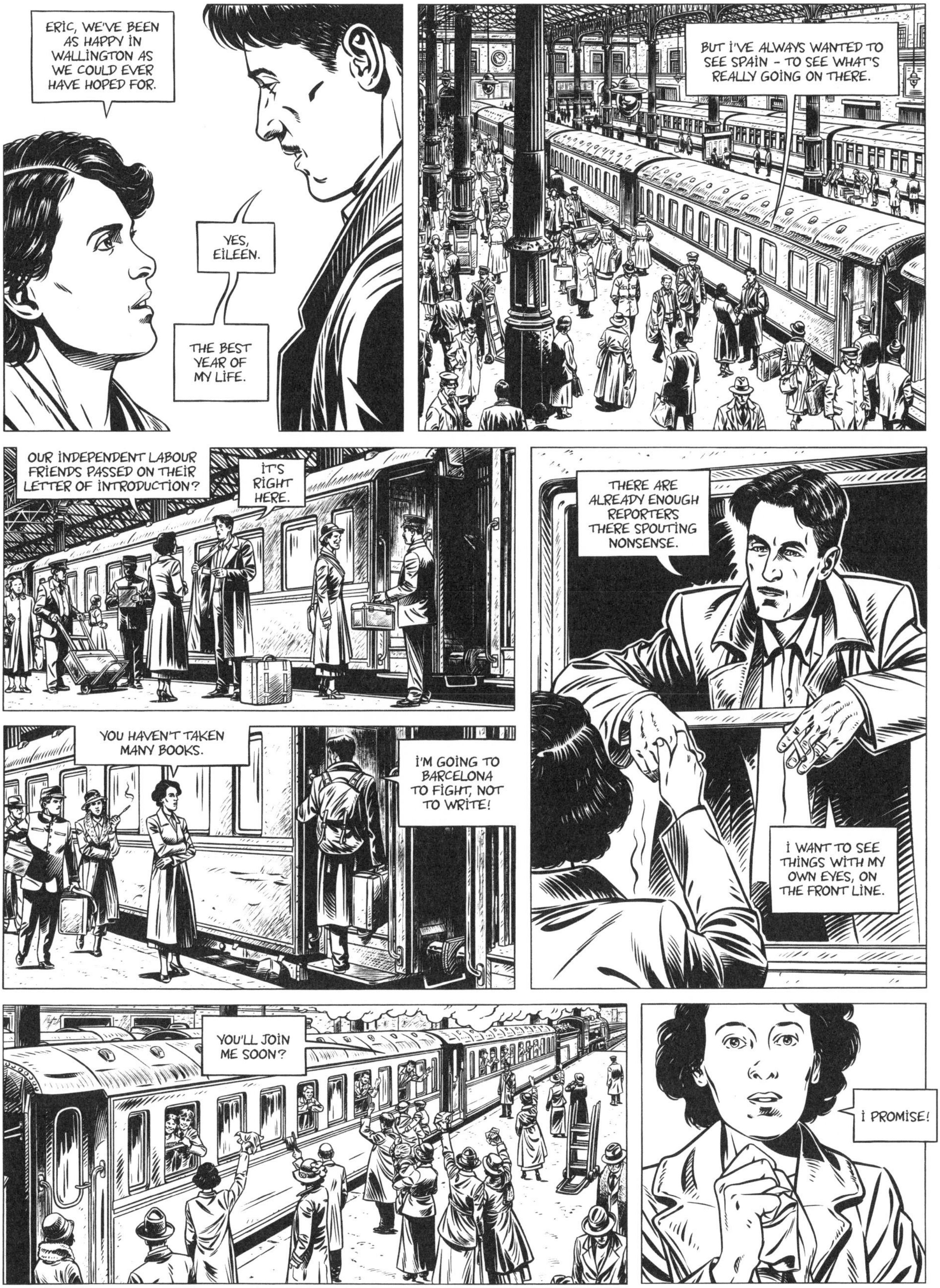
ERIC, WE'VE BEEN AS HAPPY IN WALLINGTON AS WE COULD EVER HAVE HOPED FOR.
YES, EILEEN.
THE BEST YEAR OF MY LIFE.
BUT I'VE ALWAYS WANTED TO SEE SPAIN - TO SEE WHAT'S REALLY GOING ON THERE.
OUR INDEPENDENT LABOUR FRIENDS PASSED ON THEIR LETTER OF INTRODUCTION?
IT'S RIGHT HERE.
THERE ARE ALREADY ENOUGH REPORTERS THERE SPOUTING NONSENSE.
YOU HAVEN'T TAKEN MANY BOOKS.
I'M GOING TO BARCELONA TO FIGHT, NOT TO WRITE!
I WANT TO SEE THINGS WITH MY OWN EYES, ON THE FRONT LINE.
YOU'LL JOIN ME SOON?
I PROMISE!

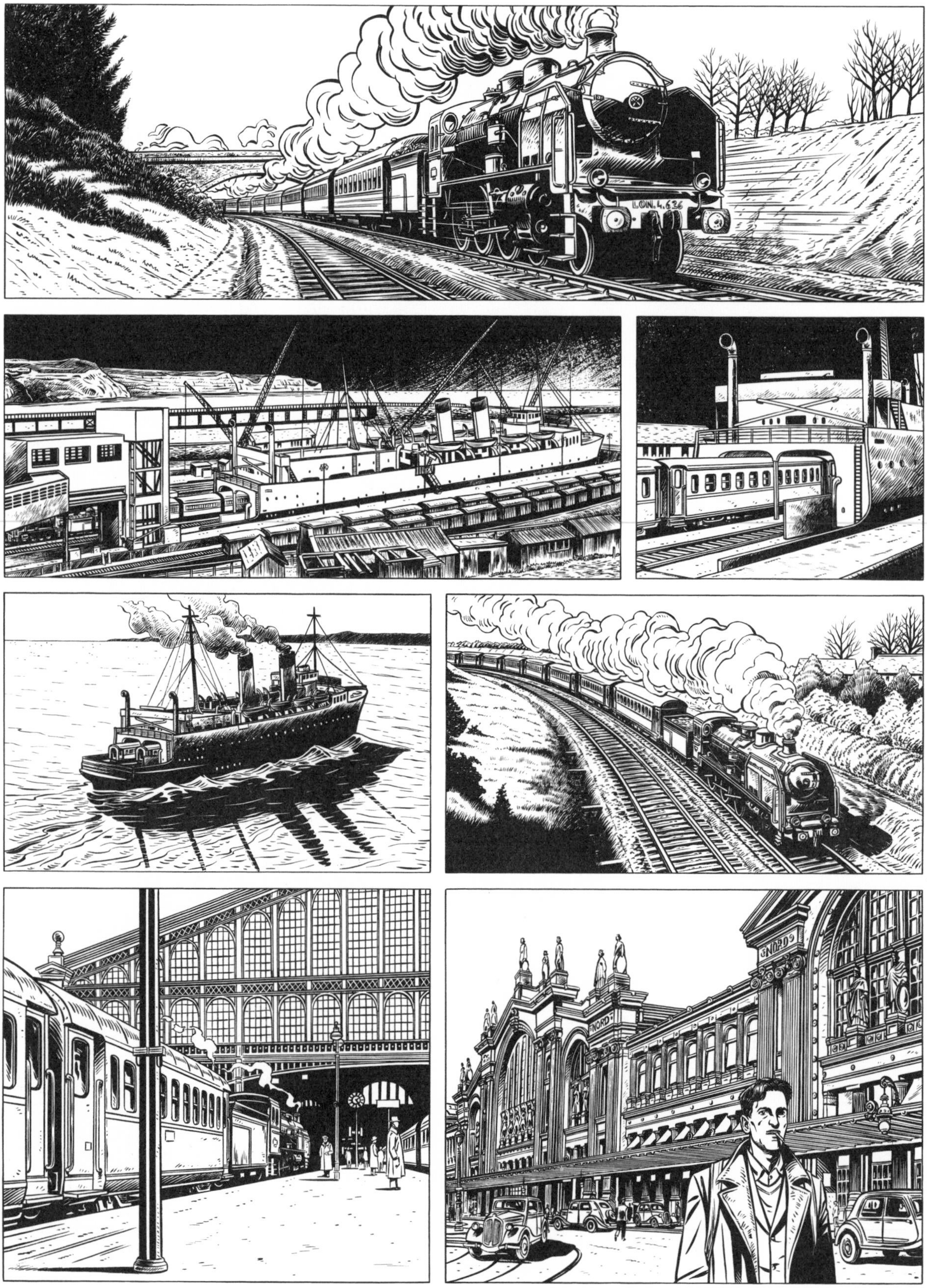
LON.4.626
NORD
NORD

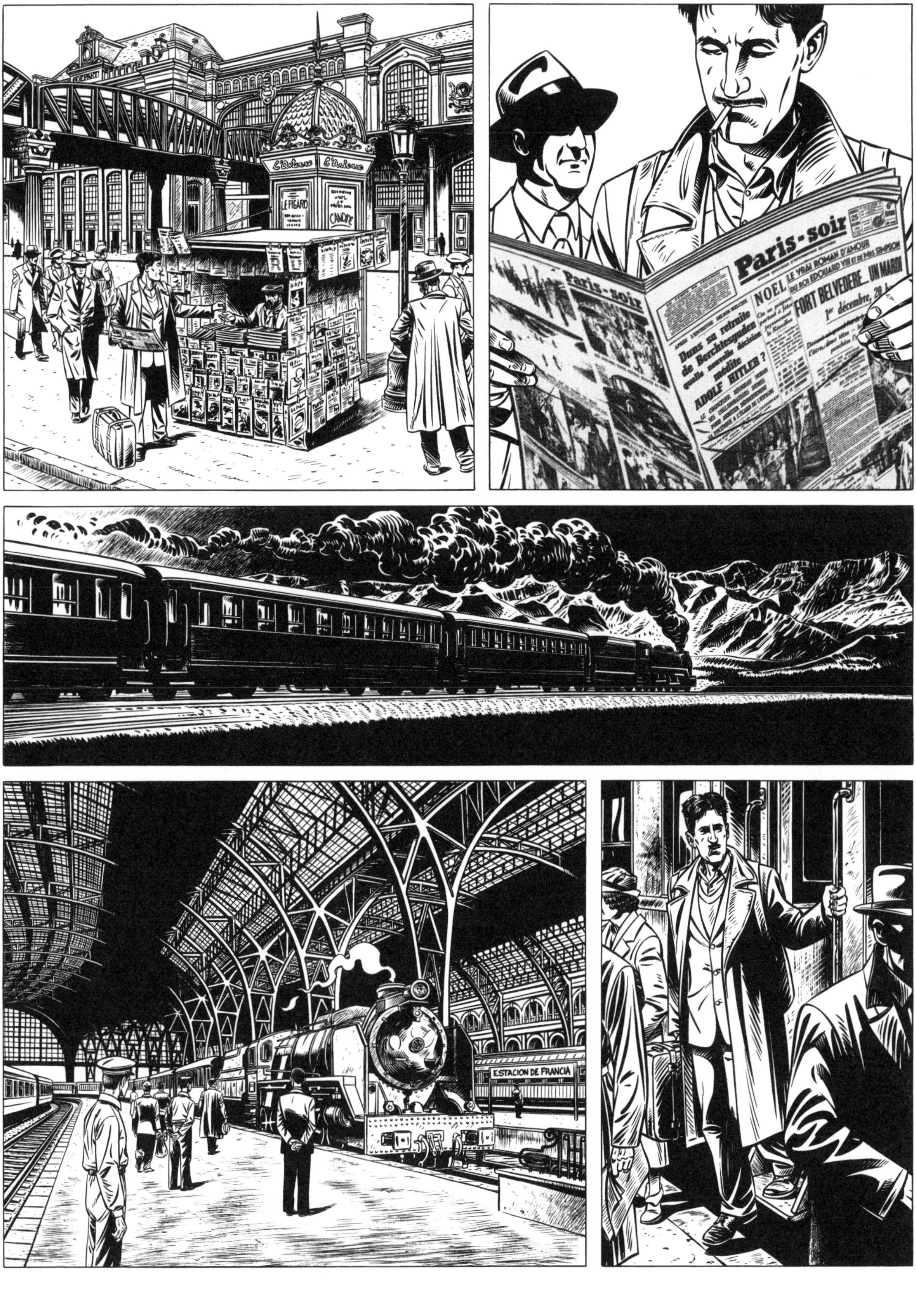
LE FIGARO
CANDIDE
Paris-soir
LE VRAI ROMAN D'AMOUR DU ROI EDOUARD VIII ET DE Mrs SIMPSON
NOEL
FORT BELVEDERE... UN MARDI
1er décembre
Dans sa retraite de Berchtesgaden quelle nouvelle décision médite ADOLF HITLER ?
ESTACION DE FRANCIA

It was the first time that I had ever been in a town where the working class was in the saddle.

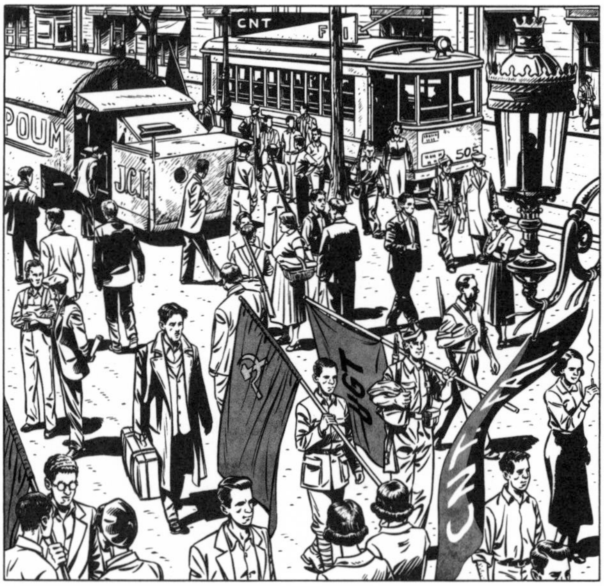
CNT
POUM
UGT

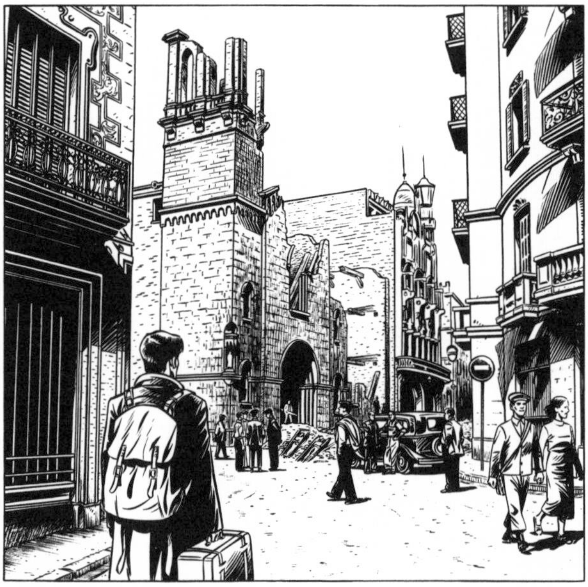

Churches here and there were being systematically demolished by gangs of workmen.

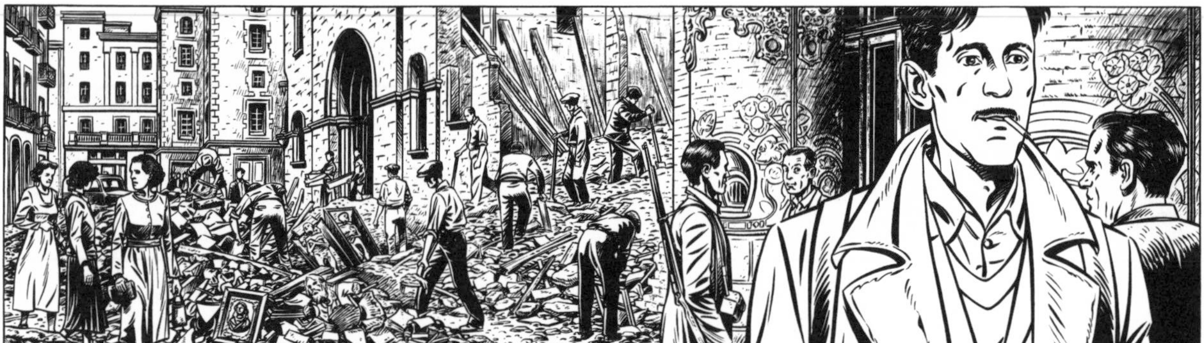

Nobody said "Señor" or "Don" or even "Usted"; everyone called everyone else "Comrade"... and said "Salud!" instead of "Buenos dias".

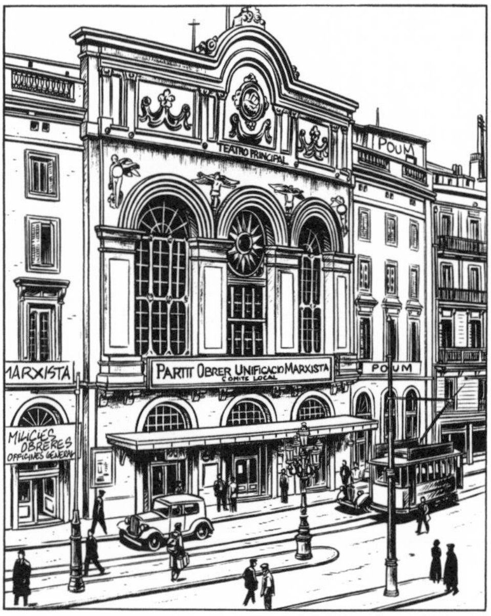
POUM
PARTIT OBRER UNIFICACIO MARXISTA
COMITE LOCAL
MARXISTA
POUM

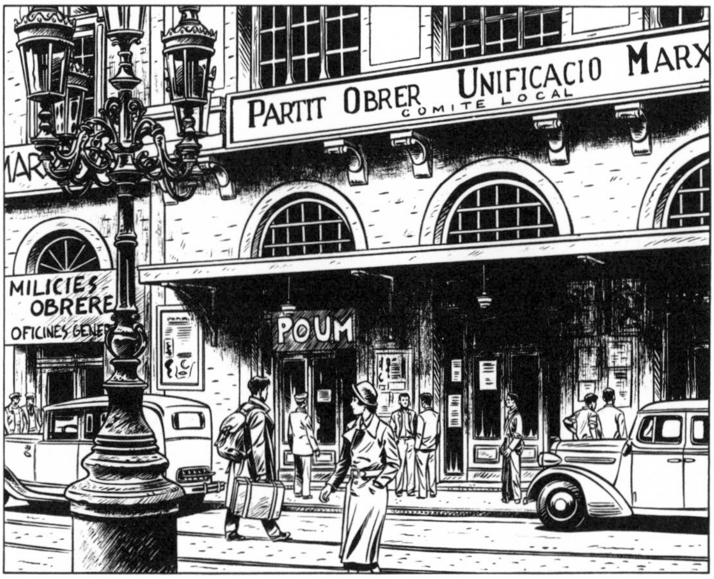
PARTIT OBRER UNIFICACIO
COMITE LOCAL
MILICIES
POUM

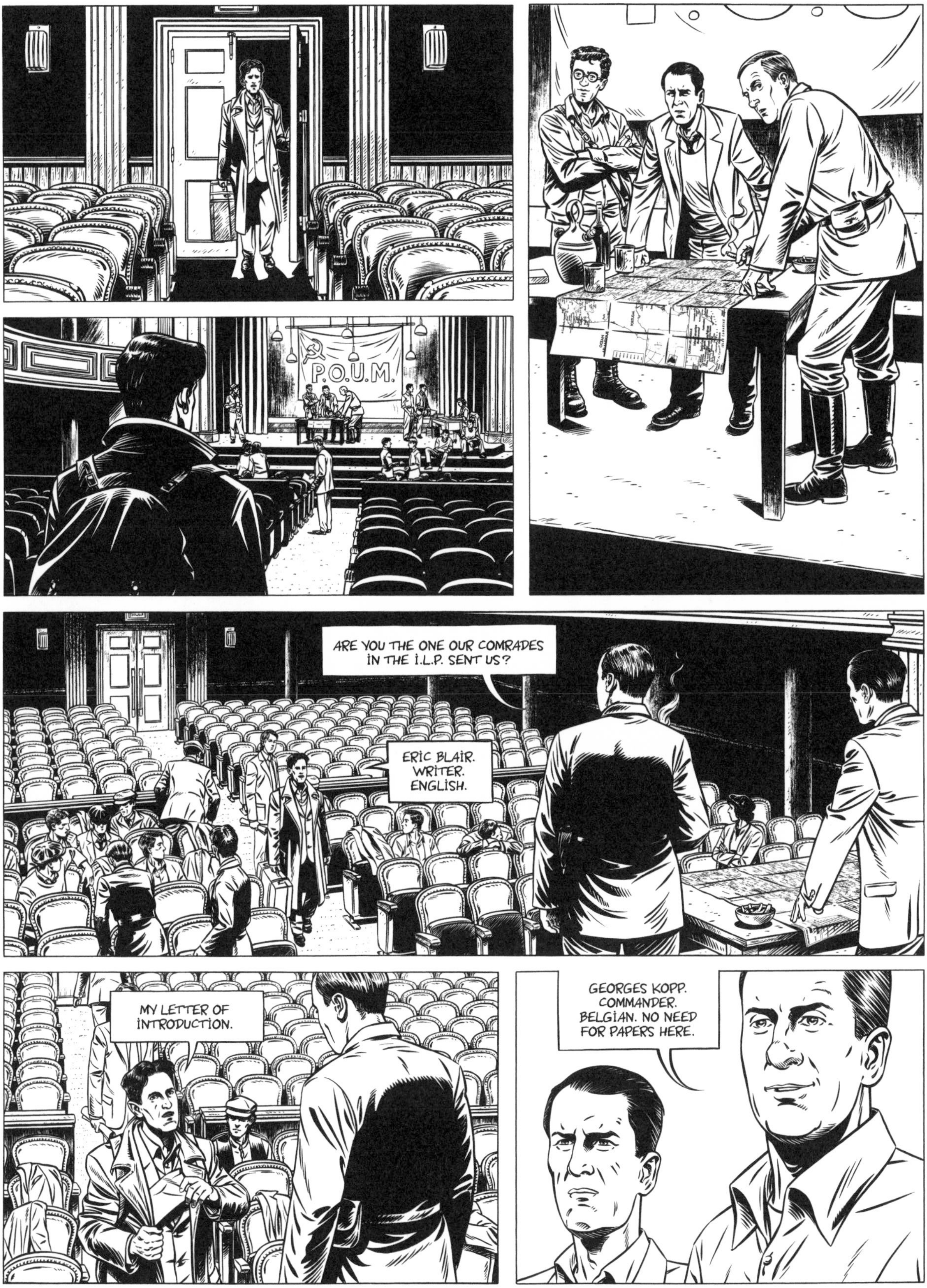
P.O.U.M.
ARE YOU THE ONE OUR COMRADES IN THE I.L.P. SENT US?
ERIC BLAIR. WRITER. ENGLISH.
MY LETTER OF INTRODUCTION.
GEORGES KOPP. COMMANDER. BELGIAN. NO NEED FOR PAPERS HERE.

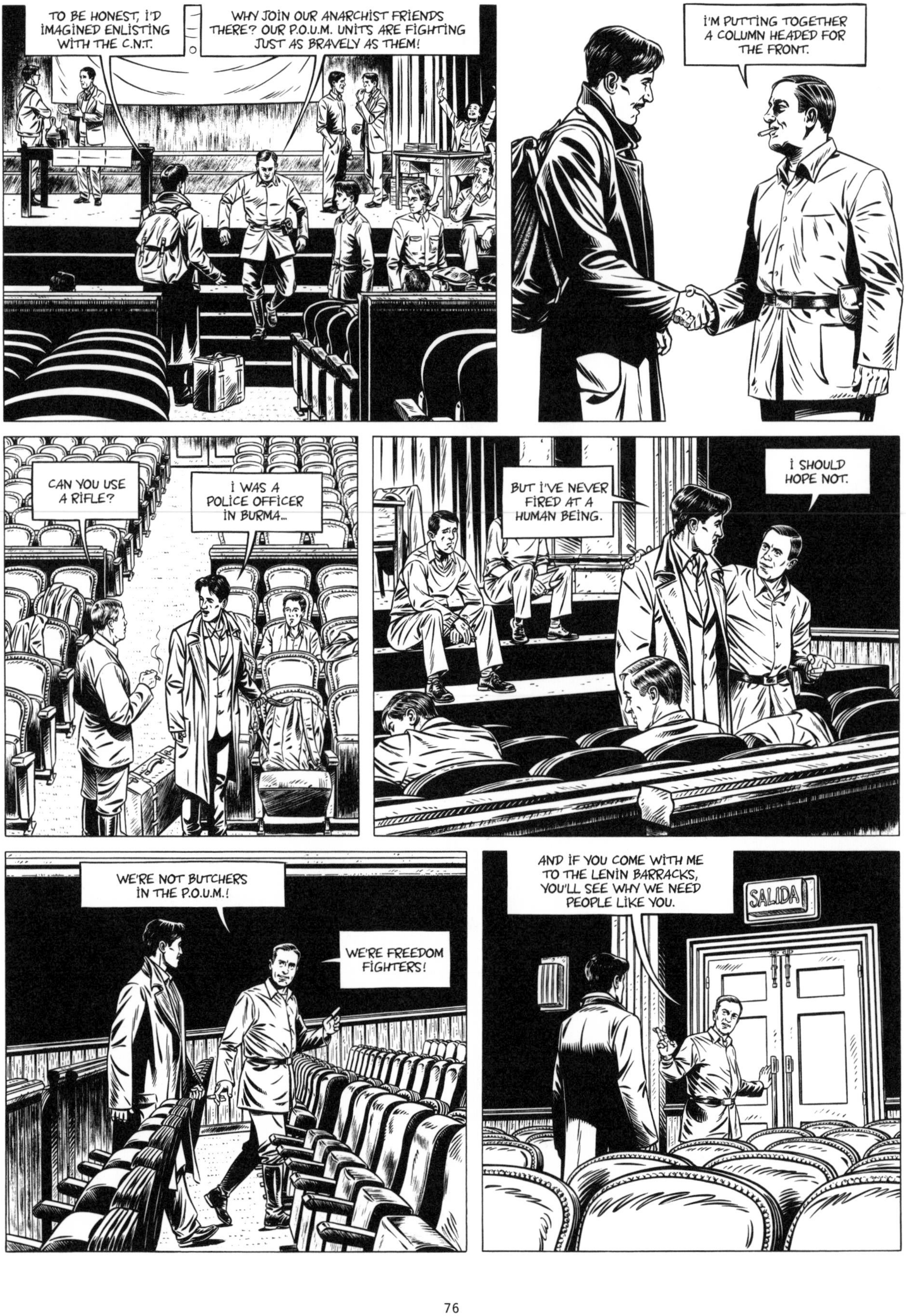
TO BE HONEST, I'D IMAGINED ENLISTING WITH THE C.N.T.
WHY JOIN OUR ANARCHIST FRIENDS THERE? OUR P.O.U.M. UNITS ARE FIGHTING JUST AS BRAVELY AS THEM!
I'M PUTTING TOGETHER A COLUMN HEADED FOR THE FRONT.
CAN YOU USE A RIFLE?
I WAS A POLICE OFFICER IN BURMA...
BUT I'VE NEVER FIRED AT A HUMAN BEING.
I SHOULD HOPE NOT.
WE'RE NOT BUTCHERS IN THE P.O.U.M.!
WE'RE FREEDOM FIGHTERS!
AND IF YOU COME WITH ME TO THE LENIN BARRACKS, YOU'LL SEE WHY WE NEED PEOPLE LIKE YOU.
SALIDA

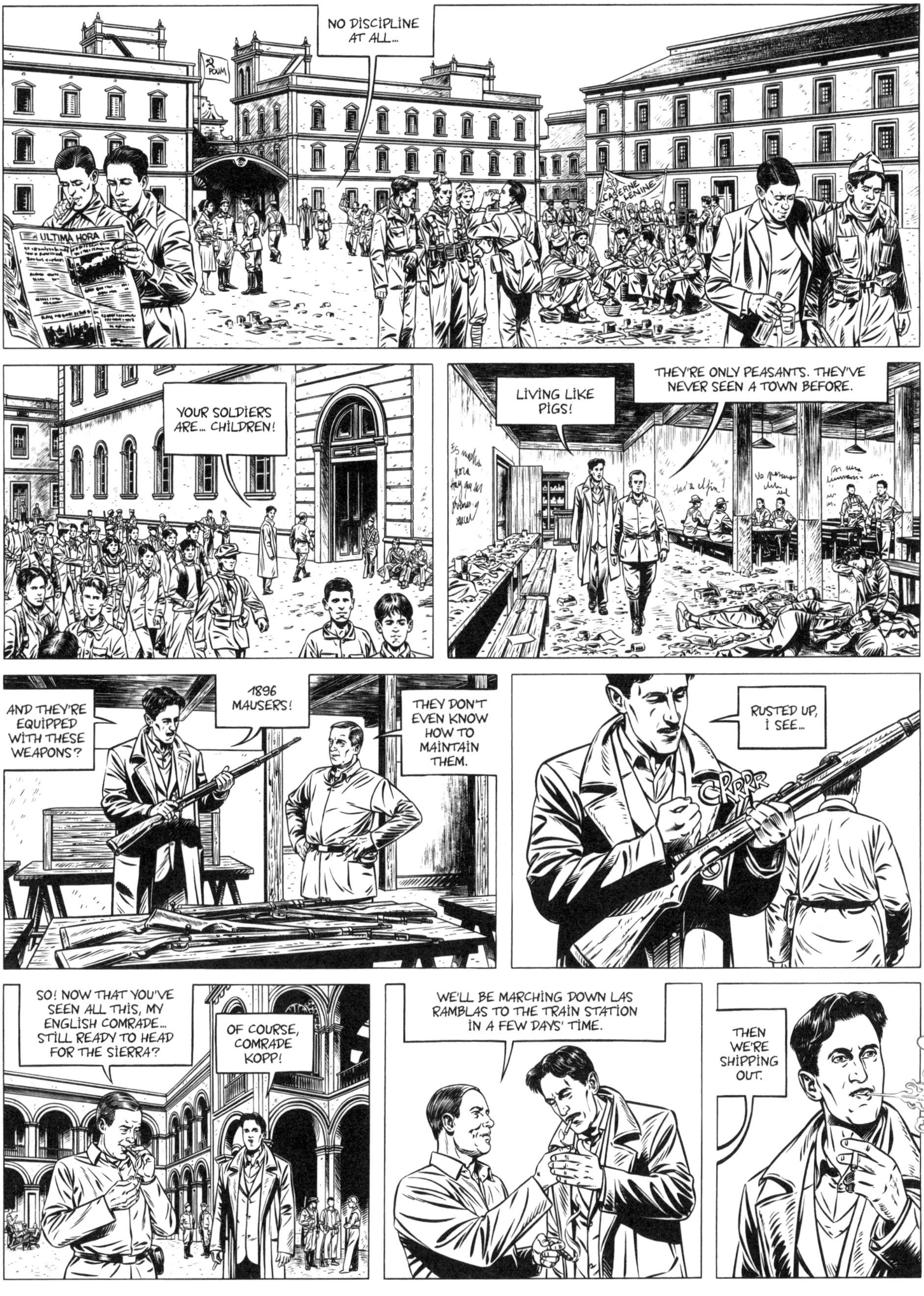
NO DISCIPLINE AT ALL...
POUM
ULTIMA HORA
CASERNE LENINE
YOUR SOLDIERS ARE... CHILDREN!
LIVING LIKE PIGS!
THEY'RE ONLY PEASANTS. THEY'VE NEVER SEEN A TOWN BEFORE.
AND THEY'RE EQUIPPED WITH THESE WEAPONS?
1896 MAUSERS!
THEY DON'T EVEN KNOW HOW TO MAINTAIN THEM.
RUSTED UP, I SEE...
CRRRR
SO! NOW THAT YOU'VE SEEN ALL THIS, MY ENGLISH COMRADE... STILL READY TO HEAD FOR THE SIERRA?
OF COURSE, COMRADE KOPP!
WE'LL BE MARCHING DOWN LAS RAMBLAS TO THE TRAIN STATION IN A FEW DAYS' TIME.
THEN WE'RE SHIPPING OUT.

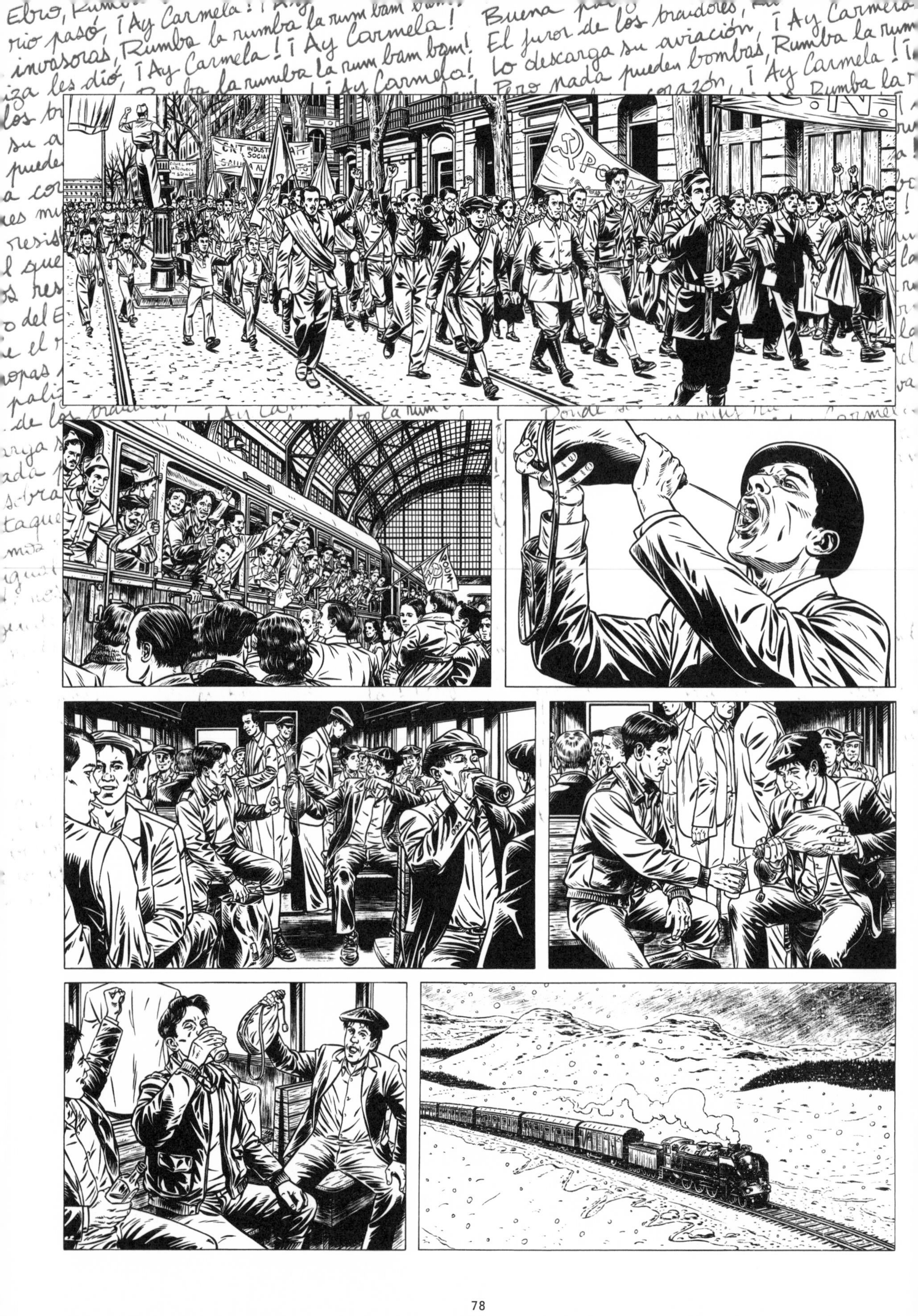
rio pasó, ¡Ay Carmela! Rumba la rumba la rum bam bam!
invasoras, Rumba la rumba la rum ¡Ay Carmela!
iza les dió, ¡Ay Carmela! ¡Ay Carmela!
Rumba la rumba la rum bam bam!
El furor de los traidores, ¡Ay Carmela
Lo descarga su aviación, ¡Ay Carmela! Rumba la rum
Pero nada pueden bombas, Rumba la rumba
corazón, ¡Ay Carmela!
CNT
POUM

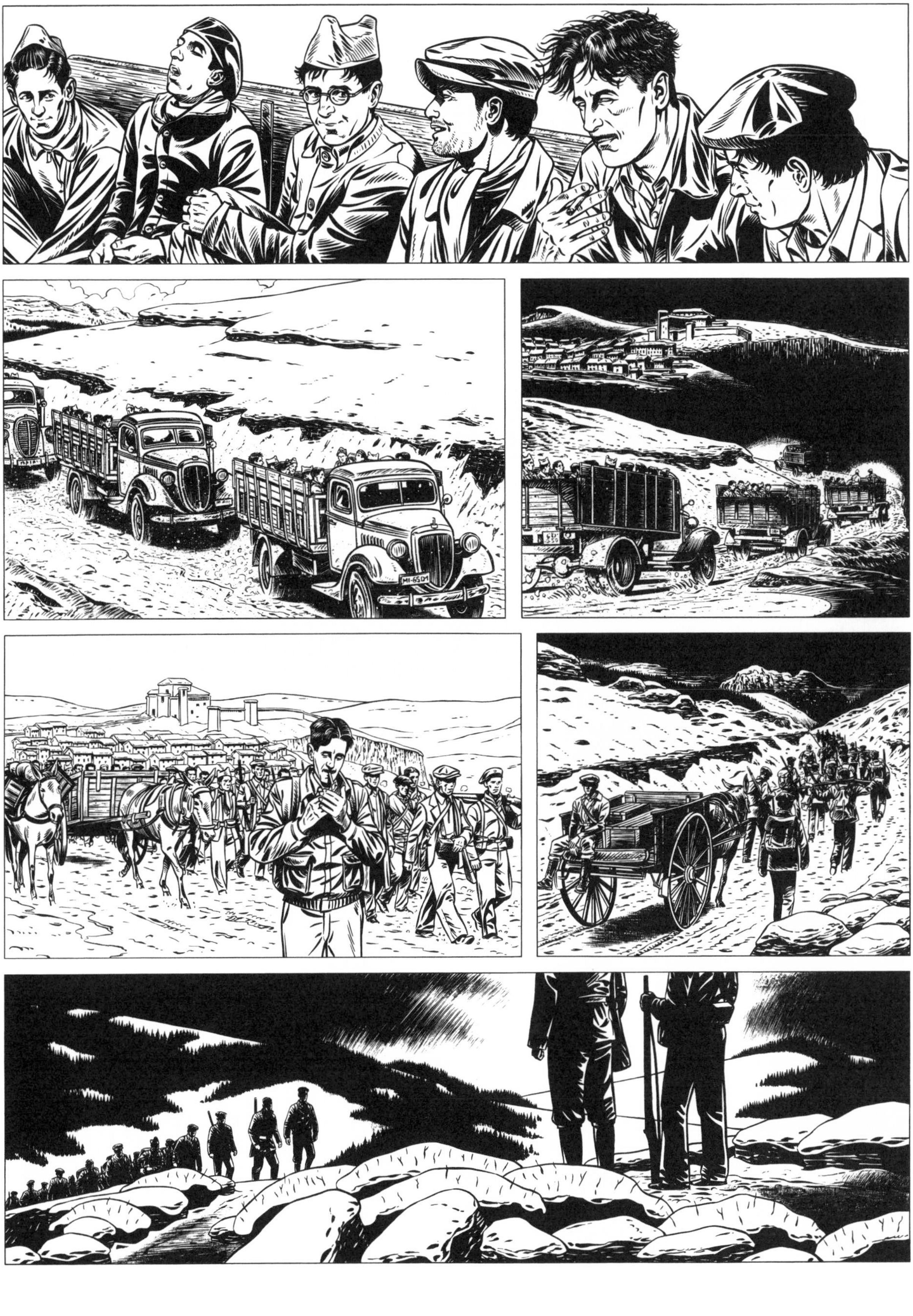

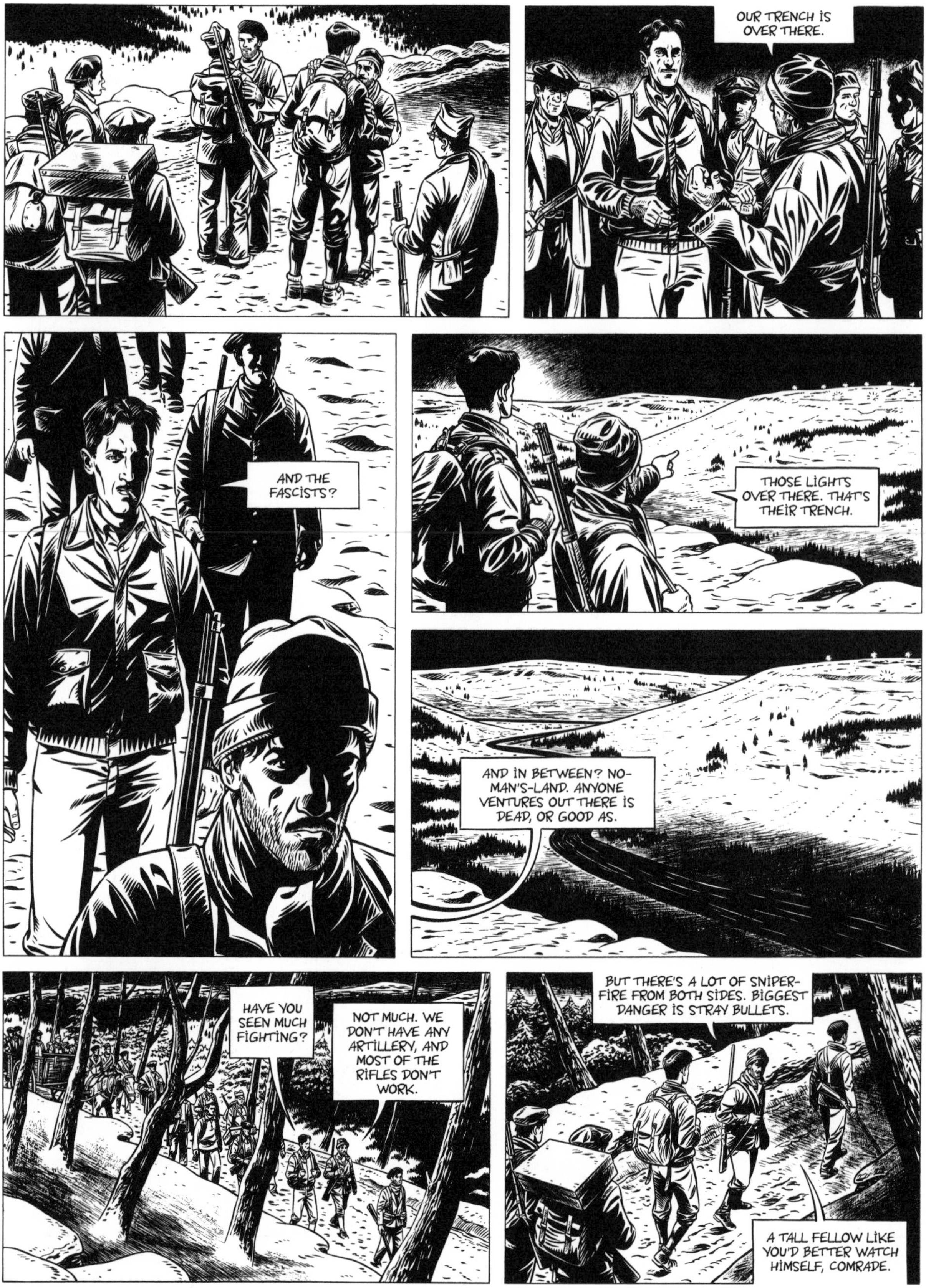
OUR TRENCH IS OVER THERE.
AND THE FASCISTS?
THOSE LIGHTS OVER THERE. THAT'S THEIR TRENCH.
AND IN BETWEEN? NO-MAN'S-LAND. ANYONE VENTURES OUT THERE IS DEAD, OR GOOD AS.
HAVE YOU SEEN MUCH FIGHTING?
NOT MUCH. WE DON'T HAVE ANY ARTILLERY, AND MOST OF THE RIFLES DON'T WORK.
BUT THERE'S A LOT OF SNIPER-FIRE FROM BOTH SIDES. BIGGEST DANGER IS STRAY BULLETS.
A TALL FELLOW LIKE YOU'D BETTER WATCH HIMSELF, COMRADE.

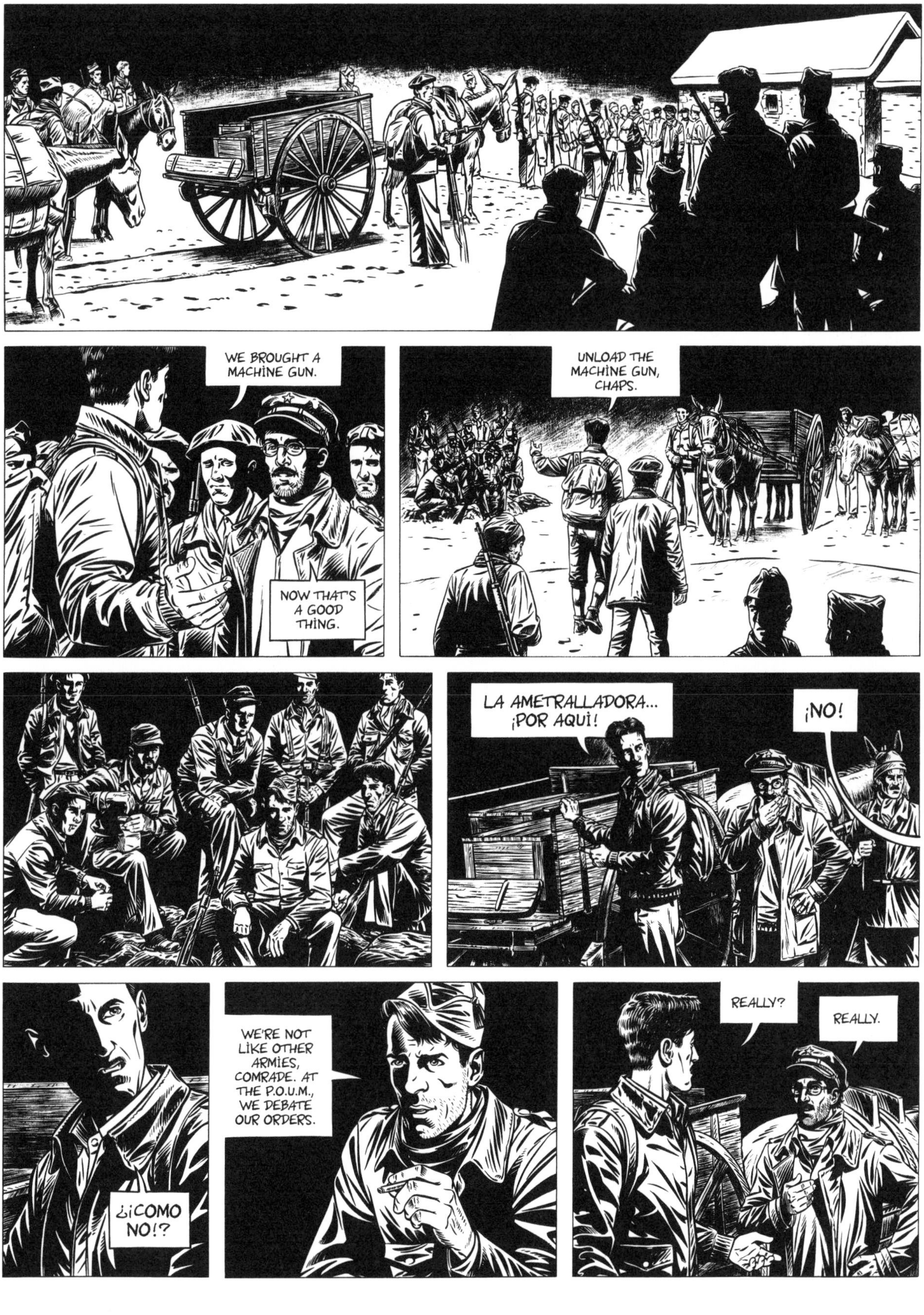
WE BROUGHT A MACHINE GUN.
NOW THAT'S A GOOD THING.
UNLOAD THE MACHINE GUN, CHAPS.
LA AMETRALLADORA... ¡POR AQUÍ!
¡NO!
¿¡COMO NO!?
WE'RE NOT LIKE OTHER ARMIES, COMRADE. AT THE P.O.U.M., WE DEBATE OUR ORDERS.
REALLY?
REALLY.

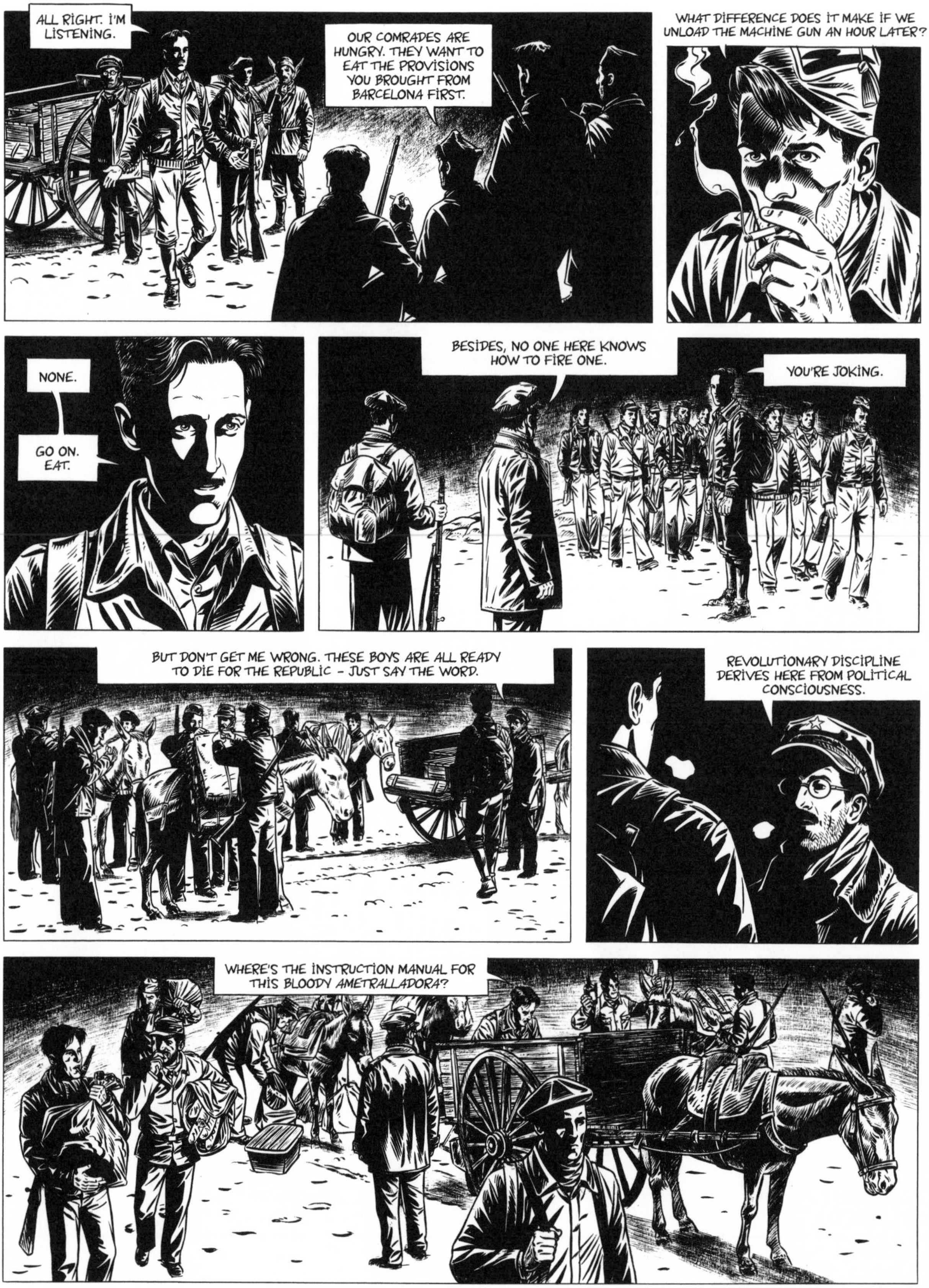
ALL RIGHT. I'M LISTENING.
OUR COMRADES ARE HUNGRY. THEY WANT TO EAT THE PROVISIONS YOU BROUGHT FROM BARCELONA FIRST.
WHAT DIFFERENCE DOES IT MAKE IF WE UNLOAD THE MACHINE GUN AN HOUR LATER?
NONE.
GO ON. EAT.
BESIDES, NO ONE HERE KNOWS HOW TO FIRE ONE.
YOU'RE JOKING.
BUT DON'T GET ME WRONG. THESE BOYS ARE ALL READY TO DIE FOR THE REPUBLIC - JUST SAY THE WORD.
REVOLUTIONARY DISCIPLINE DERIVES HERE FROM POLITICAL CONSCIOUSNESS.
WHERE'S THE INSTRUCTION MANUAL FOR THIS BLOODY *AMETRALLADORA*?

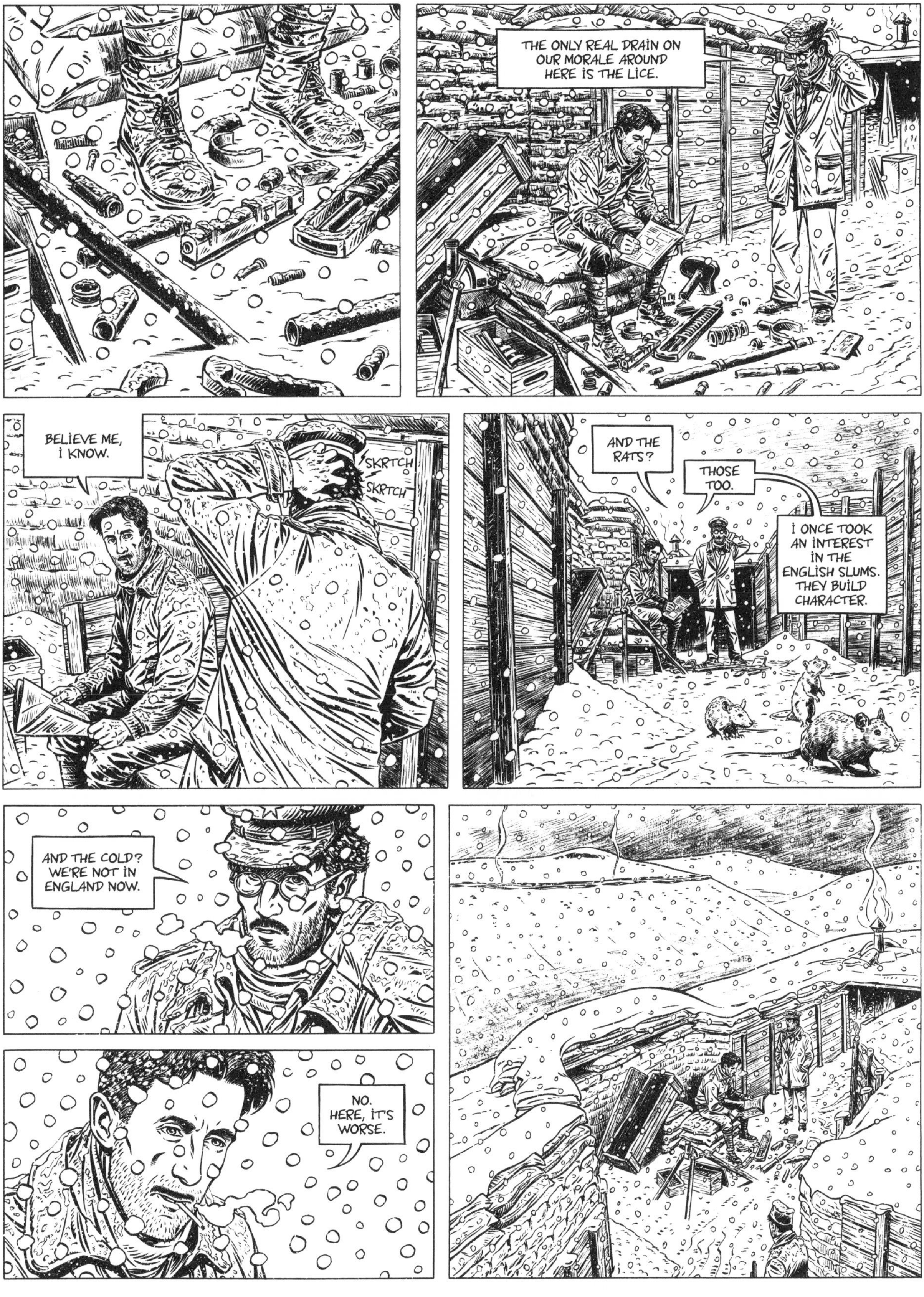
THE ONLY REAL DRAIN ON OUR MORALE AROUND HERE IS THE LICE.
BELIEVE ME, I KNOW.
SKRTCH
SKRTCH
AND THE RATS?
THOSE TOO.
I ONCE TOOK AN INTEREST IN THE ENGLISH SLUMS. THEY BUILD CHARACTER.
AND THE COLD? WE'RE NOT IN ENGLAND NOW.
NO. HERE, IT'S WORSE.

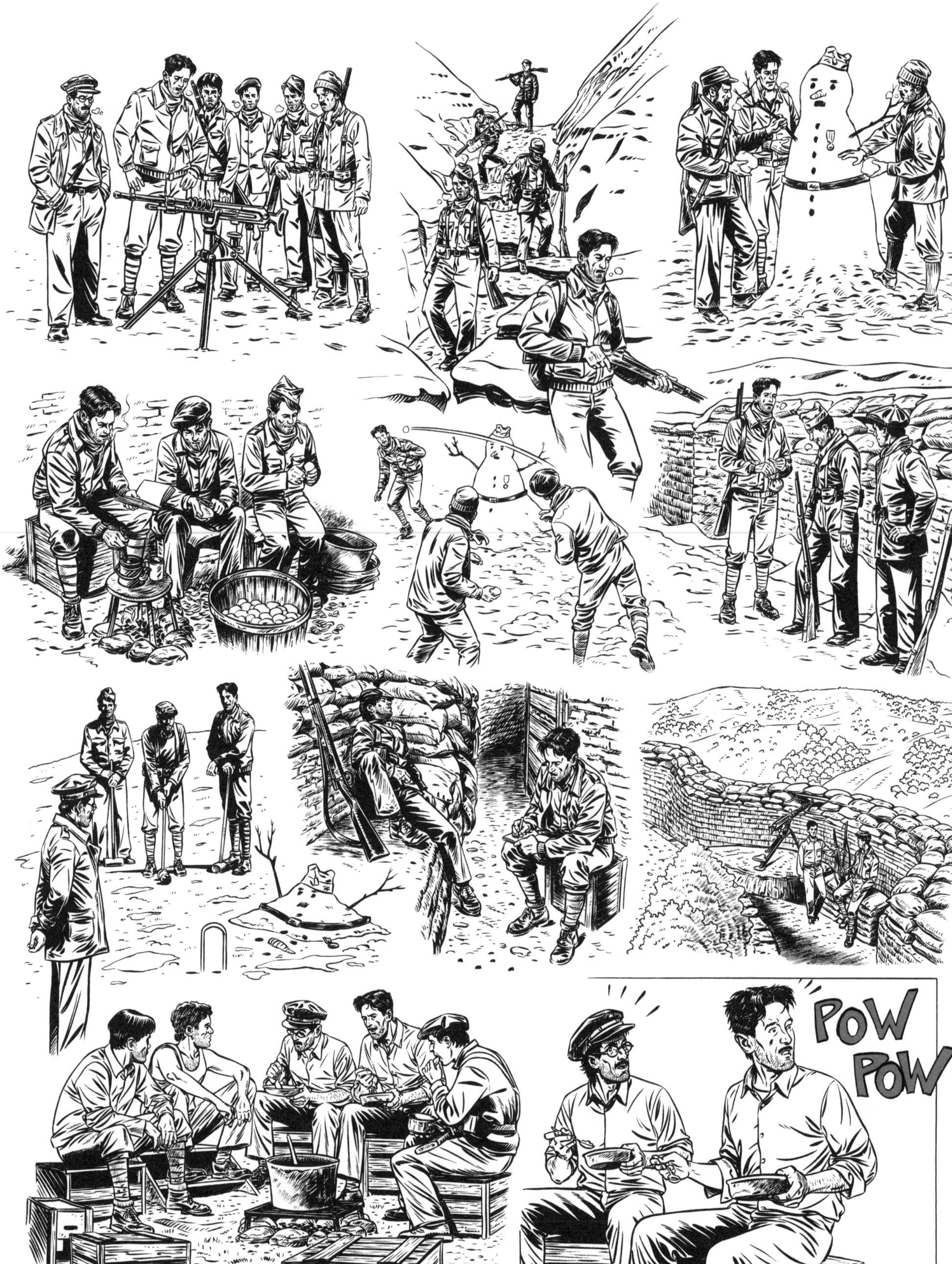
POW
POW

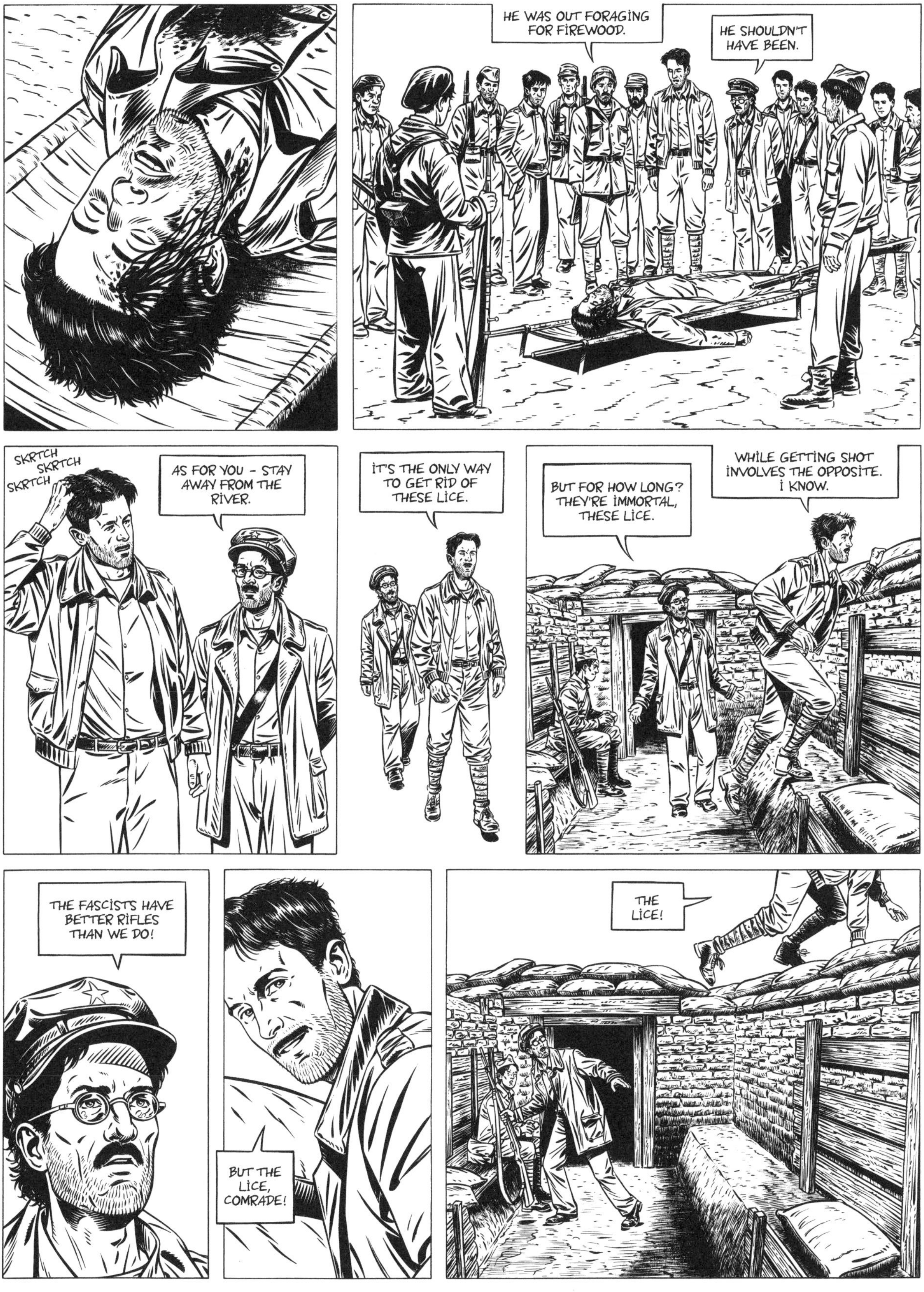
HE WAS OUT FORAGING FOR FIREWOOD.
HE SHOULDN'T HAVE BEEN.
SKRTCH SKRTCH SKRTCH
AS FOR YOU - STAY AWAY FROM THE RIVER.
IT'S THE ONLY WAY TO GET RID OF THESE LICE.
BUT FOR HOW LONG? THEY'RE IMMORTAL, THESE LICE.
WHILE GETTING SHOT INVOLVES THE OPPOSITE. I KNOW.
THE FASCISTS HAVE BETTER RIFLES THAN WE DO!
BUT THE LICE, COMRADE!
THE LICE!

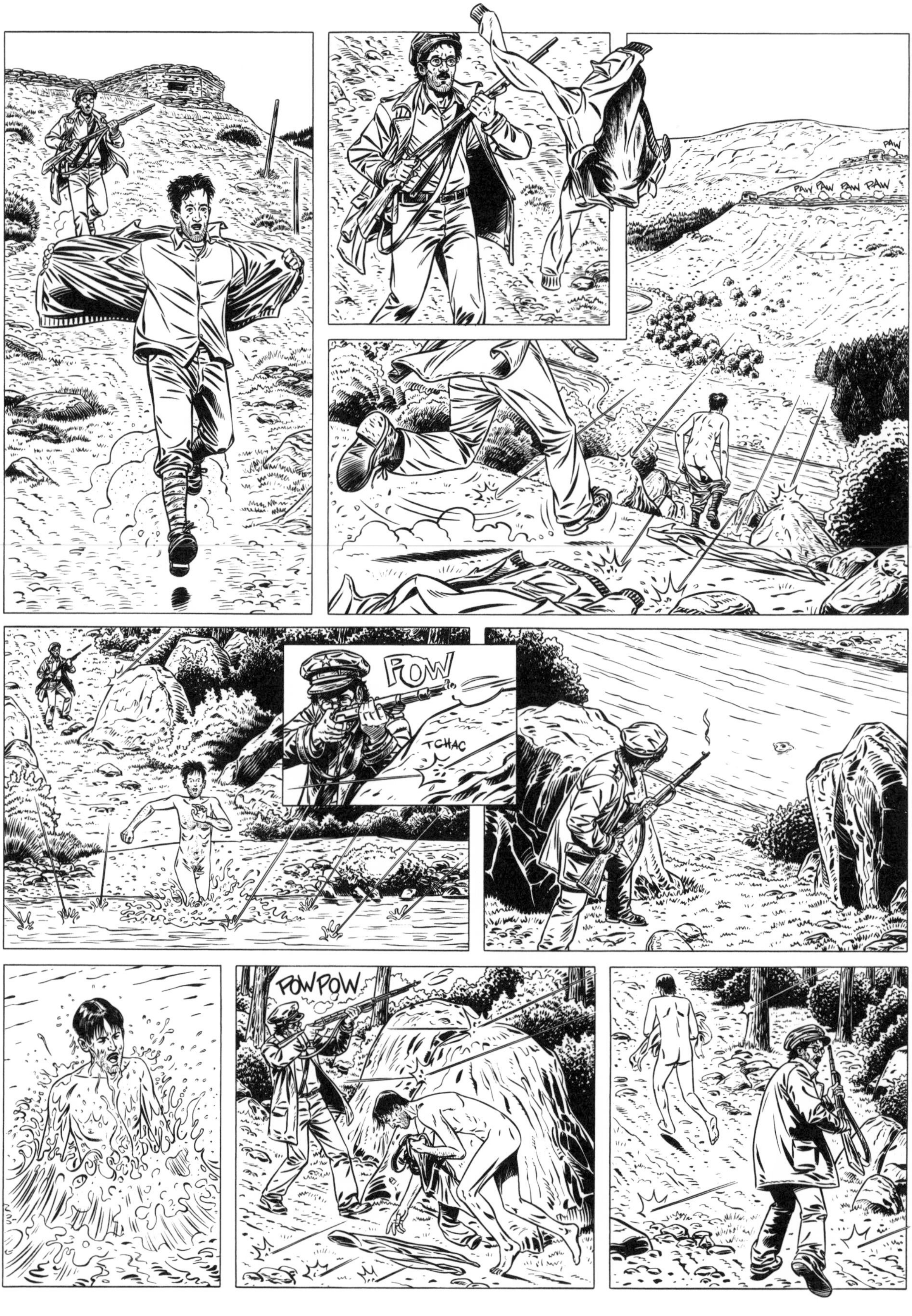
PAW
PAW PAW PAW PAW
POW
TCHAC
POWPOW

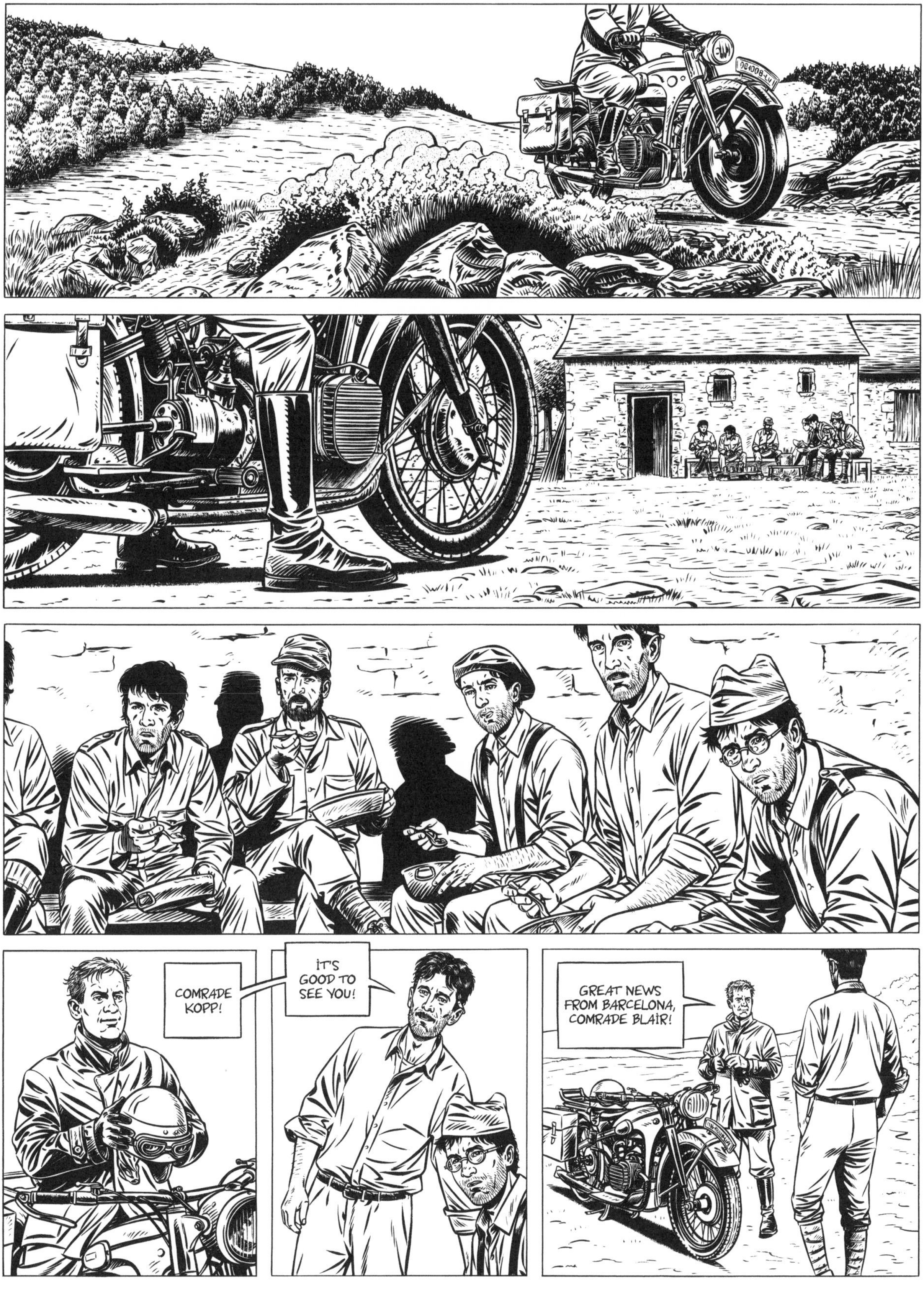
COMRADE KOPP!
IT'S GOOD TO SEE YOU!
GREAT NEWS FROM BARCELONA, COMRADE BLAIR!

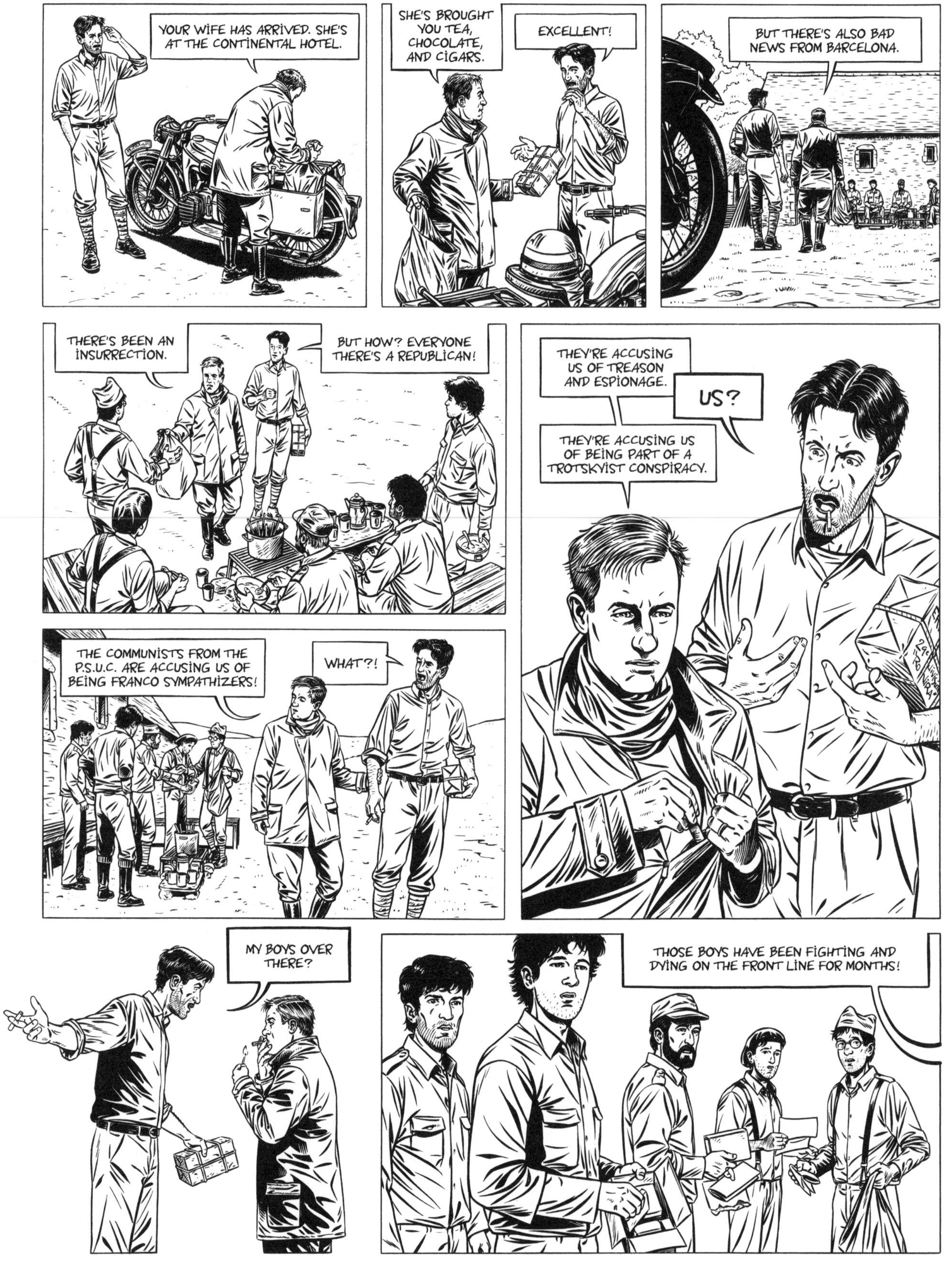
YOUR WIFE HAS ARRIVED. SHE'S AT THE CONTINENTAL HOTEL.
SHE'S BROUGHT YOU TEA, CHOCOLATE, AND CIGARS.
EXCELLENT!
BUT THERE'S ALSO BAD NEWS FROM BARCELONA.
THERE'S BEEN AN INSURRECTION.
BUT HOW? EVERYONE THERE'S A REPUBLICAN!
THEY'RE ACCUSING US OF TREASON AND ESPIONAGE.
US?
THEY'RE ACCUSING US OF BEING PART OF A TROTSKYIST CONSPIRACY.
THE COMMUNISTS FROM THE P.S.U.C. ARE ACCUSING US OF BEING FRANCO SYMPATHIZERS!
WHAT?!
MY BOYS OVER THERE?
THOSE BOYS HAVE BEEN FIGHTING AND DYING ON THE FRONT LINE FOR MONTHS!

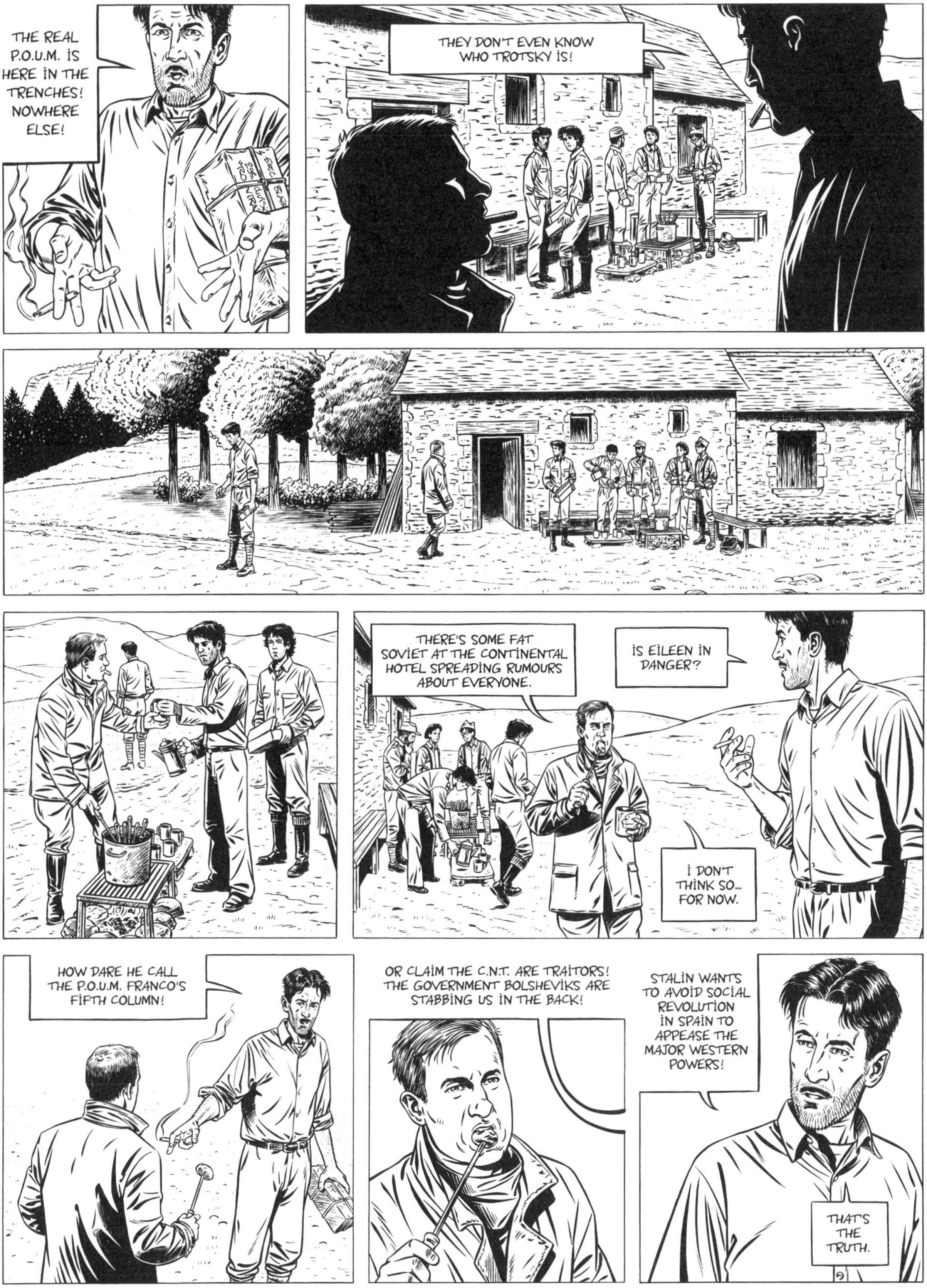
THE REAL P.O.U.M. IS HERE IN THE TRENCHES! NOWHERE ELSE!
THEY DON'T EVEN KNOW WHO TROTSKY IS!
THERE'S SOME FAT SOVIET AT THE CONTINENTAL HOTEL SPREADING RUMOURS ABOUT EVERYONE.
IS EILEEN IN DANGER?
I DON'T THINK SO... FOR NOW.
HOW DARE HE CALL THE P.O.U.M. FRANCO'S FIFTH COLUMN!
OR CLAIM THE C.N.T. ARE TRAITORS! THE GOVERNMENT BOLSHEVIKS ARE STABBING US IN THE BACK!
STALIN WANTS TO AVOID SOCIAL REVOLUTION IN SPAIN TO APPEASE THE MAJOR WESTERN POWERS!
THAT'S THE TRUTH.

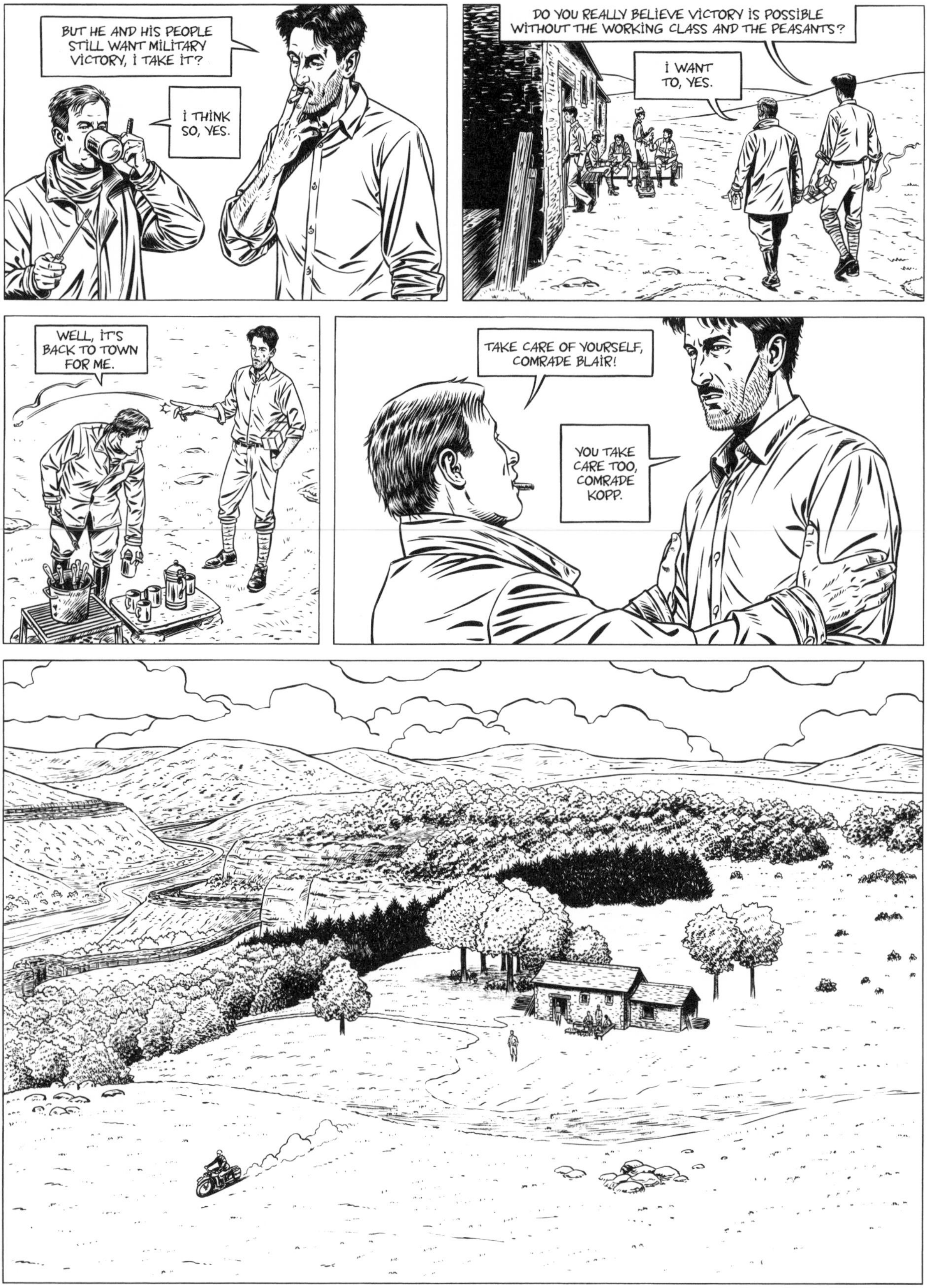

BUT HE AND HIS PEOPLE STILL WANT MILITARY VICTORY, I TAKE IT?
I THINK SO, YES.
DO YOU REALLY BELIEVE VICTORY IS POSSIBLE WITHOUT THE WORKING CLASS AND THE PEASANTS?
I WANT TO, YES.
WELL, IT'S BACK TO TOWN FOR ME.
TAKE CARE OF YOURSELF, COMRADE BLAIR!
YOU TAKE CARE TOO, COMRADE KOPP.

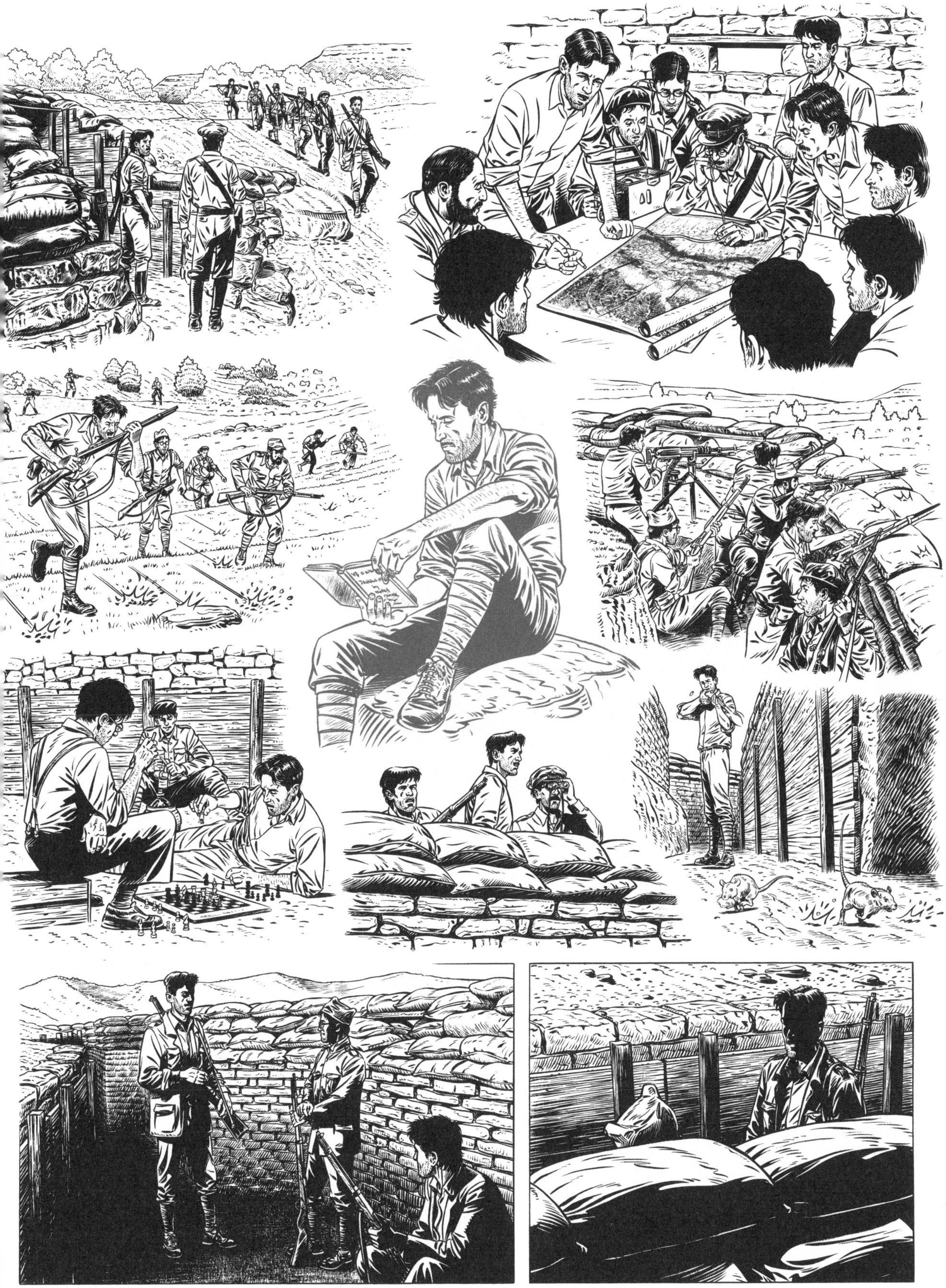

It was at the corner of the parapet, at five o'clock in the morning. This was always a dangerous time, because we had the dawn at our backs, and if you stuck your head above the parapet it was clearly outlined against the sky.

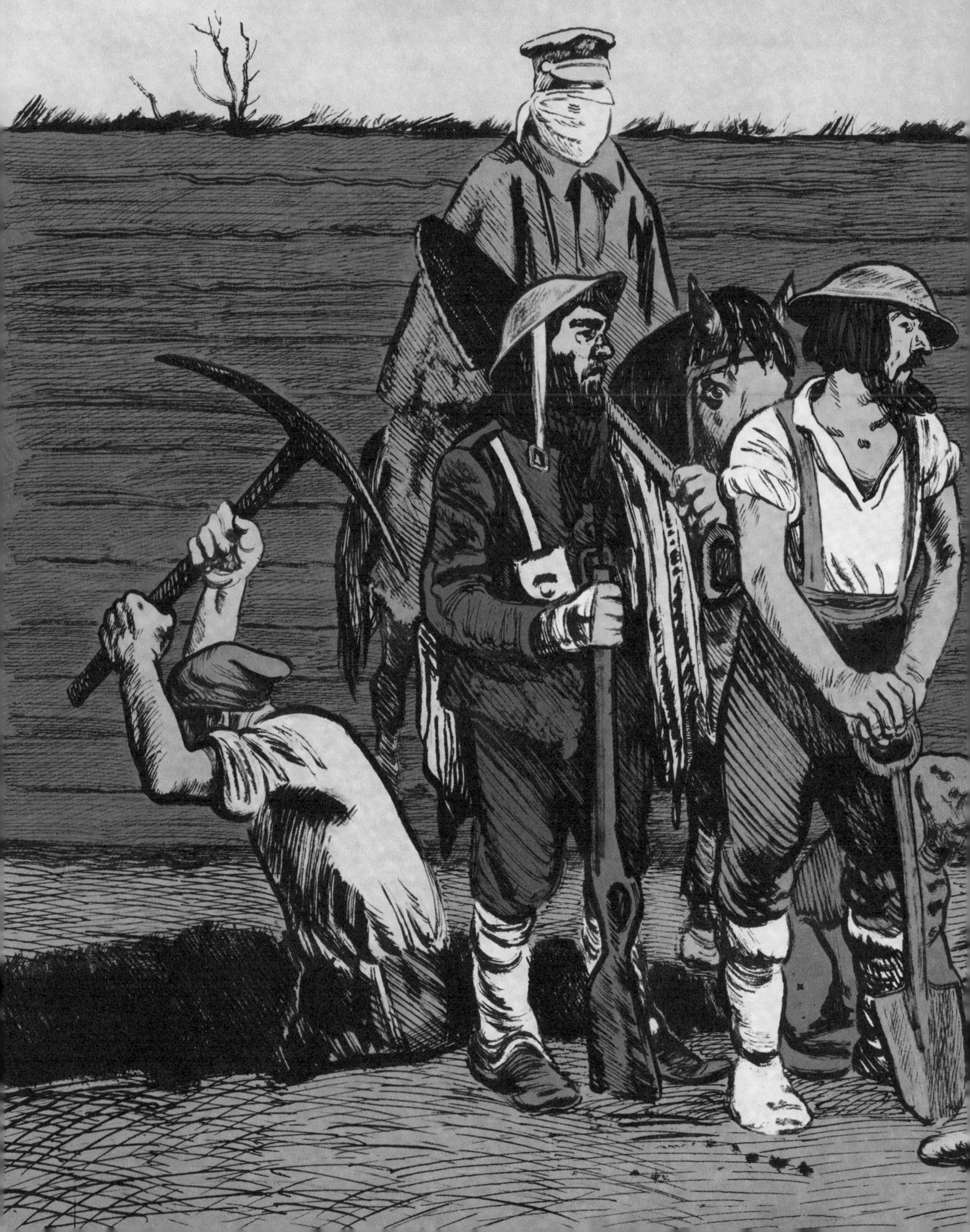

I was talking to the sentries preparatory to changing the guard. Suddenly, in the very middle of saying something, I felt - it is very hard to describe what I felt... There seemed to be a loud bang and a blinding flash of light all round me... The next moment my knees crumpled up...

I had... a consciousness of being very badly hurt... In the throat, they said... As soon as I knew that the bullet had gone clean through my neck I took it for granted that I was done for.

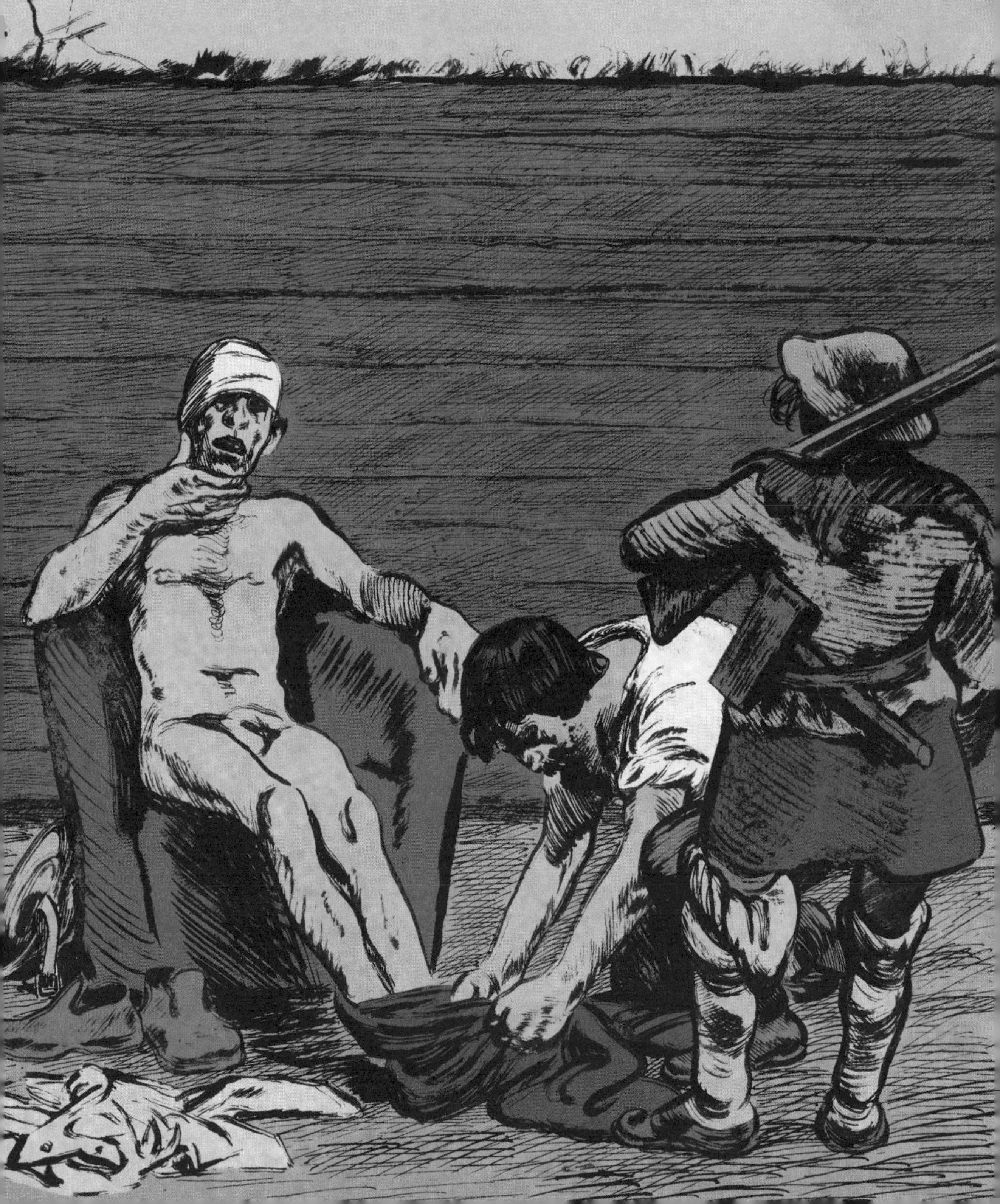

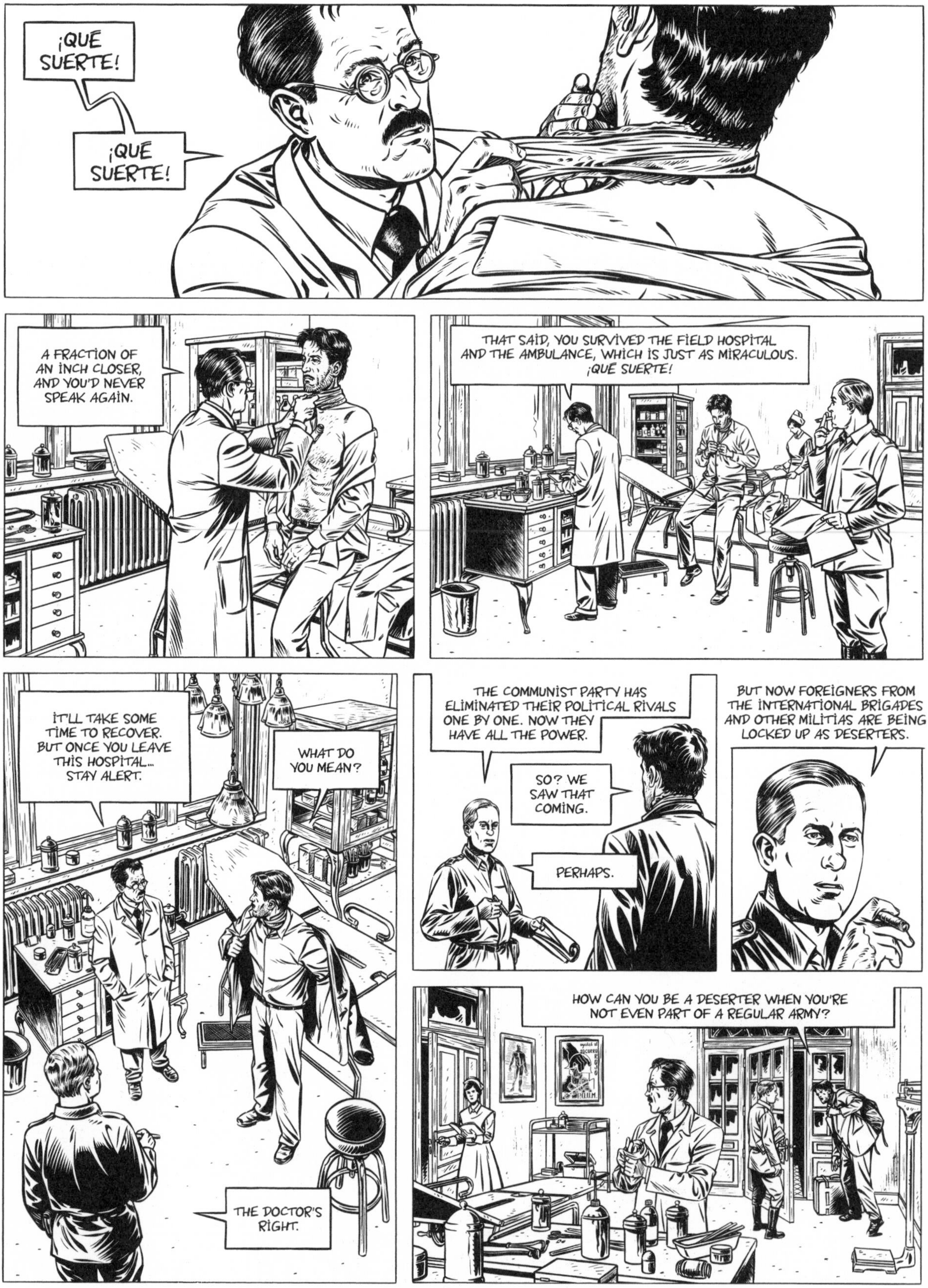

¡QUE SUERTE!
¡QUE SUERTE!
A FRACTION OF AN INCH CLOSER, AND YOU'D NEVER SPEAK AGAIN.
THAT SAID, YOU SURVIVED THE FIELD HOSPITAL AND THE AMBULANCE, WHICH IS JUST AS MIRACULOUS. ¡QUE SUERTE!
IT'LL TAKE SOME TIME TO RECOVER. BUT ONCE YOU LEAVE THIS HOSPITAL... STAY ALERT.
WHAT DO YOU MEAN?
THE DOCTOR'S RIGHT.
THE COMMUNIST PARTY HAS ELIMINATED THEIR POLITICAL RIVALS ONE BY ONE. NOW THEY HAVE ALL THE POWER.
SO? WE SAW THAT COMING.
PERHAPS.
BUT NOW FOREIGNERS FROM THE INTERNATIONAL BRIGADES AND OTHER MILITIAS ARE BEING LOCKED UP AS DESERTERS.
HOW CAN YOU BE A DESERTER WHEN YOU'RE NOT EVEN PART OF A REGULAR ARMY?

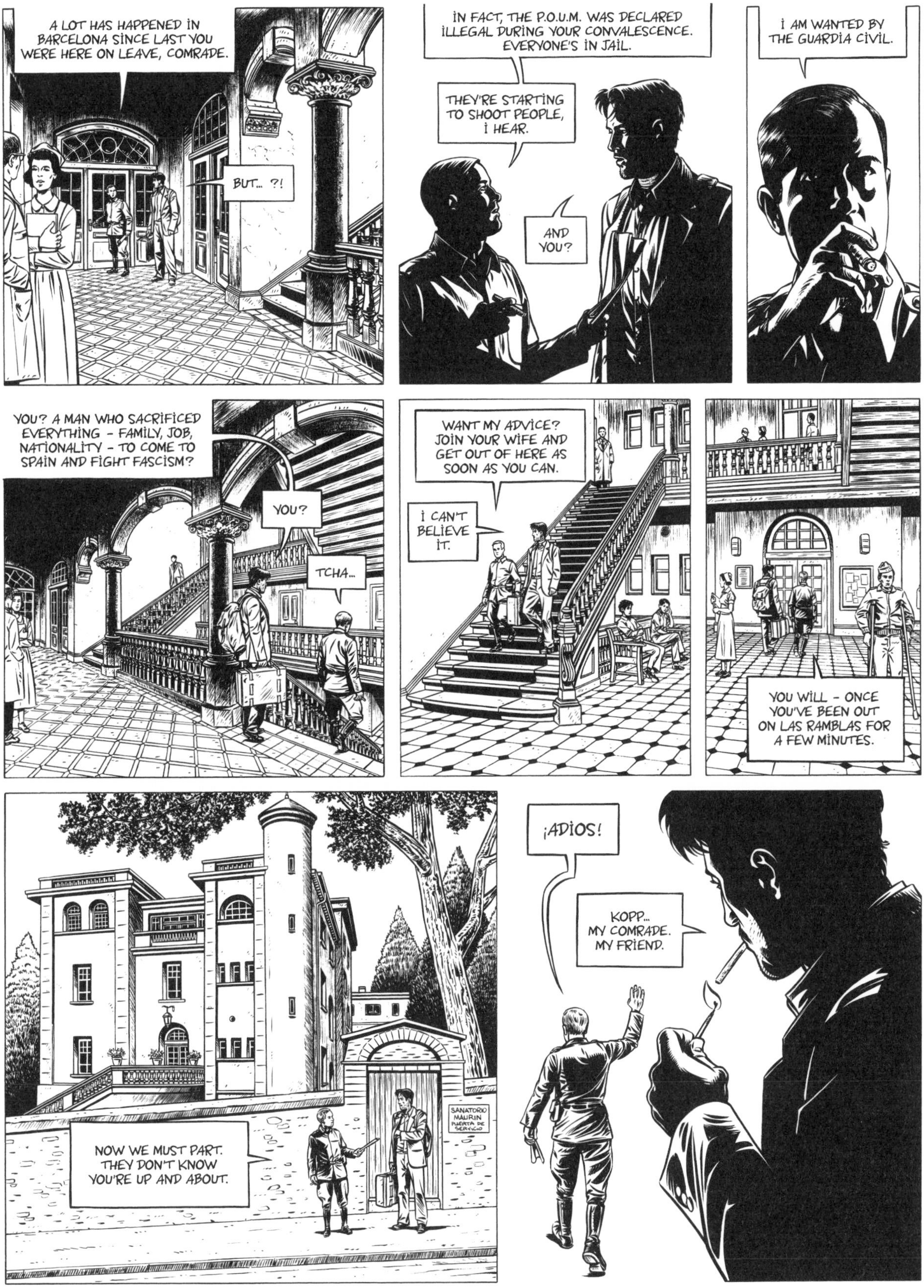
A LOT HAS HAPPENED IN BARCELONA SINCE LAST YOU WERE HERE ON LEAVE, COMRADE.
BUT... ?!
IN FACT, THE P.O.U.M. WAS DECLARED ILLEGAL DURING YOUR CONVALESCENCE. EVERYONE'S IN JAIL.
THEY'RE STARTING TO SHOOT PEOPLE, I HEAR.
AND YOU?
I AM WANTED BY THE GUARDIA CIVIL.
YOU? A MAN WHO SACRIFICED EVERYTHING - FAMILY, JOB, NATIONALITY - TO COME TO SPAIN AND FIGHT FASCISM?
YOU?
TCHA...
WANT MY ADVICE? JOIN YOUR WIFE AND GET OUT OF HERE AS SOON AS YOU CAN.
I CAN'T BELIEVE IT.
YOU WILL - ONCE YOU'VE BEEN OUT ON LAS RAMBLAS FOR A FEW MINUTES.
NOW WE MUST PART. THEY DON'T KNOW YOU'RE UP AND ABOUT.
SANATORIO MAURIN PUERTA DE SERVICIO
¡ADIOS!
KOPP... MY COMRADE. MY FRIEND.

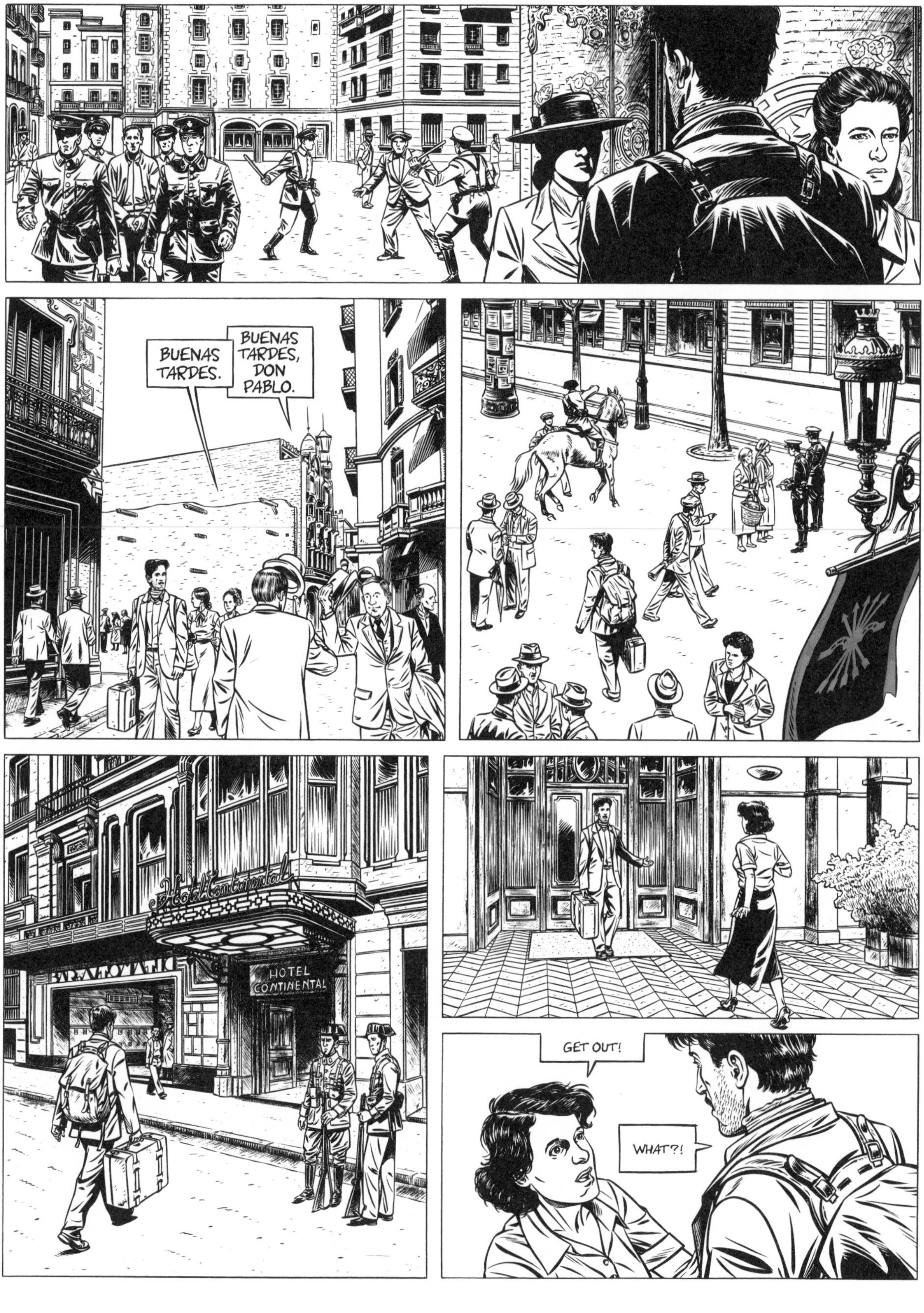
BUENAS TARDES.
BUENAS TARDES, DON PABLO.
Hotel Continental
HOTEL CONTINENTAL
GET OUT!
WHAT?!

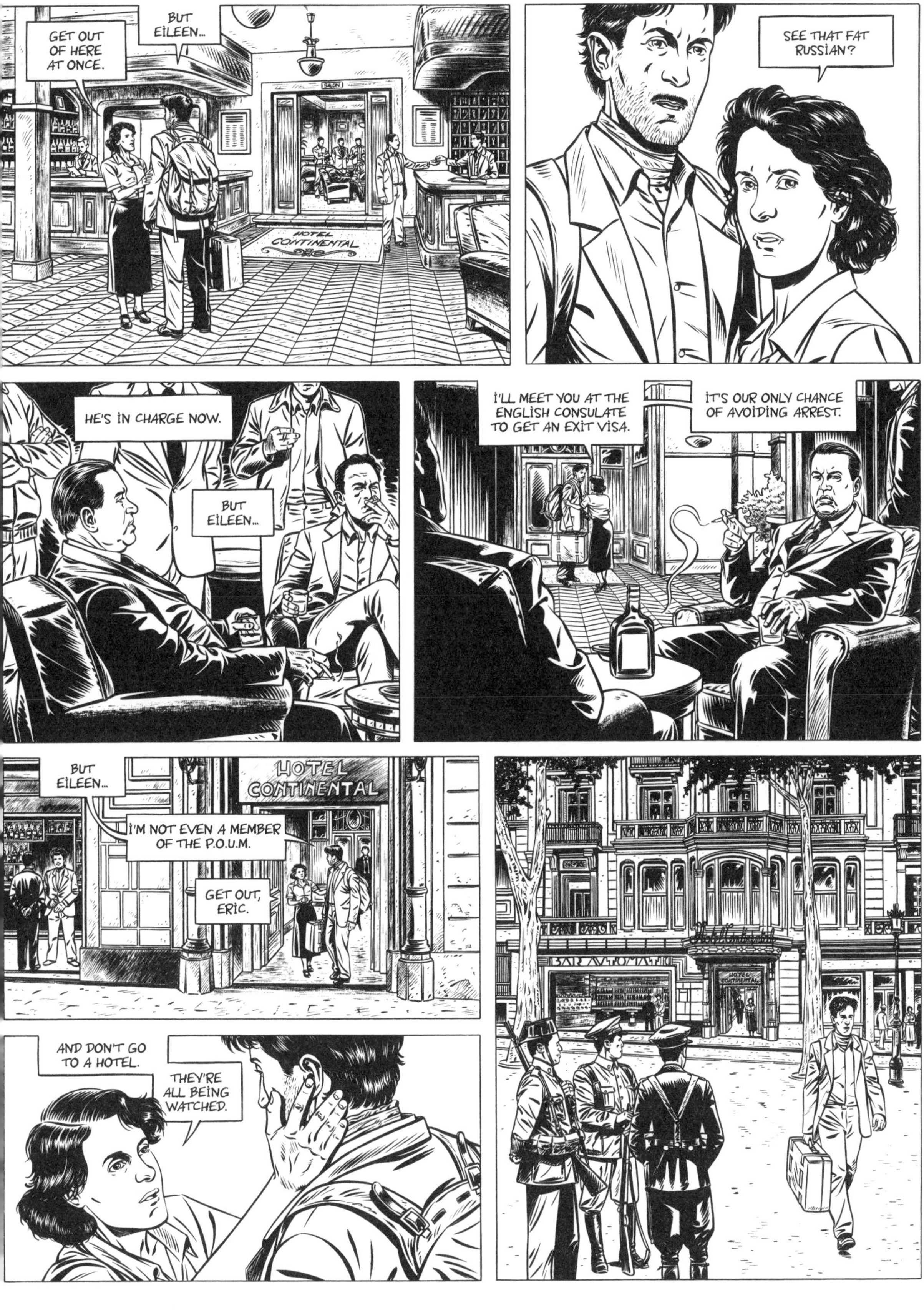

GET OUT OF HERE AT ONCE.
BUT EILEEN...
HOTEL CONTINENTAL
SEE THAT FAT RUSSIAN?
HE'S IN CHARGE NOW.
BUT EILEEN...
I'LL MEET YOU AT THE ENGLISH CONSULATE TO GET AN EXIT VISA.
IT'S OUR ONLY CHANCE OF AVOIDING ARREST.
HOTEL CONTINENTAL
BUT EILEEN...
I'M NOT EVEN A MEMBER OF THE P.O.U.M.
GET OUT, ERIC.
AND DON'T GO TO A HOTEL.
THEY'RE ALL BEING WATCHED.
BAR AUTOMATIC
HOTEL CONTINENTAL

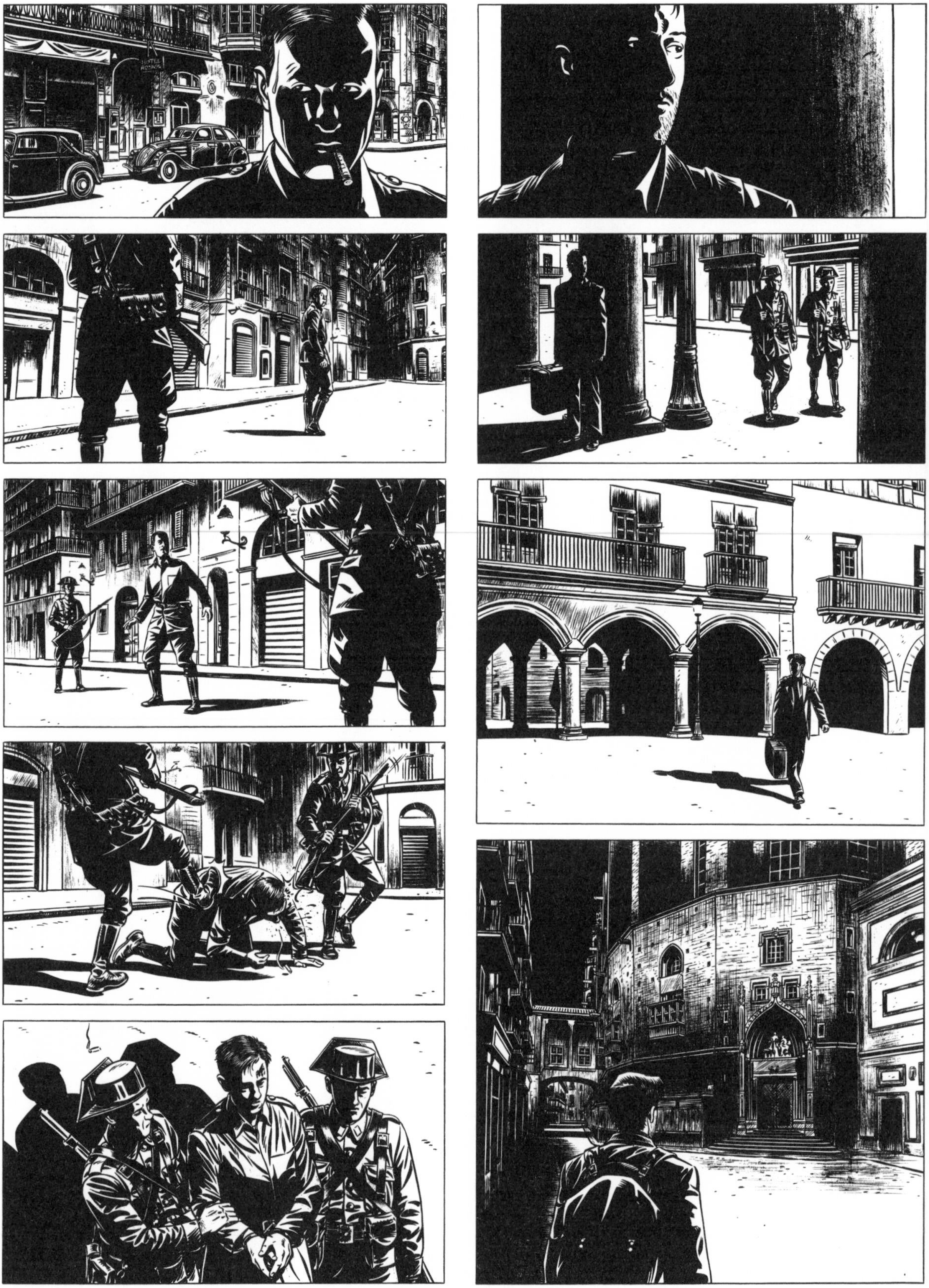

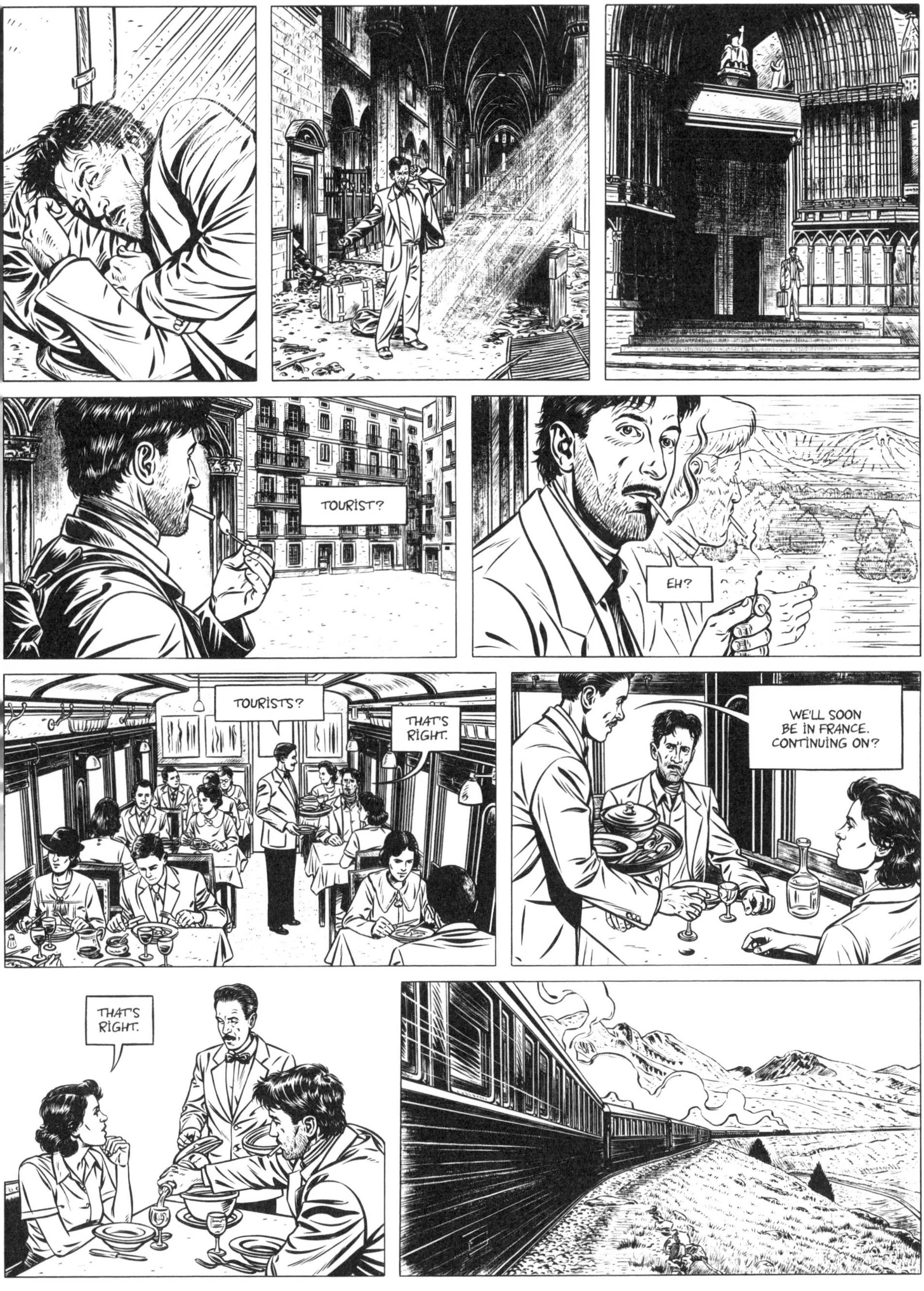
TOURIST?
EH?
TOURISTS?
THAT'S RIGHT.
WE'LL SOON BE IN FRANCE. CONTINUING ON?
THAT'S RIGHT.

GEORGE ORWELL CAME HOME.

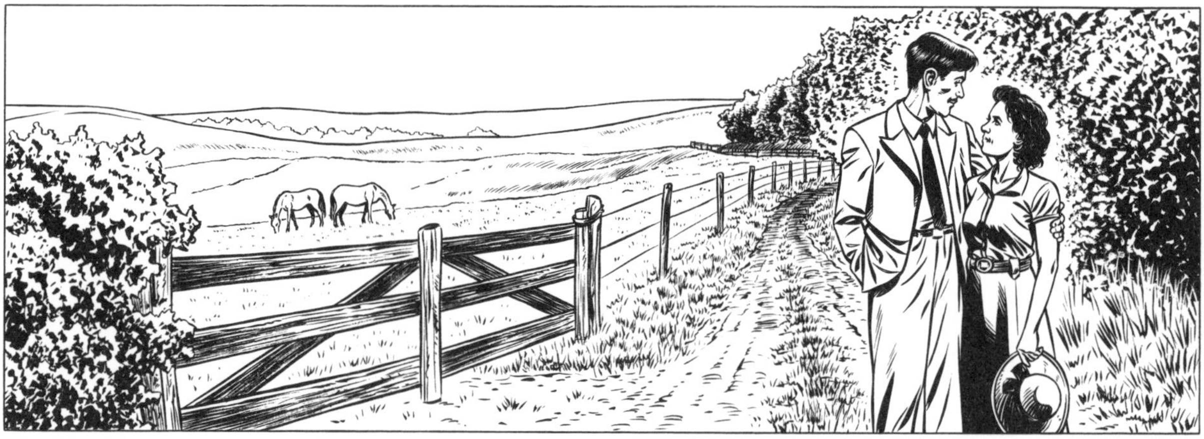

HE PUBLISHED *HOMAGE TO CATALONIA* IN 1938 – THE YEAR OF THE BATTLE OF THE EBRO, WHICH FORCED THE REPUBLICANS TO RETREAT.

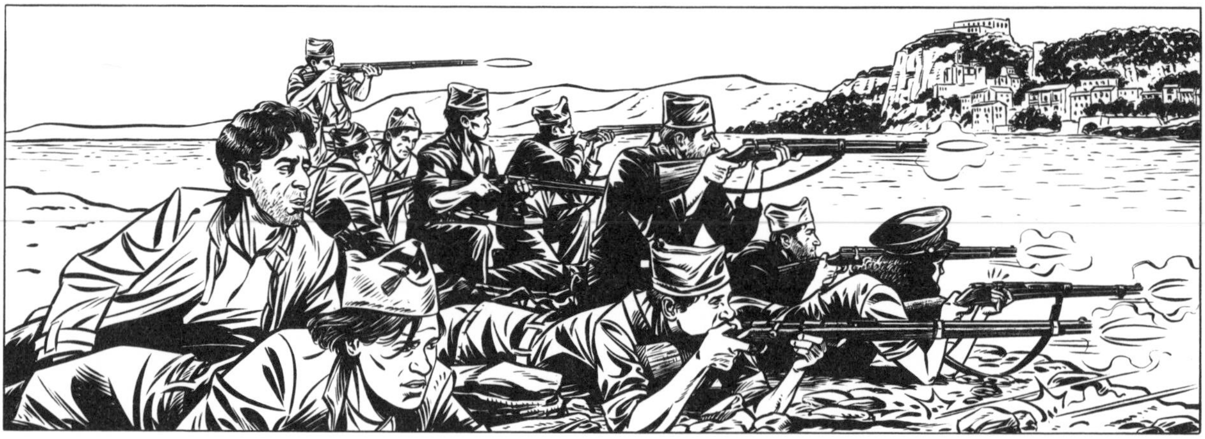

THE INTERNATIONAL BRIGADES LEFT SPAIN.

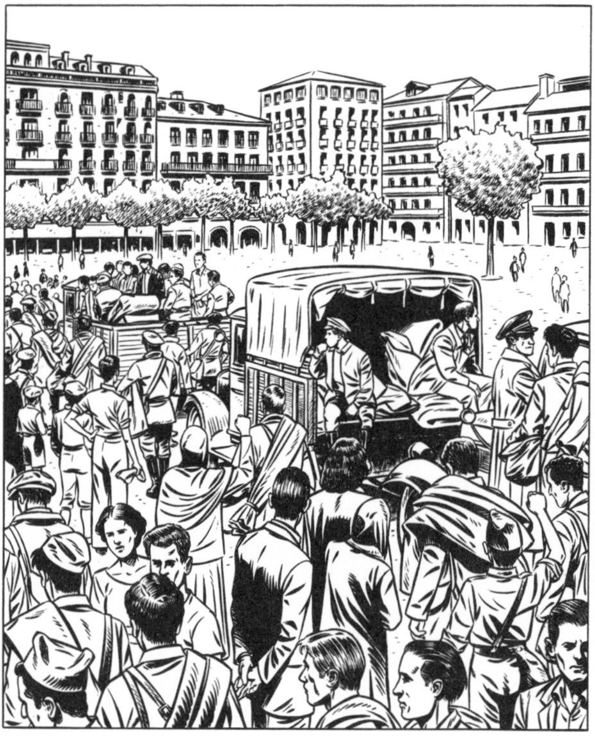

FRANCO'S TROOPS MARCHED INTO BARCELONA.

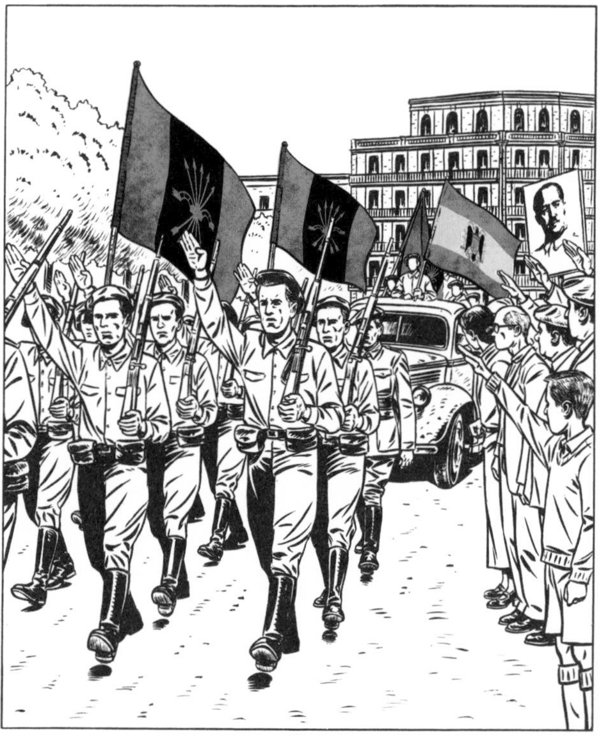

IT WAS OVER.

CHAPTER III

ORWELLIAN ORWELL

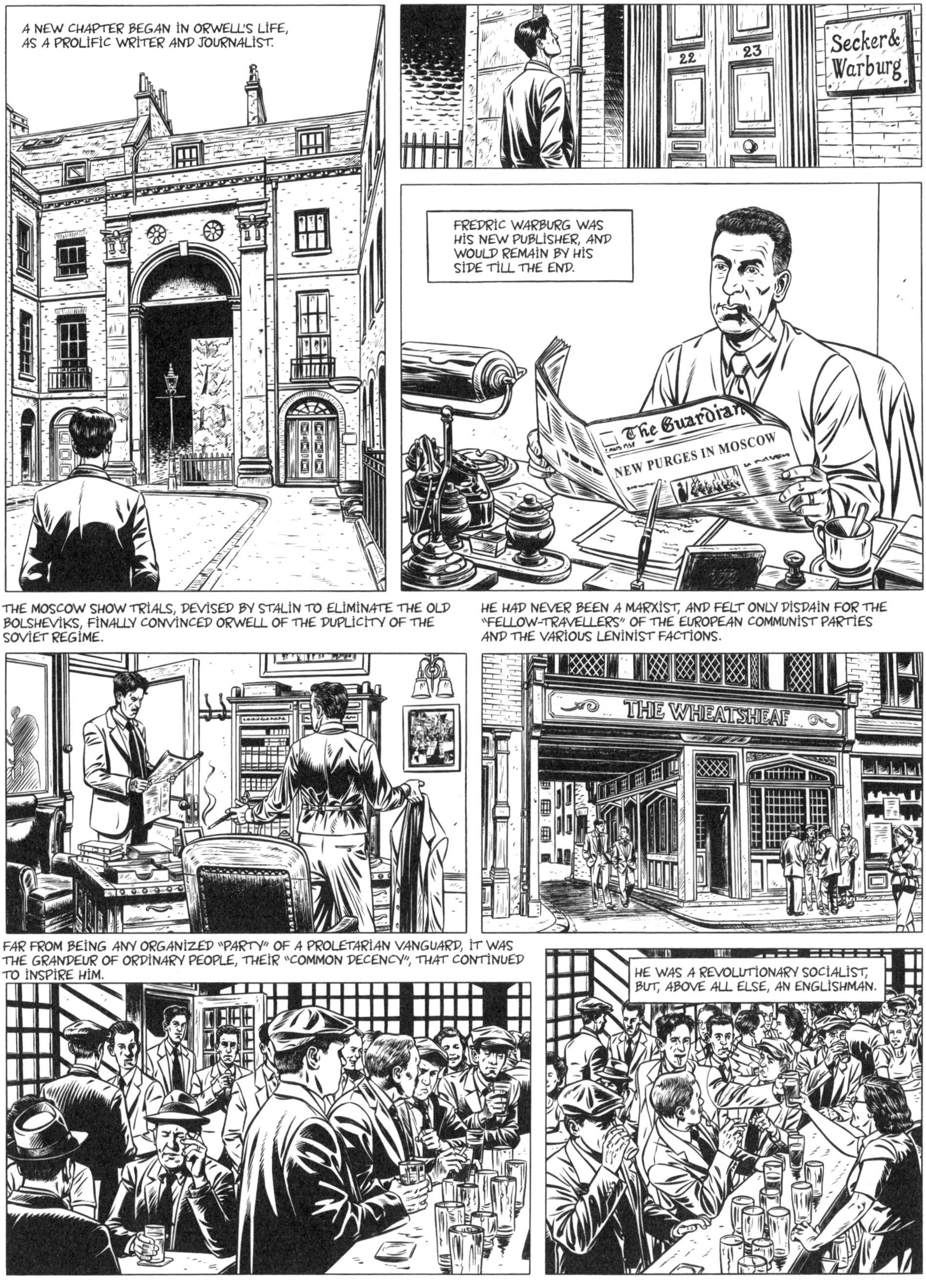
A NEW CHAPTER BEGAN IN ORWELL'S LIFE, AS A PROLIFIC WRITER AND JOURNALIST.
22
23
Secker& Warburg
FREDRIC WARBURG WAS HIS NEW PUBLISHER, AND WOULD REMAIN BY HIS SIDE TILL THE END.
The Guardian
NEW PURGES IN MOSCOW
THE MOSCOW SHOW TRIALS, DEVISED BY STALIN TO ELIMINATE THE OLD BOLSHEVIKS, FINALLY CONVINCED ORWELL OF THE DUPLICITY OF THE SOVIET REGIME.
HE HAD NEVER BEEN A MARXIST, AND FELT ONLY DISDAIN FOR THE "FELLOW-TRAVELLERS" OF THE EUROPEAN COMMUNIST PARTIES AND THE VARIOUS LENINIST FACTIONS.
THE WHEATSHEAF
FAR FROM BEING ANY ORGANIZED "PARTY" OF A PROLETARIAN VANGUARD, IT WAS THE GRANDEUR OF ORDINARY PEOPLE, THEIR "COMMON DECENCY", THAT CONTINUED TO INSPIRE HIM.
HE WAS A REVOLUTIONARY SOCIALIST, BUT, ABOVE ALL ELSE, AN ENGLISHMAN.

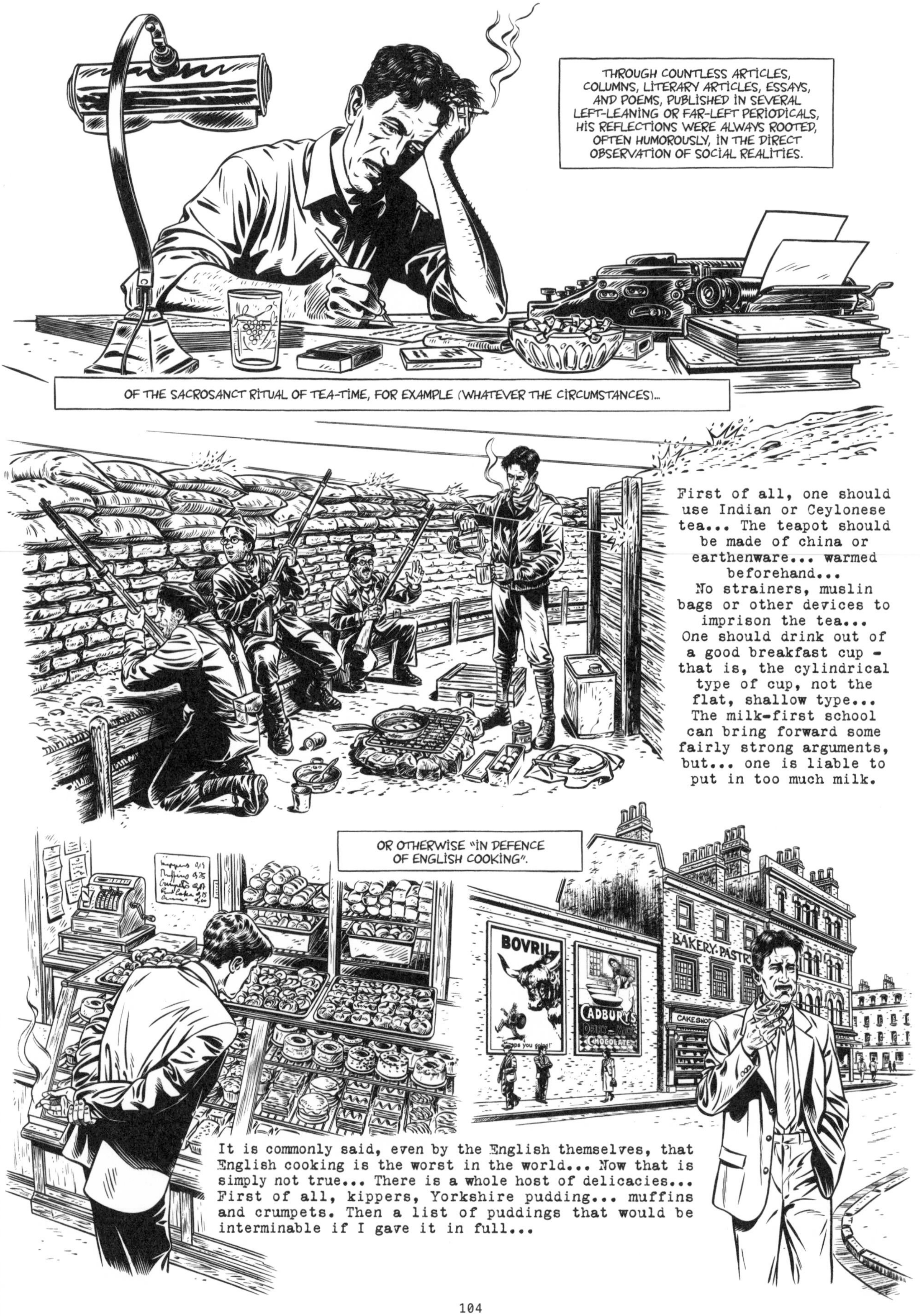
THROUGH COUNTLESS ARTICLES, COLUMNS, LITERARY ARTICLES, ESSAYS, AND POEMS, PUBLISHED IN SEVERAL LEFT-LEANING OR FAR-LEFT PERIODICALS, HIS REFLECTIONS WERE ALWAYS ROOTED, OFTEN HUMOROUSLY, IN THE DIRECT OBSERVATION OF SOCIAL REALITIES.
OF THE SACROSANCT RITUAL OF TEA-TIME, FOR EXAMPLE (WHATEVER THE CIRCUMSTANCES)...
First of all, one should use Indian or Ceylonese tea... The teapot should be made of china or earthenware... warmed beforehand... No strainers, muslin bags or other devices to imprison the tea... One should drink out of a good breakfast cup - that is, the cylindrical type of cup, not the flat, shallow type... The milk-first school can bring forward some fairly strong arguments, but... one is liable to put in too much milk.
OR OTHERWISE "IN DEFENCE OF ENGLISH COOKING".
BOVRIL
CADBURY'S
CHOCOLATE
BAKERY·PASTR
It is commonly said, even by the English themselves, that English cooking is the worst in the world... Now that is simply not true... There is a whole host of delicacies... First of all, kippers, Yorkshire pudding... muffins and crumpets. Then a list of puddings that would be interminable if I gave it in full...

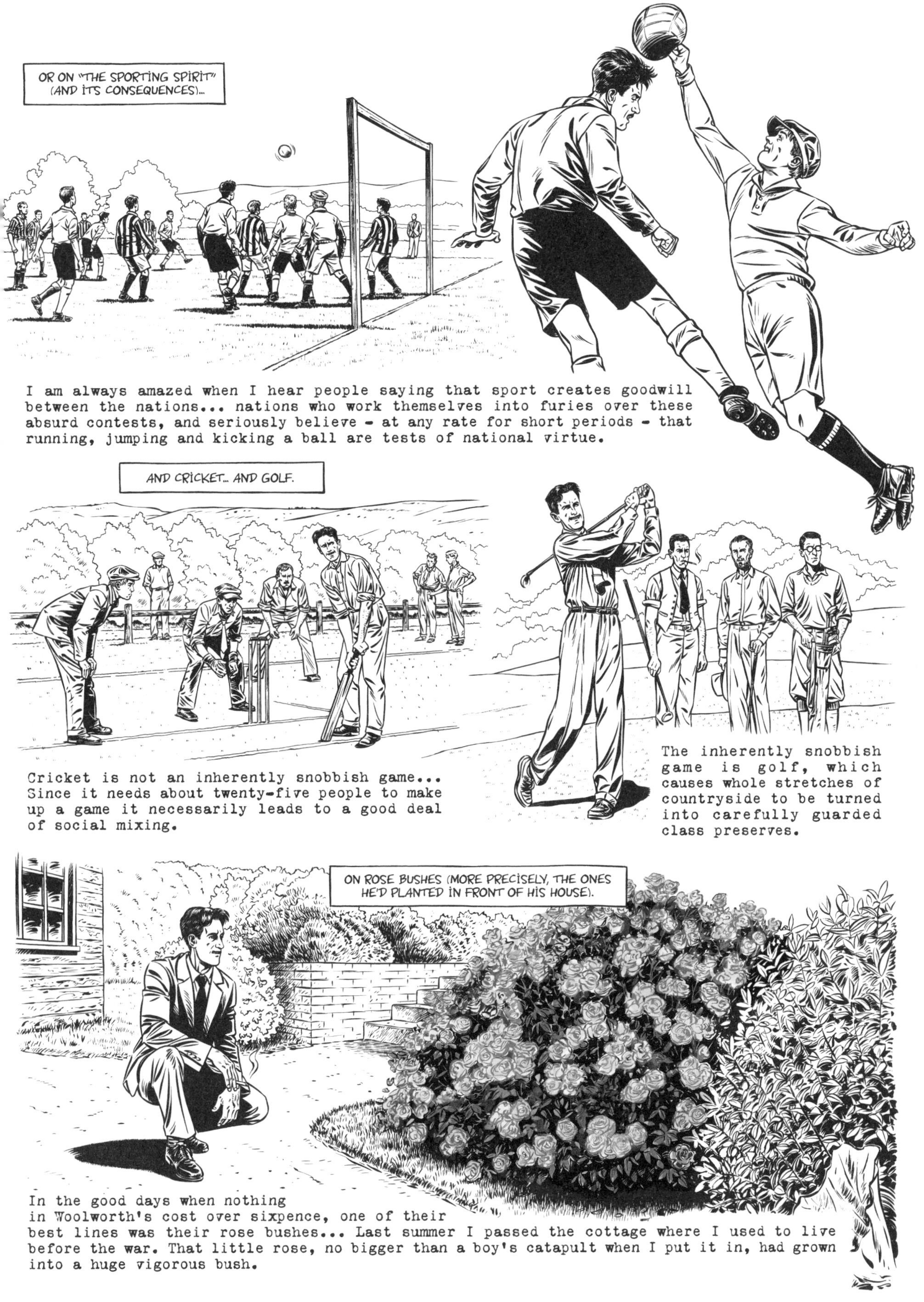
OR ON "THE SPORTING SPIRIT" (AND ITS CONSEQUENCES)...
I am always amazed when I hear people saying that sport creates goodwill between the nations... nations who work themselves into furies over these absurd contests, and seriously believe - at any rate for short periods - that running, jumping and kicking a ball are tests of national virtue.
AND CRICKET... AND GOLF.
Cricket is not an inherently snobbish game... Since it needs about twenty-five people to make up a game it necessarily leads to a good deal of social mixing.
The inherently snobbish game is golf, which causes whole stretches of countryside to be turned into carefully guarded class preserves.
ON ROSE BUSHES (MORE PRECISELY, THE ONES HE'D PLANTED IN FRONT OF HIS HOUSE).
In the good days when nothing in Woolworth's cost over sixpence, one of their best lines was their rose bushes... Last summer I passed the cottage where I used to live before the war. That little rose, no bigger than a boy's catapult when I put it in, had grown into a huge vigorous bush.

ON RAFFLES (AND MISS BLANDISH):

Raffles, "the amateur cracksman", is still one of the best-known characters in English fiction... He and his exploits make a suitable background against which to examine a more modern crime story such as *No Orchids for Miss Blandish*... Rafflles... is of upper-middle-class origin... by modern standards Raffles's crimes are very petty ones.

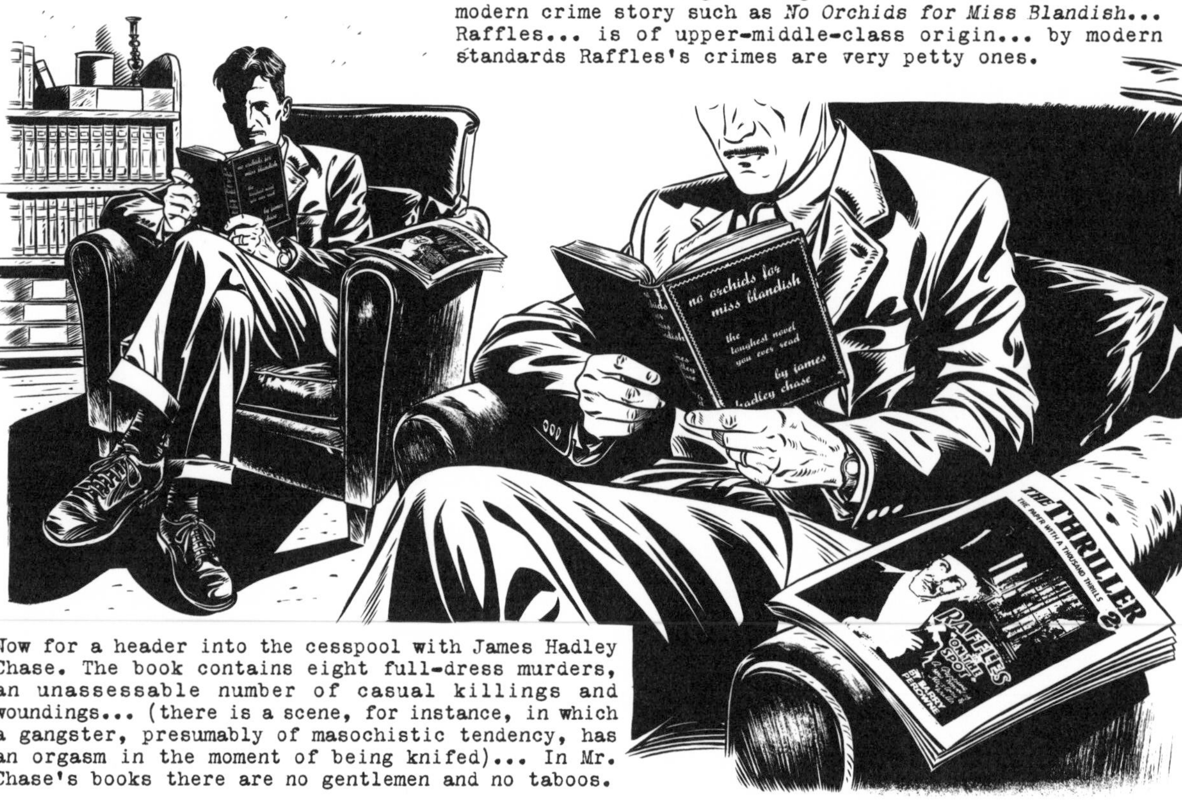
no orchids for miss blandish
the toughest novel you ever read
by james hadley chase
THE THRILLER
THE PAPER WITH A THOUSAND THRILLS
RAFFLES

Now for a header into the cesspool with James Hadley Chase. The book contains eight full-dress murders, an unassessable number of casual killings and woundings... (there is a scene, for instance, in which a gangster, presumably of masochistic tendency, has an orgasm in the moment of being knifed)... In Mr. Chase's books there are no gentlemen and no taboos.

ON AMERICAN COMICS ("DISGUSTING"):

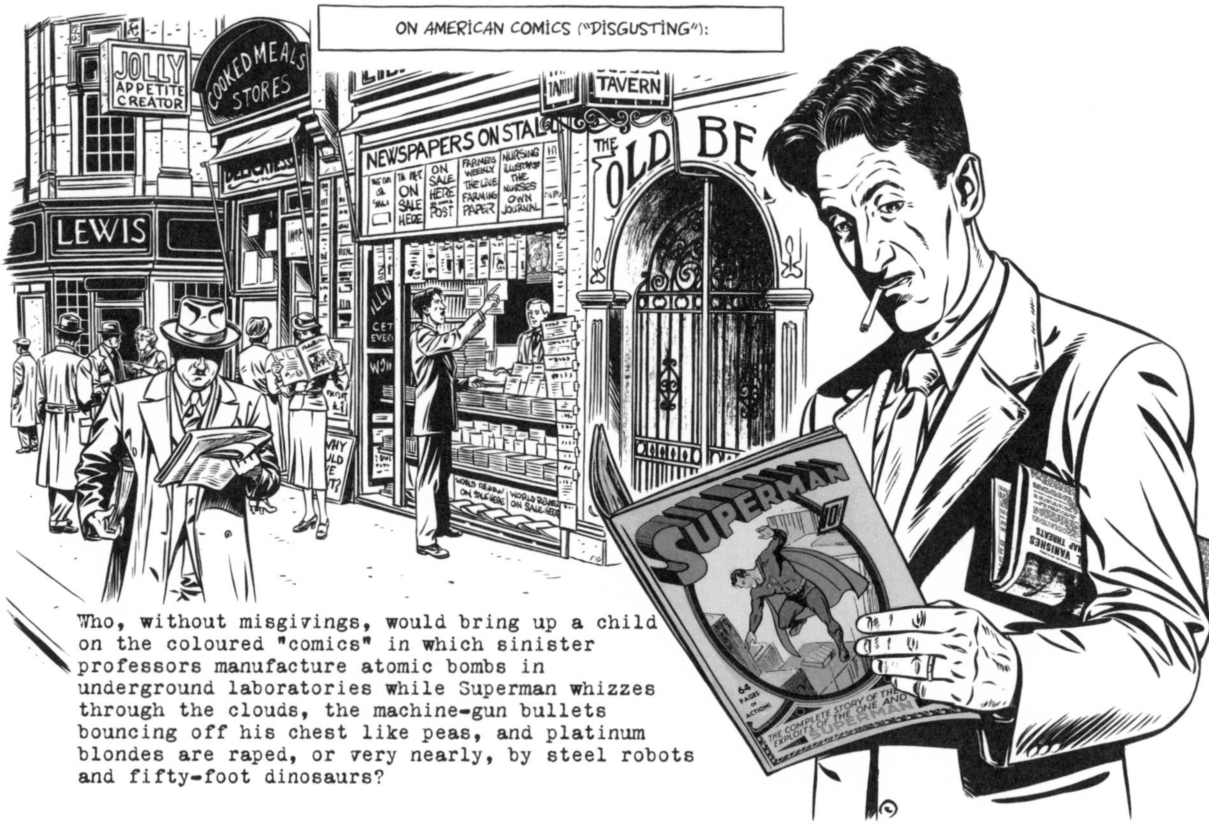
JOLLY
APPETITE CREATOR
COOKED MEALS
STORES
LEWIS
TAVERN
NEWSPAPERS ON STAL
THE OLD BE
ON SALE HERE
SUPERMAN
64 PAGES OF ACTION!

Who, without misgivings, would bring up a child on the coloured "comics" in which sinister professors manufacture atomic bombs in underground laboratories while Superman whizzes through the clouds, the machine-gun bullets bouncing off his chest like peas, and platinum blondes are raped, or very nearly, by steel robots and fifty-foot dinosaurs?

ON "PLEASURE SPOTS" (AS EARLY AS THE 1940S):

1. One is never alone.
2. One never does anything for oneself.
3. One is never within sight of wild vegetation or natural objects of any kind.
4. Light and temperature are always artificially regulated.
5. One is never out of the sound of music.

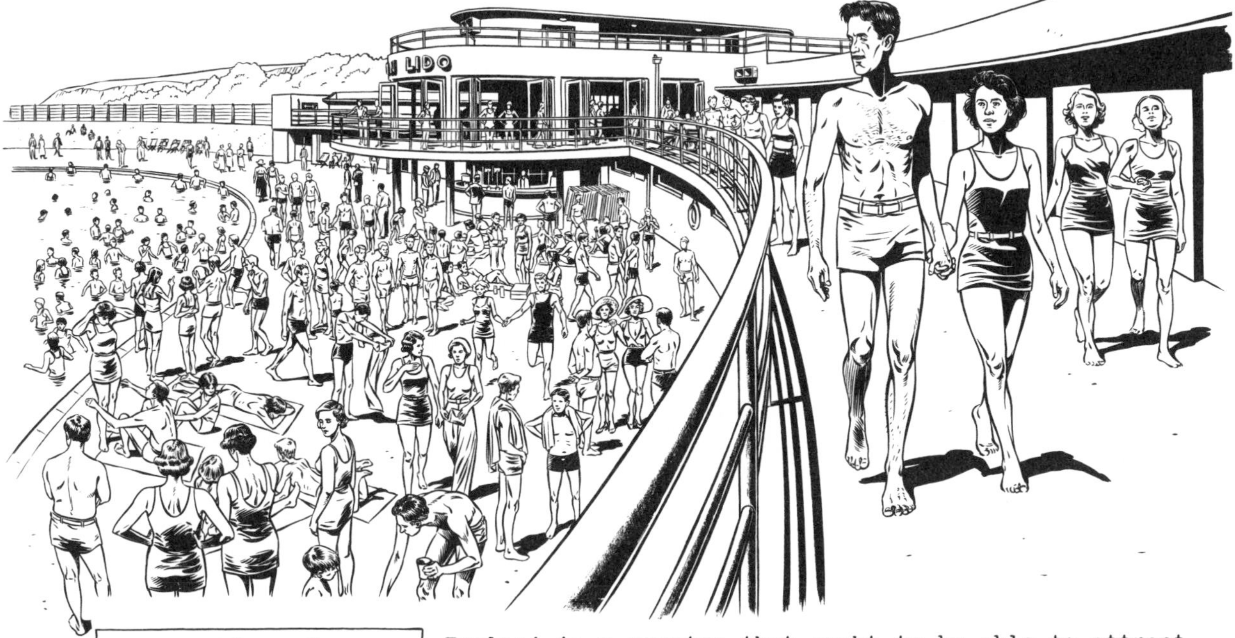
LIDO

ON FOREIGN TOURISTS:

England is a country that ought to be able to attract tourists... If you could walk where you chose instead of being fenced in by barbed wire and "Trespassers will be Prosecuted" boards, if speculative builders had not been allowed to ruin every pleasant view... and if Sunday were not artificially made into a day of misery... But if those things were true England would no longer be England.

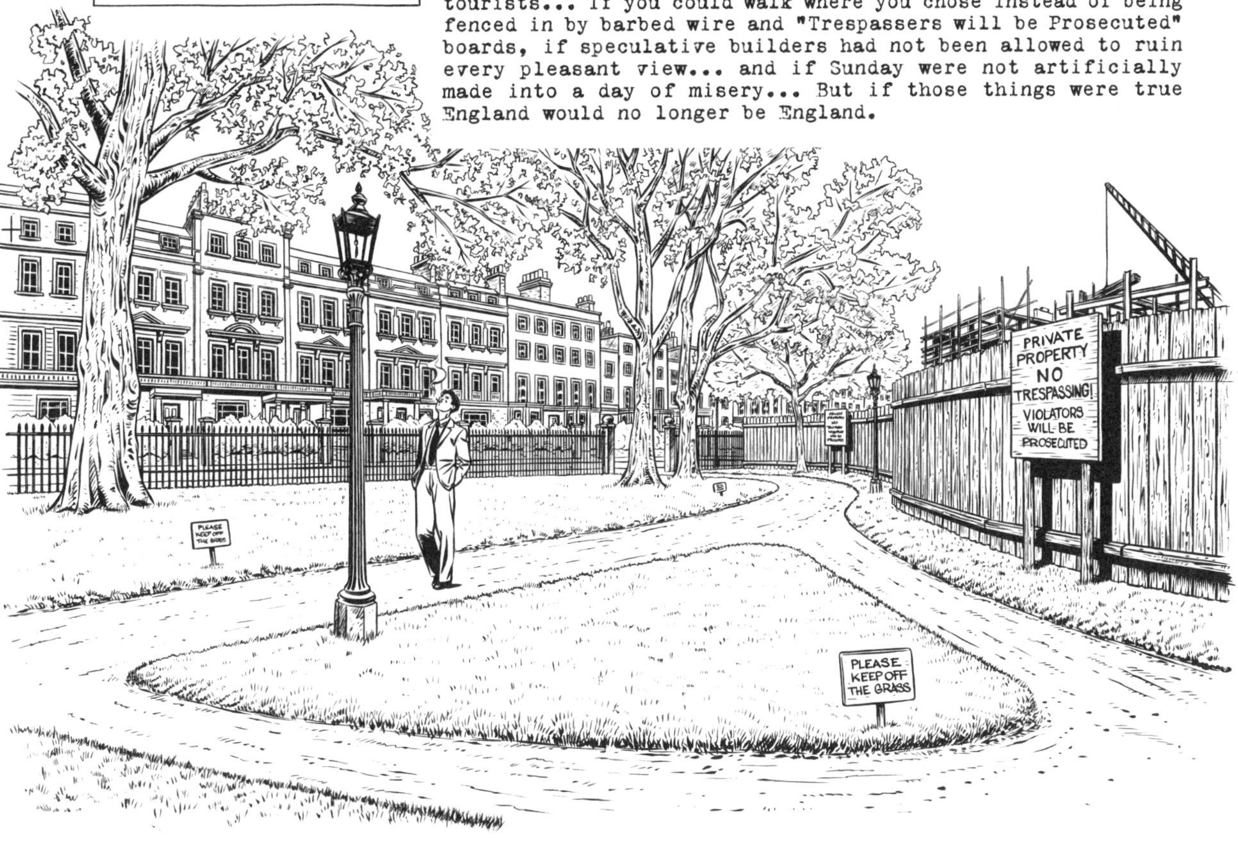
PRIVATE PROPERTY NO TRESPASSING
VIOLATORS WILL BE PROSECUTED
PLEASE KEEP OFF THE GRASS

ON THE KNIGHTING OF BUSINESSMEN:

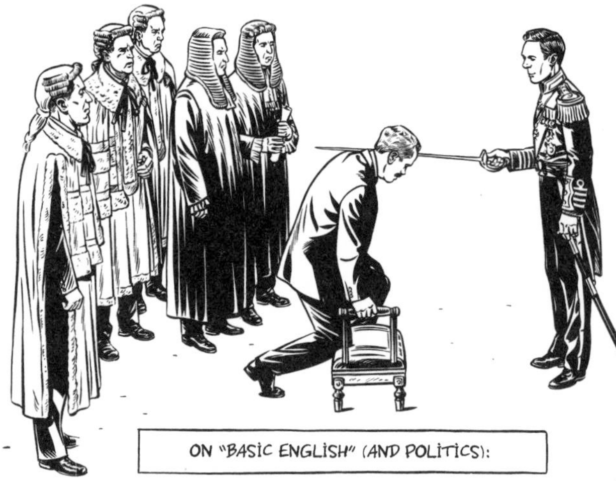

Looking through the photographs of the New Year's Honours List, I am struck (as usual) by the quite exceptional ugliness and vulgarity of the faces displayed there. It seems to be almost the rule that the kind of person who earns the right to call himself Lord Percy de Falcontowers should look at best like an overfed publican and at worst like a tax collector with a duodenal ulcer.

ON "BASIC ENGLISH" (AND POLITICS):

In Basic, I am told, you cannot make a meaningless statement without it being apparent that it is meaningless - which is quite enough to explain why so many schoolmasters, editors, politicians and literary critics object to it.

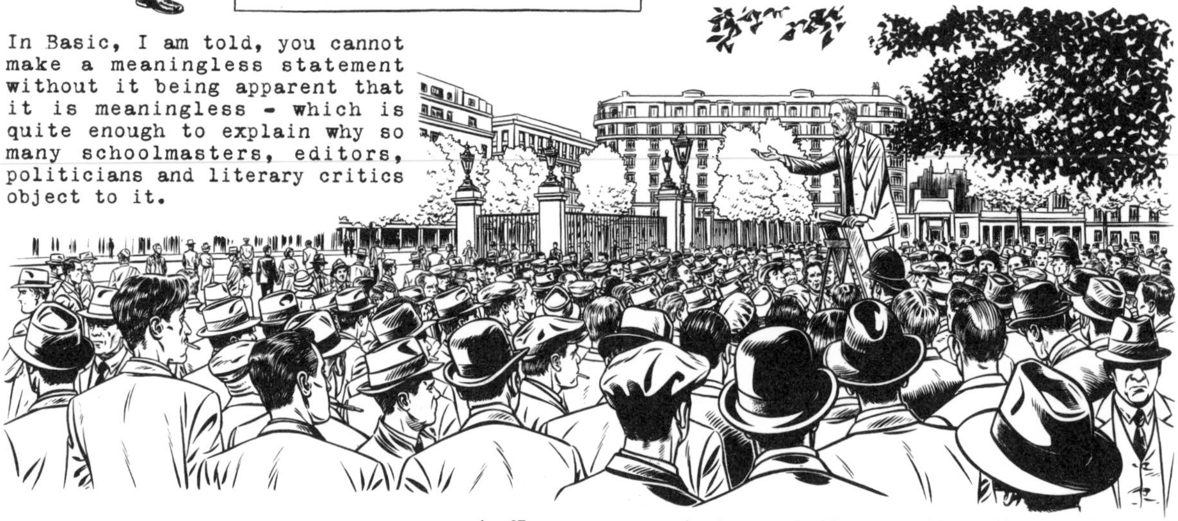

ON POLITICS (AND THE ENGLISH LANGUAGE):

i. Never use a metaphor, simile, or other figure of speech which you are used to seeing in print.
ii. Never use a long word where a short one will do.
iii. If it is possible to cut a word out, always cut it out.
iv. Never use the passive where you can use the active.
v. Never use a foreign phrase, a scientific word, or a jargon word if you can think of an everyday English equivalent.
vi. Break any of these rules sooner than say anything outright barbarous.

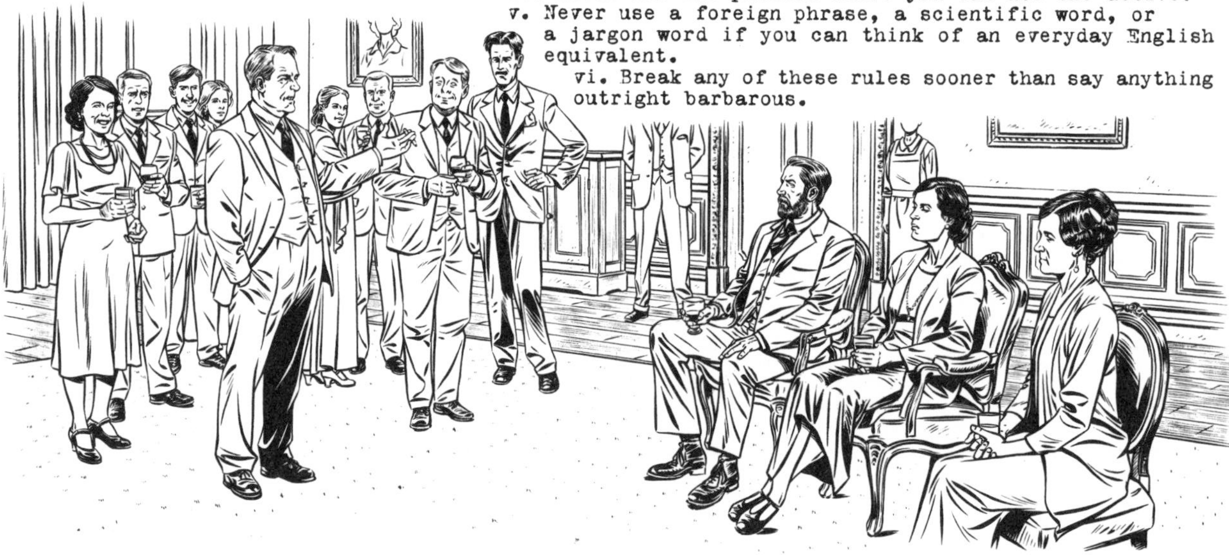

ORWELL HAD HIS HEROES. THE PHILOSOPHER BERTRAND RUSSELL, FOR EXAMPLE...

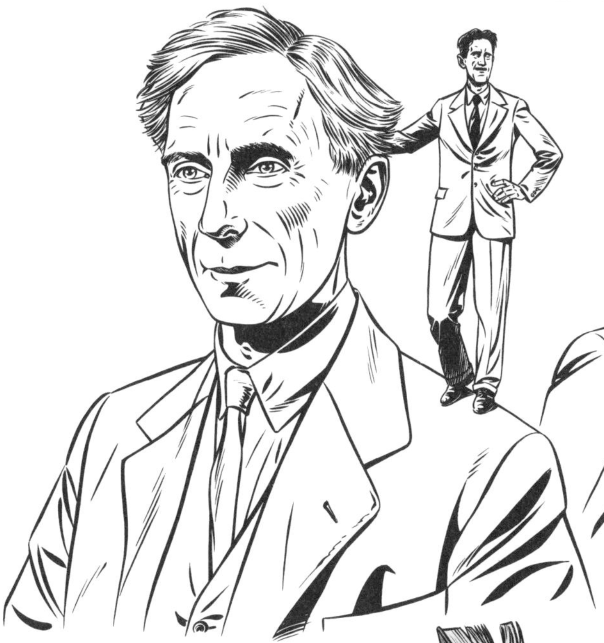

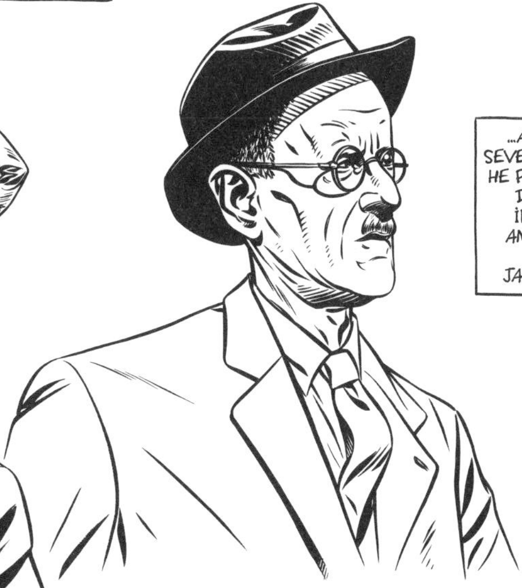

...AS WELL AS SEVERAL WRITERS HE PASSIONATELY DEFENDED, INCLUDING, AMONG MANY OTHERS, JAMES JOYCE.

SURPRISINGLY ENOUGH, HE EVEN FORGAVE P.G. WODEHOUSE, THE HILARIOUS AUTHOR OF THE JEEVES BOOKS, FOR NEGLECTING TO NOTICE HE WAS COLLABORATING WITH NAZI GERMANY.

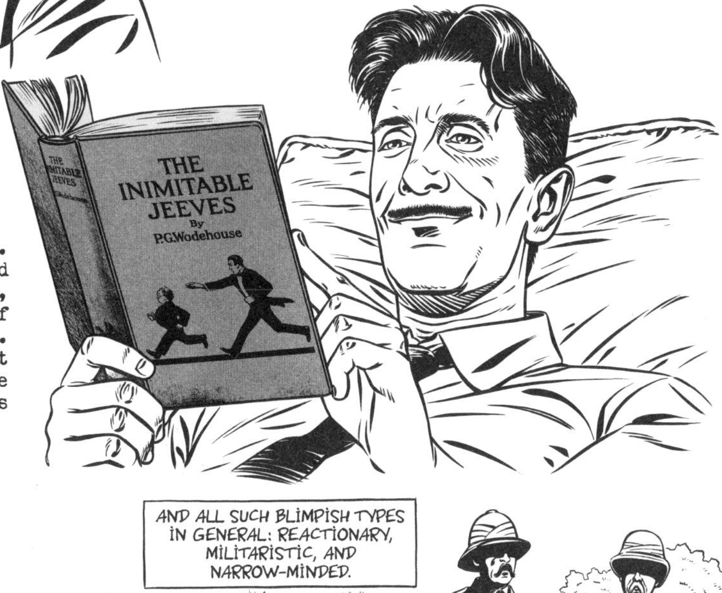
THE INIMITABLE JEEVES
By
P.G.Wodehouse
THE INIMITABLE JEEVES

Still, it was a great day for Mr. Wodehouse when he created Jeeves, and thus escaped from the realm of comedy, which in England always stinks of virtue, into the realm of pure farce. The great charm of Jeeves is that (although he did pronounce Nietzsche to be "fundamentally unsound") he is beyond good and evil.

BUT HE ALSO HAD HIS BÊTES NOIRS, EMBODIED IN COLONEL BLIMP, THE CARTOON CHARACTER INVENTED BY DAVID LOW IN 1930.

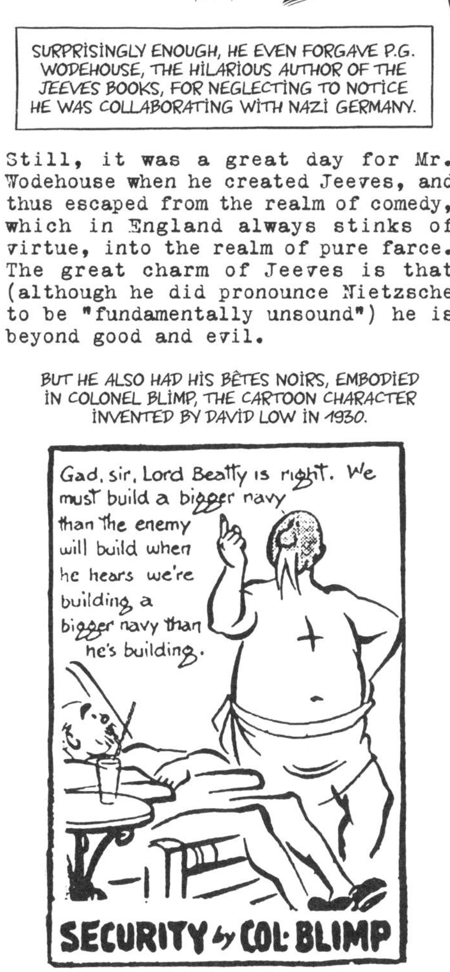
Gad, sir, Lord Beatty is right. We must build a bigger navy than the enemy will build when he hears we're building a bigger navy than he's building.
SECURITY by COL. BLIMP

AND ALL SUCH BLIMPISH TYPES IN GENERAL: REACTIONARY, MILITARISTIC, AND NARROW-MINDED.

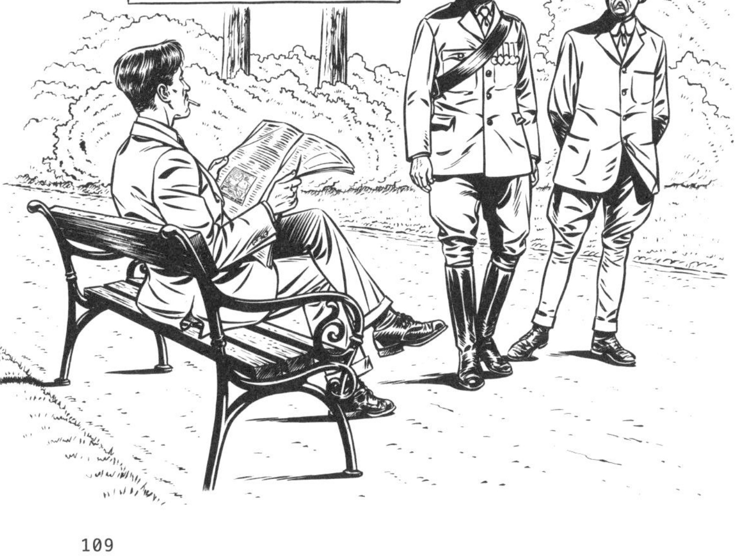

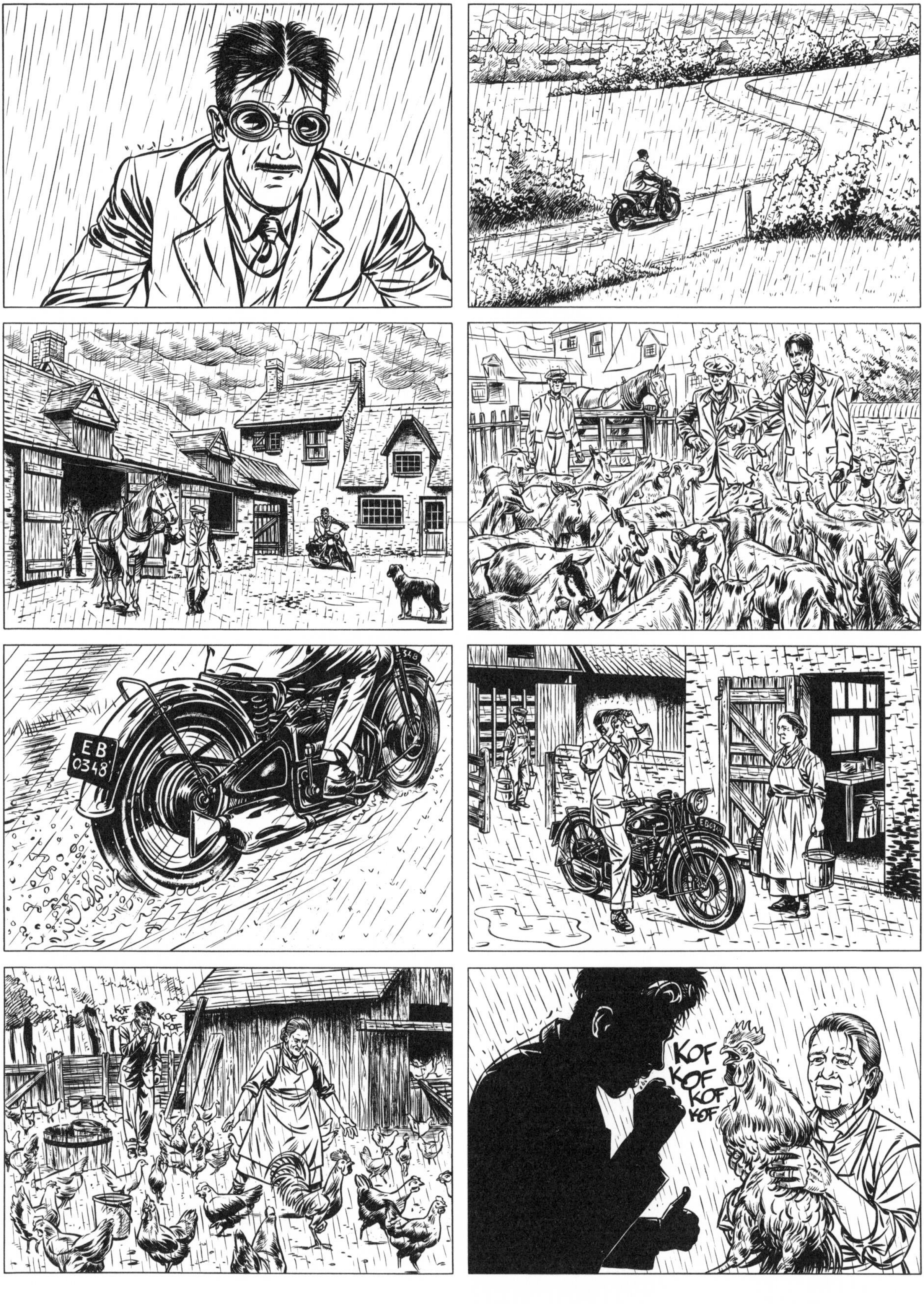
EB
0348
KOF KOF
KOF KOF
KOF KOF KOF KOF

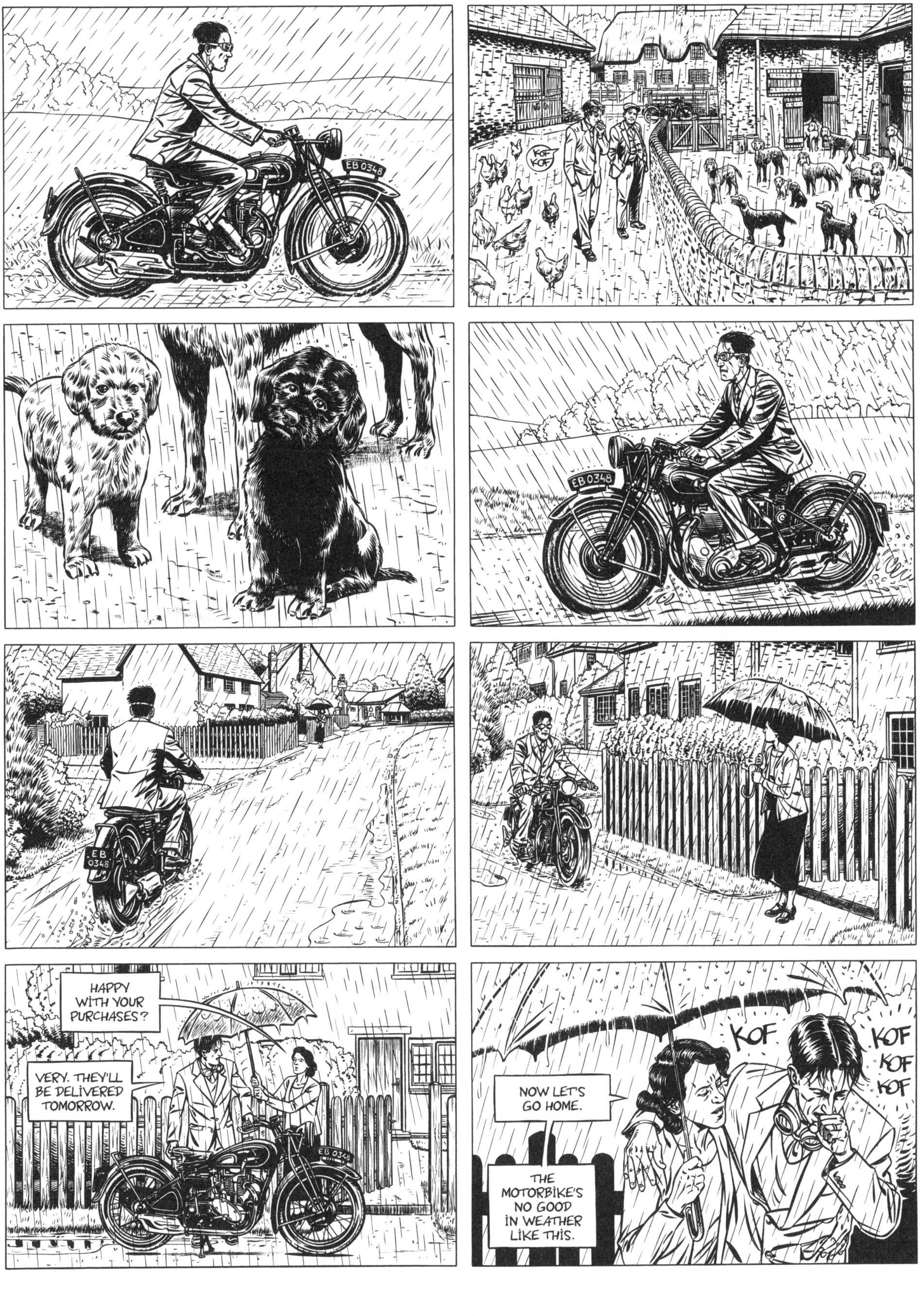
EB 0348
KOF KOF
EB 0348
EB 0348
HAPPY WITH YOUR PURCHASES?
VERY. THEY'LL BE DELIVERED TOMORROW.
EB 0348
NOW LET'S GO HOME.
KOF
KOF KOF KOF
THE MOTORBIKE'S NO GOOD IN WEATHER LIKE THIS.

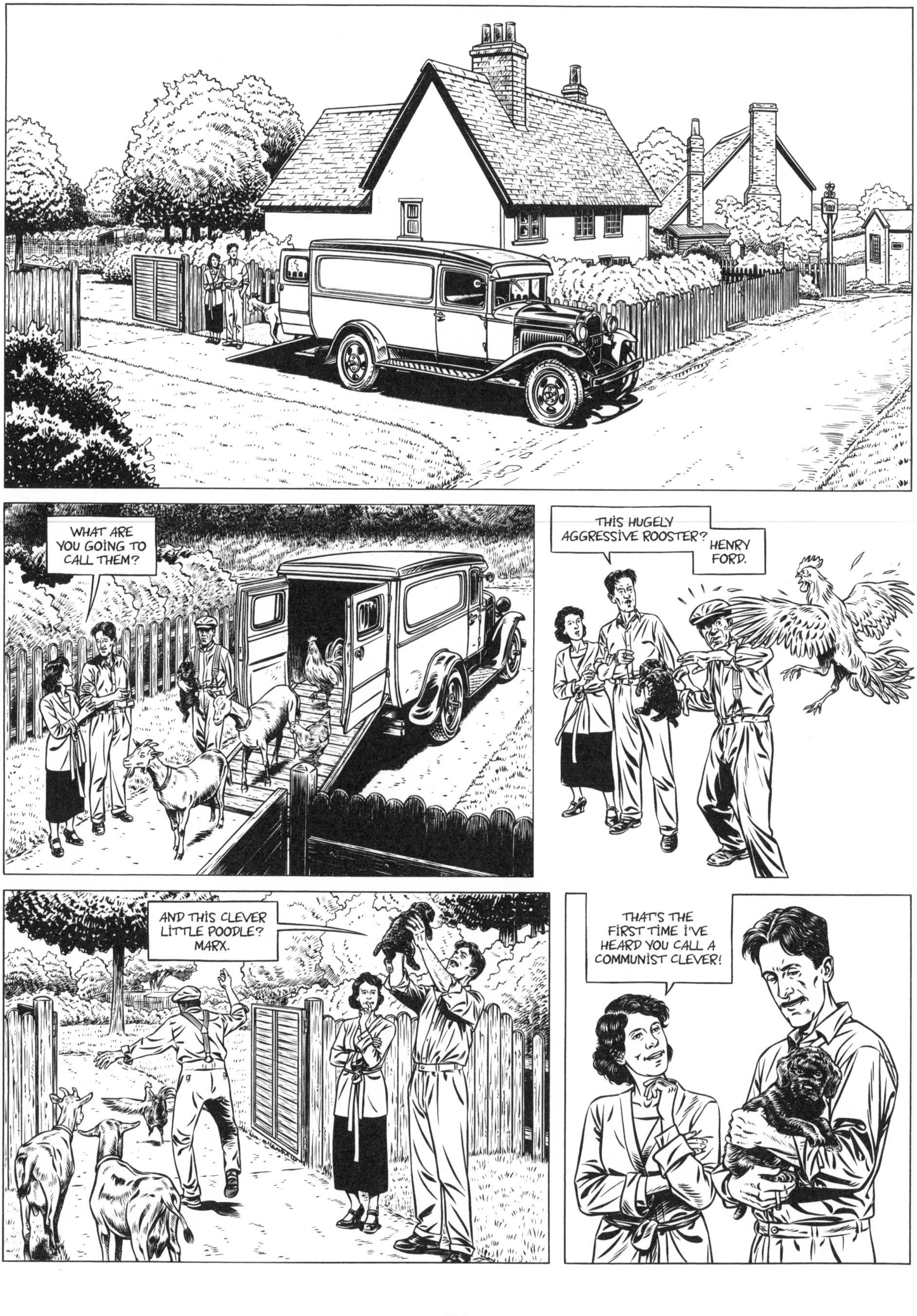
WHAT ARE YOU GOING TO CALL THEM?
THIS HUGELY AGGRESSIVE ROOSTER?
HENRY FORD.
AND THIS CLEVER LITTLE POODLE? MARX.
THAT'S THE FIRST TIME I'VE HEARD YOU CALL A COMMUNIST CLEVER!

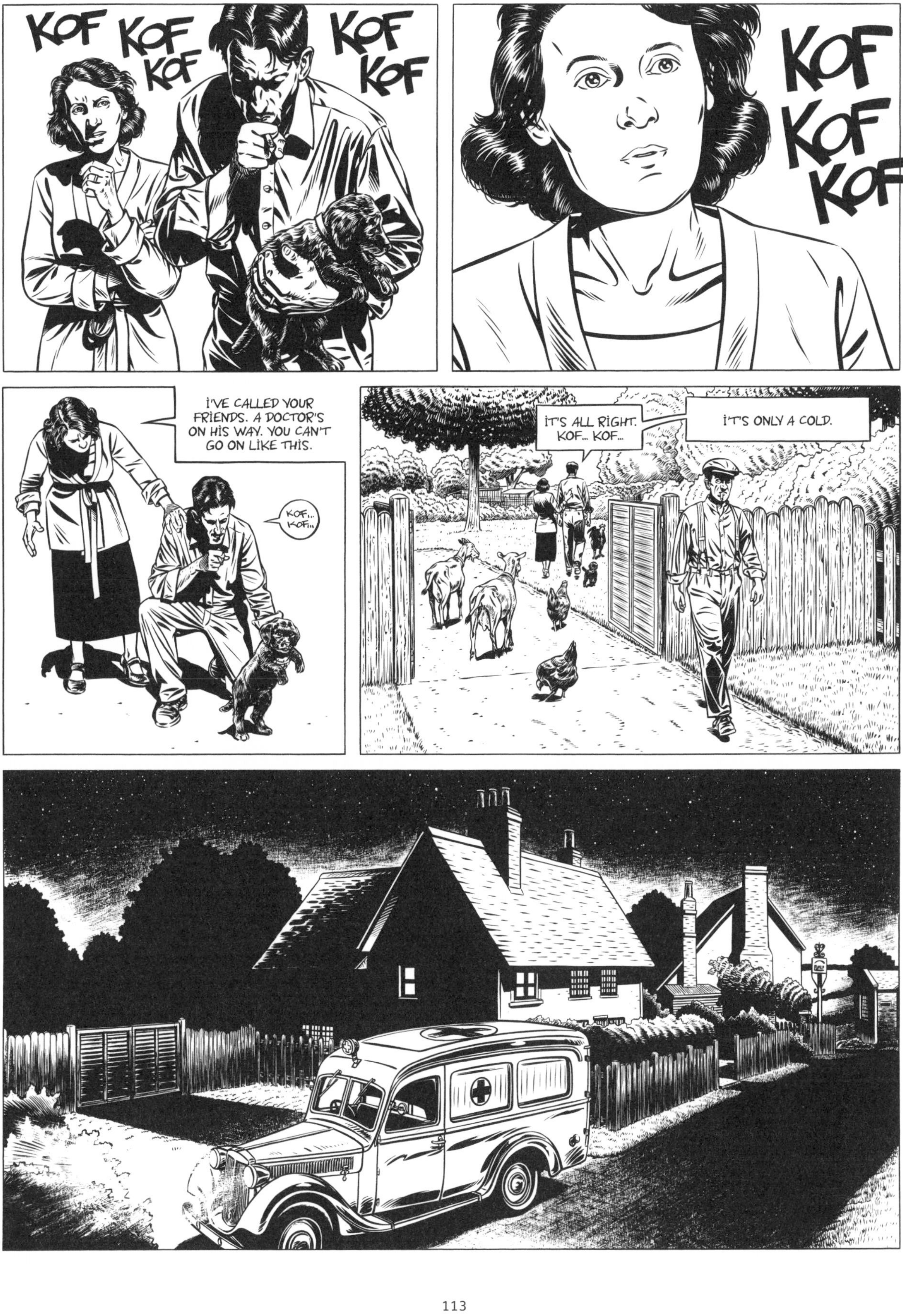
KOF
KOF KOF
KOF KOF
KOF KOF KOF
I'VE CALLED YOUR FRIENDS. A DOCTOR'S ON HIS WAY. YOU CAN'T GO ON LIKE THIS.
KOF... KOF...
IT'S ALL RIGHT. KOF... KOF...
IT'S ONLY A COLD.

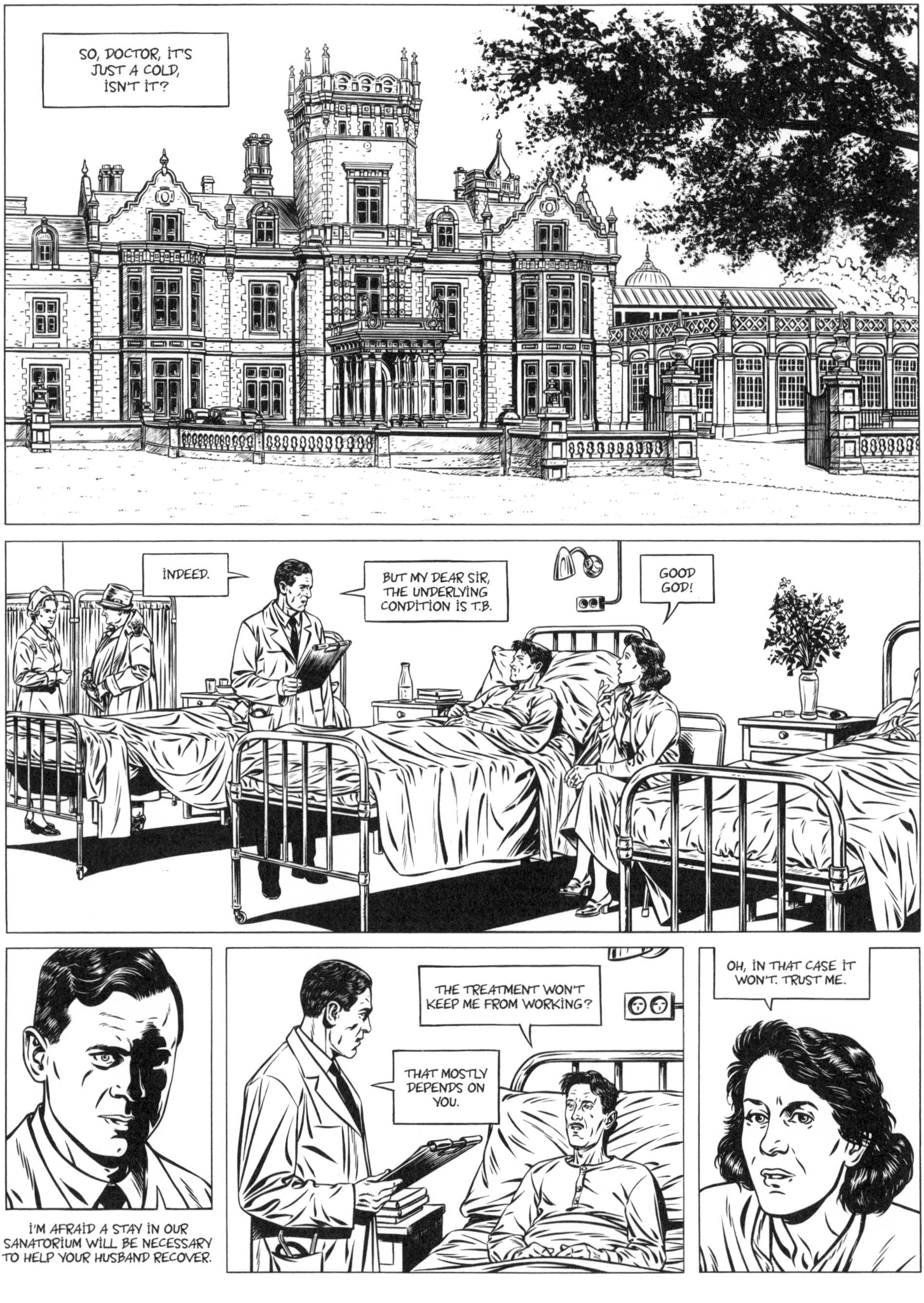
SO, DOCTOR, IT'S JUST A COLD, ISN'T IT?
INDEED.
BUT MY DEAR SIR, THE UNDERLYING CONDITION IS T.B.
GOOD GOD!
I'M AFRAID A STAY IN OUR SANATORIUM WILL BE NECESSARY TO HELP YOUR HUSBAND RECOVER.
THE TREATMENT WON'T KEEP ME FROM WORKING?
THAT MOSTLY DEPENDS ON YOU.
OH, IN THAT CASE IT WON'T. TRUST ME.

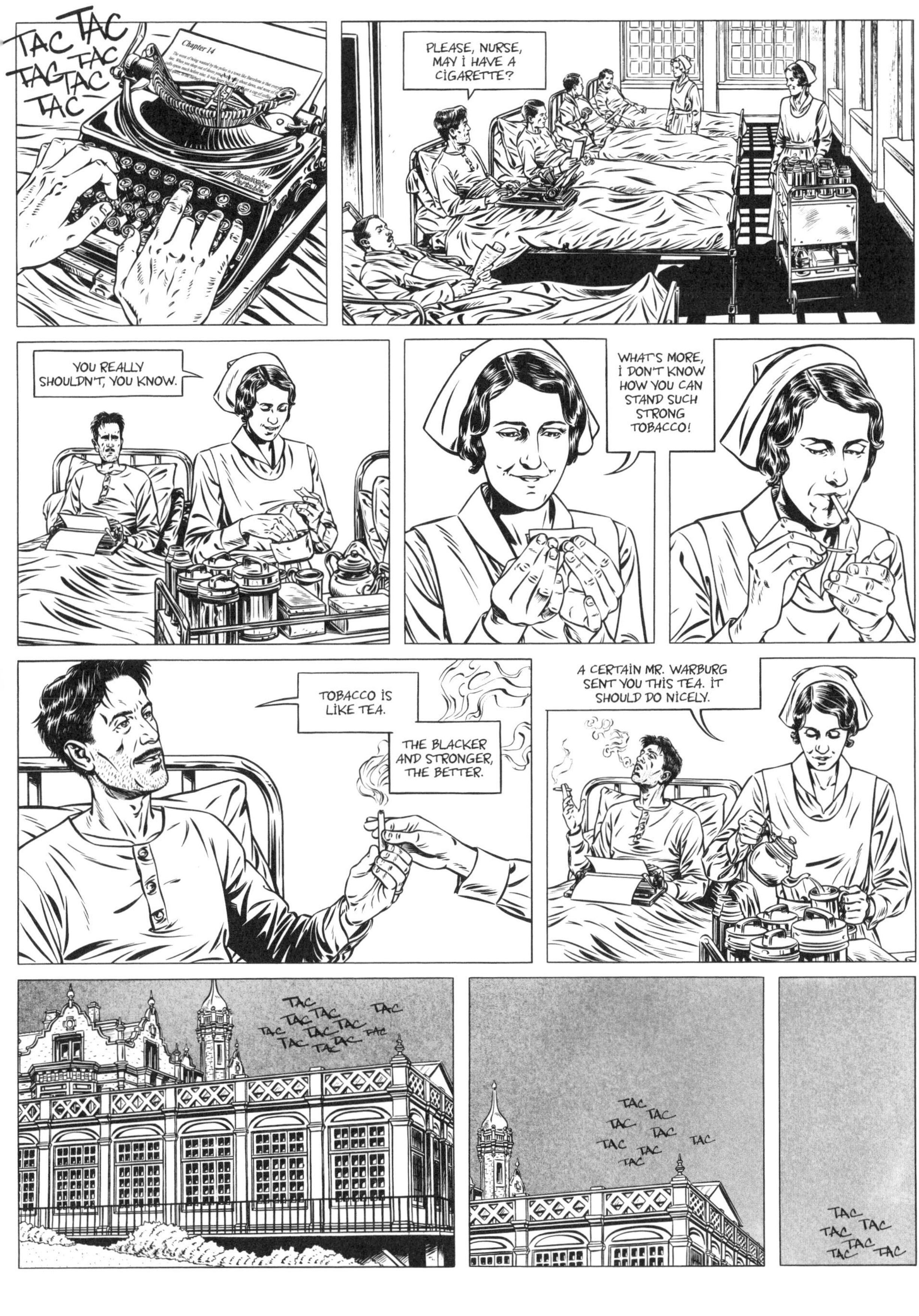
TAC TAC TAC TAC TAC TAC
Chapter 14
PLEASE, NURSE, MAY I HAVE A CIGARETTE?
YOU REALLY SHOULDN'T, YOU KNOW.
WHAT'S MORE, I DON'T KNOW HOW YOU CAN STAND SUCH STRONG TOBACCO!
TOBACCO IS LIKE TEA.
THE BLACKER AND STRONGER, THE BETTER.
A CERTAIN MR. WARBURG SENT YOU THIS TEA. IT SHOULD DO NICELY.
TAC TAC TAC TAC TAC TAC TAC TAC TAC TAC TAC
TAC TAC TAC TAC TAC TAC TAC TAC
TAC TAC TAC TAC TAC TAC

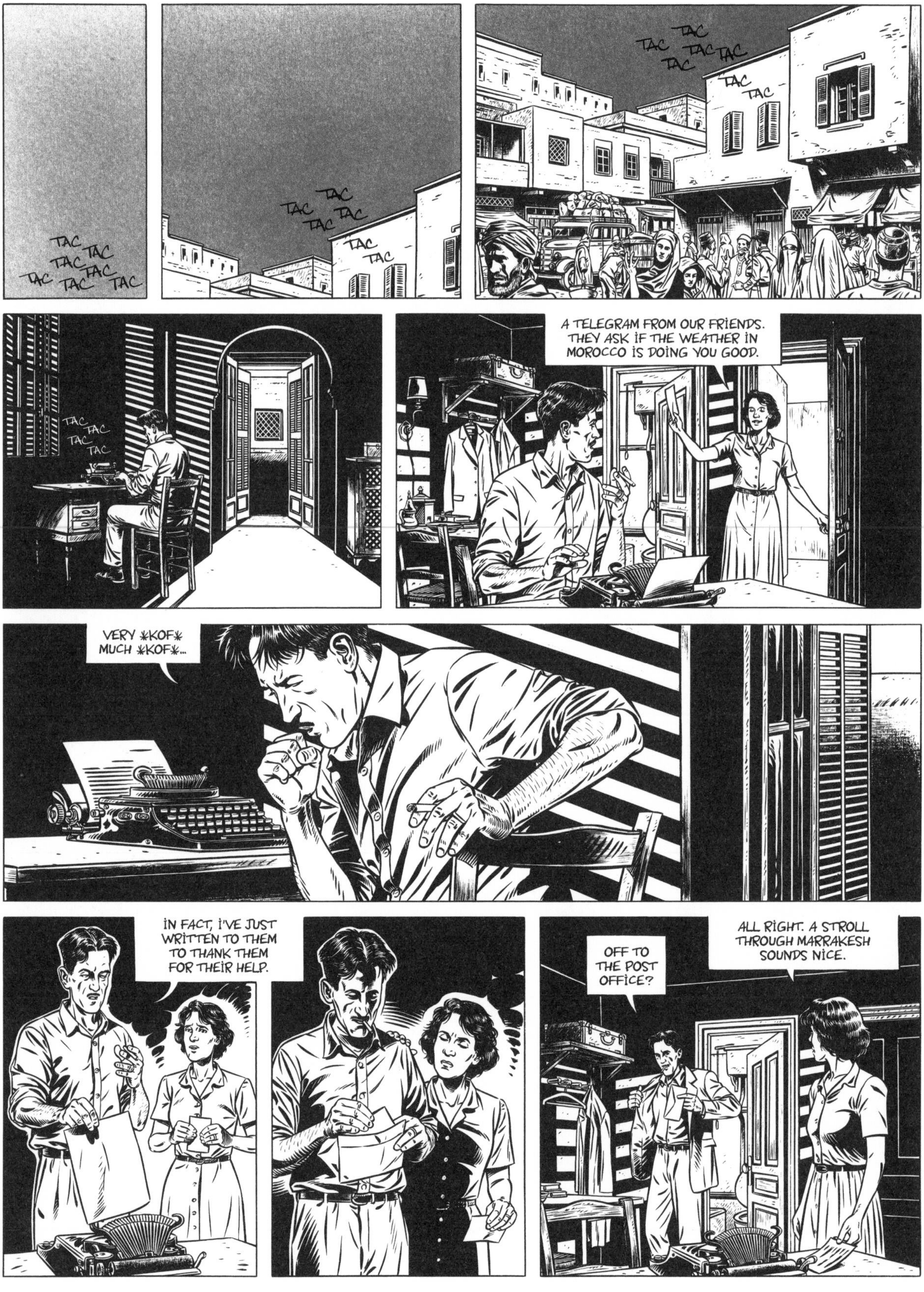
TAC TAC TAC TAC TAC TAC TAC TAC
TAC TAC TAC TAC TAC TAC
TAC TAC TAC TAC TAC TAC TAC
TAC TAC TAC TAC
A TELEGRAM FROM OUR FRIENDS. THEY ASK IF THE WEATHER IN MOROCCO IS DOING YOU GOOD.
VERY *KOF* MUCH *KOF*...
IN FACT, I'VE JUST WRITTEN TO THEM TO THANK THEM FOR THEIR HELP.
OFF TO THE POST OFFICE?
ALL RIGHT. A STROLL THROUGH MARRAKESH SOUNDS NICE.

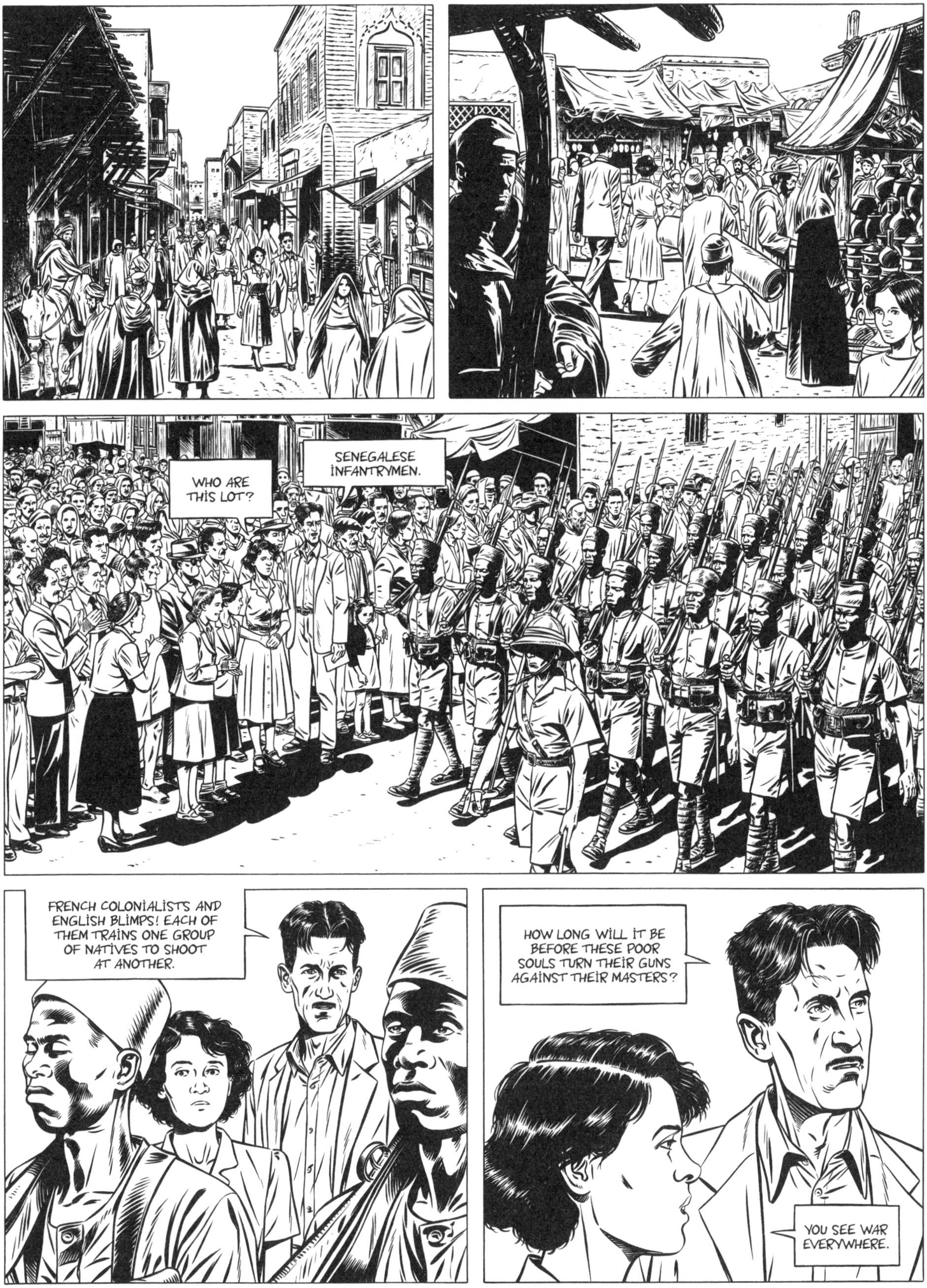
WHO ARE THIS LOT?
SENEGALESE INFANTRYMEN.
FRENCH COLONIALISTS AND ENGLISH BLIMPS! EACH OF THEM TRAINS ONE GROUP OF NATIVES TO SHOOT AT ANOTHER.
HOW LONG WILL IT BE BEFORE THESE POOR SOULS TURN THEIR GUNS AGAINST THEIR MASTERS?
YOU SEE WAR EVERYWHERE.

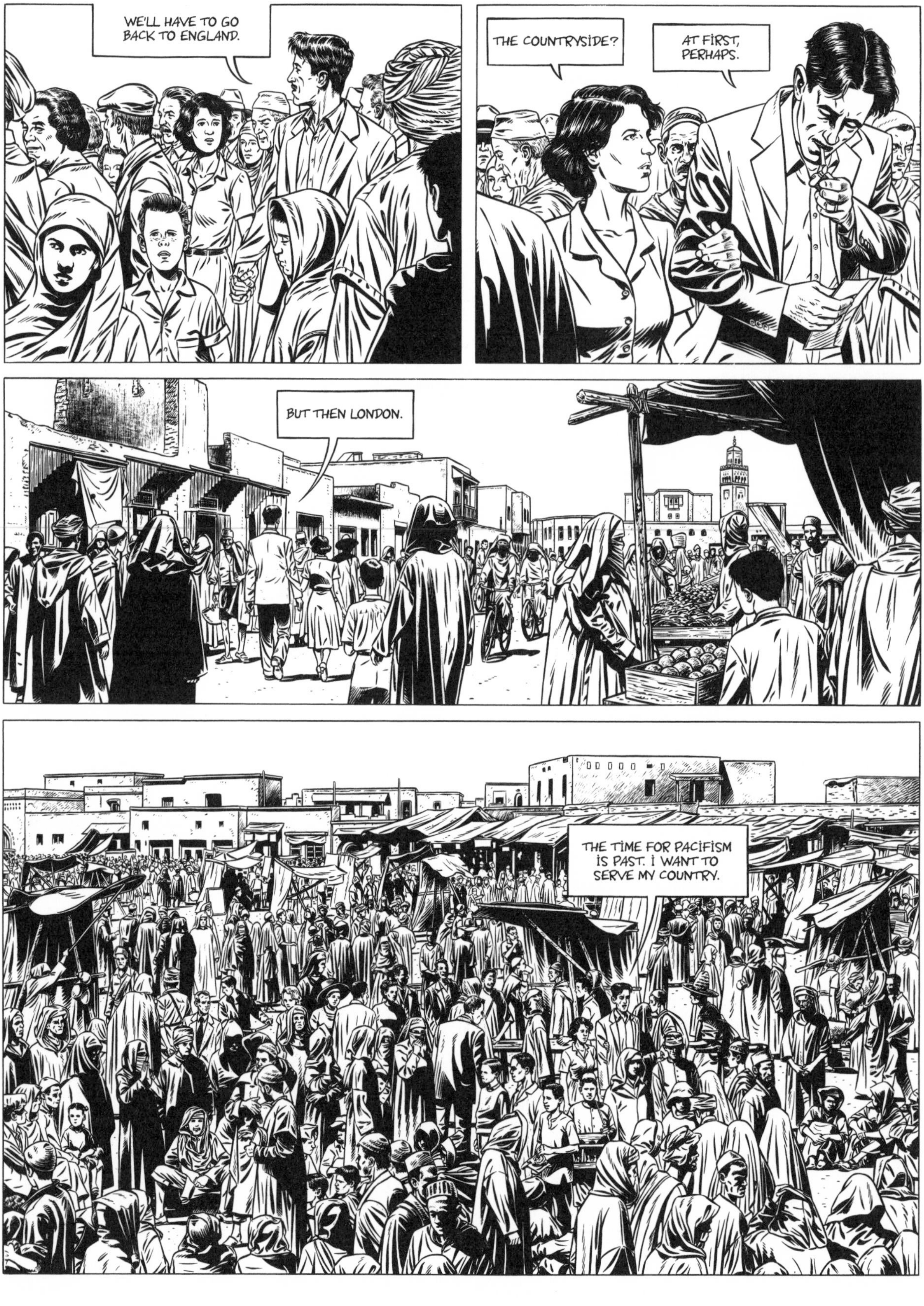
WE'LL HAVE TO GO BACK TO ENGLAND.
THE COUNTRYSIDE?
AT FIRST, PERHAPS.
BUT THEN LONDON.
THE TIME FOR PACIFISM IS PAST. I WANT TO SERVE MY COUNTRY.

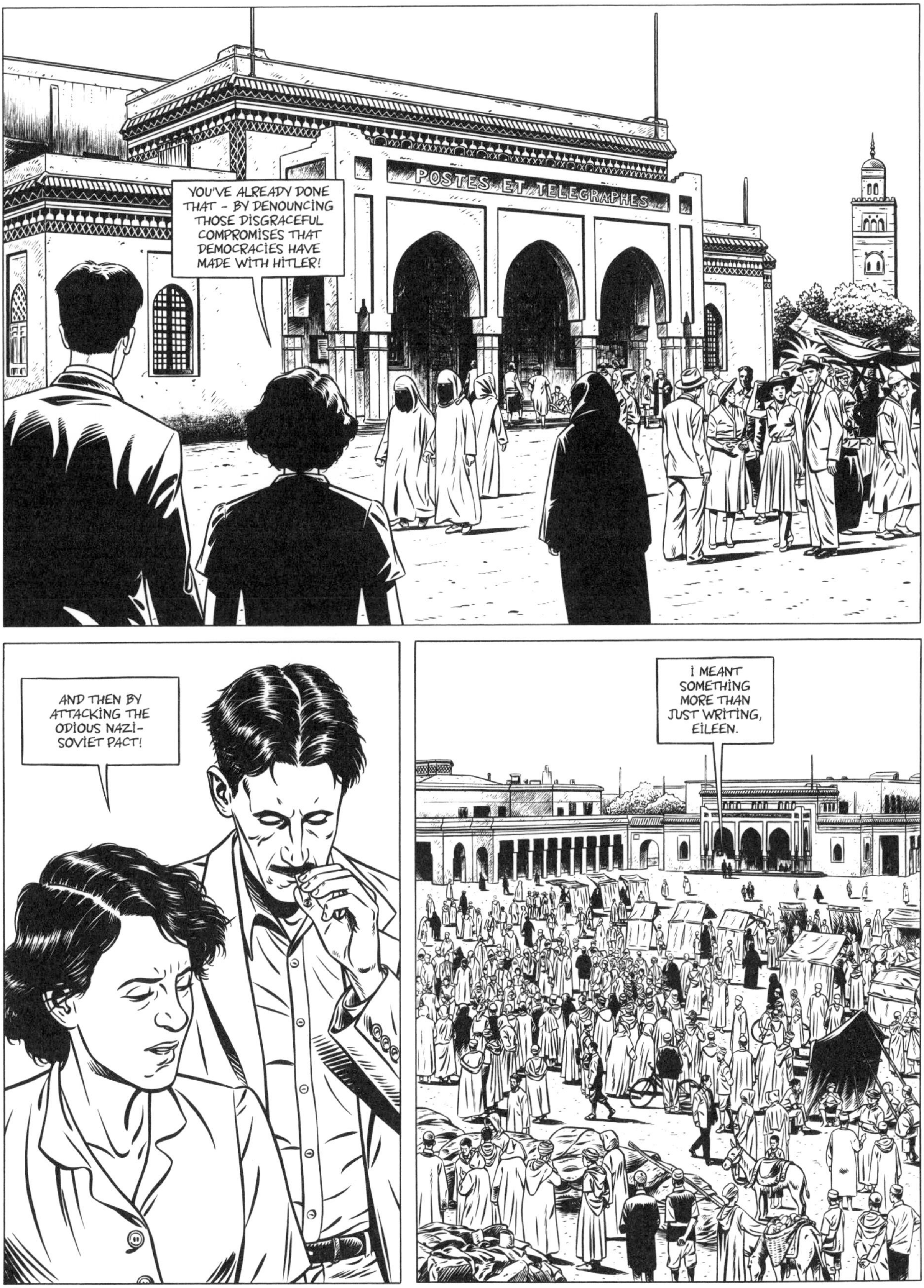
POSTES ET TELEGRAPHES
YOU'VE ALREADY DONE THAT - BY DENOUNCING THOSE DISGRACEFUL COMPROMISES THAT DEMOCRACIES HAVE MADE WITH HITLER!
AND THEN BY ATTACKING THE ODIOUS NAZI-SOVIET PACT!
I MEANT SOMETHING MORE THAN JUST WRITING, EILEEN.

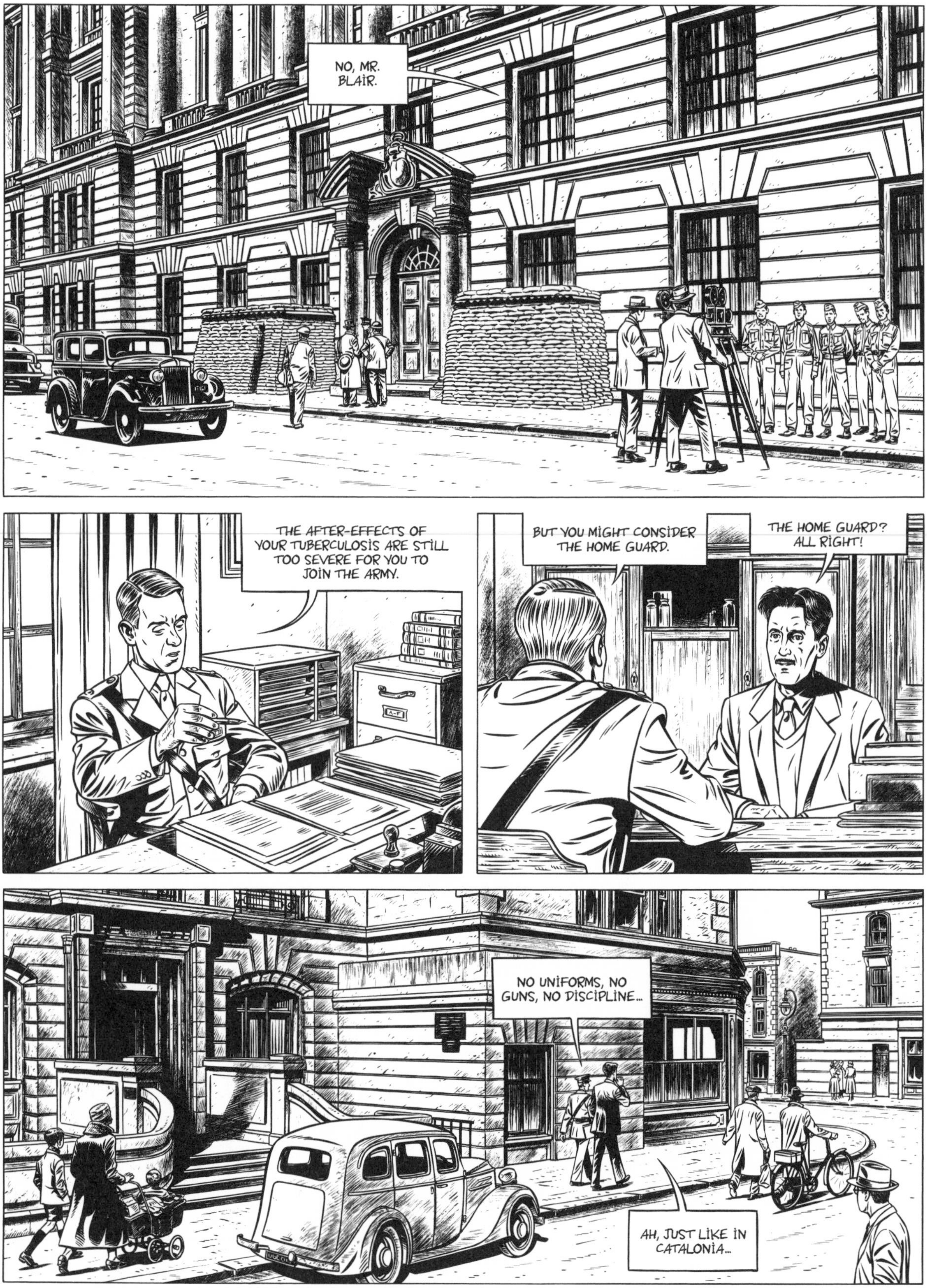
NO, MR. BLAIR.
THE AFTER-EFFECTS OF YOUR TUBERCULOSIS ARE STILL TOO SEVERE FOR YOU TO JOIN THE ARMY.
BUT YOU MIGHT CONSIDER THE HOME GUARD.
THE HOME GUARD? ALL RIGHT!
NO UNIFORMS, NO GUNS, NO DISCIPLINE...
AH, JUST LIKE IN CATALONIA...

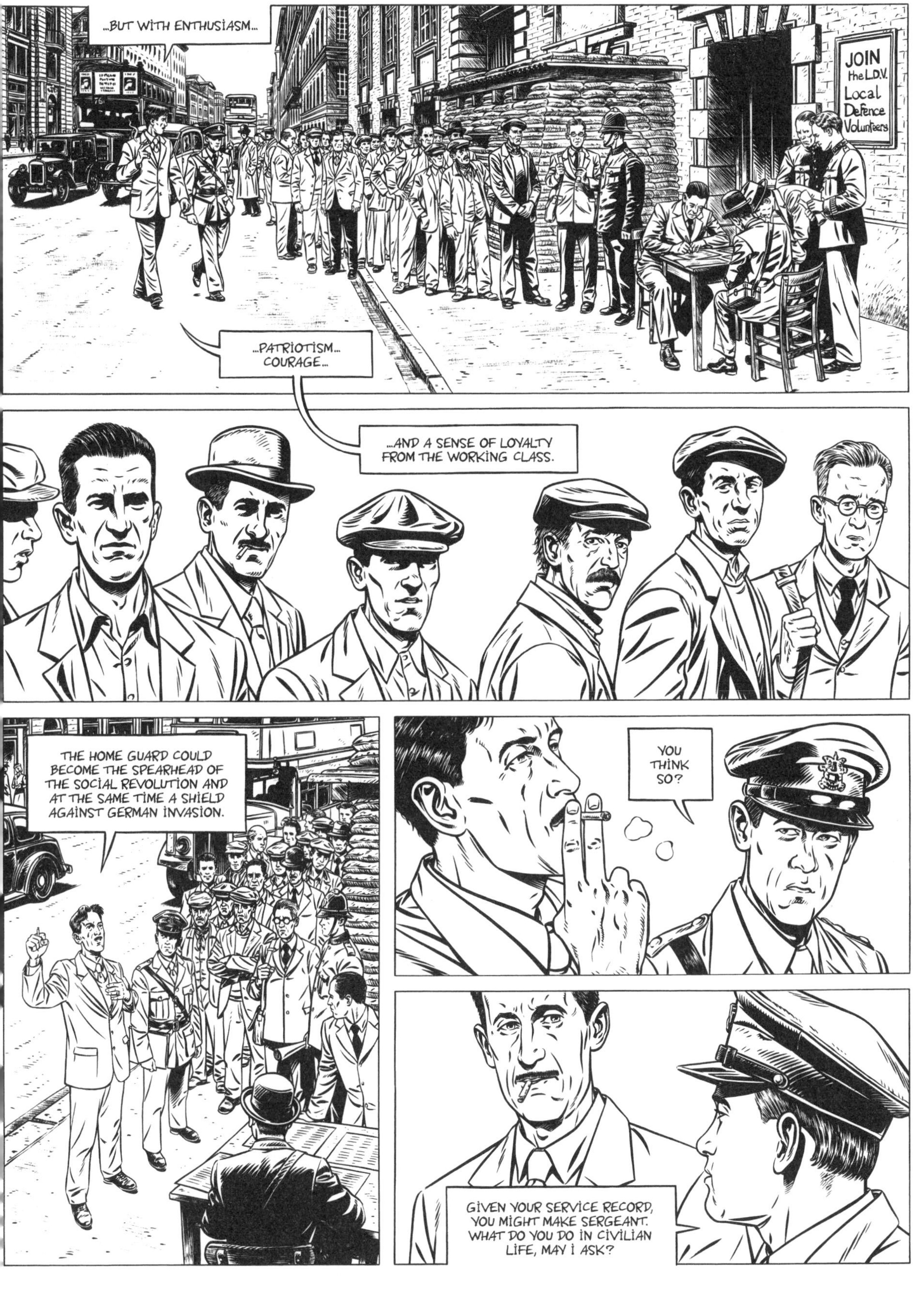

...BUT WITH ENTHUSIASM...
JOIN the L.D.V. Local Defence Volunteers
...PATRIOTISM... COURAGE...
...AND A SENSE OF LOYALTY FROM THE WORKING CLASS.
THE HOME GUARD COULD BECOME THE SPEARHEAD OF THE SOCIAL REVOLUTION AND AT THE SAME TIME A SHIELD AGAINST GERMAN INVASION.
YOU THINK SO?
GIVEN YOUR SERVICE RECORD, YOU MIGHT MAKE SERGEANT. WHAT DO YOU DO IN CIVILIAN LIFE, MAY I ASK?

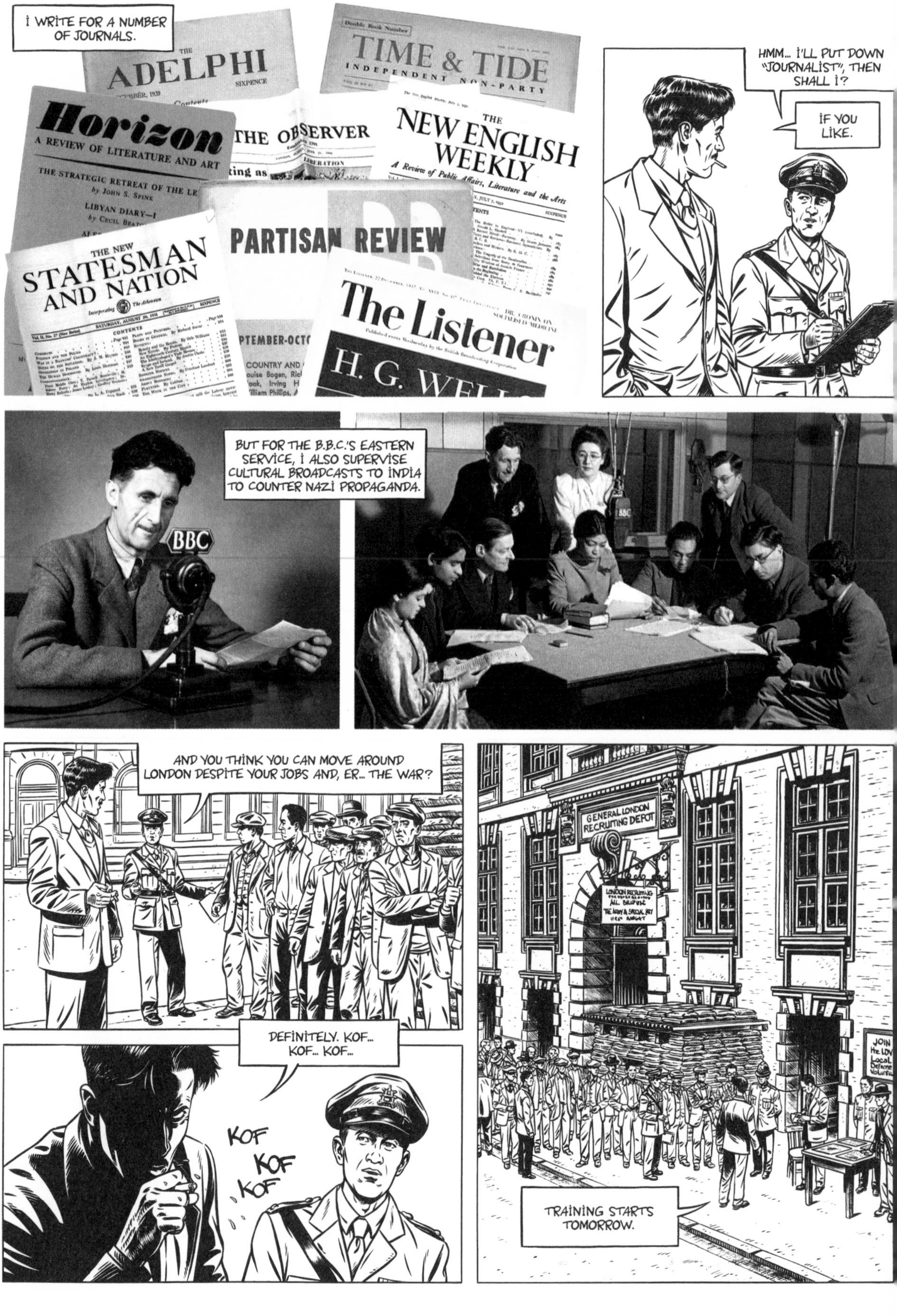

I WRITE FOR A NUMBER OF JOURNALS.
THE ADELPHI
TIME & TIDE
INDEPENDENT NON-PARTY
Horizon
A REVIEW OF LITERATURE AND ART
THE OBSERVER
THE NEW ENGLISH WEEKLY
A Review of Public Affairs, Literature and the Arts
PARTISAN REVIEW
THE NEW STATESMAN AND NATION
The Listener
H. G. WELLS
HMM... I'LL PUT DOWN "JOURNALIST", THEN SHALL I?
IF YOU LIKE.
BUT FOR THE B.B.C.'S EASTERN SERVICE, I ALSO SUPERVISE CULTURAL BROADCASTS TO INDIA TO COUNTER NAZI PROPAGANDA.
BBC
AND YOU THINK YOU CAN MOVE AROUND LONDON DESPITE YOUR JOBS AND, ER... THE WAR?
DEFINITELY. KOF... KOF... KOF...
KOF
KOF
KOF
GENERAL LONDON RECRUITING DEPOT
TRAINING STARTS TOMORROW.

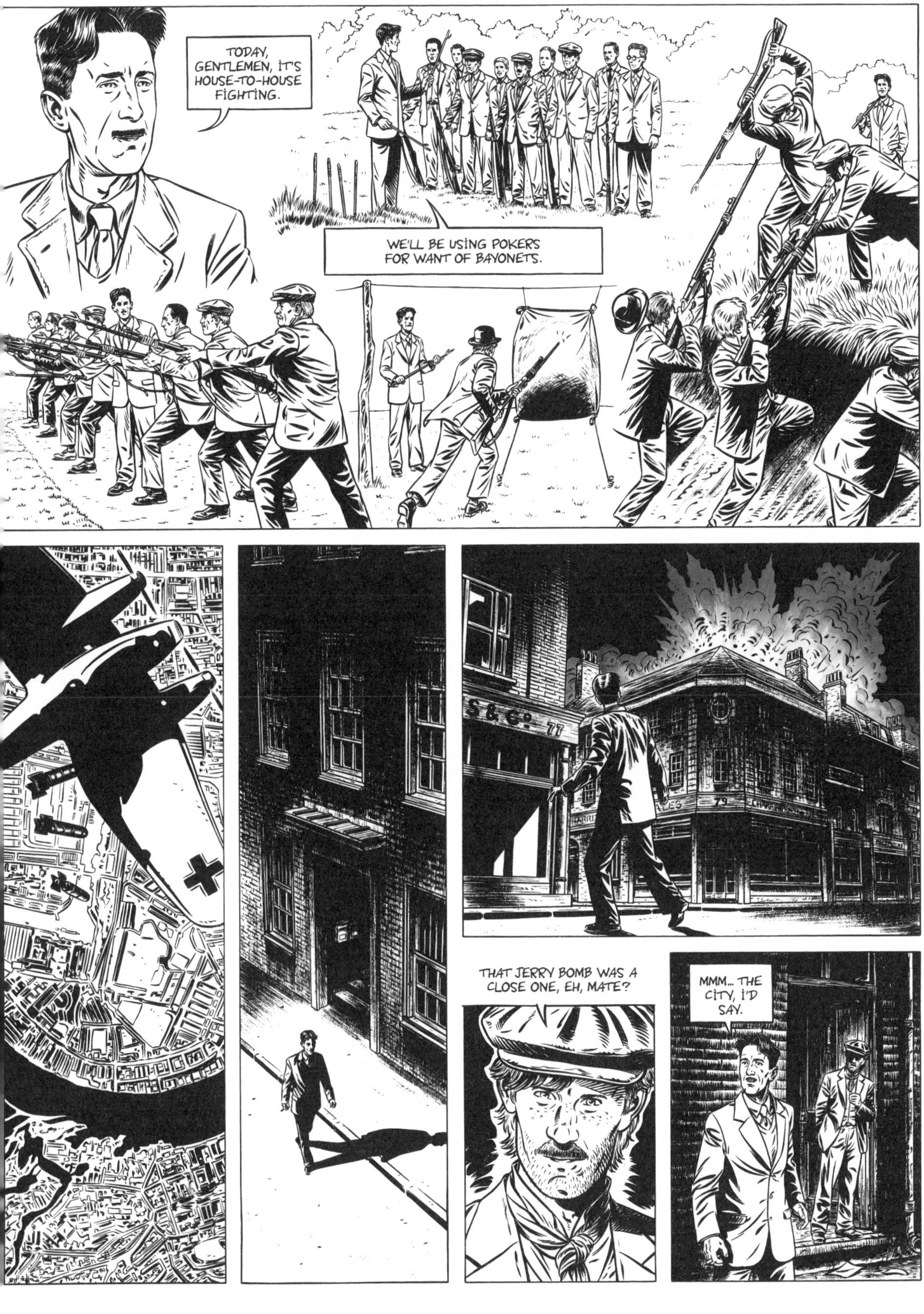
TODAY, GENTLEMEN, IT'S HOUSE-TO-HOUSE FIGHTING.
WE'LL BE USING POKERS FOR WANT OF BAYONETS.
THAT JERRY BOMB WAS A CLOSE ONE, EH, MATE?
MMM... THE CITY, I'D SAY.

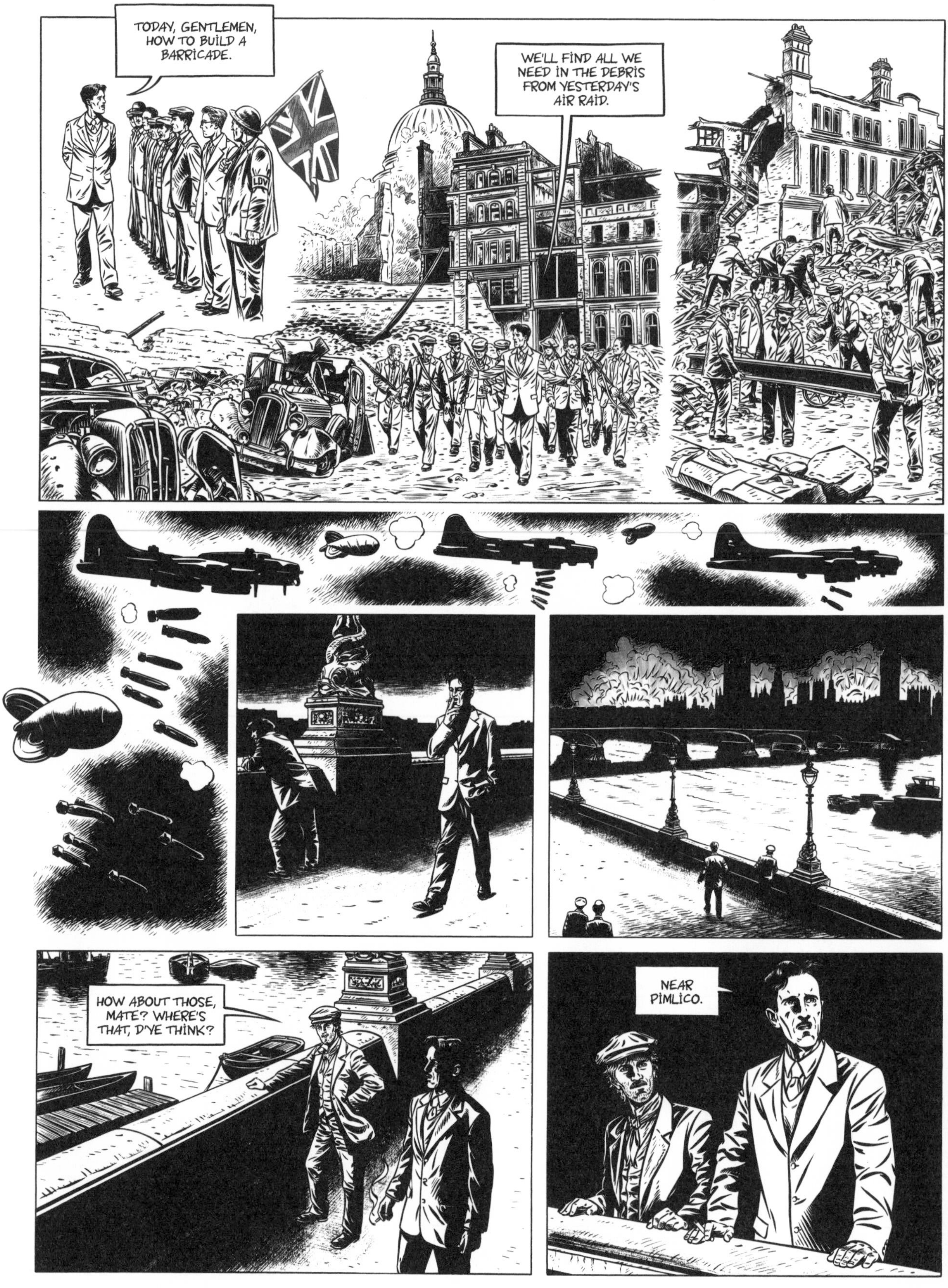
TODAY, GENTLEMEN, HOW TO BUILD A BARRICADE.
LDV
WE'LL FIND ALL WE NEED IN THE DEBRIS FROM YESTERDAY'S AIR RAID.
HOW ABOUT THOSE, MATE? WHERE'S THAT, D'YE THINK?
NEAR PIMLICO.

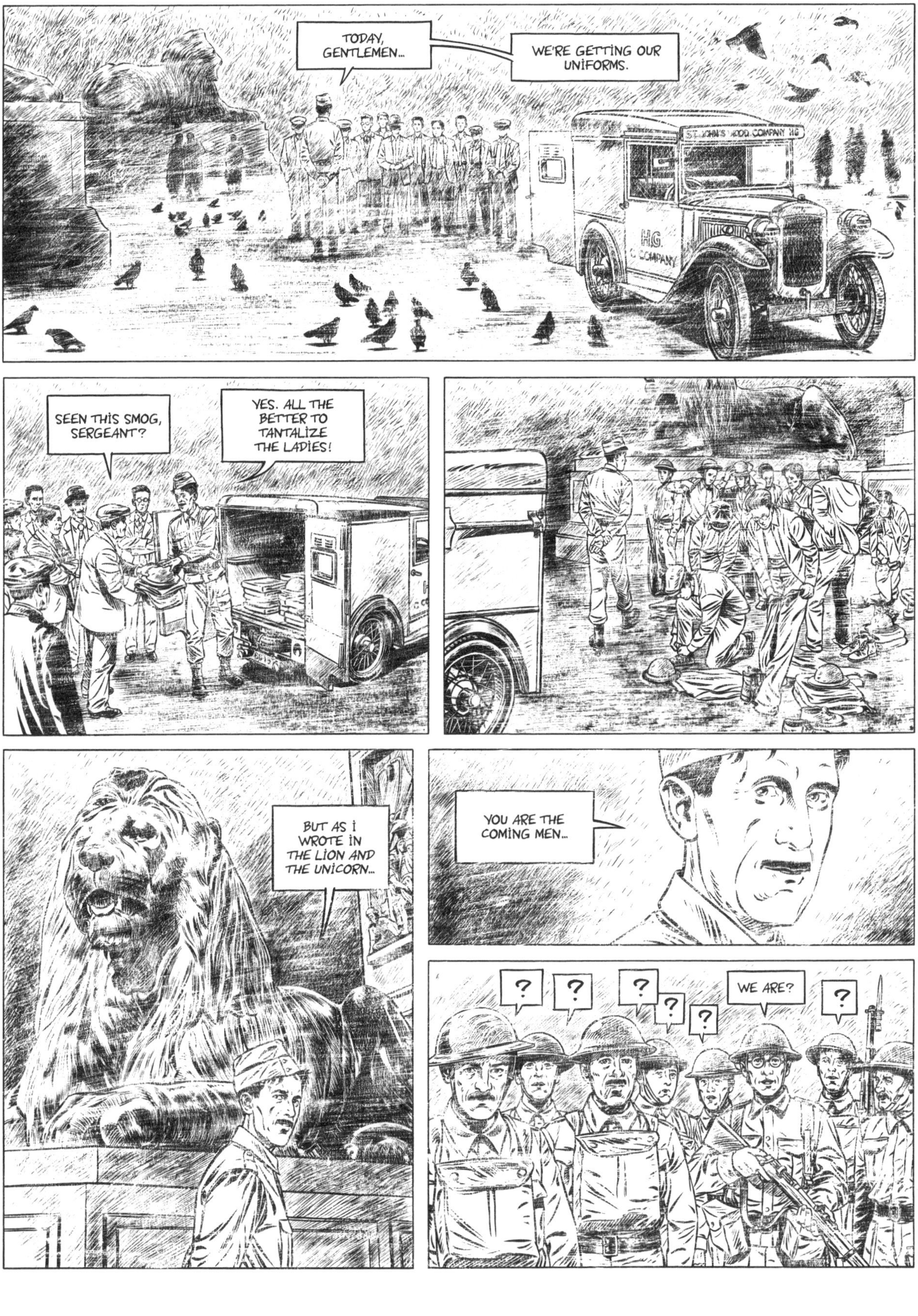
TODAY, GENTLEMEN...
WE'RE GETTING OUR UNIFORMS.
ST. JOHN'S WOOD COMPANY HG
H.G. C COMPANY
SEEN THIS SMOG, SERGEANT?
YES. ALL THE BETTER TO TANTALIZE THE LADIES!
BUT AS I WROTE IN THE LION AND THE UNICORN...
YOU ARE THE COMING MEN...
?
?
?
?
?
WE ARE?
?

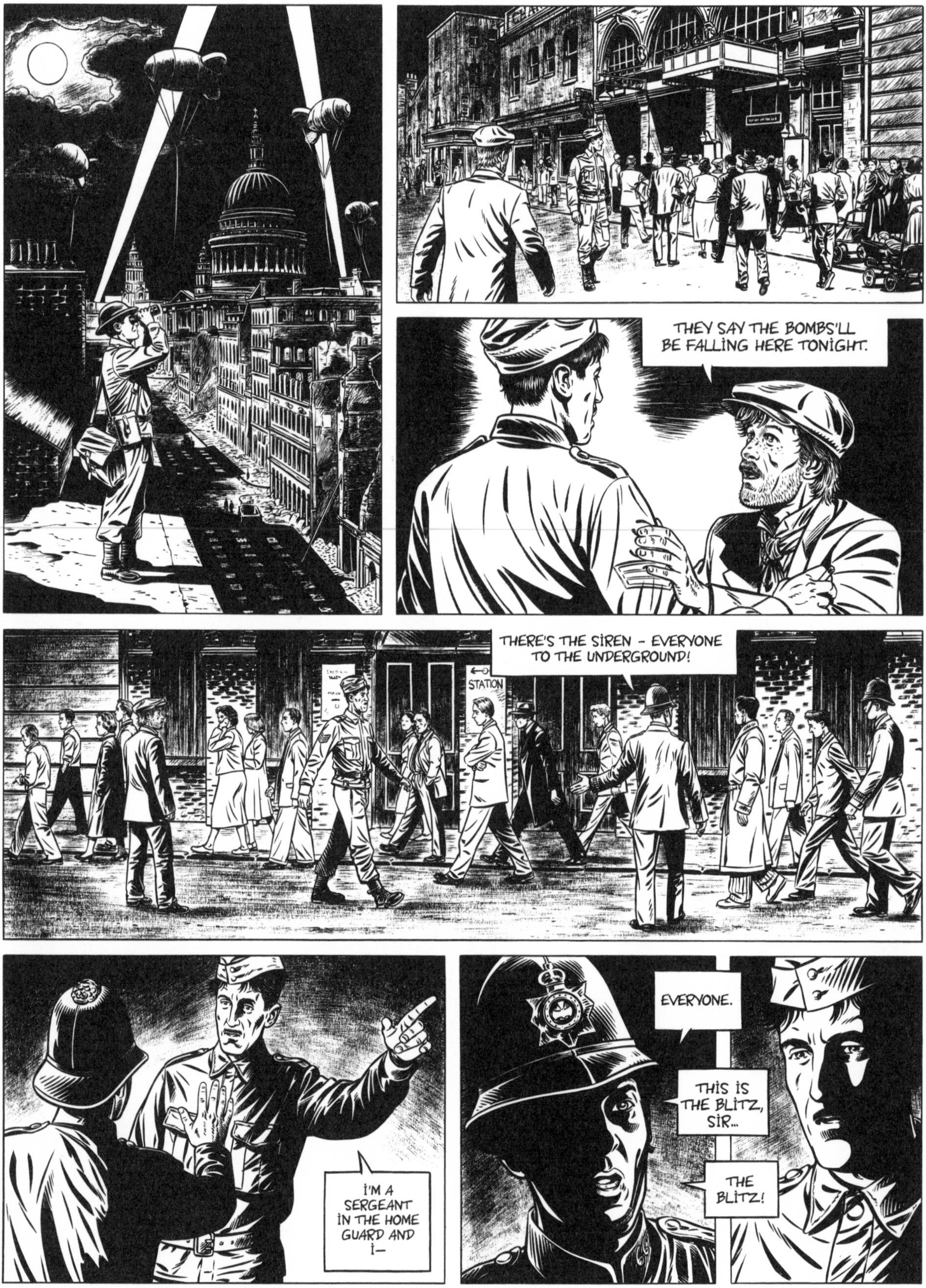
THEY SAY THE BOMBS'LL BE FALLING HERE TONIGHT.
THERE'S THE SIREN - EVERYONE TO THE UNDERGROUND!
STATION
I'M A SERGEANT IN THE HOME GUARD AND I–
EVERYONE.
THIS IS THE BLITZ, SIR...
THE BLITZ!

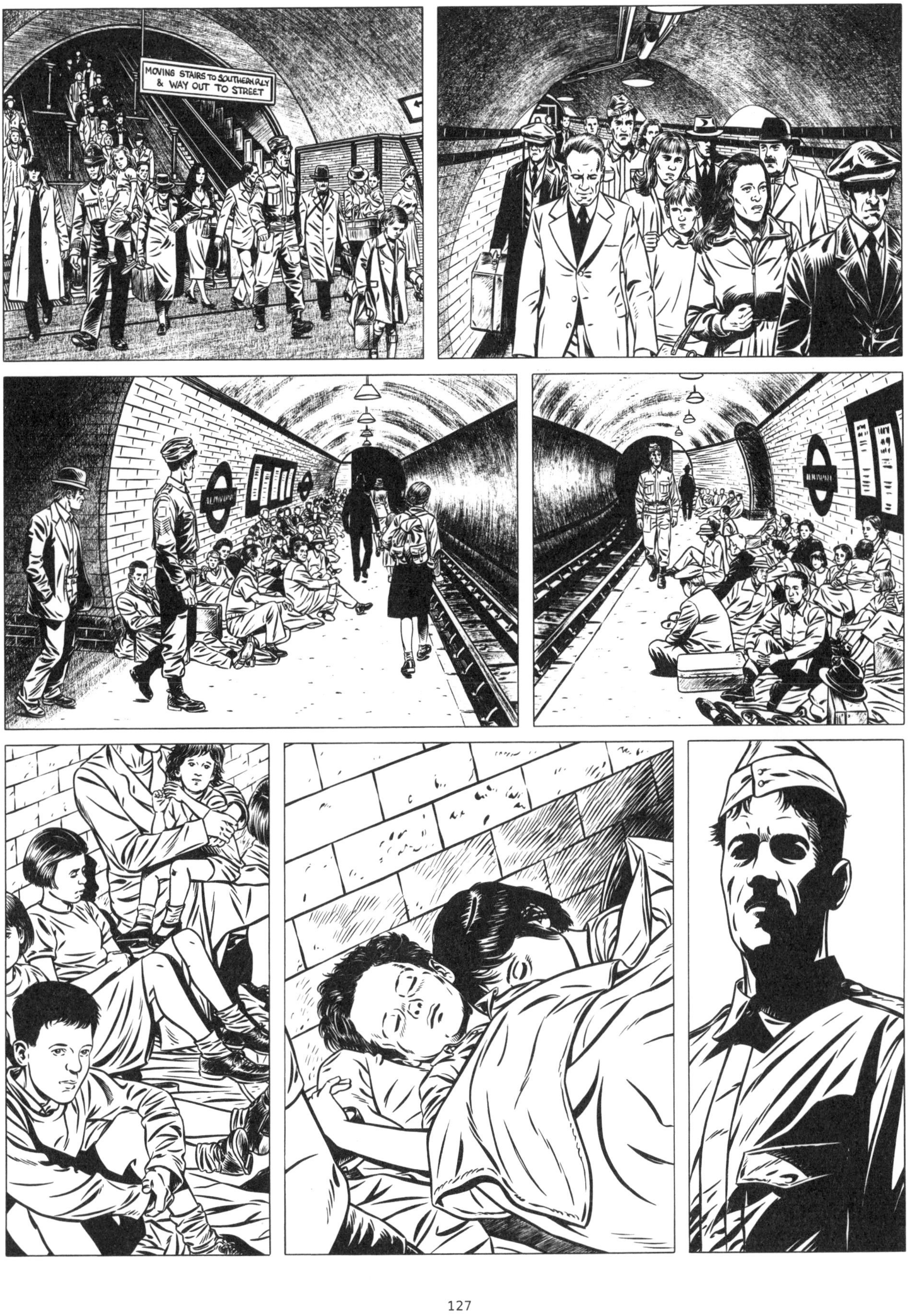
MOVING STAIRS TO SOUTHERN RLY
& WAY OUT TO STREET

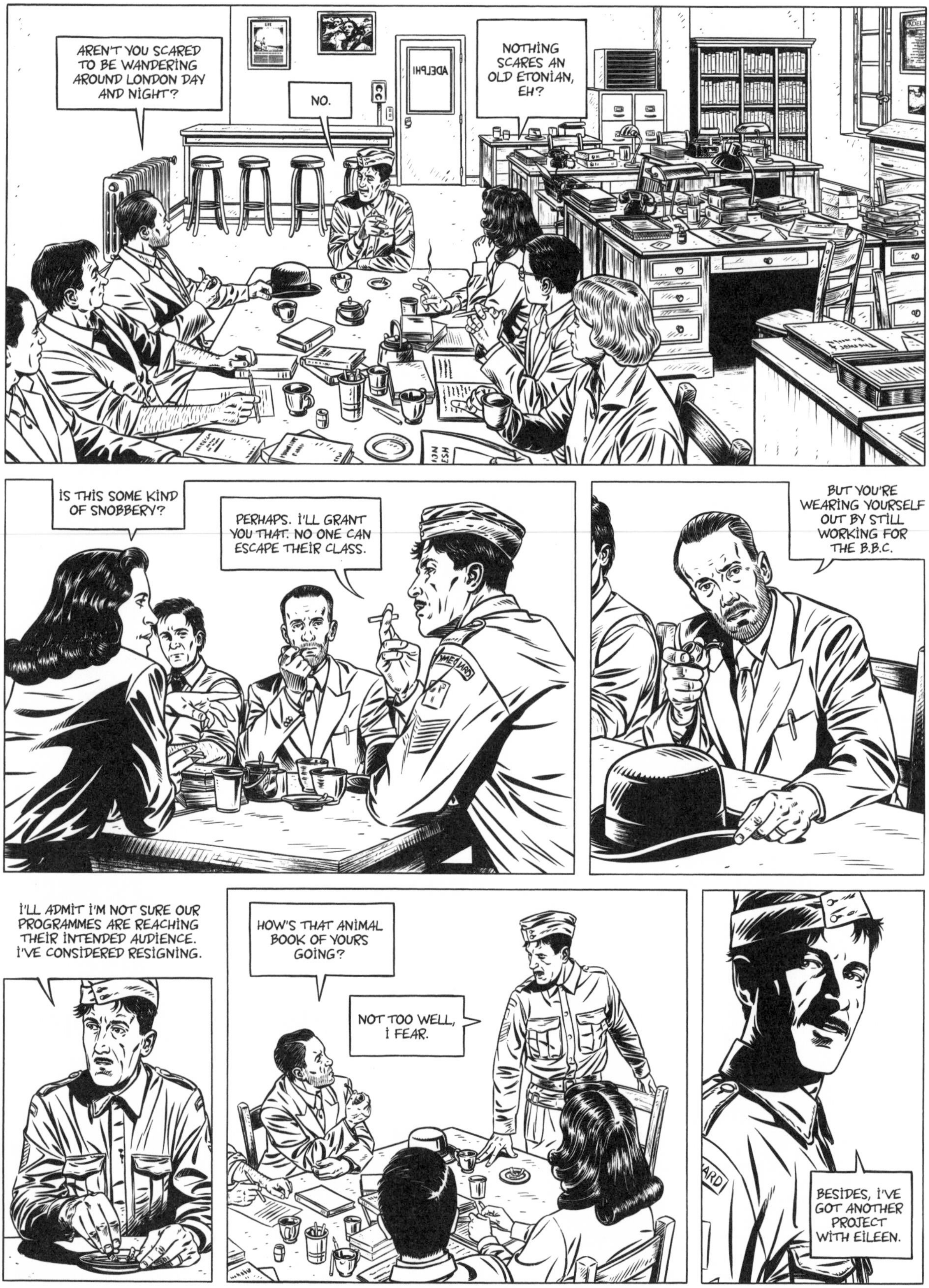
AREN'T YOU SCARED TO BE WANDERING AROUND LONDON DAY AND NIGHT?
NO.
NOTHING SCARES AN OLD ETONIAN, EH?
ADELPHI
IS THIS SOME KIND OF SNOBBERY?
PERHAPS. I'LL GRANT YOU THAT. NO ONE CAN ESCAPE THEIR CLASS.
BUT YOU'RE WEARING YOURSELF OUT BY STILL WORKING FOR THE B.B.C.
I'LL ADMIT I'M NOT SURE OUR PROGRAMMES ARE REACHING THEIR INTENDED AUDIENCE. I'VE CONSIDERED RESIGNING.
HOW'S THAT ANIMAL BOOK OF YOURS GOING?
NOT TOO WELL, I FEAR.
BESIDES, I'VE GOT ANOTHER PROJECT WITH EILEEN.

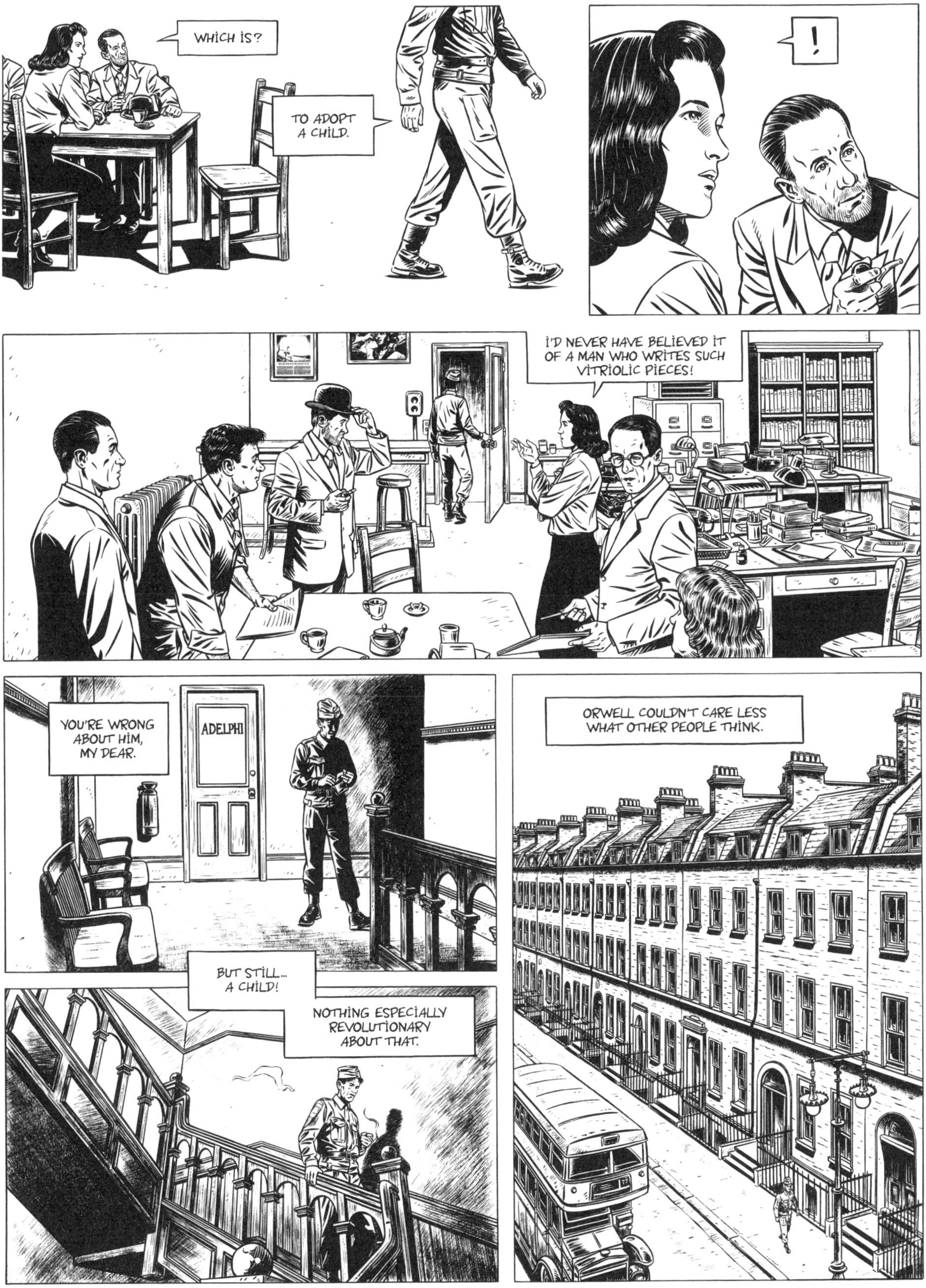
WHICH IS?
TO ADOPT A CHILD.
!
I'D NEVER HAVE BELIEVED IT OF A MAN WHO WRITES SUCH VITRIOLIC PIECES!
YOU'RE WRONG ABOUT HIM, MY DEAR.
ADELPHI
ORWELL COULDN'T CARE LESS WHAT OTHER PEOPLE THINK.
BUT STILL... A CHILD!
NOTHING ESPECIALLY REVOLUTIONARY ABOUT THAT.

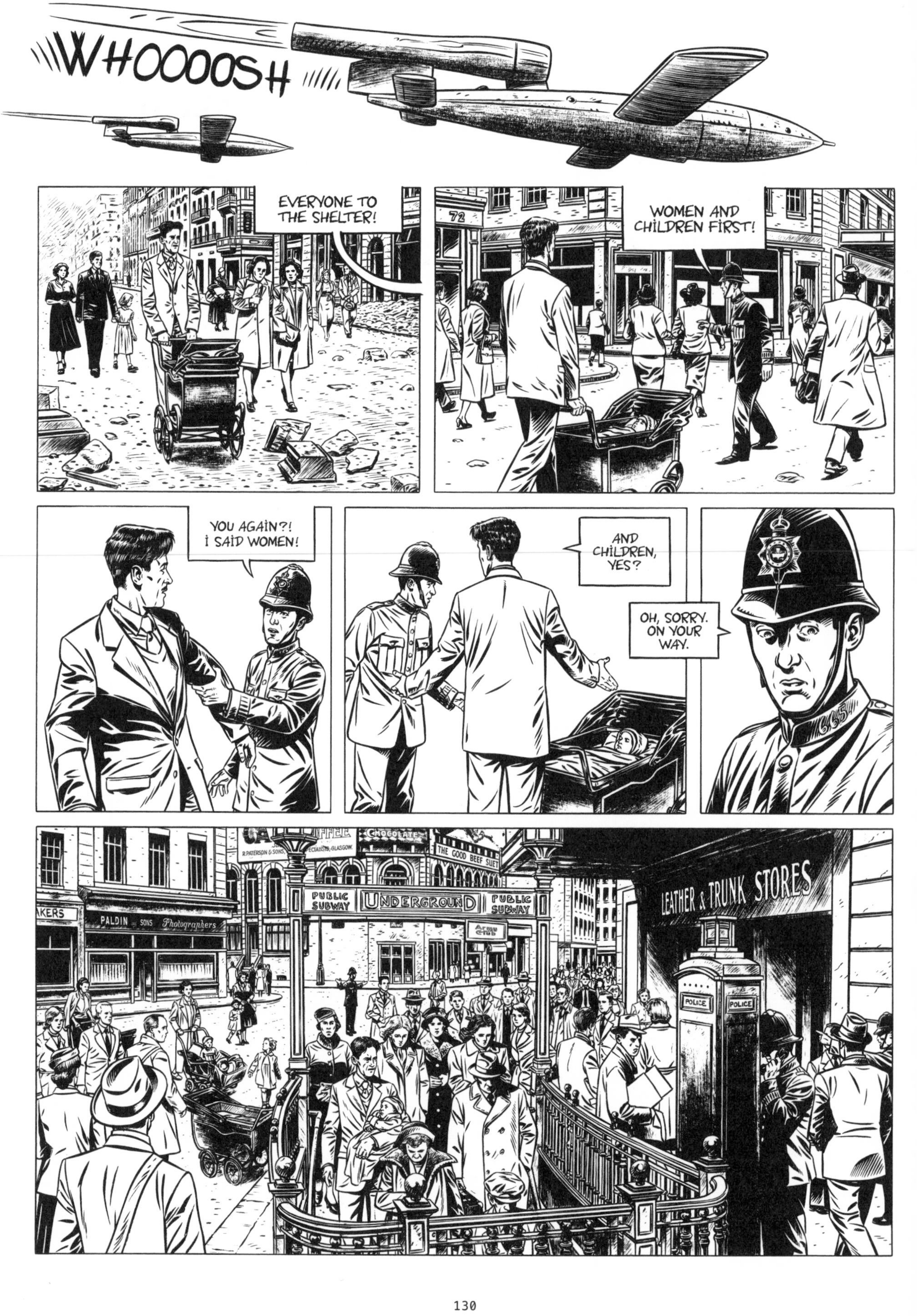
WHOOOOSH
EVERYONE TO THE SHELTER!
72
WOMEN AND CHILDREN FIRST!
YOU AGAIN?! I SAID WOMEN!
AND CHILDREN, YES?
OH, SORRY. ON YOUR WAY.
CHOCOLATE
THE GOOD BEEF SUET
AKERS
PALDIN & SONS Photographers
PUBLIC SUBWAY
UNDERGROUND
PUBLIC SUBWAY
LEATHER & TRUNK STORES
POLICE
POLICE

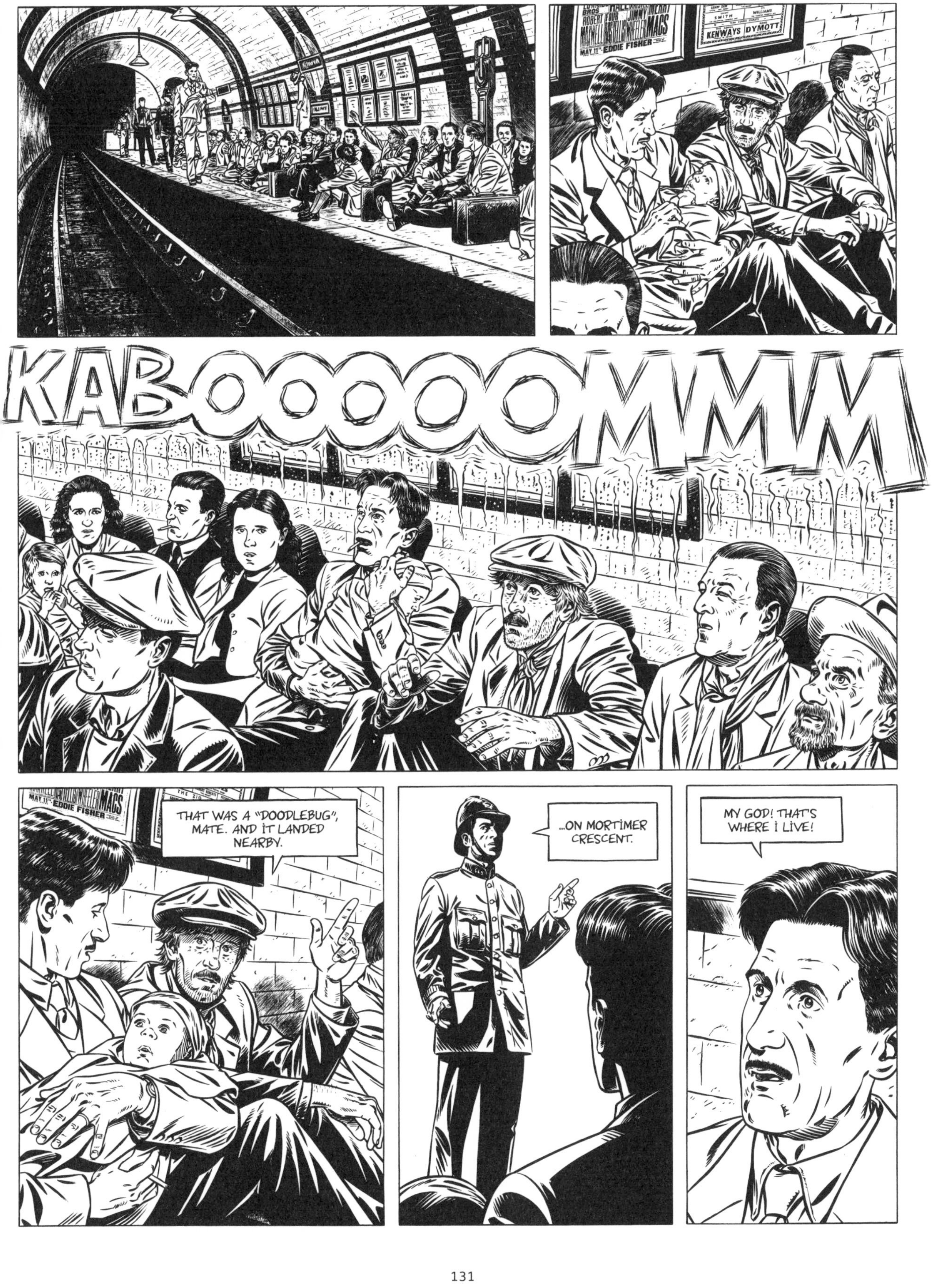
EDDIE FISHER
KENWAYS
DYMOTT
KABOOOOOMMMM
THAT WAS A "DOODLEBUG", MATE. AND IT LANDED NEARBY.
...ON MORTIMER CRESCENT.
MY GOD! THAT'S WHERE I LIVE!

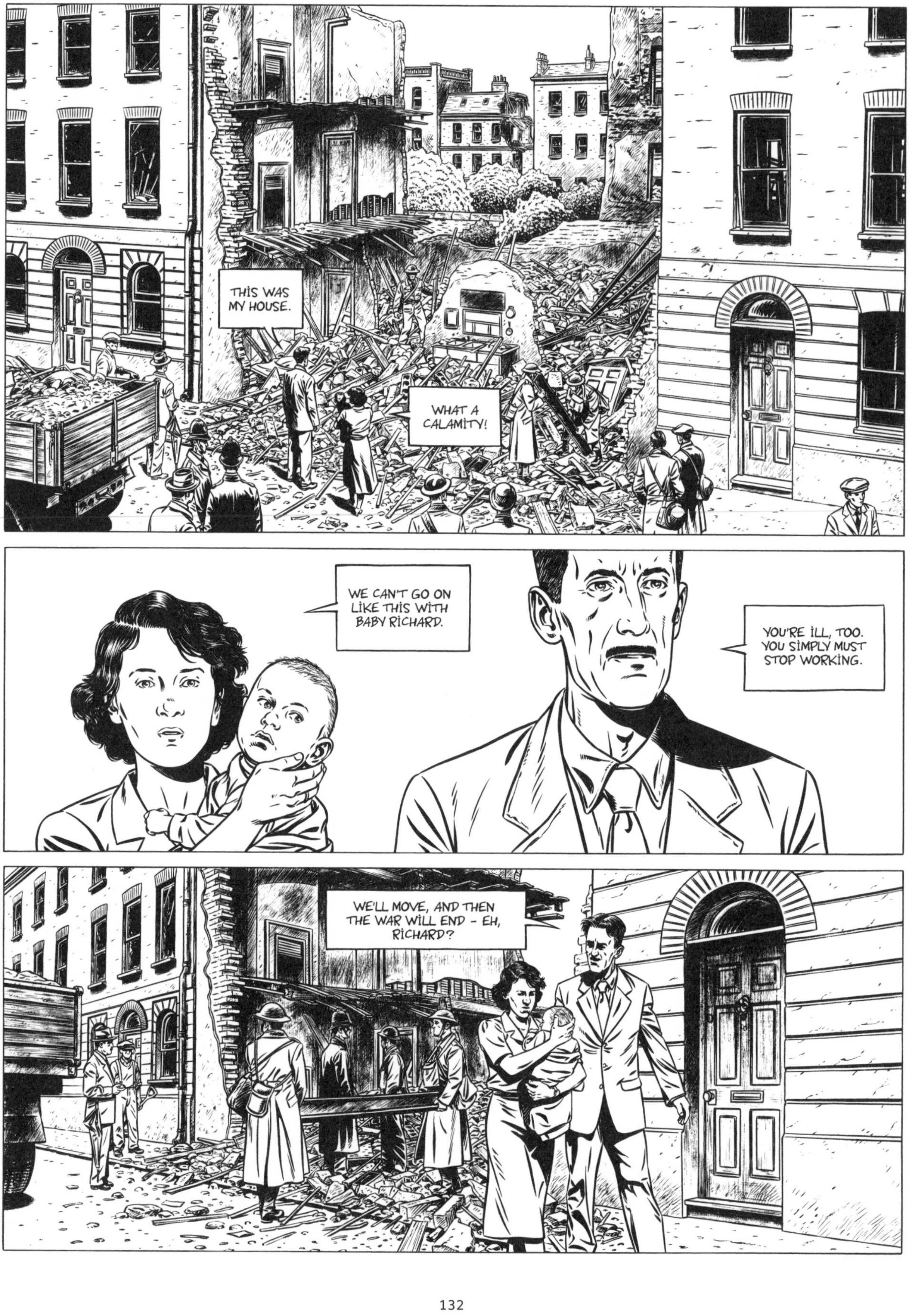
THIS WAS MY HOUSE.
WHAT A CALAMITY!
WE CAN'T GO ON LIKE THIS WITH BABY RICHARD.
YOU'RE ILL, TOO. YOU SIMPLY MUST STOP WORKING.
WE'LL MOVE, AND THEN THE WAR WILL END - EH, RICHARD?

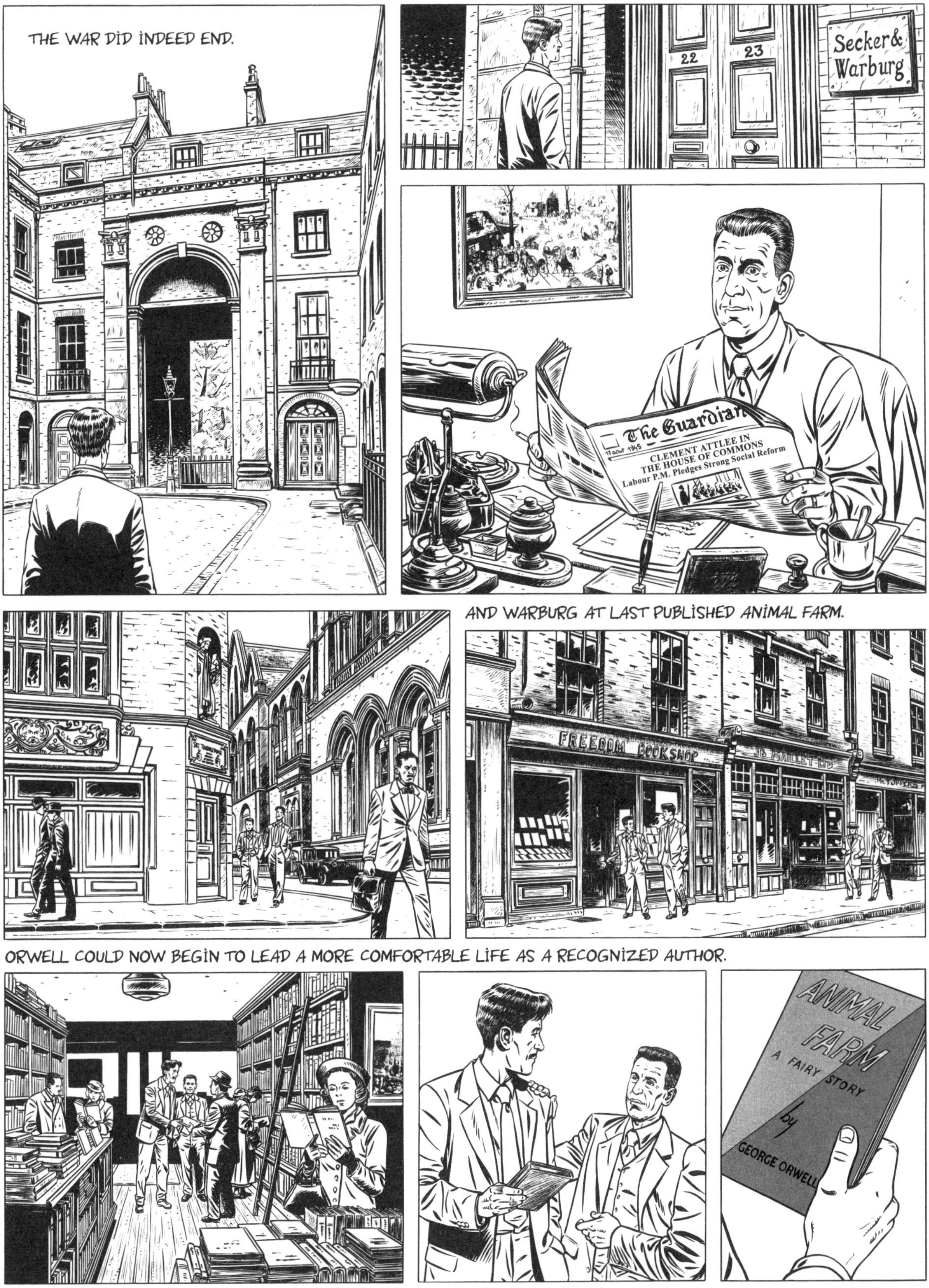
THE WAR DID INDEED END.
Secker & Warburg
22
23
The Guardian
17 août 1945
CLEMENT ATTLEE IN THE HOUSE OF COMMONS
Labour P.M. Pledges Strong Social Reform
AND WARBURG AT LAST PUBLISHED ANIMAL FARM.
FREEDOM BOOKSHOP
JB MAILLET LTD
ORWELL COULD NOW BEGIN TO LEAD A MORE COMFORTABLE LIFE AS A RECOGNIZED AUTHOR.
ANIMAL FARM
A FAIRY STORY
by
GEORGE ORWELL

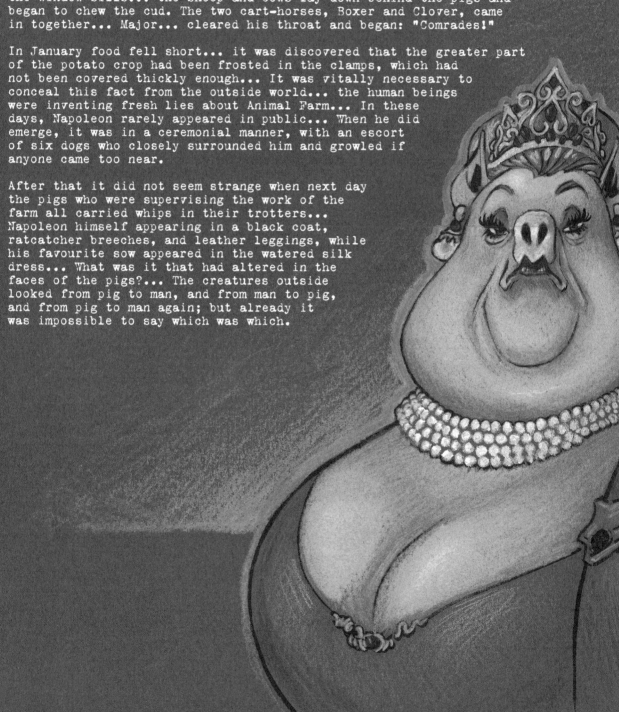

ALL ANIMALS ARE EQUAL
BUT SOME ANIMALS ARE MORE
EQUAL THAN OTHERS

Before long the other animals began to arrive... First came the three
dogs, Bluebell, Jessie, and Pincher... The hens perched themselves on
the window-sills... the sheep and cows lay down behind the pigs and
began to chew the cud. The two cart-horses, Boxer and Clover, came
in together... Major... cleared his throat and began: "Comrades!"

In January food fell short... it was discovered that the greater part
of the potato crop had been frosted in the clamps, which had
not been covered thickly enough... It was vitally necessary to
conceal this fact from the outside world... the human beings
were inventing fresh lies about Animal Farm... In these
days, Napoleon rarely appeared in public... When he did
emerge, it was in a ceremonial manner, with an escort
of six dogs who closely surrounded him and growled if
anyone came too near.

After that it did not seem strange when next day
the pigs who were supervising the work of the
farm all carried whips in their trotters...
Napoleon himself appearing in a black coat,
ratcatcher breeches, and leather leggings, while
his favourite sow appeared in the watered silk
dress... What was it that had altered in the
faces of the pigs?... The creatures outside
looked from pig to man, and from man to pig,
and from pig to man again; but already it
was impossible to say which was which.

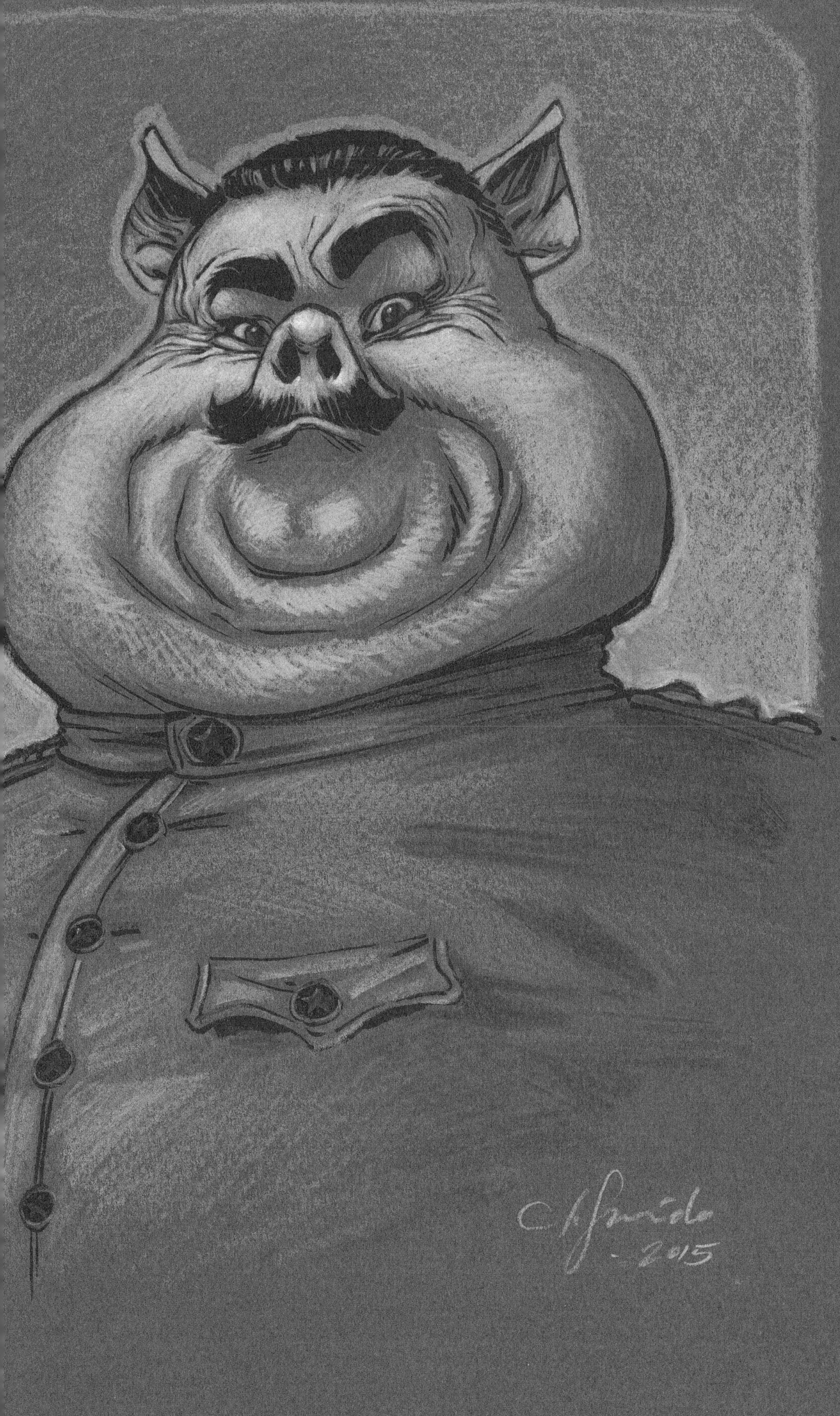

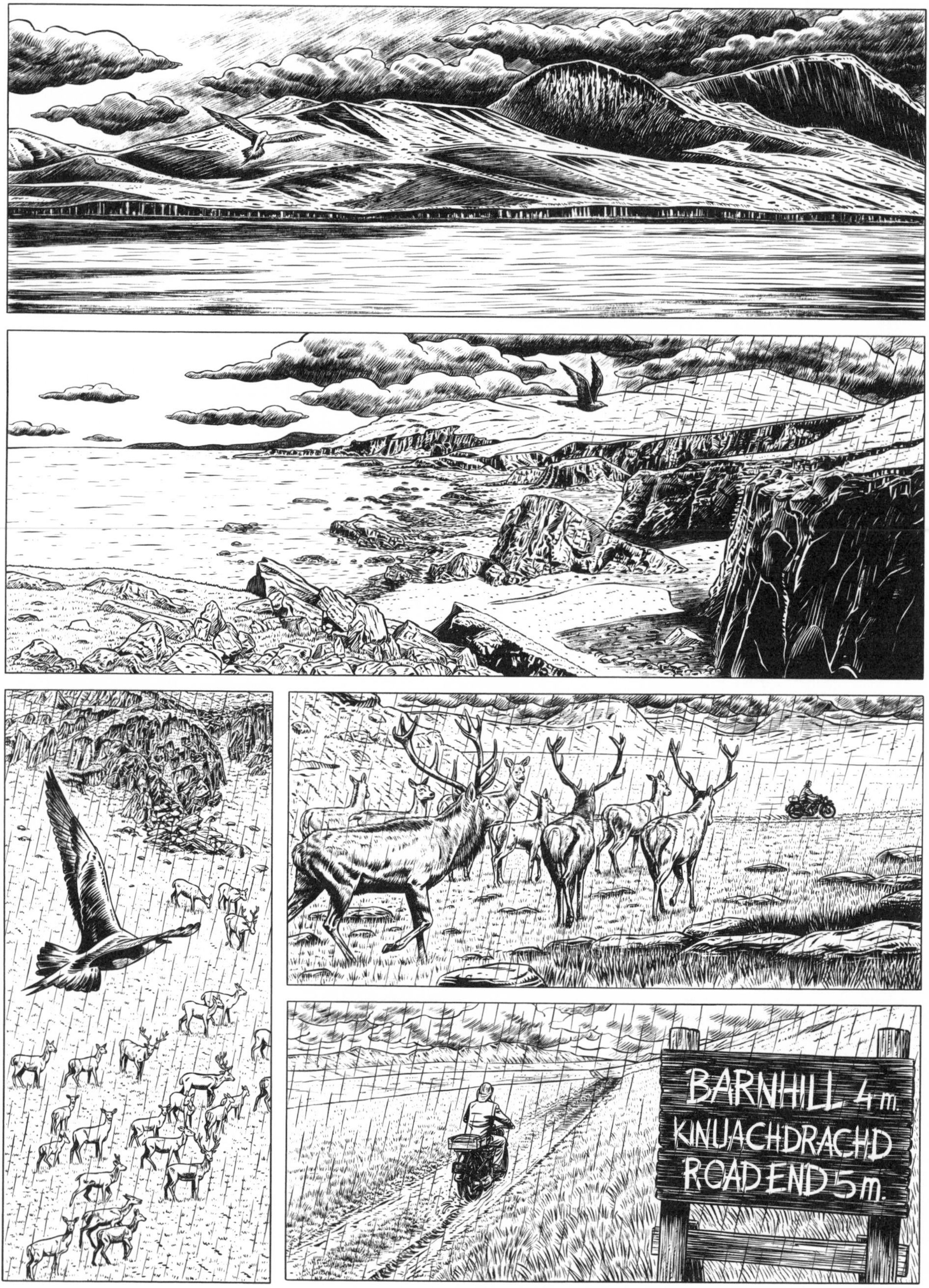
BARNHILL 4 m.
KINUACHDRACHD
ROAD END 5 m.

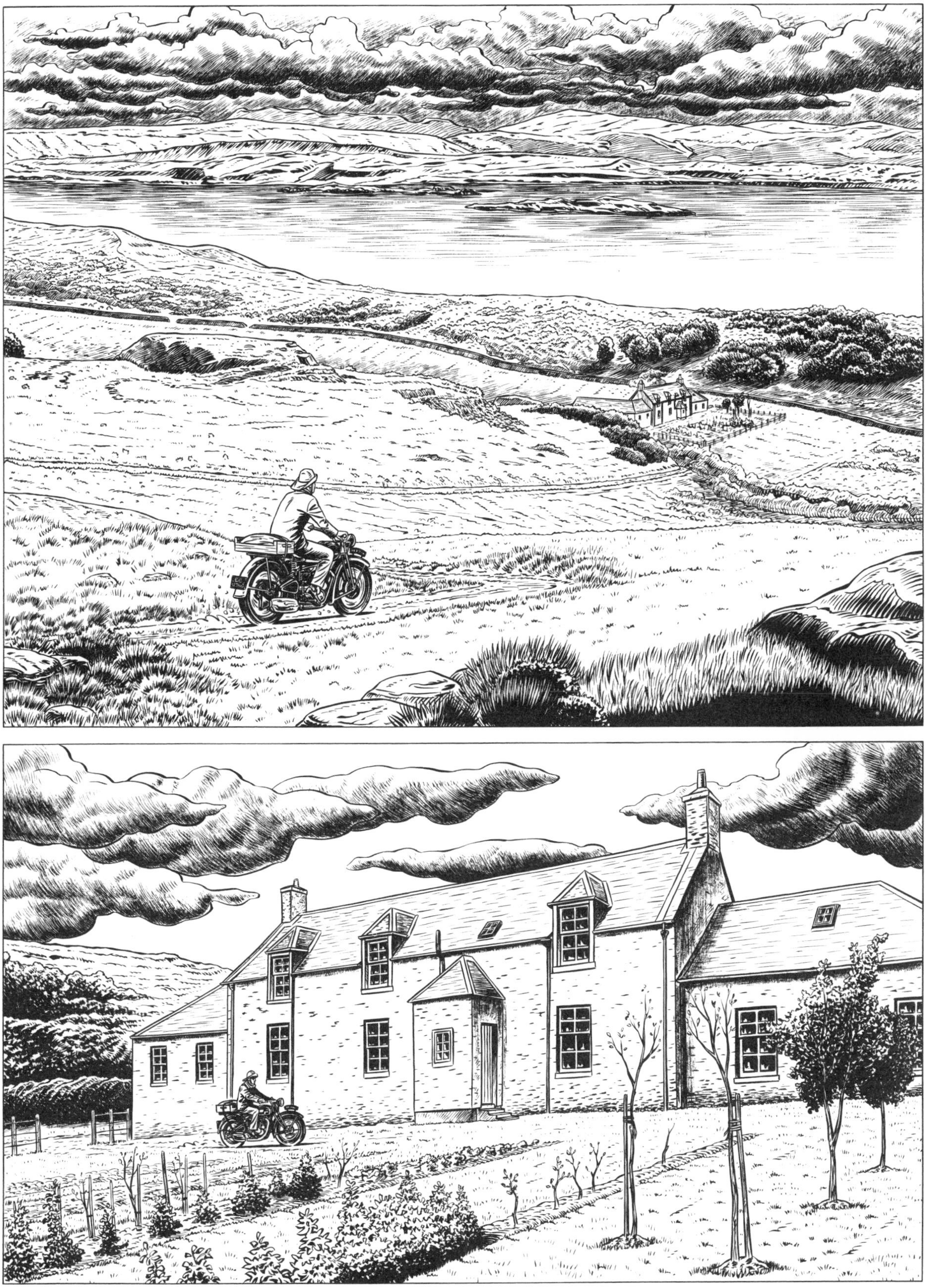

AVRIL?

THERE YOU ARE AT LAST!

I'VE BROUGHT LOTS OF NICE THINGS FOR RICHARD TO EAT.

AND ALSO SOME SEEDLINGS FOR THE GARDEN.

WE'LL PLANT THINGS TOGETHER, EH, LITTLE CHAP?

AND... SOME FOOD FOR US?

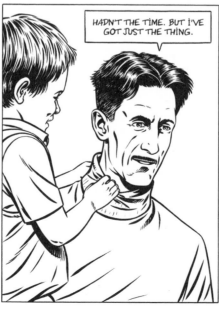

HADN'T THE TIME. BUT I'VE GOT JUST THE THING.

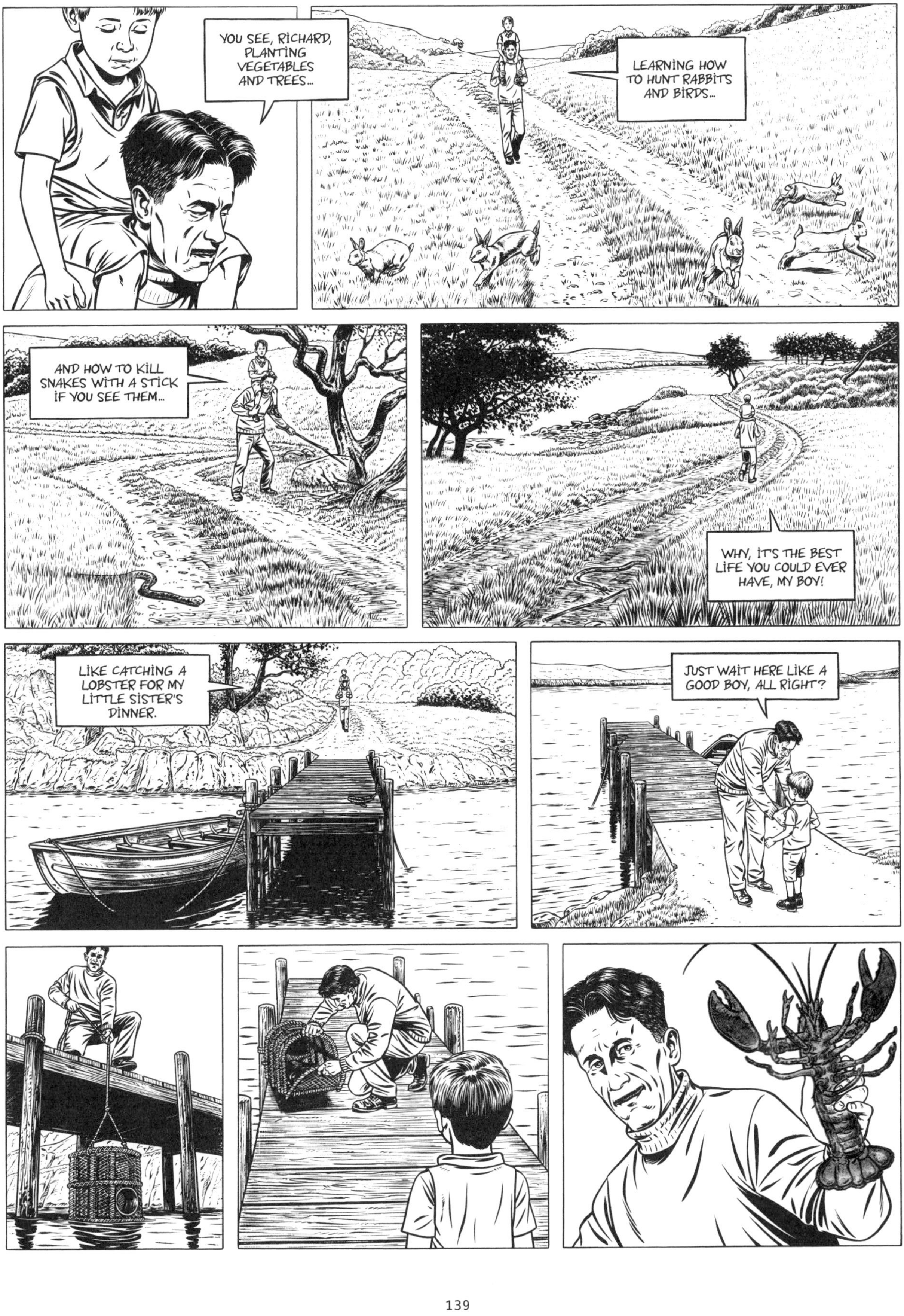
YOU SEE, RICHARD, PLANTING VEGETABLES AND TREES...
LEARNING HOW TO HUNT RABBITS AND BIRDS...
AND HOW TO KILL SNAKES WITH A STICK IF YOU SEE THEM...
WHY, IT'S THE BEST LIFE YOU COULD EVER HAVE, MY BOY!
LIKE CATCHING A LOBSTER FOR MY LITTLE SISTER'S DINNER.
JUST WAIT HERE LIKE A GOOD BOY, ALL RIGHT?

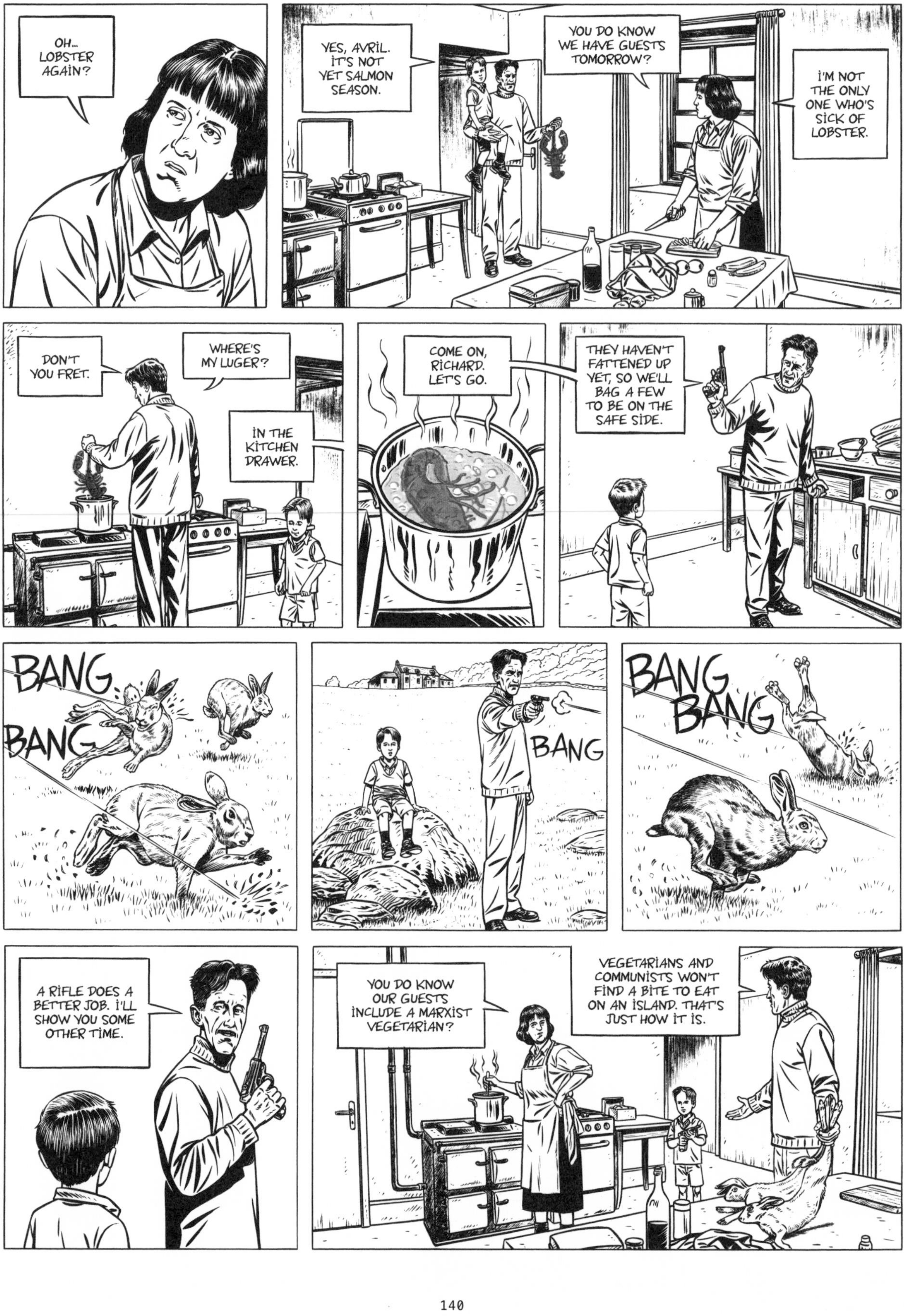
OH... LOBSTER AGAIN?
YES, AVRIL. IT'S NOT YET SALMON SEASON.
YOU DO KNOW WE HAVE GUESTS TOMORROW?
I'M NOT THE ONLY ONE WHO'S SICK OF LOBSTER.
DON'T YOU FRET.
WHERE'S MY LUGER?
IN THE KITCHEN DRAWER.
COME ON, RICHARD. LET'S GO.
THEY HAVEN'T FATTENED UP YET, SO WE'LL BAG A FEW TO BE ON THE SAFE SIDE.
BANG
BANG
BANG
BANG
BANG
A RIFLE DOES A BETTER JOB. I'LL SHOW YOU SOME OTHER TIME.
YOU DO KNOW OUR GUESTS INCLUDE A MARXIST VEGETARIAN?
VEGETARIANS AND COMMUNISTS WON'T FIND A BITE TO EAT ON AN ISLAND. THAT'S JUST HOW IT IS.

ORWELL WAS NOW A FAMOUS AUTHOR AND JOURNALIST, RUBBING SHOULDERS WITH SOME OF THE GREAT NAMES OF LITERATURE, SUCH AS HIS FRIEND ARTHUR KOESTLER, ANOTHER OUTSPOKEN CRITIC OF THE SOVIET REGIME.

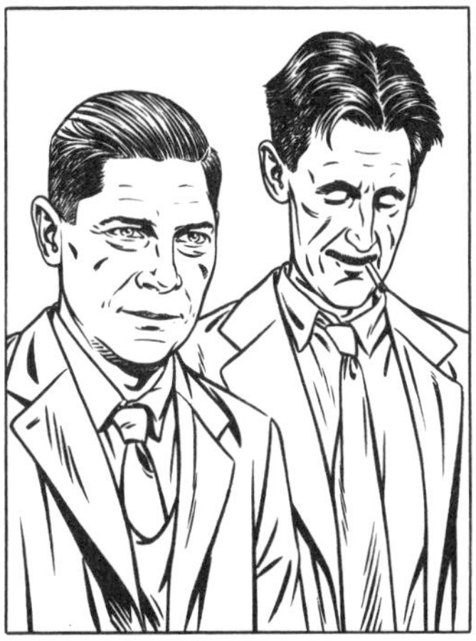

DURING ONE OF HIS TRIPS AWAY, EILEEN DIED DURING AN OPERATION. DEVASTATED, ORWELL PROPOSED MARRIAGE TO EVERY WOMAN HE MET IN THE LONDON SALONS.

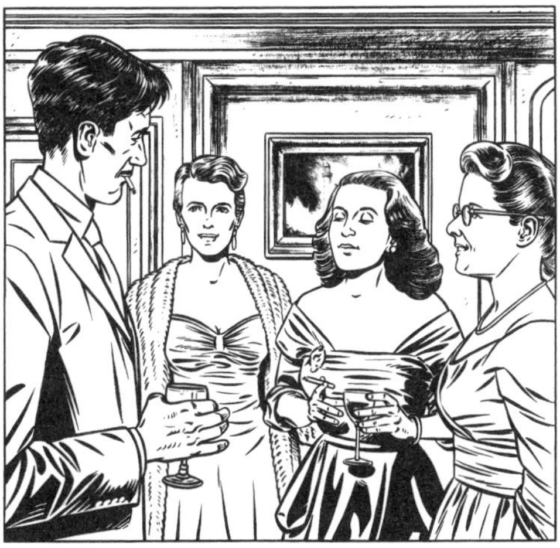

ONE OF THEM, THE BEAUTIFUL SONIA BROWNELL - LATER A MODEL FOR A CHARACTER IN A MARGUERITE DURAS NOVEL - WAS PLAYING HARD-TO-GET.

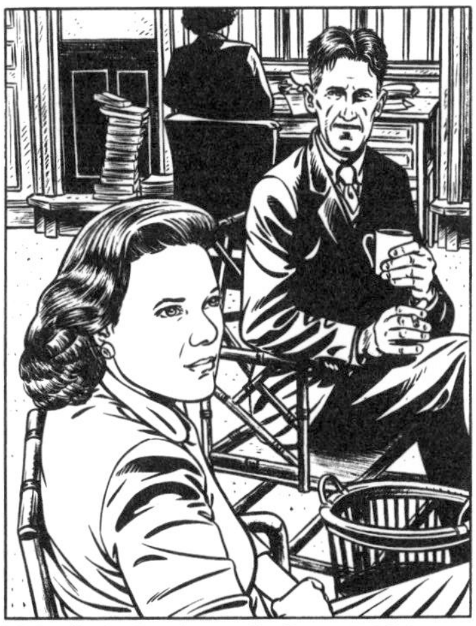

SHE NEVER VISITED THE HEBRIDEAN ISLAND OF JURA, TO WHERE ORWELL HAD DECIDED TO RETIRE IN 1946, TO WRITE WHAT HE WAS THEN STILL CALLING "THE LAST MAN IN EUROPE".

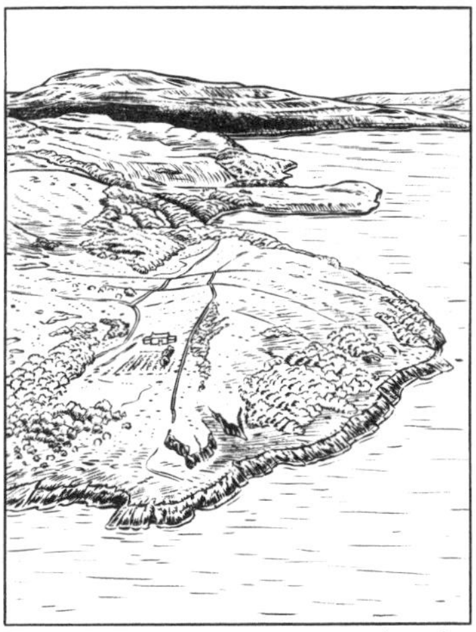

DESPITE THE LACK OF HOME COMFORTS, AND HIS OWN PHYSICAL FRAILTY, ORWELL ENTHUSIASTICALLY SET ABOUT A SERIES OF PROJECTS ABOUT THE HOUSE AND GARDEN OF BARNHILL.

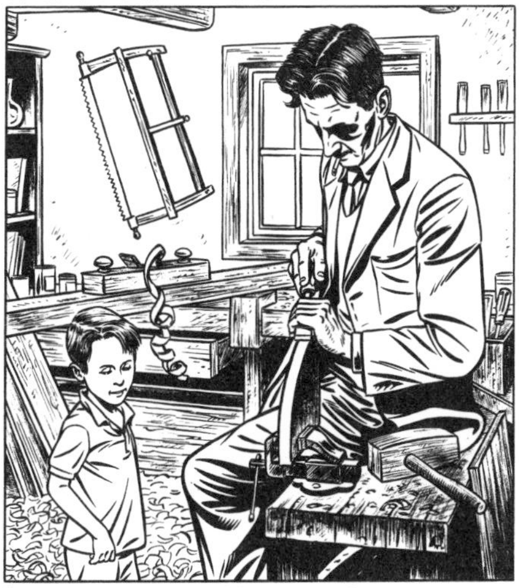

HE REMAINED PASSIONATE ABOUT FLORA AND FAUNA, AND, ASIDE FROM HIS WORK AS A WRITER, THE SUBJECT OF POLITICS WAS BANNED FROM ALL CONVERSATION, AS WELL AS FROM HIS PERSONAL DIARIES.

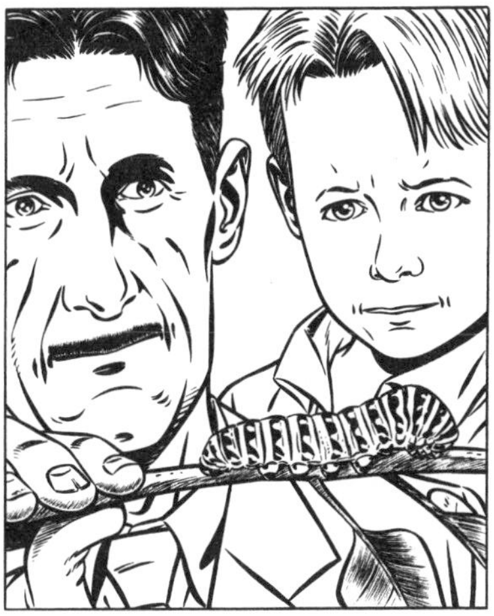

HIS SISTER AVRIL CAME TO HELP HIM RAISE RICHARD, WHOM HE ADORED, AND A FEW OLD FRIENDS LIKE RICHARD REES CAME TO VISIT - SOMETIMES EVEN A FEW CHILDREN FROM THE MAINLAND.

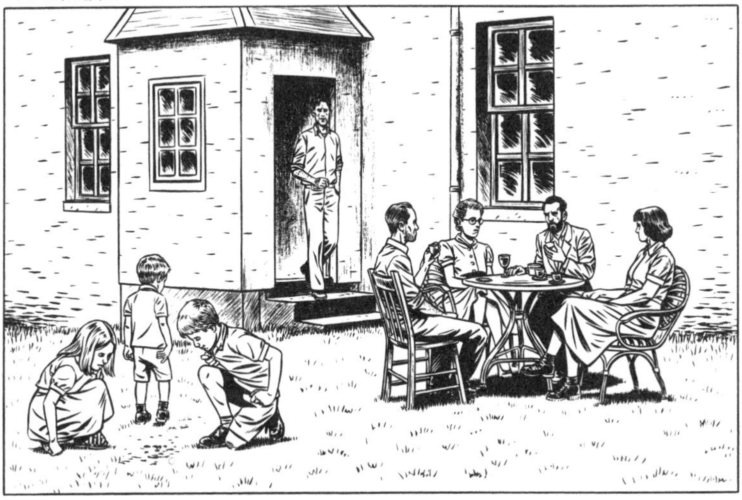

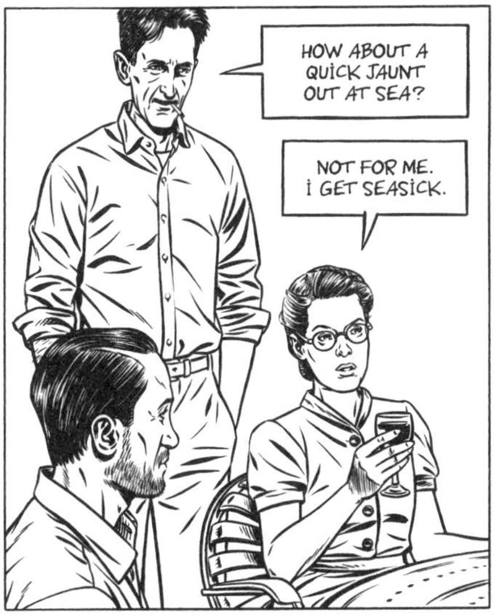
HOW ABOUT A QUICK JAUNT OUT AT SEA?
NOT FOR ME. I GET SEASICK.

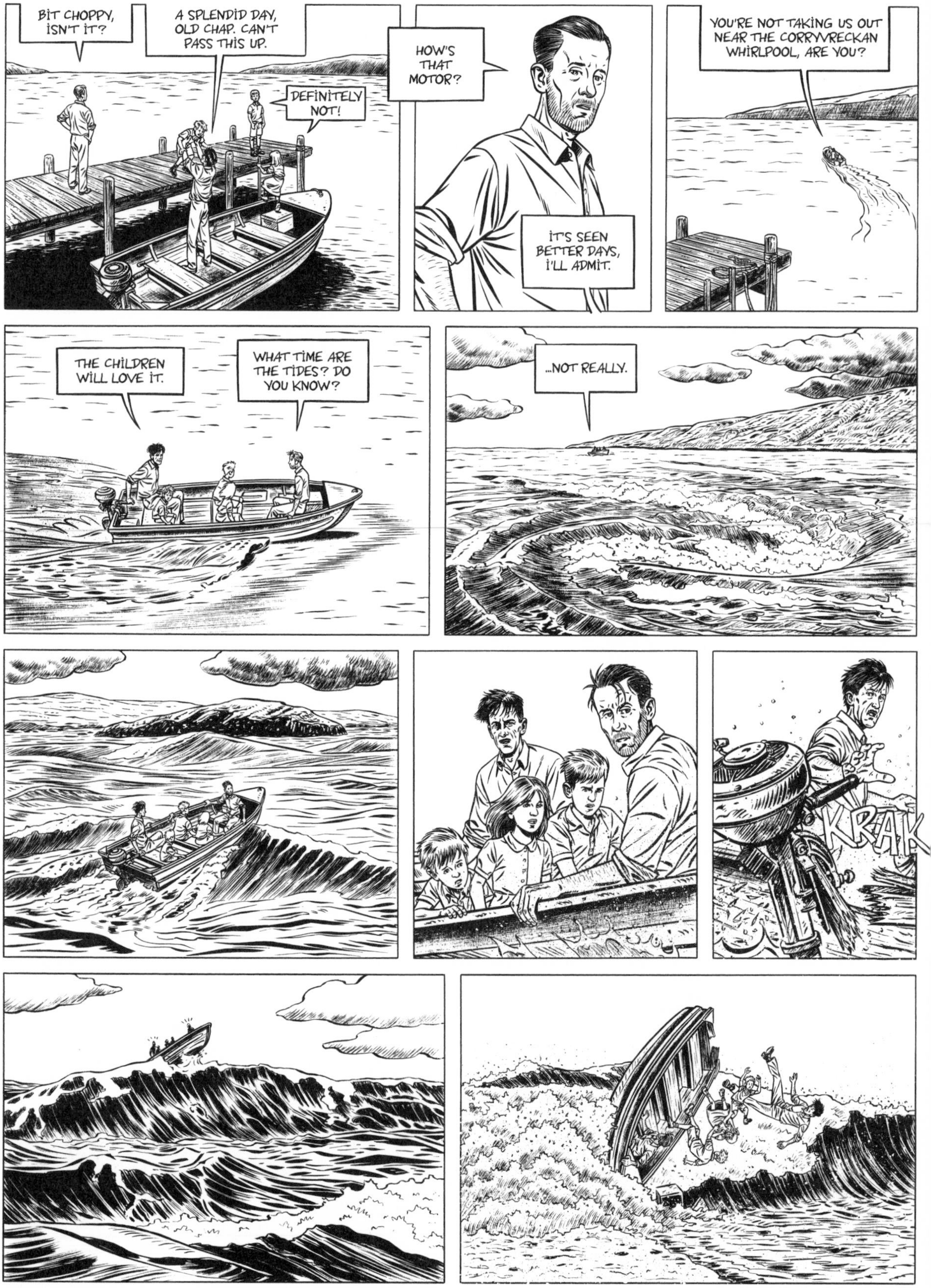
BIT CHOPPY, ISN'T IT?
A SPLENDID DAY, OLD CHAP. CAN'T PASS THIS UP.
DEFINITELY NOT!
HOW'S THAT MOTOR?
IT'S SEEN BETTER DAYS, I'LL ADMIT.
YOU'RE NOT TAKING US OUT NEAR THE CORRYVRECKAN WHIRLPOOL, ARE YOU?
THE CHILDREN WILL LOVE IT.
WHAT TIME ARE THE TIDES? DO YOU KNOW?
...NOT REALLY.
KRAK

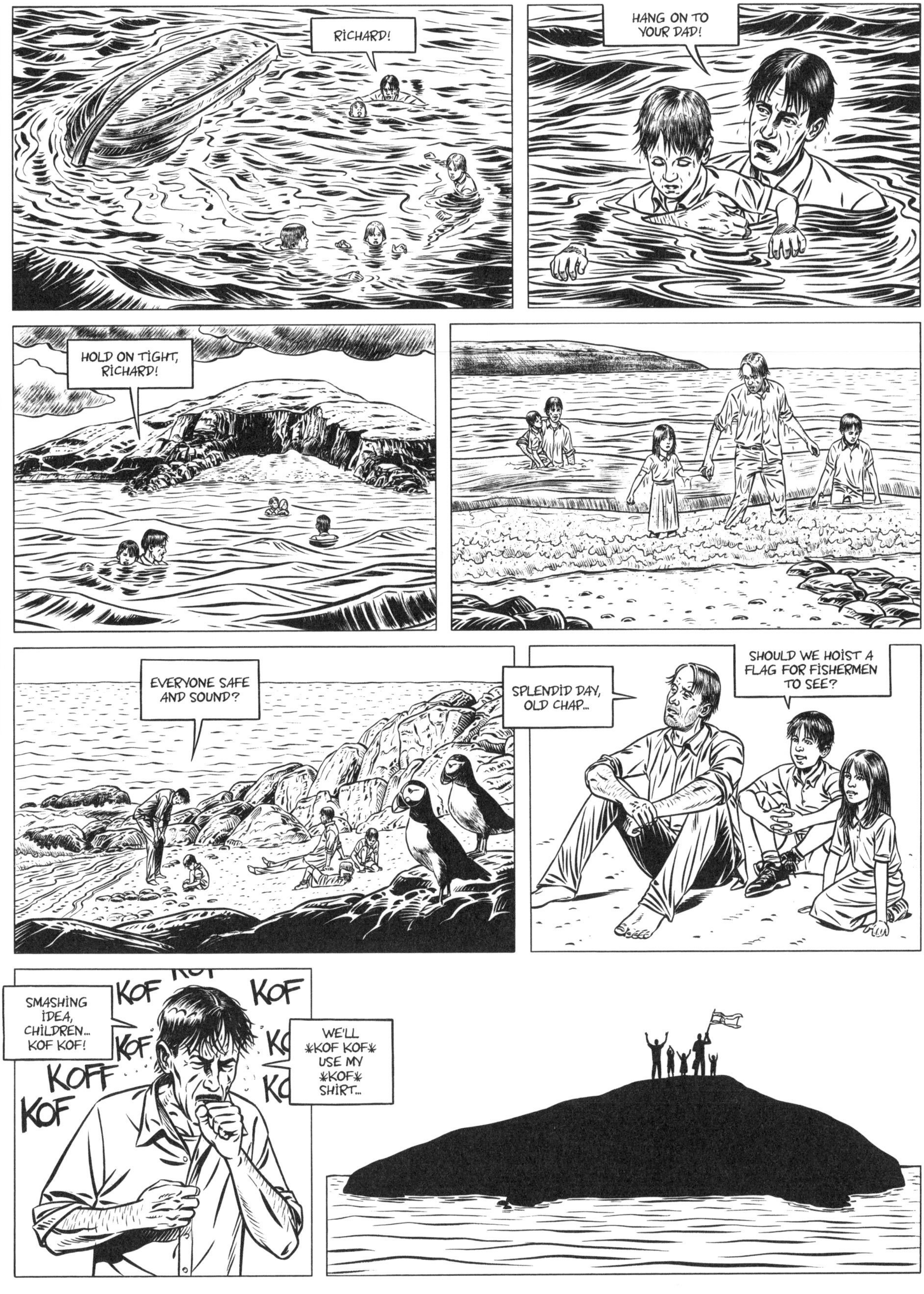
RICHARD!
HANG ON TO YOUR DAD!
HOLD ON TIGHT, RICHARD!
EVERYONE SAFE AND SOUND?
SPLENDID DAY, OLD CHAP...
SHOULD WE HOIST A FLAG FOR FISHERMEN TO SEE?
SMASHING IDEA, CHILDREN... KOF KOF!
KOF
KOF
KOF
KOFF
KOF
WE'LL *KOF KOF* USE MY *KOF* SHIRT...

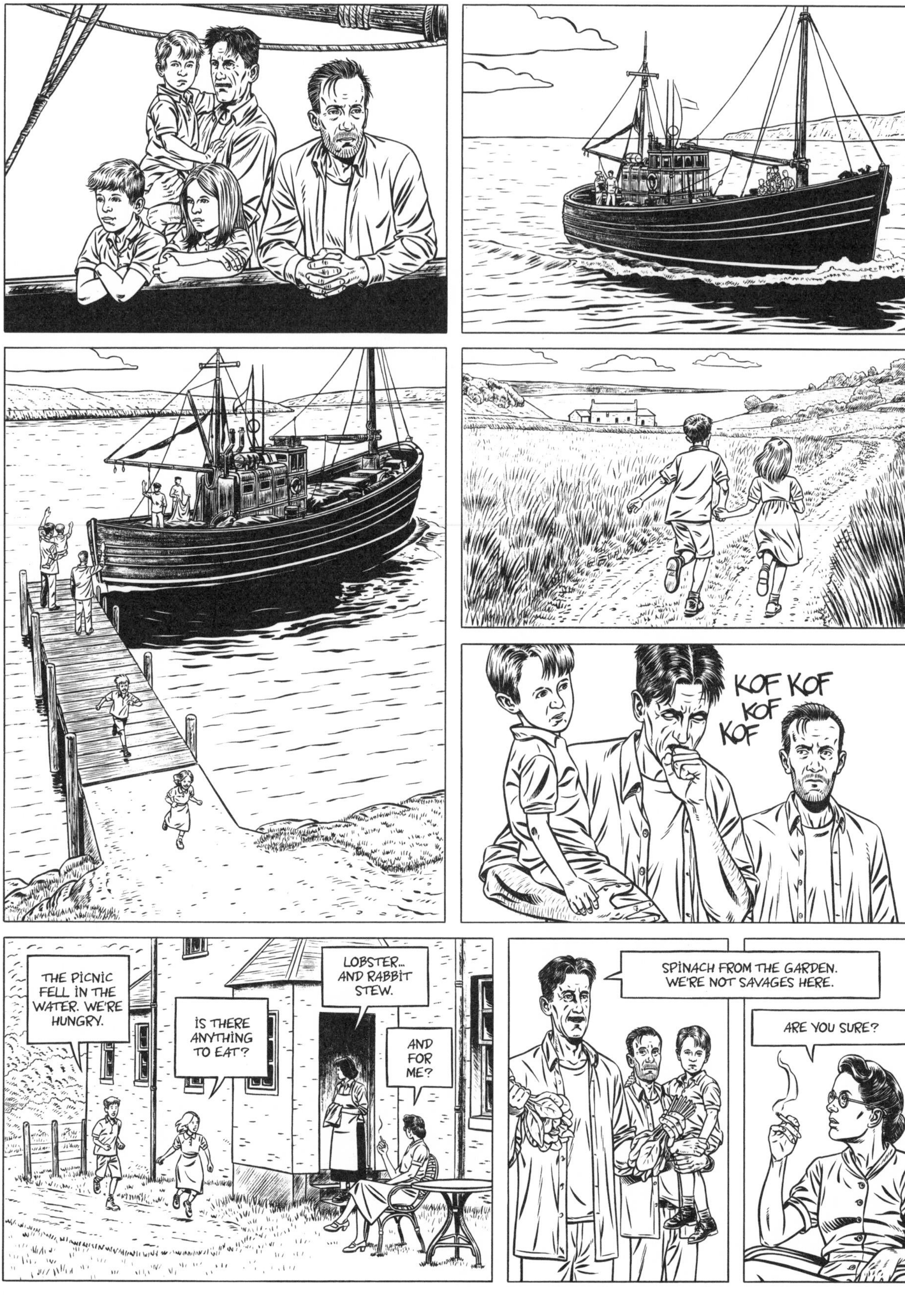
KOF KOF
KOF
KOF
THE PICNIC FELL IN THE WATER. WE'RE HUNGRY.
IS THERE ANYTHING TO EAT?
LOBSTER... AND RABBIT STEW.
AND FOR ME?
SPINACH FROM THE GARDEN. WE'RE NOT SAVAGES HERE.
ARE YOU SURE?

Since the Spanish Civil War, I cannot honestly say that I have done anything except write books and raise hens and vegetables. What I saw in Spain, and what I have since of the inner workings of left-wing political parties, have given me a horror of politics.

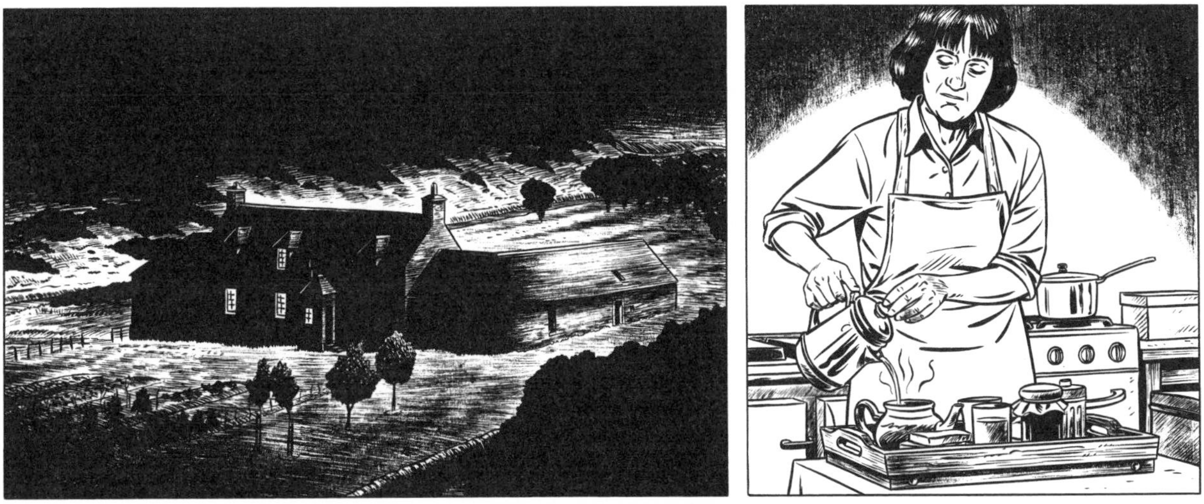

Outside of my work the thing I care most about is gardening, especially vegetable gardening. I dislike big towns, noise, motor cars, the radio, tinned food, central heating, and "modern" furniture.

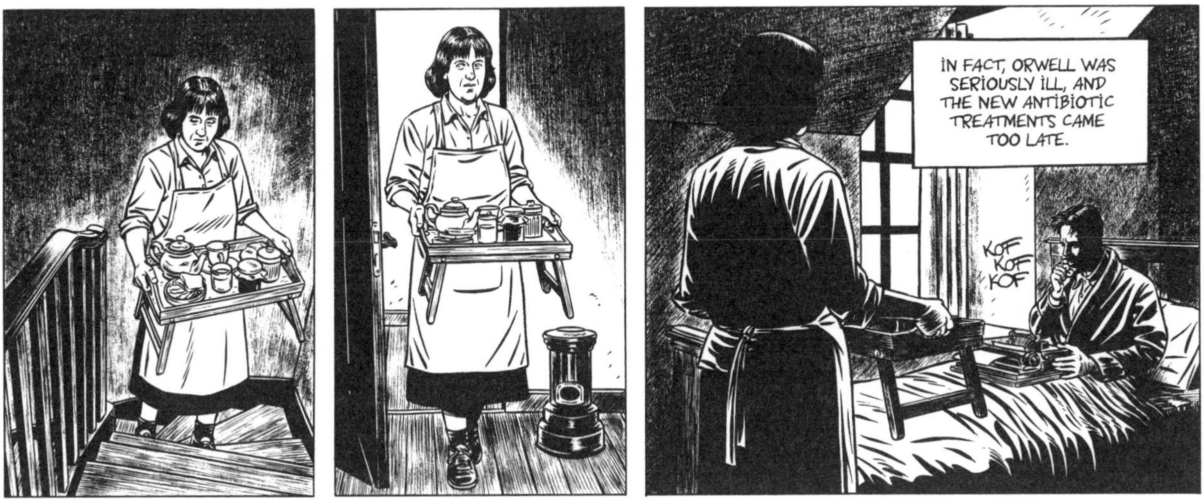
IN FACT, ORWELL WAS SERIOUSLY ILL, AND THE NEW ANTIBIOTIC TREATMENTS CAME TOO LATE.
KOF KOF KOF

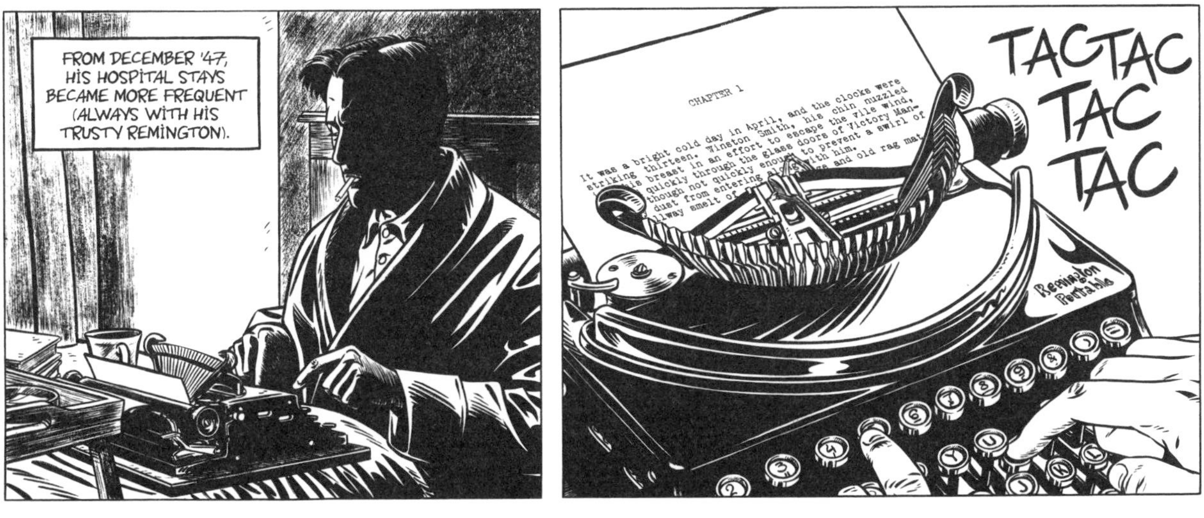
FROM DECEMBER '47, HIS HOSPITAL STAYS BECAME MORE FREQUENT (ALWAYS WITH HIS TRUSTY REMINGTON).
CHAPTER 1
TACTAC TAC TAC
Remington Portable

The hallway smelt of boiled cabbage and old rag mats. At one end of it a coloured poster, too large for indoor display, had been tacked to the wall. It depicted simply an enormous face, more than a metre wide: the face of a man of about forty-five, with a heavy black moustache and ruggedly handsome features.

Winston made for the stairs. It was no use trying the lift. Even at the best of times it was seldom working, and at present the electric current was cut off during daylight hours. It was part of the economy drive in preparation for Hate Week. The flat was seven flights up, and Winston, who was thirty-nine and had a varicose ulcer above his right ankle, went slowly, resting several times on the way. On each landing, opposite the lift-shaft, the poster with the enormous face gazed from the wall. It was one of those pictures which are so contrived that the eyes follow you about when you move. BIG BROTHER IS WATCHING YOU, the caption beneath it ran.

Inside the flat a fruity voice was reading out a list of figures which had something to do with the production of pig-iron. The voice came from an oblong metal plaque like a dulled mirror which formed part of the surface of the right-hand wall. Winston turned a switch and the voice sank somewhat, though the words were still distinguishable. The instrument (the telescreen, it was called) could be dimmed, but there was no way of shutting it off completely. He moved over to the window...
Behind Winston's back the voice from the telescreen was still babbling away about pig-iron and the overfulfilment of the Ninth Three-Year Plan. The telescreen received and transmitted simultaneously. Any sound that Winston made, above the level of a very low whisper, would be picked up by it; moreover, so long as he remained within the field of vision which the metal plaque commanded, he could be seen as well as heard. There was of course no way of knowing whether you were being watched at any given moment...
Winston kept his back turned to the telescreen. It was safer; though, as he well knew, even a back can be revealing. A kilometre away the Ministry of Truth, his place of work, towered vast and white above the grimy landscape. This, he thought with a sort of vague distaste - this was London, chief city of Airstrip One, itself the third most populous of the provinces of Oceania...
The Ministry of Truth - Minitrue, in Newspeak - was startlingly different from any other object in sight. It was an enormous pyramidal structure of glittering white concrete, soaring up, terrace after terrace, 300 metres into the air. From where Winston stood it was just possible to read, picked out on its white face in elegant lettering, the three slogans of the Party:

WAR IS PEACE
FREEDOM IS SLAVERY
IGNORANCE IS STRENGTH

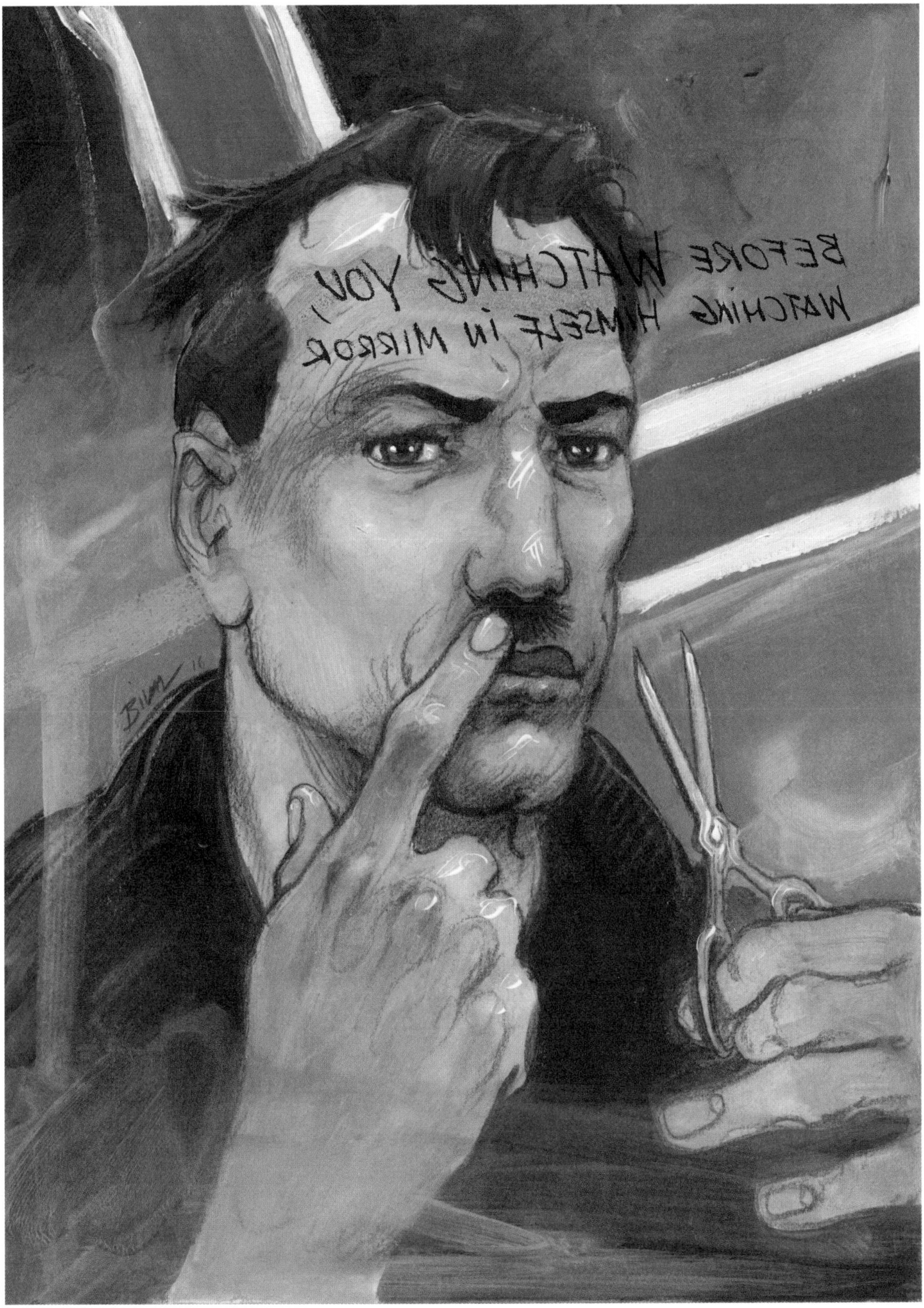
BEFORE WATCHING YOU,
WATCHING HIMSELF IN MIRROR

ORWELL MARRIED SONIA BROWNELL IN 1949.

HE DIED IN JANUARY 1950. AS ALL LONDON'S CEMETERIES WERE FULL, HE WAS GIVEN AN ANGLICAN BURIAL IN A SMALL VILLAGE IN OXFORDSHIRE.

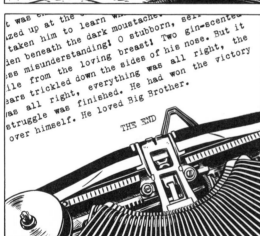

t was ...
...azed up at the ...
...taken him to learn wi...
...en beneath the dark moustach...
...ess misunderstanding! O stubborn, sel...
...ile from the loving breast! Two gin-scented
...ears trickled down the sides of his nose. But it
...was all right, everything was all right, the
...struggle was finished. He had won the victory
over himself. He loved Big Brother.

THE END

HE HAD COMPLETED THE TYPESCRIPT HE HAD BEEN WORKING ON FOR SO LONG IN 1948.

HE REVERSED THE LAST TWO DIGITS OF THAT YEAR TO MAKE 1984 – THE NOVEL THAT WOULD SECURE ORWELL'S REPUTATION AS ONE OF THE 20TH CENTURY'S GREATEST VISIONARIES.

AFTER ORWELL

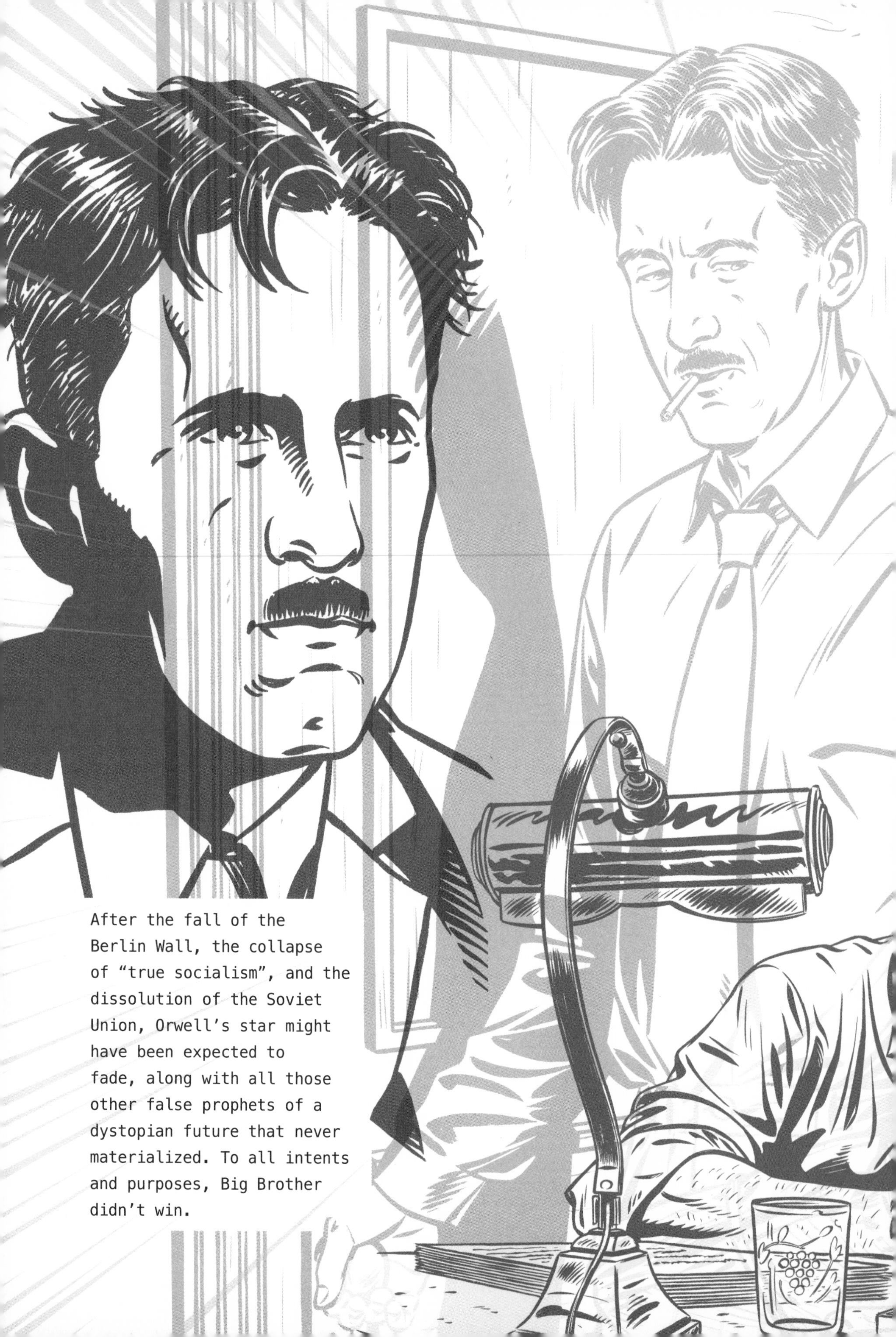
After the fall of the Berlin Wall, the collapse of "true socialism", and the dissolution of the Soviet Union, Orwell's star might have been expected to fade, along with all those other false prophets of a dystopian future that never materialized. To all intents and purposes, Big Brother didn't win.

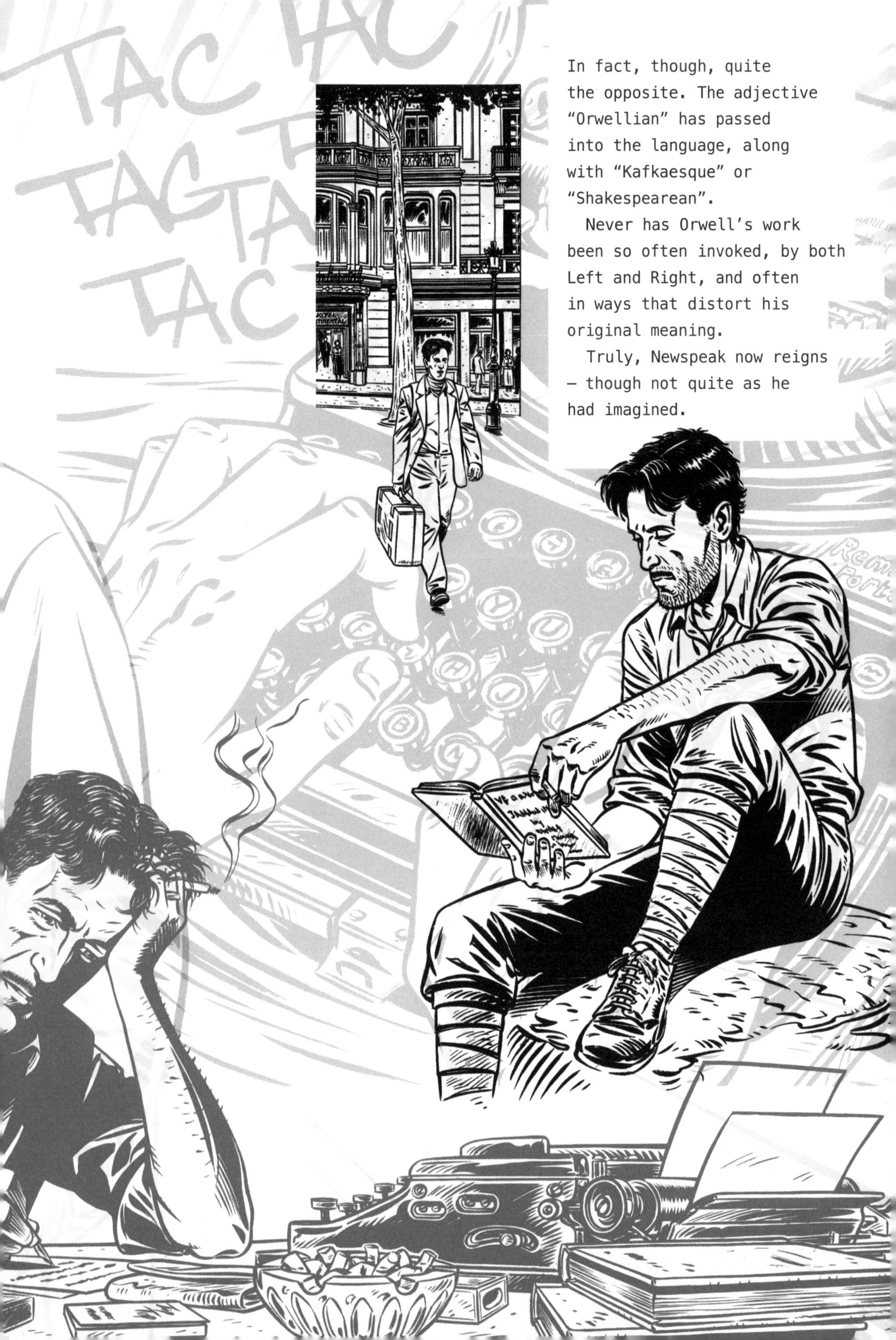
In fact, though, quite the opposite. The adjective "Orwellian" has passed into the language, along with "Kafkaesque" or "Shakespearean".
Never has Orwell's work been so often invoked, by both Left and Right, and often in ways that distort his original meaning.
Truly, Newspeak now reigns – though not quite as he had imagined.

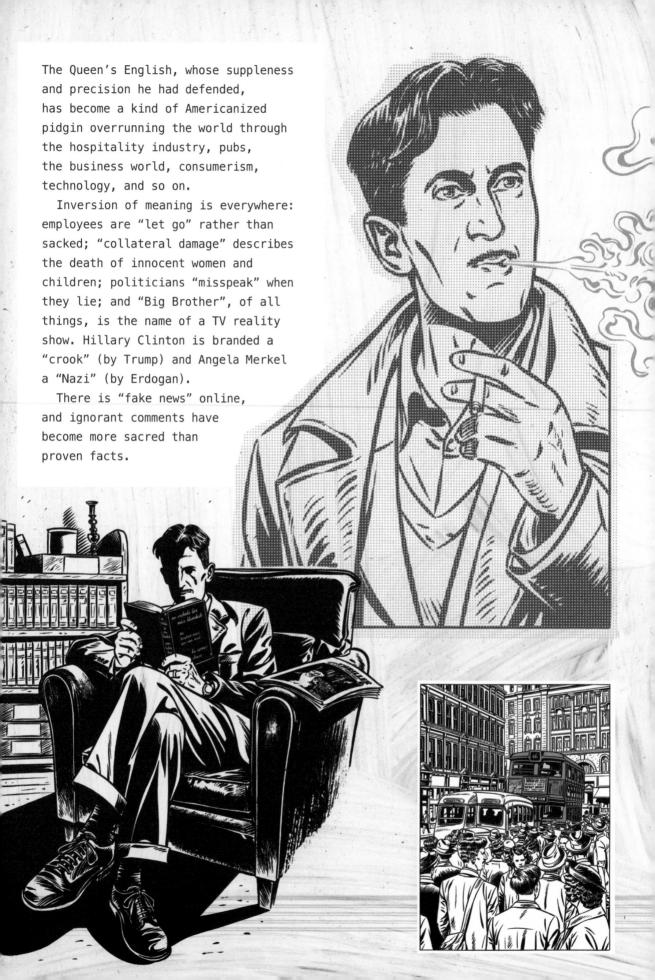

The Queen's English, whose suppleness and precision he had defended, has become a kind of Americanized pidgin overrunning the world through the hospitality industry, pubs, the business world, consumerism, technology, and so on.

Inversion of meaning is everywhere: employees are "let go" rather than sacked; "collateral damage" describes the death of innocent women and children; politicians "misspeak" when they lie; and "Big Brother", of all things, is the name of a TV reality show. Hillary Clinton is branded a "crook" (by Trump) and Angela Merkel a "Nazi" (by Erdogan).

There is "fake news" online, and ignorant comments have become more sacred than proven facts.

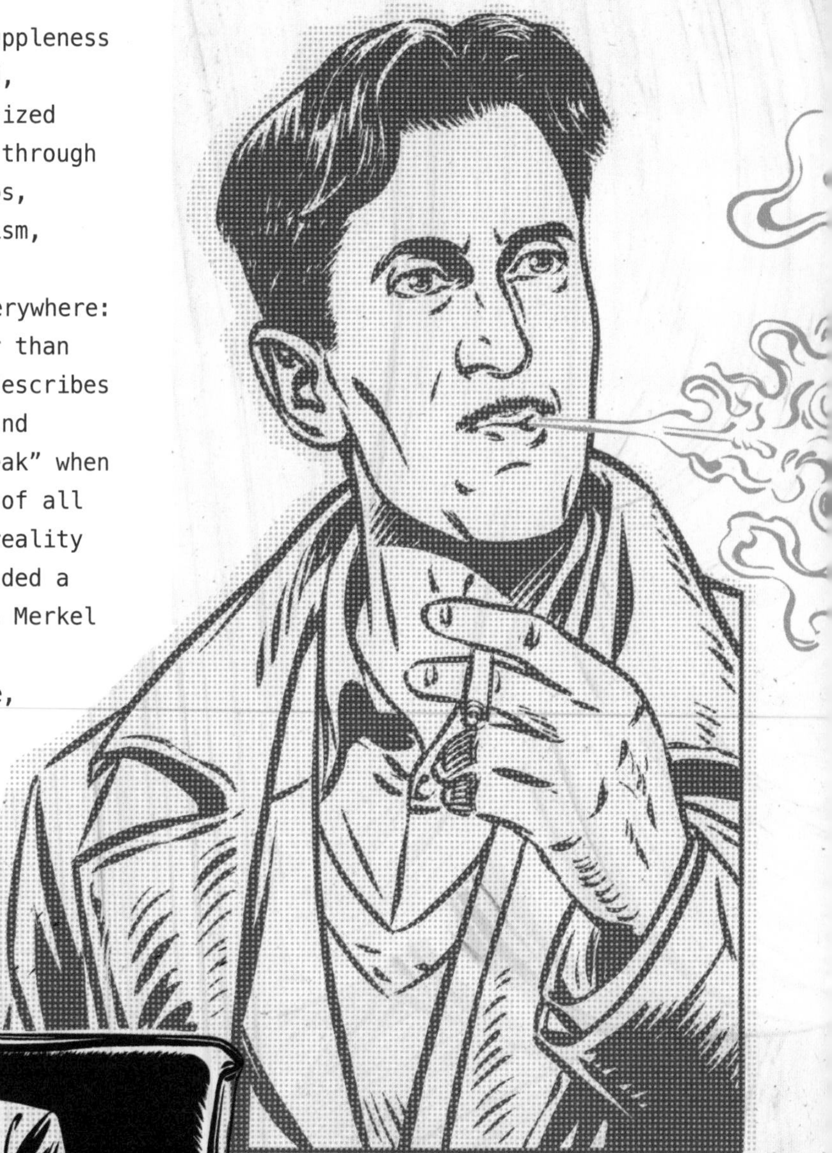

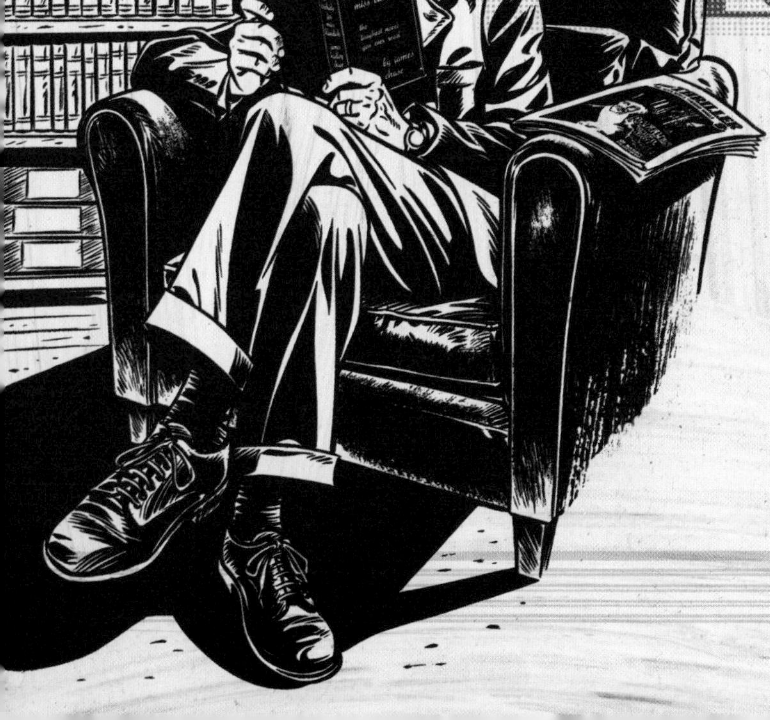

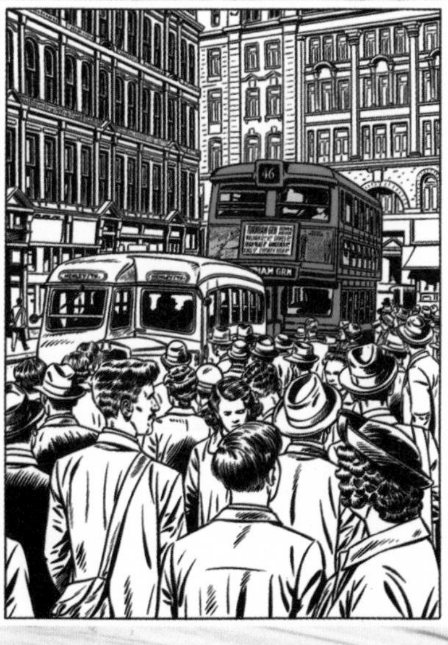

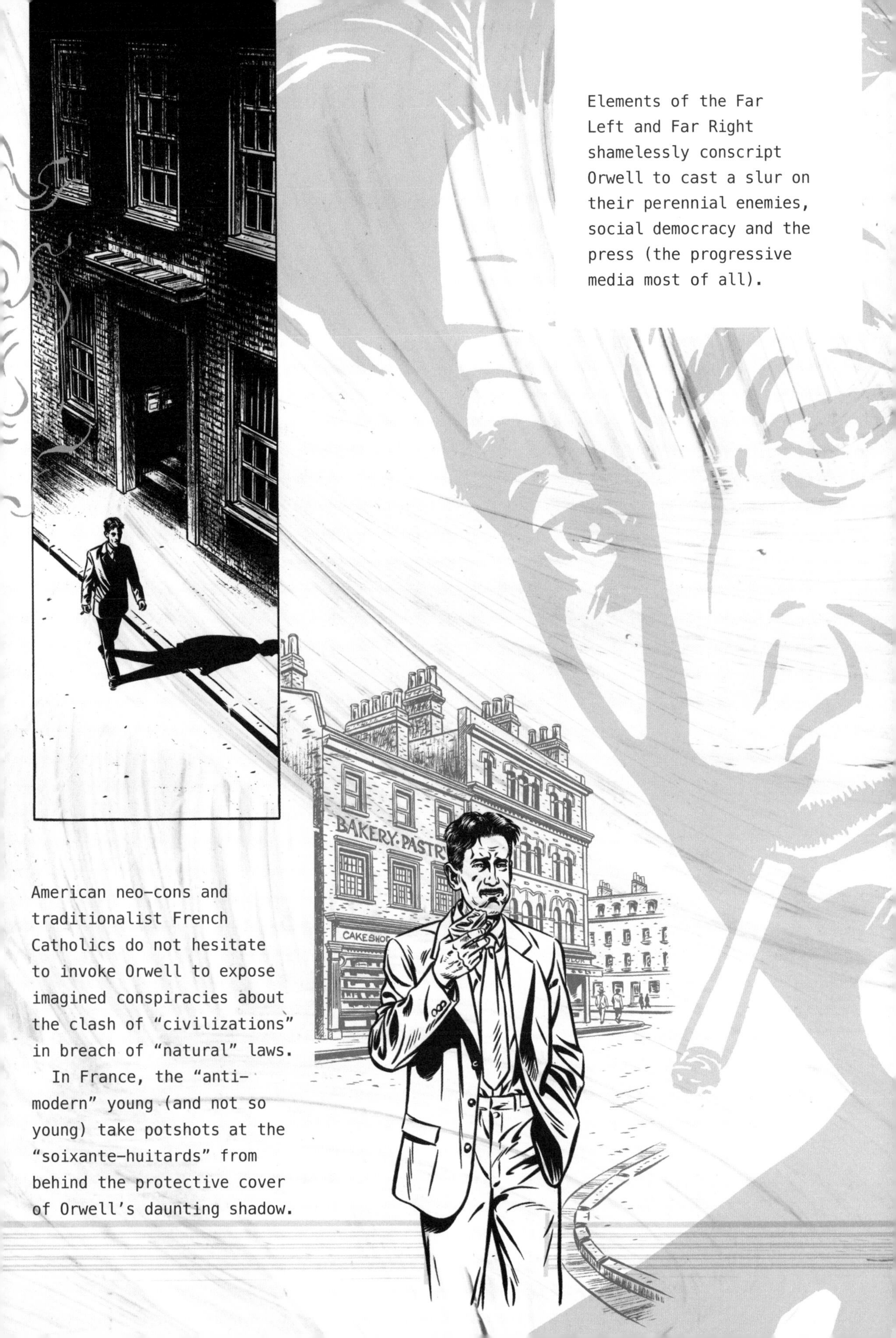
Elements of the Far Left and Far Right shamelessly conscript Orwell to cast a slur on their perennial enemies, social democracy and the press (the progressive media most of all).
BAKERY
American neo-cons and traditionalist French Catholics do not hesitate to invoke Orwell to expose imagined conspiracies about the clash of "civilizations" in breach of "natural" laws.
In France, the "anti-modern" young (and not so young) take potshots at the "soixante-huitards" from behind the protective cover of Orwell's daunting shadow.

It is less dispiriting to look for traces of his enduring cultural influence in countless fields.

For example, in film, with Terry Gilliam's *Brazil*, perhaps the most brilliant take on *1984*, along with Andrew Niccol's unsettling dystopian vision *Gattaca*.

We might also look, among modern historians, to the abrasive author Simon Leys, whose polemic against Mao's "Little Red Book" in *The Chairman's New Clothes* (1971) was clearly inspired by Orwell, to whom he would later devote an essay…

And in journalism, a range of sociological reportage, of varying degrees of anonymity, such as Florence Aubenas's poignant *Le Quai de Ouistreham* (2010), all of which owe a debt to *The Road to Wigan Pier*.

Nor can we ignore graphic novels, since the old reporter in *The Black Order Brigade* (1979) could almost be Orwell himself – had he survived, let his beard grow, and retired to his Hebridean island of Jura to compose his final work.

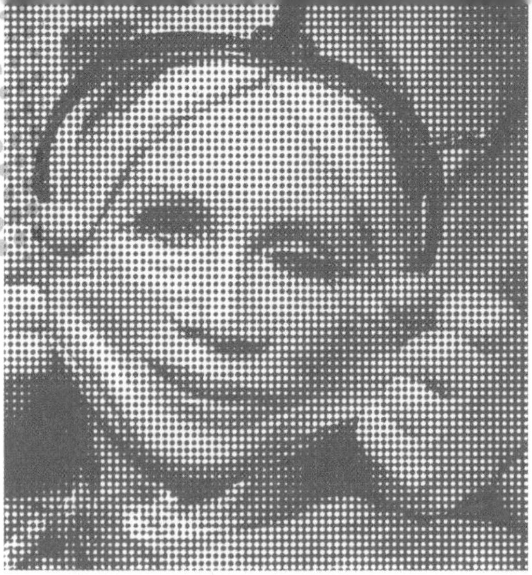

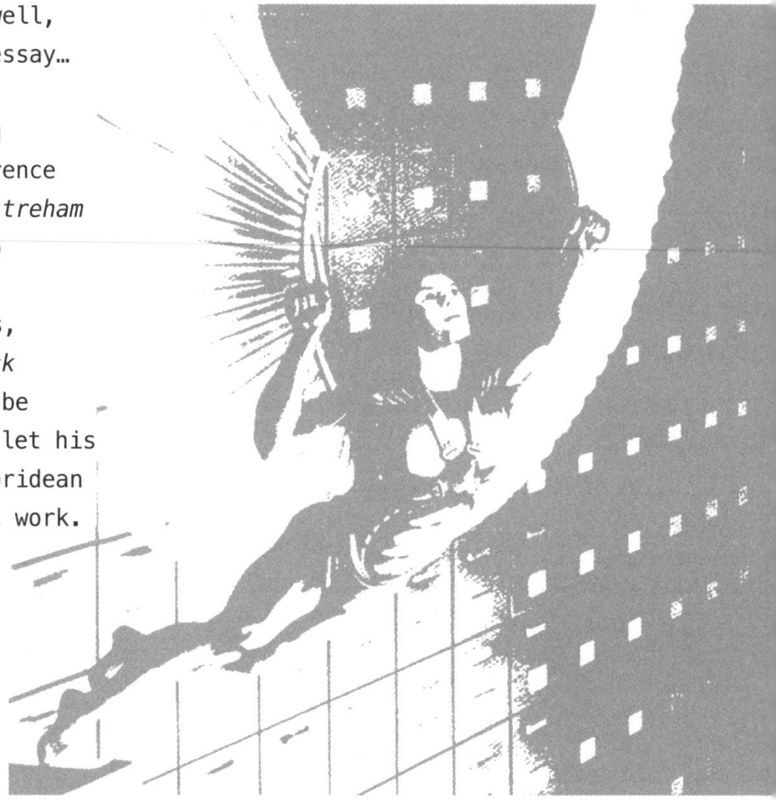

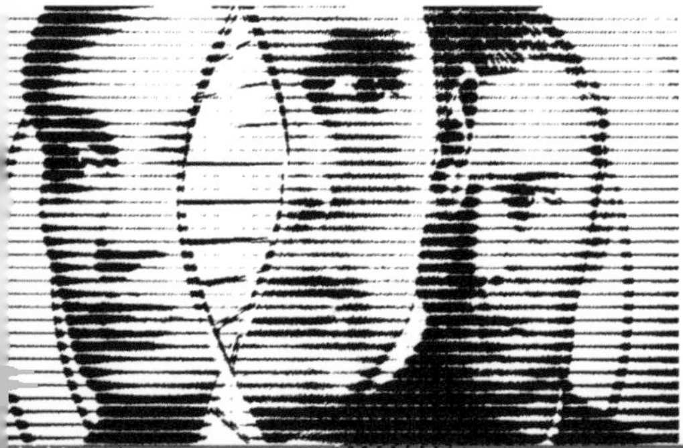

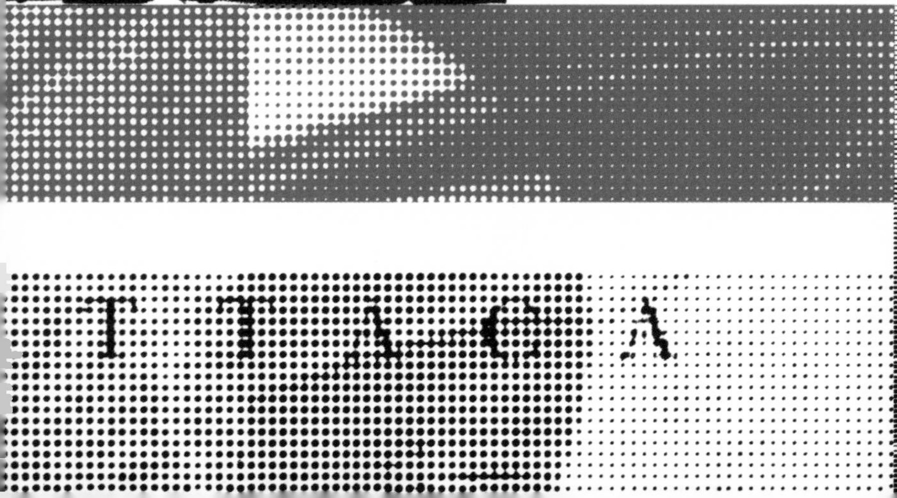
T TA C A

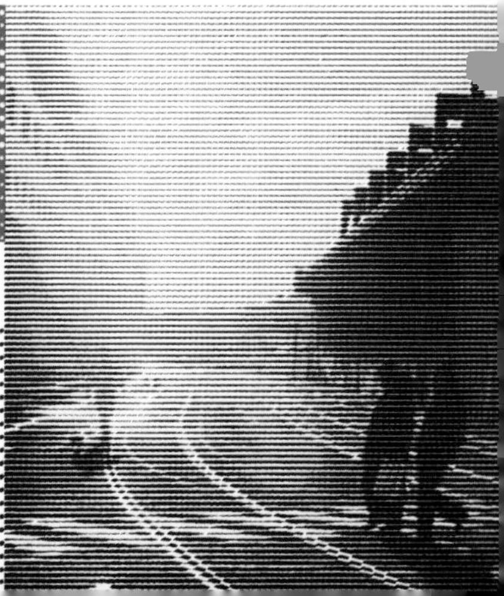

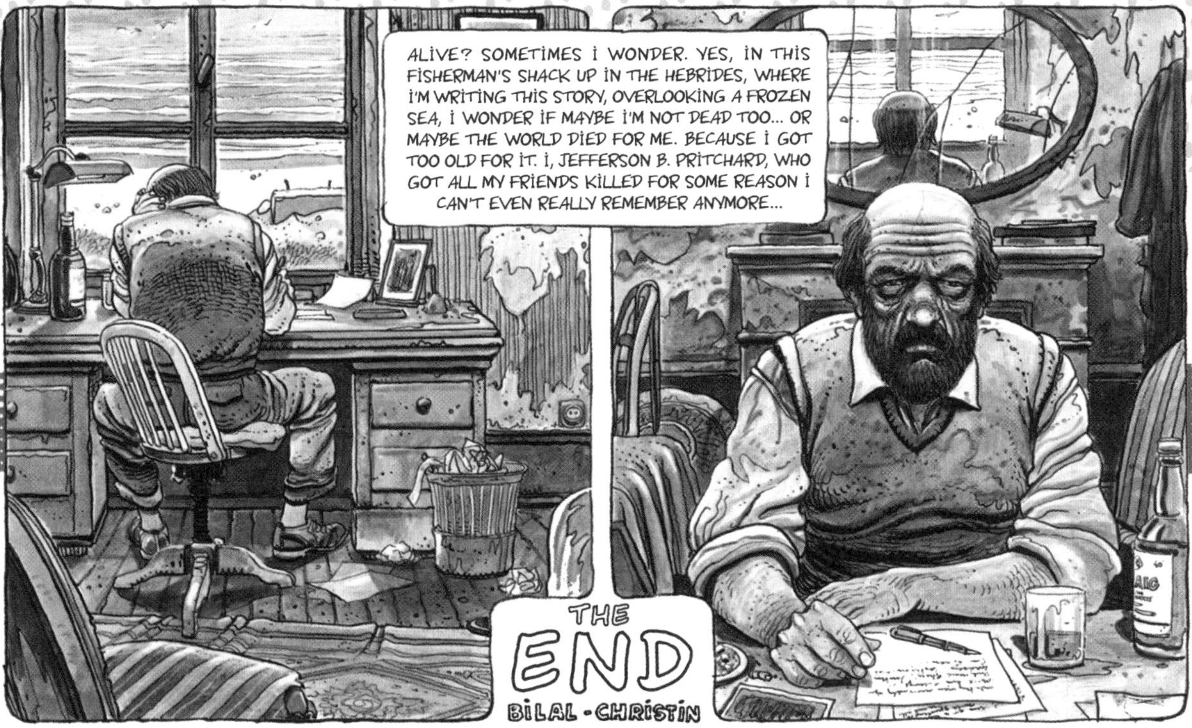
ALIVE? SOMETIMES I WONDER. YES, IN THIS FISHERMAN'S SHACK UP IN THE HEBRIDES, WHERE I'M WRITING THIS STORY, OVERLOOKING A FROZEN SEA, I WONDER IF MAYBE I'M NOT DEAD TOO... OR MAYBE THE WORLD DIED FOR ME. BECAUSE I GOT TOO OLD FOR IT. I, JEFFERSON B. PRITCHARD, WHO GOT ALL MY FRIENDS KILLED FOR SOME REASON I CAN'T EVEN REALLY REMEMBER ANYMORE...
THE END
BILAL - CHRISTIN

Still, the man and his work remain shrouded in a certain mystery, like one of those beautiful English rivers, with their calm surfaces and cloudy depths, whose name he adopted for his own.

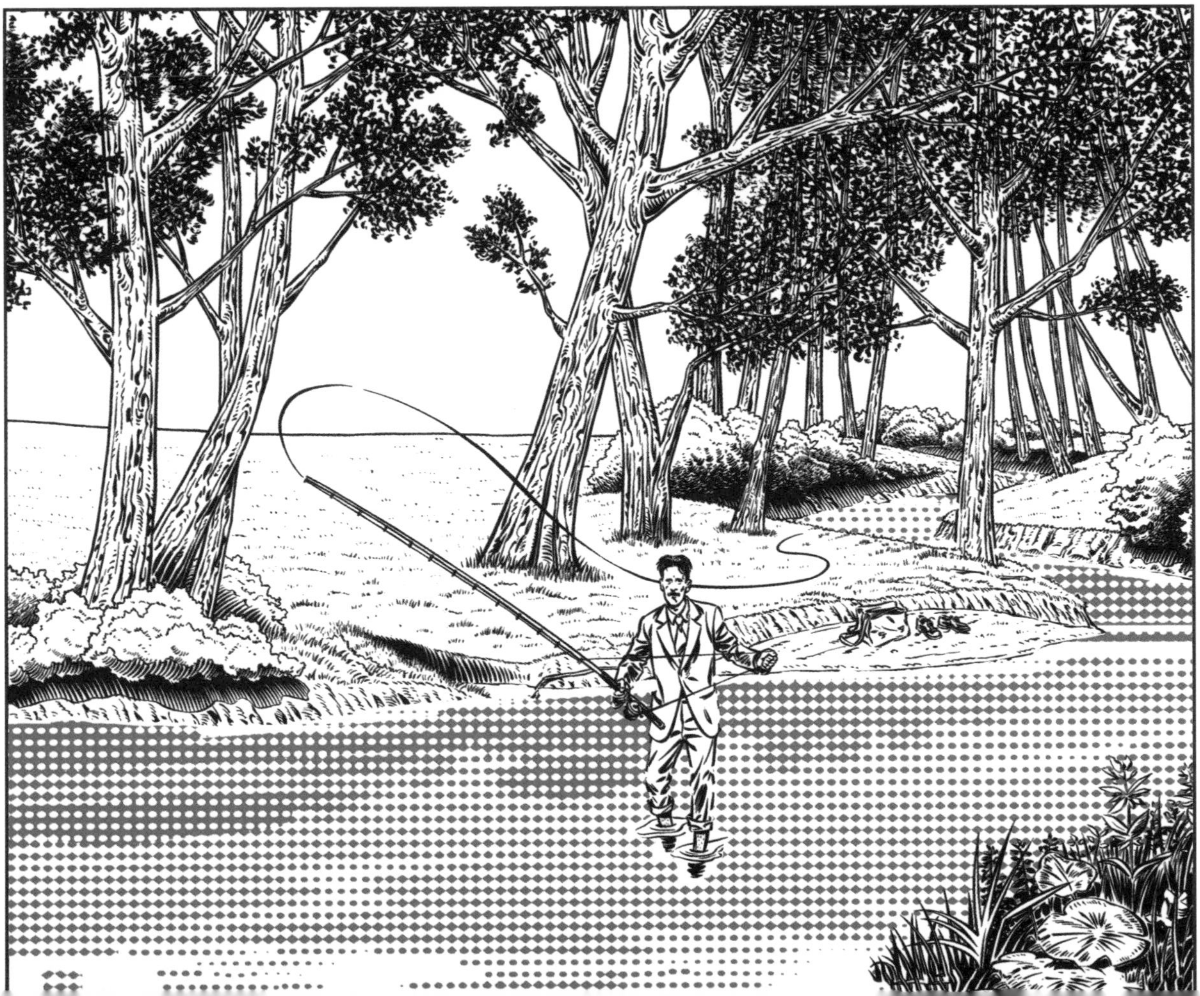

Afterword

Many works and articles have been devoted to George Orwell in England and the U.S. I have relied heavily on Bernard Crick's monumental biography, *George Orwell: A Life* (Secker & Warburg Ltd., 1980); on Orwell's own *Diaries* (ed. Peter Davison, W.W. Norton, 2012); and on articles in *The New Yorker*, *The Guardian*, and others.

In France, the bulk of his body of work, and commentaries upon it, have been published by Éditions Ivrea and Éditions Agone. In general, but not always, I have referred to the available translations; and, in French translation, to Simon Leys's sparkling essay "Orwell: The Horror of Politics" in *The Angel and the Octopus: Collected Essays*, 1983–1998 (Duffy & Snellgrove, 1999); Jean-Claude Martin's moving tale, *L'Autre Vie d'Orwell* (*Orwell's Other Life*, Gallimard, 2013); and Emmanuel Roux's conceptual analysis, *La Politique de l'écrivain* (*The Writer's Politics*, Michalon, 2015), not to mention the latest post-Orwell work to date, Jean-Claude Michéa's *Notre ennemi, le capital* (*Our Enemy Capital*, French and European Publications Inc., 2017).

To suit the needs of the graphic medium, I was forced to make a few chronological elisions, dramatize scenes, and make up dialogue between people Orwell knew, as well, of course, as privileging purely visual scenes. Unwilling to reduce, wherever possible, Orwell's words to paraphrase, I have flagged my direct quotation of them in typewritten font.

I also called on certain artist friends — André Juillard, Olivier Balez, Manu Larcenet, Blutch, Juanjo Guarnido, Enki Bilal — to immerse themselves in the landmark works of Orwell's literary career and provide their visions of a few scenes, rather than merely subject readers to my own soulless excerpts.

From the Irrawady Delta in Burma to the Isle of Jura off the Scottish coast, by way of Hampstead and the rocky wastes of the Catalan, I have been quietly following in Orwell's footsteps all my life. This graphic novel, co-created with Sébastien Verdier, seeks to do justice to the man who has inspired the greater part of my dystopian fiction.

Pierre Christin, April 2019

Quotations from Orwell in this book are taken from the following works:

Such, Such Were the Joys
(Harcourt, Brace, Jovanovich, 1953)

Inside the Whale and Other Essays
(Victor Gollancz Ltd., 1940)

Down and Out in Paris and London
(Victor Gollancz Ltd., 1933)

The Road to Wigan Pier
(Left Book Club, 1937)

Homage to Catalonia
(Secker and Warburg, 1938)

Animal Farm
(Secker and Warburg, 1945)

Nineteen Eighty-Four
(Secker and Warburg, 1949)

The Collected Essays, Journalism and Letters of George Orwell
(Harcourt, Brace & World 1968; Mariner Books, 1971; David R. Godine, 2000; Penguin UK, 2003)

– Volume 1: An Age Like This 1920–1940
– Volume 2: My Country Right or Left 1940–1943
– Volume 3: As I Please, 1943–1945
– Volume 4: In Front of Your Nose, 1945–1950

Special Contributors:

Pages 18–21: André Juillard
Pages 42–43: Olivier Balez
Pages 56–57: Manu Larcenet
Pages 92–93: Blutch
(colors: Isabelle Merlet)
Pages 134–135: Juanjo Guarnido
Page 147: Enki Bilal

Photographic credits on pages 28, 38, 122: all rights reserved
Page 106: all rights reserved DC Comics
Page 109: "Security by Col. Blimp", David Low, all rights reserved

Illustration on page 9: Reynold Brown for *The Time Machine* Poster (1960)

Illustrations on page 154 taken from *Brazil* (dir. Terry Gilliam, Embassy International Pictures
And Universal Pictures, 1985), and *Gattaca* (dir. Andrew Nicol, Colombia Pictures and Jersey Films, 1997).

Illustration on page 155 (upper) is excerpted from *The Black Order Brigade* by Christin/Bilal © Casterman.
With kind permission from the creators and Éditions Casterman.

Layout and design for appendix: Philippe Ravon

Philippe Ravon was the colourist for Sébastien Verdier's
outlines, except on pages 34–37 and 50–51,
which Verdier coloured himself.